THE GOLDEN TRADE OF THE MOORS

West African Kingdoms in the Fourteenth Century

EDWARD WILLIAM BOVILL

with a new introduction
by Robert O. Collins

Markus Wiener Publishers
Princeton

D1449269

For information write to:
Markus Wiener Publishers,
114 Jefferson Road, Princeton, NJ 08540

Library of Congress Cataloging-in-Publication Data

Bovill, E.W.
    The golden trade of the Moors/Edward W. Bovill;
with a new introduction by Robert O. Collins.—2nd ed.,
rev./and with additional material by Robin Hallett.
    Originally published: London: Oxford University Press, 1958.
With new introduction.
    Includes bibliographical references and index.
    ISBN 1-55876-091-1 (pbk.)
    1. Sudan (Region)—History. 2. Africa—Commerce—History.
I. Hallett, Robin.   II. Title.
DT356.B6 1994   94-27190
382'.0966—dc20   CIP

Cover Design by Cheryl Mirkin

Printed by Princeton Academic Press on acid-free paper

Preface to First Edition

THIS book has been written in response to a request for a new edition of my *Caravans of the Old Sahara*. It covers the same field and tells much the same story, but not in quite the same way. There are several reasons for this.

First, I found the mere revision of what I wrote a quarter of a century ago humiliating and tedious. There was too much that should have been written better, and not a little that should not have been written at all. In the meanwhile, too, I had gathered new material much of which had to be used, if only to show how wrong some of my earlier conclusions had been. The need to rewrite the whole book was plainly inescapable.

But more than that was required. The passage of years had brought changes which seemed to call for a different treatment of the subject, a new approach to the story. The purpose of my *Caravans* was, as the Preface said, to show how the trans-Saharan trade routes had woven ties of blood and culture between the peoples north and south of the desert, and to win a measure of recognition for the part which the Western Sudanese have played in the history of civilization. The emphasis was on the influence of the peoples of the north on those of the interior, of the whites and browns on the blacks. The book was conceived in Kano, looking northwards across the great wastes of the Sahara towards the teeming cities of Barbary with which the Western Sudanese were linked by ties forged over the centuries. The book was consequently addressed primarily to those interested in West Africa.

Since then I have become better acquainted with Barbary, from Marrakech to Lepcis, and with its literature. My modest travels and my reading have taught me much, especially that the Sahara dominates the history of the north not less than that of the south. But this ascendancy is little recognized by the historians of Barbary, and not at all by the masses who gaze enthralled at the splendour of the ancient monuments with which that arid land is strewn.

There seemed to me a need for a book showing how the Sahara enriched the Carthaginian and bewildered the Roman; how in later times the great caravan routes, linking the sophisticated cities of the north with the great markets and modest seats of learning of the south, not only influenced the course of events in Barbary, and even beyond, but sometimes determined it; how, all down the centuries, Berbers and Arabs, Jews and Christians, never ceased to draw on the wealth and industry of the Sudanese. This book seeks to satisfy that need.

The history of North Africa has engaged many illustrious scholars some of whom have made its study their life's work. This incursion into a field in which I have had so many distinguished predecessors has therefore been undertaken with humility, but not so humbly that I have not sometimes dared to question the conclusions of the great.

Although this book, unlike my earlier one, is partly addressed to those who are interested in North Africa, in writing it I have borne constantly in mind the needs of students of West African history to whom alone I owe the call for a new edition of my *Caravans*. Barbary gold, like Morocco leather, had its origin in the Sudan, the land to which every thread in my story leads.

I have recorded, in Bibliography and footnotes, the sources of my material. But acknowledgment is also due to those who from time to time suggested corrections, amendments, and additions to my earlier work. My indebtedness accumulated through the years, but only to be further swelled in recent times by the generous response of those to whom I have turned for help and guidance in writing the present book.

Among those to whom I am particularly grateful are: the late E. J. Arnett, Mrs. Olwen Brogan, Mr. G. R. Crone, Mr. F. de F. Daniel, Professor Henri Labouret, Sir Gordon Lethem, Mrs. A. R. McDougall, Sir Richmond Palmer, Mr. R. A. Skelton and his staff in the Map Room of the British Museum, Professor E. G. R. Taylor, my daughter Mrs. James Blackett-Ord, and finally my wife who adds to the critical sense of our daughter a gift for unselfish endurance which is beyond praise or reward.

LITTLE LAVER HALL   E. W. BOVILL
    HARLOW
1 February 1957

Note to Second Impression. I am grateful to M. Raymond Mauny for his help in correcting this impression.

Contents

NINETEENTH-CENTURY REVOLUTIONS

Maps

Introduction

EDWARD William Bovill (1892-1966) was born on Christmas Day 1892, the son of Wedward Merewether Bovill and Mary Larkins. In the traditions of the English gentry he was educated at Rugby and upon demonstrating an interest in learning went up to Trinity College, Cambridge, and like his classmates in 1914 patriotically responded to the call to war and served with the Royal Hussars (S.R.) and the W.A. "Frontier Force" in Nigeria. Like Basil Davidson, perhaps the most influential popularizer of the African past in this century who arrived in Kano, Nigeria, to continue his military service in the Second World War only to discover Africa, Bovill's experiences a quarter of a century before with The West African Frontier Force stationed in Kano had a profound impact upon his future life. Upon demobilization in 1919 he married Sylvia Mary Cheston and returned to the family estates at Moreton, Ongar, Essex where he combined the life of the quintessential English country gentleman with a fascination for the history of the Western Sudan and the trans-Saharan trade stimulated by the English country life which provided him with the leisure to write about the empires of the Western Sudan whose culture history he had briefly experienced as an officer and a gentleman in Kano.

The result was the publication in 1933 of *Caravans of the Old Sahara* (Oxford: Oxford University Press, 1933). His motivation was not only intellectual curiosity about different cultures with which the vicissitudes of war had brought him into contact, but, as he once told my colleague Anthony Kirk-Greene, a certain repugnance to "the toffee-nosed administration in Kano" he had encountered during his service with the West African Frontier Force. Although Arab chroniclers and later European explorers of the nineteenth century had written of the expansive medieval kingdoms of the Western Sudan, Bovill distilled their commentaries into a single volume, which not only demonstrated the importance of trans-Saharan trade in the state-building of the medieval empires of Ghana, Mali, and Songhay but which through his clarity of style, vigor, and supreme gift as a teller of tales captivated a wide audience which hitherto had regarded the Western Sudan as a wasteland.

With the publication of *Caravans of the Old Sahara* an English country gentleman was transformed into an authority on a land whose history had remained locked in the traditions and records of its indigenous inhabitants and the accounts of travelers. He continued his interest in the history of the trans-Saharan trade and, of course, its relationship with the rise and fall of the medieval empires of the Western Sudan with country and commercial life in Britain and combined them all with equal skill. From 1942 until 1961 he was Chairman of R.C. Treat and Co. Ltd. as well as a director of Matheson and Co. Ltd. from 1936-45. But real estate, commerce, and the export-import trade were not his primary interests which remained the English countryside and the Western Sudan, geographically thousands of miles apart but not all that dissimilar in the management of political and social life.

As a result of the publication of *Caravans of the Old Sahara* he received in 1935, somewhat to his astonishment for he was a modest man, the Medal of the Royal Society of Arts and membership in the Society of Arts as a fellow. This appeared to stimulate his continuing interest in the history of the Western Sudan and English country life. Beginning in the 1950's there was a veritable torrent of publications which undoubtedly reflected his decision to retire gracefully from commercial responsibilities and devote more time to research and writing. The results were not without reward. In 1950 he became joint editor of *East African Agriculture* (London: Oxford University Press, 1950), but this was more a diversion than a commitment to a region of Africa in which his interests were more agricultural than historical. He was much more confident after twenty-five years of continuous inquiry into the trans-Saharan trade and the West African past. *The Battle of Alcazar* (London: Batchwerth Press, 1952) was a set-piece battle, but its narrow subject attracted only those interested in the conflict between Muslims and Christians in the Iberian peninsula. During these years he kept up research to enlarge his knowledge of the caravans of the old Sahara motivated by the constant requests to produce a revised edition of his earlier work on the subject which he did in 1958 under the title *The Golden Trade of the*

Moors (Oxford: Oxford University Press, 1958). It told essentially the same story as *Caravans* but in a different way. S.N. Fisher, himself an authority on the Western Sudan, wrote in the *American Historical Review* (January, 1959) that "The style in the more recent publication reveals a more mature scholar, for the text is smoother and more even and his points are made with greater clarity and assurance. Beyond these superficialities, two points should be made. First, new material has been added and the author utilizes the fruits of scholarship on this subject made by others since 1933, although it is painfully obvious that in the last quarter century too few students have been digging in this field. The other and major objective in rewriting his book has been the realization that the Sahara and its trade routes had even more influence on North Africa than they did in the Western Sudan".

New material and a "broader view", however, did not diminish Bovill's enthralling ability as a "teller of tales" whose narrative of style which attracted an audience far beyond the academic community is the primary reason why this work with its firm grasp of anthropology, economic geography, and history all delightfully written should be made available to the generation born after *The Golden Trade of the Moors* had gone out of print. With the assistance of Robin Hallett's knowledge of the Western Sudan the Oxford University Press reprinted *The Golden Trade of the Moors* in 1968. It is now long out of print.

Bovill's research and writing on the Western Sudan beginning after the First World War received increasing recognition. In 1946 he became a member of the Council of the Hakluyt Society and a trustee and a member of the Council of the Society for Nautical Research in 1954. This was a welcome change from his previous real estate and commercial interests. In 1964 he was elected vice president of the Hakluyt Society. This was followed by *Missions to the Niger.* 3 vols. (New York: Cambridge University Press on behalf of the Hakluyt Society, 1964 and 1966). Volume I (1964) was an edition of Frederick Hornemann and A. Gordon Laing, *Travels in Timmannee* (London, 1825); volumes II and III (1966), entitled *The Bornu Mission,* was an edition of Dixon Denham and High Clapperton. *Narrative of Travels and Discoveries in Northern and Central Africa* (London, 1826). A final volume was published posthumously. *The Niger Explored.* ed. E.W. Bovill (Oxford:

Oxford University Press, 1968).

Although Bovill is best remembered for his books on the Western Sudan and its trans-Saharan trade, his love of the English countryside, where he resided throughout most of his life was equally strong and resulted in two sentimental books about the land that he loved so much: *The England of Nimrod and Surtees* (London: Oxford University Press, 1959) and *English Country Life: 1780-1830* (London: Oxford University Press, 1962), where his narrative skill combined with his life in the English countryside established him in the literature of Britain's writers who shunned the cities for the country.

But it is *The Golden Trade of the Moors* for which he will be best remembered. Over half a century after the publication of *Caravans of the Old Sahara* and a generation after its revision as *The Golden Trade of the Moors*, the work remains not only required reading for the student and scholar but a delightful safari for anyone interested in that fascinating, romantic, and vital history of the far-flung empires of the Western Sudan and the caravan routes across the arid and implacable hostility of the Saharan wastes which connected the land of the Blacks with the Mediterranean world. Long out of print, it is time that this wonderful book be made available to those who do not have access to the intimidating portals of a research library.

> *Robert O. Collins*
> *Santa Barbara, California*
> *August 1994*

AFRICA ANTIQUA

1

Arid Nurse of Lions

'Caelo terraque penuria aquarum.'—SALLUST.

NORTHERN AFRICA is divided into a series of natural zones
running roughly parallel to each other from west to east. Along
the Mediterranean sea-board lies a narrow strip of undulating
country, generally known as the Tell, which enjoys a climate
similar to that of southern Europe and is peopled by an agricultural peasantry. Behind these coastal hills lie the arid uplands
of the High Plateaux which, although they culminate in the peaks
of the Atlas, are for the most part steppe-like in character and
support a pastoral and semi-nomadic population. These highlands
drop sharply into the Sahara, the largest continuous desert on the
earth's surface, where extreme aridity imposes a nomadic existence
on its sparse population. No natural frontier bounds the Sahara on
the south. It gradually merges into steppes and these in turn give
place first to savanna and then to parklands, which, like the Tell,
are peopled by a sedentary agricultural population. Beyond the
parklands lies the equatorial forest.

The broad belt of broken country separating the Mediterranean
from the Sahara and extending from Tripoli in the east to the
Atlantic in the west has come to be loosely termed Barbary. The
great plains which lie south of the Sahara, separating it from the
equatorial forest, form the Bilad as Sudan, an Arabic name meaning
the Land of the Blacks. It extends from the Red Sea to the
Atlantic, that part which lies to the west of Lake Chad forming
the Western Sudan.

Although Barbary and the Western Sudan are separated by a
desert which forms one of the world's greatest barriers to human
movement the cultural and economic development of both has
been profoundly affected by intercourse between the two. The

Sahara consequently dominates the whole of the history of the interior of northern Africa.

A slight increase in the aridity of this immense desert would produce far-reaching political consequences. It would drive the wild desert tribes into the settled uplands and plains of Barbary and the Sudan, and it would so extend the waterless stages that the caravan routes would become impassable to camels and therefore to men. A correspondingly slight increase in rainfall would quickly multiply the water-holes and desert pastures, render man independent of the now necessary camel, and, by making his life more endurable, tame the nomad. Whether there has been any material change in the climate of the Sahara in historical times is therefore a question of great importance to the student of history.

Probably no part of the world is richer in outward signs of a deterioration in climate than North Africa. Nowhere, apparently, is there less room for doubt that things have gone from bad to worse. On every hand to the east of Morocco (much of which is comparatively well watered) is a desolation which seemingly springs from lack of rain. From Algeria to the Nile the land is strewn with the ruins of deserted towns, waterless cisterns, and dry river-beds. In the hinterland, which Herodotus called the 'wild beast region',[1] the larger animals are virtually extinct. The weight of evidence appears to be overwhelmingly in favour of a grievously diminished rainfall.

The world has few more impressive monuments than the vast amphitheatre of el-Jem (Thysdrus), built to seat 60,000 spectators, but today a ruin set amid utter desolation. Only less impressive are the ruins of Thamugadi (Timgad). The grassy uplands in which they lie are today peopled only by nomads, and one looks in vain for any vestige of the water which once flowed perpetually through every street. The visitor to Lepcis Magna may well wonder, as he views those superb ruins, where its 60,000 or more inhabitants got their water and how the great cisterns and public baths were filled if the rainfall was not far more abundant than the precarious seven or eight inches a year which are all Lepcis gets today. Countless other examples of depopulation, all apparently due to the failure of the water supply, could be quoted, but these suffice to illustrate the type of evidence which most impresses the traveller. Scarcely less striking are the dry river-beds, some of great depth, which score the countryside and clearly point to progressive desiccation over a long period.

If any further confirmation of the apparent deterioration of the climate since classical times were required it is ready at hand in the museums where are gathered the best of the mosaics which have so far been recovered by the excavators of Roman remains. They show how men lived, what their houses and farms were like, how they cultivated the soil, their field sports and, best of all, the wild life of their countryside. The overall picture is of a land very different from what we see today. It approaches much more to Kenya than to the countries of Barbary, more to what one would expect the Granary of Rome to have been like than to what in fact it is. The most striking change is the loss of the country's fauna which in Roman times included a wide variety of animals, apparently in great numbers, and which today we can only see in a wild state in tropical Africa. Perhaps the most delightful of these mosaics is one in the Bardo (Musée Alaoui) at Tunis of Orpheus charming the animals, which includes even a hartebeest. History tells the same story. The elephants, great herds of which roamed North Africa in Carthaginian times, were still there with the Romans. Herodotus's oft-repeated description of the hinterland as the wild beast region was evidently apt.

The natural conclusion to be drawn from this great mass of evidence is that the arid conditions of today have supervened since Roman times, and that the Sahara is encroaching on the once well-favoured lands fringing Africa's northern shore. What other explanation can there be of how in Tripolitania, where the process appears to have reached its culmination, the ancient seaports of Lepcis Magna and Sabratha were found buried under an immense depth of drifted sand?

Yet there is another explanation, not only of the sand-buried ruins, but also of the abandoned cities in waterless wastes, the dry river-beds, and the lost fauna. The weight of evidence is wholly against a significant climatic change, and the probability is that the rainfall is much as it was two and a half *millenia* ago.

When, for economic, political, or military reasons, the Romans wanted to establish a settlement anywhere, or to expand an established settlement beyond its immediate resources, they did not allow lack of water to stand in their way. If water was not close at hand, or lacked the high standard of purity they required, they brought it from far afield. Cirta (Constantine) drew its water from 20 miles away, Caesarea (Cherchel) from 19, and Carthage from nearly 90 miles. The great aqueducts striding across the desolate plains and piercing mountain ranges remain as impressive monuments to the genius of the Roman water engineers, the *aquilegi,* under whose care came also the springs from which, far or near, the towns were supplied. But there were not always springs to tap. This was particularly so in Tripolitania where the water problem was, as today, much more acute than farther west. Here one method, which the Italians copied when establishing new settlements in the 1930's, was to collect rainwater from catchment areas and store it in cisterns. The catchment areas varied from rock faces to domestic roofs.* Another method was to build dams across the river-beds behind which in the short wet season the flood water could be stored or led off into cisterns. This lent itself to great elaboration. In fairness to the Greeks it should be added that farther east they did just as well as, if not better than, the Romans in still more difficult circumstances. They so successfully developed the rock cistern method that they had a chain of thriving towns and villages, surrounded by fields and vineyards, extending all the way from Cyrene to Alexandria.

In these very dry regions east of the Lesser Syrtis the threat of the desert was constant, and the encroaching sand was kept at bay only so long as the country was cultivated. When tillage had to cease through the destruction or decay of the dams and cisterns the desert advanced with the consequences we now see at Lepcis and Sabratha.

The aqueducts, dams, and cisterns constructed by the Roman engineers made possible the building of the dead cities which astonish us today. That these works are now all in ruins is not due to the failure of the rainfall and the springs. It is sometimes due to earth movements, but more usually to the hand of man. For nearly 2,000 years the people of the country have been using Roman monuments as stone quarries for the building of houses and mosques. The great mosque at Kairwan, the Djama al-Kabir, contains about 300 columns from neighbouring Roman and Byzantine buildings of which no traces survive. In a sixteenth-century mosque at Tagiura, a few miles east of Tripoli, there are forty-eight columns taken from Lepcis. At Ghadames, down in the

---

* The total annual water requirements of an Arab cultivator under Mediterranean conditions have been estimated at 550 gallons per head (about $1\frac{1}{2}$ gallons a day or a fifth of what a native cultivator in tropical Africa requires). In Tripolitania, with an 8-inch rainfall, this quantity of water could be obtained from a catchment area of only 150 square feet, say a roof measuring $12\frac{1}{2} \times 12\frac{1}{2}$ feet. This, however, would allow little or no margin for loss by evaporation.

desert, the only remains of the long Roman occupation are a few Doric and Corinthian columns in the two principal mosques. But wilful destruction by invaders also played havoc with the magnificent buildings the Romans left behind them.

The wilful destroyer was usually a Hilalian Arab. It was an evil day for North Africa when, in the eleventh century, the Banu Hilal poured out of Egypt westwards, along the coast. Knowing no home but a tent and abhorring any more lasting structure, the Bani Hilal systematically pillaged every town and destroyed every solid building they encountered. Cities, towns, villages, aqueducts, dams, cisterns, and bridges went down before a savage horde far more destructive than any of the earlier invaders of the country. Land dependent on irrigation went out of cultivation and reverted to desert. Even great expanses of forest were destroyed by the invaders and their herds, thus further aggravating the water problem by hastening the surface run-off. Unlike the earlier Arab invaders of the seventh and eighth centuries, the Bani Hilal gave the country nothing. So the land fell into a decay from which, despite the remarkable achievements of the French and Italians, it has never wholly recovered.

The dry river-beds are easily explained. For the most part they were carved out in the quaternary age when, a very long time before the dawn of history, the country enjoyed a heavy rainfall. Many of them still flow for a brief period during the wet season of the year.

Climatic change was certainly not responsible for the loss of the country's fauna. The animals pictured so vividly in the Roman mosaics, if alive today, would have little difficulty in living off a great part of the country, were it not that under modern conditions their interests would conflict with those of man. But not all these animals are extinct or have been extinct as long as one might think. The hartebeest in the Bardo mosaic in Tunis is the bubal hartebeest which survived in Morocco up to the Second World War. There were lions in the Middle Atlas till at least 1922 and there may still be leopards in Morocco. The ostrich has disappeared, but only within living memory.

There is no doubt that the extinction of the elephant occurred early in the Christian era. This was the elephant which the Greeks hunted after having learnt its use on Alexander's campaigns in the East, and which they taught the Carthaginians to catch and train. It was the same animal that roams central Africa today but smaller,

modified by isolation and environment. Those who are familiar
with the elephant in tropical Africa, where it thrives under surprisingly varied conditions, will have no difficulty in accepting
the repeated assurance of naturalists that there are many parts of
North Africa where the elephant could prosper today. Its last
habitat was probably the High Atlas.

Man, like the animals, is prone to increase and outgrow his
immediate resources. Hunger leads to inter-tribal feuds, then to
war and eventually to mass movements of peoples such as have
repeatedly changed the course of history in Asia and Europe.
But the first victims of human privation, before hunger drives
man to war with his neighbours, are the beasts of the field. They
are hunted for their flesh and to save the crops they destroy. Today
the greatest threat to the game animals of tropical Africa is the
increase in the human population accompanied by a vast extension in tillage and an insistent demand for more grazing. There is
no longer enough room for both man and game, and so the game
has to give way. In the twenty-five years, 1929 to 1954, the Uganda
Government had to shoot over 26,000 elephants, and it is still
shooting several hundreds a year because of the damage they do to
farmers' crops, cultivation having extended into traditional elephant territory from which the herds, tenacious of their rights,
refuse to be driven. Similarly, the vast herds of zebra, which little
more than a generation ago used to roam the Kenya plains, have
been reduced to negligible proportions because there was not
enough grazing for them and the farmers' cattle. The great game
drives which have repeatedly shocked public sentiment in southern
Africa obey the same pressing need. That this need had also to be
obeyed in North Africa, when the human population, primarily
dependent for its subsistence on husbandry, was enormously
swelled by successive waves of invaders and the natural increase
which resulted from the advent of orderly government, cannot be
doubted. The animals had to go.

But a main cause of the destruction of wild life was the insatiable
demand of the Romans for beasts for their games, the *venationes*,
from the supply of which the *munerarii* grew rich. The baser
instincts of a people so insensitive as to enjoy the crucifixion of a
rogue on the stage during a play, as the Romans did under
Domitian, were not satisfied by the slaughter of a dozen or so
beasts in the arena. So their consuls and emperors gave them
holocausts. On one occasion Caesar put into the arena 400 lions

to battle with the gladiators; Pompey went one better with 600.
In the twenty-six *venationes* given by Augustus 3,500 animals were
slaughtered. Titus celebrated so notable an occasion as the in-
auguration of the Colosseum with 9,000 animals for the gladiators
to destroy or be destroyed by. On a lesser occasion, not many
years later, Trajan had 2,246 killed in a single day.[2]

These were spectacles made memorable by the magnitude of the
slaughter. The animals killed then can have been but an insigni-
ficant percentage of the total sacrificed during the century and a
half the records cover, not to mention the slaughter of earlier and
later decades. Some of these animals came from Asia and some
from Egypt, but that the great majority came from Barbary is
beyond doubt. Knowing as we do the difficulty of capturing
dangerous animals without maiming them and how few of those
secured survive their capture except in very skilled hands, it is
obvious that the cost of the Roman games to Africa in terms of
wild life must have reached astronomical figures.

The elephant seems to have had comparatively little arena-
value, chiefly because when Pompey had a number slaughtered
in the circus by some Gaetuli specially brought over from Africa
the spectacle was so ghastly that it horrified even the unfeeling
Roman public.[3] But the elephant did not escape persecution. In
Rome there was a great demand for ivory and, rather surprisingly,
the cartilage of the elephant's trunk was, according to Pliny, one of
the delicacies served up from Roman kitchens.[4]

Strabo leaves us in no doubt that it was the combination of
the competing interests of farmers and game on the one hand and
the insatiable demand for animals for the arena on the other
which led to the reduction of the country's fauna to the point of
extinction.

> The whole land from the Pillars of Hercules to Carthage [he wrote],
> . . . abounds in wild beasts no less than the interior; and it does not
> seem improbable that the cause why the name Nomads, or Wanderers,
> was bestowed on certain of these people originated in their not being
> able anciently to devote themselves to husbandry on account of wild
> beasts. At the present day, when they are well skilled in hunting, and
> are besides assisted by the Romans in their rage for the spectacle of
> fights with beasts, they are both masters of the beasts and of husbandry.[5]

That is to say, by the end of the first century before Christ, the
game had been sufficiently reduced to make farming possible

where before it had not been. But, as we know, its persecution continued for long after that.

What is surprising is not that many of the animals pictured in the mosaics no longer survive or are so rare that their survival is in doubt, but that they did not become extinct long before the end of the Roman occupation. Like the dead cities and dry river-beds, the lost fauna is in no way attributable to climatic change.

It would be wrong to assume that there have been no variations in climate. The destruction of the forests probably led to minor local modifications in rainfall. There have also been slight changes for reasons we do not know. Archaeologists think it probable that in Roman times Tripolitania was more humid than it is now. To take another example from just outside our field, the rainfall records kept by Ptolemy the geographer in the second century A.D. show that in Egypt although the rainy days were about as numerous as they are today, they were better distributed.[6] But had the changes been more than slight, had the rainfall been materially heavier, some of the Roman bridges would not have spanned the rivers, and many fords would have been unfordable.

When reading descriptions of the country by Roman authors it is impossible not to be impressed by how applicable they are to present-day conditions of climate and water supply. To the Romans, for all their dependence on North Africa for corn (though they depended much more on Egypt), it was a country to be dreaded for its waterless wastes and wild beasts. It is a theme which constantly recurs in their literature, but it remained for Horace to sum it up in three words, 'leonum arida nutrix'.[7] Sallust's comment was equally apt, 'caelo terraque penuria aquarum.'[8] In historical records the problem of water supply frequently recurs. When Caesar was campaigning near Hadrumentum (Sousse) lack of water was a constant anxiety to him, as it was to Belisarius six centuries later. Droughts, too, were seemingly no less common than they are today. Hadrian was beloved of Africans because rain fell for the first time in five years on the day of his arrival in the country. The conclusion that climatically the Maghrib has changed but little in the last 2,000 years is impossible to resist.

*   *   *   *   *

The climatic history of the Sahara is even more striking than that of Barbary. There can be little doubt that two thousand years ago the Sahara must have been almost as arid and formidable a desert as it is today. Classical authors all paint a sombre picture of what the Sahara was like. 'Libya is full of wild beasts', wrote Herodotus, 'while beyond the wild beast region there is a tract which is wholly sand, very scant of water, and utterly and entirely a desert.[9] To Pliny, five hundred years later, the Sahara was just 'a desert abandoned to the sand and swarming with serpents'.[10]

At no time was a journey into the Sahara regarded as other than a hazardous enterprise. Even before Herodotus's time it was possible for a whole army to be overwhelmed. Such was the fate of the expedition which Cambyses sent to destroy the oracle at Jupiter Ammon, the modern Siwa. 'A wind arose from the south, strong and deadly, bringing with it vast columns of whirling sand, which entirely covered up the troops, and caused them wholly to disappear.' Thus, according to the Ammonians, did it fare with this army![11]

Cambyses's expedition took place about 525 B.C. But if one presses further back in time, the face of the Sahara changes. 'Long, long ago', Lloyd Cabot Briggs, one of the leading students of Saharan prehistory has written, 'during the prehistoric ages before the dawn of written history, the Sahara was very different from what it is today, for much of it was fertile and relatively thickly populated. Stone implements of all shapes and sizes are scattered nearly all over the desert, in a profusion which proves beyond doubt that the land once supported a very substantial human population, thanks to a climate far more salubrious than that it now enjoys. Fishhooks and barbed harpoon points made of bone have been found as far north as the centre of the western Sahara, and so there must have been good fishing once upon a time. Indeed recent excavations have shown that, up until perhaps as recently as three or four thousand years ago, much of what is now desert was relatively fertile and well watered country, dotted with shallow lakes and swamps, and even clumps of trees, shrubs, and ferns belonging to species which are no longer found south of the Atlas Mountains.'[12]

The fishing implements of neolithic man are not the only evidence left by him to suggest a remarkable change in climate. On certain rock sites in the central and northern Sahara there have been discovered life-size engravings done by an early race of hunters. Among the animals depicted are elephant, rhinoceros, hippopotamus, and the extinct *bubalus antiquus*. (We shall have

cause to discuss these engravings more fully in the next chapter.)
Although the residual fauna of the Sahara and the Sahel is still
remarkably rich and varied,* all the larger species shown on the
rock pictures have disappeared. When all the evidence is considered, prehistorians have reached the conclusion that, for reasons
which are still somewhat obscure, a marked climatic change took
place in the Sahara between 3000 and 1500 B.C.[13]

But climatic change has not been the only cause of desiccation.
In the southern Sahara and the Sahel river beds have silted up, the
levels of major streams have fallen and lesser streams have been
forced into different channels. Changes of this nature are most
dramatically illustrated in the area of Lake Chad. In neolithic
times the waters of Lake Chad flowed for four hundred miles along
the valley, known as the Bahr al-Ghazal, into the Bodele depression, whose level is more than two hundred feet lower than that of
the lake. Rich neolithic sites have been reported in the Bodele
area and, even more remarkable, enormous slag-heaps, providing
evidence of iron-working. Iron-working can hardly have been
carried on much earlier than the beginning of the Christian era,
so the Bodele area must have been inhabited by a sedentary population long after neolithic times. Today the whole length of the
Bahr al-Ghazal is dry, but on one occasion as late as 1874 water is
said to have flowed from Lake Chad for a hundred miles down the
Bahr al-Ghazal. It appears that the level of Lake Chad has been
steadily falling. One cause may be the gradual capture of the
Logone, one of the main sources of water for Lake Chad, by the
Benue, for when the waters of the Logone reach a certain height
they do not continue to flow northwards into the lake but spill over
into a marshy area before passing by way of the Mayo Kebbi into
the Benue.[14]

Finally, human action appears to have played some part in the
'desertification' of the Sahara. Rock paintings show that in neolithic times the Sahara was occupied by a race of pastoralists.
The destruction done by their herds to the existing vegetation
occurred at a time when the decrease in rainfall made it impossible
for a natural regeneration of the vegetation to occur. This is a
continuing process: overgrazing by the flocks and herds of nomadic

* The most notable animals are the lion, giraffe, Barbary sheep, a monkey, the white
oryx, three gazelles, and of course the most widely distributed of the larger desert
game, the addax antelope. These animals, and many lesser ones, manage to thrive
on conditions which prohibit their drinking for months, and often for years on end,
and some do not drink from birth to death.

people still contributes to the process of desiccation. This is not the only way in which man has helped to enlarge the desert area. In some areas, around Kumbi Saleh, for example, the ancient capital of Ghana, the desert has crept in when the original population of sedentary agriculturalists was driven out by the nomads. Elsewhere, trade-routes across the desert have fallen into disuse and the wells that served them have been abandoned and become choked with sand, not on account of any natural reason, but simply because the trade has been diverted down other channels.[15]

Outside the polar regions there are few parts of the world less encouraging to human occupation than the Sahara. It has been peopled from the days of Herodotus onwards to the limit of its meagre capacity. Its inhabitants are governed by the rigorous conditions which the desert imposes. Most of them are pastoral nomads because only by keeping constantly on the move can the penurious resources of the desert in water and pasture be made to support human life. The margin between plenty and starvation is so narrow and sensitive that life is always precarious, the future never secure. This breeds a tough, virile race who are ever ready to defend to their last breath their wells and pastures, or, if these should fail, to fight with equal determination for those of their neighbours. In order to support life, or at least make it tolerable, they must supplement their meagre natural resources by every available means. They therefore blackmail caravans passing through their country and make seasonal migrations into the better-favoured areas surrounding the desert. As the nomads of the Arabian and Syrian deserts move seasonally into the valleys of the Nile and Euphrates, like the sons of Jacob, so do some of the Bedawin tribes of the north Sahara spend the hottest months of the year pasturing their flocks and herds on the High Plateaux of the Atlas or in the Tell of Algeria and Tunisia. Similarly in the south, the Tuareg drive their stock down on to the savannahs of the Western Sudan, into Nigeria and the great plains of the middle Niger. Such seasonal migrations are traditional and accepted by the semi-nomadic and sedentary peoples into whose countries they move. When the hot season ends the nomads return peacefully to the desert.

Sometimes desert pastures fail altogether and the wells and water-holes dry up. When this happens there is a danger of the desert overflowing, of seasonal migrations being extended beyond their traditional limits, in both extent and time. This conflicts with the interests of neighbouring tribes and trouble follows. The seasonal migrations may develop into raids, and the raids into permanent occupation with shepherd kings lording it over agriculturists. The courage, hardihood, and mobility of the nomads, and especially their proneness to overspill their frontiers, make them dangerous neighbours. The less virile semi-nomads of the peripheral areas outside the desert are powerless to resist them, and even a strong central government may be unable to hold them at bay by normal methods of defence. The Egyptians of the twelfth dynasty had to build a wall from Heliopolis to Pelusium to stop Arab incursions of this nature. The Assyrians built a barrier across the Euphrates to keep out the Medes, and the Persians a wall against the Huns. The Great Wall of China was a defence against the Mongols. Each of these great works was designed to put an end to the ever-recurring danger of raids by the desert on the sown.

The vast steppes of Central Asia repeatedly sent out hordes of pastoral nomads whose conquests shook the world. The extreme poverty of the Sahara set so strict a limit to its population that it has never in recorded history launched a conquering horde comparable with the Scythians, Aryans, Avars, Huns, Arabs, or Turks to whose spectacular migrations the arid lands of Asia gave birth. It has, however, frequently disturbed the peace of its neighbours. A notable event in the history of the Maghrib was the conquest of Morocco by the Almoravids, most of whom were desert-born. The Sanhaja were traditional raiders of Timbuktu and the middle Niger as were the Banu Hilal and Banu Sulaim of Mecca and Medina. The Tebu of Tibesti similarly raided the Nile valley. All around the inhabited periphery of the desert incursions by nomads was an ever-present danger.

It is not always realized that the reason for such raids is usually economic necessity, rather than predatory instincts or mere love of conquest. (The Almoravids were a notable exception.) The controlling factor is usually rainfall. If it is seasonally inadequate to support the nomads and their herds the tribes become seasonally predatory. If, through repeated failure of rains or the natural increase of the herds, the resources of the desert and of the traditional dry-weather grazing grounds cease to be able to support life, then invasion and conquest are the only answer. It follows, therefore, that if the climate of the Sahara had deteriorated since, say, Roman times the history of northern Africa would be one of ever-

increasing political disturbance and bloodshed. It is nothing of
the sort.

The control of the unruly desert tribes was a problem which
constantly taxed the resources and ingenuity of the Romans.
Recorded history south of the Sahara covers less than a thousand
years; but it affords no evidence of raiding of the rich countries of
the Western Sudan by the Tuareg having increased in the course
of time owing to natural causes. Despite the natural tendency of
man and his herds to multiply, the Sahara did not grow less able to
support the desert tribes until the European destroyed their economy. This is a conclusive proof that although there appears to
have been a gradual increase in aridity, there has not been since
the second millennium B.C. any decisive change for the worse.

2

Carbuncles and Gold

'Among the Carthaginians nothing is reputed infamous that is joined with gain.'
POLYBIUS.

SOMETIME about the year 450 B.C. the eminent Greek traveller
and historian, Herodotus, visited the colony established by his
compatriots at Cyrene in North Africa. There he gathered a good
deal of information about the various tribes of Libya, as North
Africa was then called by the Greeks. One of the remotest of these
tribes were the Garamantes, who occupied an area corresponding
to the modern Fezzan. 'The Geramantes', Herodotus was informed, 'hunt the Ethiopian hole-men, or troglodytes, in four-
horse chariots, for these troglodytes are exceedingly swift of foot—
more so than any people of whom we have any information. They
eat snakes and lizards and other reptiles and speak a language like
nothing upon earth—it might be bats screeching.' If the Garamantes are to be regarded as the ancestors of the modern population of the Fezzan, it seems possible that the Ethiopian troglodytes
—the black men who live in holes—were the ancestors of the
Tebu of Tibesti.[1]

Herodotus picked up another remarkable story that threw some

light on the Sahara. Five wild young men, sons of Nasamonian
chiefs from the Greater Syrtis, had set out to explore the desert
parts of Libya, with the object of penetrating farther than any
had done before. Providing themselves with a plentiful supply of
water and provisions they traversed the desert in a westerly direction. After travelling for many days over the sand they came to a
plain where there were trees laden with fruit. While they were
gathering the fruit they were surprised and seized by some dwarf-
ish negroes whose language they could not understand. They were
carried away over extensive marshes till they reached a town, the
inhabitants of which spoke the same language as their captors.
A great river containing crocodiles flowed past the town, running
from west to east. In due course the adventurous young men returned safely to their own country.[2]

These two curious pieces of information noted down by Herodotus—the Garamantes in their chariots chasing the Ethiopian
troglodytes and the strange adventure of the young Nasamones—
represented almost all that was known about the inhabitants of
the Central Sahara in the first millenium B.C. But in recent years
Herodotus's information has been both confirmed and supplemented by the evidence provided by the rock-engravings and
paintings of the desert. The existence of ancient pictures on the
rocks was first reported by Heinrich Barth, the great German
explorer, as early as 1851.[3] But it has been only in the last forty
years that the astonishing richness of Saharan rock art has been
revealed, mainly through the work of French archaeologists.

For technical reasons, the paintings and engravings are very
difficult to date, but it has been possible to classify them into
various styles, which can then be arranged in chronological order.[4]
The earliest style is distinguished by its life-size or nearly life-size
engravings, executed in a vigorous naturalistic manner, of wild
animals, including elephant, rhinoceros, and the now extinct
bubalus antiquus. Some of the engravings have scenes depicting
hunters, and it seems likely that the engravings are in fact the work
of a people who lived mainly by hunting. Engravings in this style
have been found only in the northern half of the Sahara. Some
scholars believe that the engravings must have been executed
before 5,000 B.C.; others prefer a more recent date.

The second style shows many of the same animals as the first
style, but is clearly of later date, as the bubalus antiquus is no longer
shown. Instead, domestic cattle make their appearance, being

shown both in engravings and in polychromatic paintings. Pictures of cattle have been found in many parts of the Sahara; they are particularly common in the Jebel Uweinat lying to the east of Tibesti, in Tibesti itself, and in the Tassili-n-Ajjer to the west of the Fezzan. Clearly these cattle-pictures provide evidence of the arrival of pastoral people coming from further east. Some scholars are inclined to see in these ancient pastoralists the ancestors of the nomadic Fulani of West Africa.

The third distinct style is marked by the presence of men riding in horse-drawn chariots. Over three hundred representations of chariots have been found in the Sahara, from the Fezzan to southern Morocco, in Ahaggar, and in Adrar of the Iforas. The chariots confirm Herodotus's statement about the Garamantes; they also help to provide an explanation for the strange exploit of the Nasamones, for a French archaeologist, Henri Lhote, has found chariot-drawings at various stations along an ancient caravan route leading from Ahaggar to Adrar of the Iforas. Their presence suggests that this was the route that was taken by the Nasamones and that the river which they saw flowing from west to east was in fact the Niger in the vicinity of Gao.[5]

In the fourth style, the chariots have disappeared. Instead, men armed with javelins are shown riding on horses. The fifth style— artistically the least distinguished—shows men on camels.

It will be many years before archaeologists have succeeded in extracting all the information contained in this remarkably rich material. For the paintings and engravings contain far more than men and animals. Some pictures represent strange deities; others provide detailed impressions of dress and weapons. Some paintings give clear evidence of Egyptian influence; others—notably some of the chariot pictures—recall the art-styles of the Aegean. But though much remains obscure, one fact stands out beyond the reach of controversy: for centuries before the introduction of the camel into the Sahara (an event that took place about the beginning of the Christian era) men were accustomed to move about the desert with oxen, in horse-drawn chariots, or on horse-back.

The use of horses and of oxen in the desert is not quite such a surprising fact as it might appear to those who have been brought up to think that the camel is the only beast of burden man can employ in the Sahara. Until quite recent times, many Saharan tribes maintained a small number of horses. Among some tribes, the Tuareg of Ahaggar for example, the horse was rare enough to be regarded as a symbol of prestige; among others, horses formed one of the basic elements of their strength. For in close fighting the horse is a much more reliable animal than the camel.[6]

Pack-oxen are extensively used by many people living in the Sudan, by the Shuwa Arabs of the Lake Chad area for example, and they are still employed in parts of the Sahara, in Air, and in the Fezzan, while in Tibesti the Tebu have a tradition of having used bullocks before the camel reached them.

Bullocks are no longer used outside the great oases, so it is not easy to determine how their capacity to travel without water compares with that of the camel. F. R. Rodd (now Lord Rennell) tells us that 'loaded oxen can march comfortably with water only every third day'. He also says that 'incredible as it may seem, cattle (unloaded) . . . do as much as four and five days without water.[7] The present writer's inquiries lead him to believe that cattle are capable of a far better performance than that. At the peak of the dry season in northern Tanganyika a native herdsman told him that he was not watering his cattle more than once in five days. There was nothing in their condition to suggest that they were suffering any hardship. During the last war a Kenya veterinary officer who was regularly driving cattle for slaughter from Somaliland to Mombasa found no difficulty in getting his herds through eight successive waterless days. These cattle were not carrying loads, but they were required to go much longer without water than they were used to, and if the heat by day was less than it would have been in the Sahara there was not the stimulus of the cold desert night. It seems reasonable to suppose that a beast capable of doing eight days without water in the hot coastal plains of East Africa might with time be accustomed to doing at least equally well in the Sahara. Whether it could be trained to do eight waterless days with a load is doubtful. Had these Somali cattle been of a stock accustomed for countless generations to carrying loads on the desert trade routes they probably could have done so.

A camel does not normally do more than ten days without water, so there may not be a very great difference in this respect between camel and bullock. The carrying capacity of both is much the same, and in the Western Sudan a bullock will do twenty miles a day, which is little less than a camel. The bullock on the other hand travels much more slowly, so it takes him longer to get from one watering point to another and sets a strict limit to his range of travel. It was not of course until the coming of the *mehari*, the riding camel bred for speed, that the Saharan tribes acquired their astonishing mobility.

There is certainly no reason to suppose that caravan traffic in the Sahara only became possible with the arrival of the camel. If the wells and water-holes were a little more numerous than they are now travel with bullock transport on many caravan routes may well have been little more difficult than with camels. Bullocks may also have been supplemented with donkeys which, as we have seen, have an astonishing capacity for going without water, can carry half a bullock's load and travel as many miles a day. The Pharaohs of the XXth Dynasty used donkeys to transport stores and gold to and from the mines of the Eastern Desert.* The primitive Isebetan or Djohala of the Hoggar mountains, who have never acquired camels, still use donkeys.

In Herodotus's day the general pattern of life in the Sahara cannot have differed greatly from what it was in recent times. In order to support life the tribes were under the same necessity of making the fullest possible use of the desert's meagre resources, and seasonal migrations from the Sahara into the hills and plateaux of the north were a normal feature of desert life. There was certainly no *cordon sanitaire* segregating the nomads from the sedentary tribes. Contact between the desert and the sown was continuous, and contact certainly meant trade. This may have been little more than the bartering of dates for corn, but it probably went much further. With the exchange of goods went the exchange of ideas, and of knowledge, above all of geographical knowledge.

All through history the commonest motive for geographical exploration has been trade. Until recent times discovery for discovery's sake was rare. The desire to seek the origin of strange and valued products, to discover untapped sources of wealth, to go behind the middleman's back and buy cheaply, is deeply ingrained in human nature. One cannot suppose that the people of North Africa were more free from the covetousness of man than others, that their contacts with the nomads of the desert did not awaken desires to seek out the prosperous oases, even to reach the teeming and fertile plains of the remote south. We must therefore turn to the people living on the Mediterranean coast of North

---

* The small Sudan donkey can do 85 miles between watering places if heartened after the first 50 with a single bowl of water. (Dr. C. G. Seligman, quoting A. J. Arkell, in a letter to the author.)

Africa to see what we can find out of their relations with the people of the Sahara and the Sudan.

In the fifth century B.C., when Herodotus was describing the ways of the Garamantes, there existed along the North African coast from the Gulf of Syrtis westwards to the Atlantic a string of trading posts founded by the Phoenicians in the course of the previous five hundred years. The Phoenicians were essentially merchant adventurers, too mercenary not to have been curious about the interior of Africa, but too maritime to adventure there themselves. (They were like the early Portuguese traders in India who were compared to fishes because if taken from the sea they perished.) This was less true of their kinsmen the Carthaginians, who had first established their hegemony over the Phoenician settlements in North Africa and then absorbed and developed them into colonies of the mother-city. By the fifth century B.C. Carthage had become a metropolis which owed some of its prosperity to the fertility of its hinterland, a considerable, but undefined, extent of which it directly controlled.

East and west along the coast and beyond the Pillars of Hercules Carthage had established colonies, most of which were Phoenician in origin. But whereas the Phoenicians had been content with small settlements with just enough administrators, probably temporary expatriates, to care for their mercantile interests, the Carthaginians' colonies were the permanent homes of many of their countrymen, each trading on its own account and largely self-dependent. During the thousand years of their occupation of the coast the Carthaginians' interests were almost wholly commercial and ranged all over the western Mediterranean, of which Carthage was the mistress, and far beyond the Pillars. Their existence must nevertheless have depended a great deal on Africa, on the fruits of its soil for their living and, to a less extent, on its exportable products for their trade. So, unlike their Phoenician predecessors, their relations with the people of the country were close. They were bound to them by mutual interests and, to an ever-increasing extent, by inter-marriage. Both the development of the colonies and the dependence of each on its hinterland was encouraged by isolation, for, thanks to their Phoenician ancestry, the Carthaginians were still essentially maritime and their occupation of the coast was not geographically continuous. They did not want more land than was necessary for their trade and well-being. So their colonies were no more than *enclaves*, separated one from another by harbourless stretches of coast for which they had neither need nor use.

Carthage itself, however, was too great a city for a mere *enclave* to meet its needs. For its support, as for its defence, it was directly dependent on a great part of what is now Tunisia, and it commanded the allegiance of many of the Berber tribes. Although the limits of Carthaginian rule in the city's hinterland are doubtful they must have been far-flung, for African levies formed a large part, latterly a preponderant one, of the immense armies of the Carthaginians. Himilco's shameful abandonment of his African troops at Syracuse, to be slain or enslaved by the Greeks, will be recalled, as will more certainly the light Numidian cavalry of Hannibal's army.

Political and economic necessity forced the Carthaginians to acquire a territorial empire in Africa. Its long broken coastline, rich in fine harbours, made it an admirable base from which to build up and maintain a vast maritime trade. Carthage itself combined, like so many Punic settlements, the advantages of a first-class harbour with a situation on an easily defended peninsula, but to these it added a central position commanding the Narrows of the Mediterranean, the world's greatest trade route. This happy combination of circumstances made it the perfect capital for such an empire.

The immensely strong strategical position of Carthage and the comparable one of the second city of the empire, Gades (Cadiz), beyond the Pillars, enabled the Carthaginians, who were uncompromisingly intolerant of interlopers, to prevent any interference with their trade by foreigners.

The Romans were excluded by treaty from all lands where the Carthaginians had established trading settlements. So Sicily, Sardinia, and southern Spain were closed to them. No ship of Rome forced to seek shelter in a Punic port might stay longer than weather or essential repairs necessitated. The passage of the Straits was also forbidden lest others should learn that the Carthaginians got their tin and lead from Cornwall and Brittany. Strabo relates how the captain of a ship of Gades bound for the English Channel, finding himself shadowed by an enterprising Roman galley, ran his ship aground, losing both ship and cargo, but taking the Roman with him. [8]

The North African coast west of Cyrenaica was similarly closed to foreigners. In the sixth century the Greeks were forced to abandon a settlement they had made on the coast between the Syrtes, and a century or so later they were forbidden by treaty to come farther west than the Altars of the Philaeni. This rigid exclusion of Greeks and Romans from the country west of the Greater Syrtis is reflected in the paucity of information which the classical authors give about the Carthaginians' African trade and our consequent ignorance of its nature and extent.

Carthage manufactured cheap goods for export, but the trade of herself and her satellite colonies was mainly of an *entrepôt* nature, the carriage of goods from one foreign country to another, the exchange of the raw products of one for the manufactured goods of another. The Carthaginians were not therefore particularly dependent on Africa itself for the support of their trade. Indeed, the Berber tribes of the littoral were too primitive and their country not rich enough for the Maghrib to be able to make any great contribution to the immensity of Punic commerce. Wool, skins, timber, purple dye, ivory, and ostrich feathers were the principal local products which found their way into foreign ports, but not, so far as one can tell, on an important scale. Owing to its moderate nature the purely African trade of the Carthaginians cannot have been of great consequence to them.

The Carthaginians were so successful in concealing their trade secrets that we can only draw tentative inferences from circumstantial evidence. All we know for certain is that they obtained carbuncles from the Garamantes, and that in Europe the carbuncle was known as the Carthaginian stone. Although Pliny writes very fully about African carbuncles and emphasizes the importance of Carthage as the principal *entrepôt* for them, neither he nor any other writer indicates how important the trade was.[9] It is significant, however, that after the fall of Carthage the Romans found it worth their while to carry it on.

Then, as all through history, the easiest access to the interior from the Mediterranean lay southward from midway between the Lesser and the Greater Syrtis. This barren and inhospitable coast, the Syrtica Regio, stretching east and west from the modern town of Tripoli, was significantly called the Emporia by the ancients, though to Herodotus it was the country of the Lotophagi. Along it, at short intervals, there were three important Carthaginian trading settlements, Sabratha, Oea (Tripoli), and Lepcis. This was far closer settlement than the natural resources of this part of the coast and its immediate hinterland could justify. As there were no particular political or strategic reasons for such over-crowding at this point the conclusion must be drawn that it was due to the ready access it gave to the interior. If the story Athen-aeus tells of a Carthaginian named Mago having crossed the desert three times be true, this is the way he must have gone.[10]

Tripoli has been called the gateway of the Sahara, and it con-tinued to be regarded as such till the nineteenth century when a noble line of explorers, notably Lyon, Denham, Oudney and Clapperton, and the remarkable Barth, all chose it as the base from which to set out on their travels into the heart of the con-tinent. To Tripoli, too, coming from Lake Chad up the Gara-mantian road, marched General Leclerc at the head of his gallant column in 1943. Another pointer to the importance of this coast to the Carthaginians is their having fixed the Altars of the Philaeni as the western limit of Greek dominion. It was far enough away to deny the Greeks the use of the Garamantian road to the Fezzan.

If not only carbuncles, what else was it that made the Gara-mantian road so important? What other trades could have helped to support the Emporia? For an answer we must look to the uses to which the road was put in later times when the veil of commer-cial secrecy was lifted. Until far into the last century slaves, gold, ivory, and ostrich feathers were the life-blood of the Mediterranean trade with the Fezzan. In the days of Carthage there were too many elephants and ostriches in North Africa for there to have been any need to go south for ivory and feathers. So, either slaves or gold, or both, appears to be the answer.

The Carthaginians employed vast numbers of slaves, notably on the great privately owned estates in the hinterland of the capital, the skilled cultivation of which made their agriculture famous. They also traded in slaves. The Balearics seem to have been a particularly valuable market, for the islanders were willing to sell three or four men for a woman, which suited the Cartha-ginians, and those of them who served in the Carthaginian army had an engaging habit of investing their pay in women and wine. To what extent the Carthaginians employed negro slaves is doubt-ful. Punic cemeteries have yielded numerous skulls of a negroid character, and there were some very dark-skinned Africans, per-haps negroes, in the Carthaginian army which invaded Sicily early in the fifth century B.C. Frontinus tells us that as prisoners they were paraded naked before the Greek soldiery in order to bring the Carthaginians into contempt.[11] On the other hand, as the Carthaginians customarily enslaved prisoners of war and the victims of their piracy, two sources of supply which they must have found very fruitful, they were far from being dependent on Africa for slave labour. It is unlikely that they hesitated to enslave as many Berbers as they required, nor were so brutal a people likely to have drawn the line at doing the same to their own peasantry. The evidence of negro blood is, however, significant and it seems probable that they imported slaves from the Fezzan. It was a likely source, for the Garamantes cannot have hunted the Troglodyte Ethiopians except to enslave them. The slave trade with the Fezzan may even have been important to the Carthaginians, but there are no grounds for assuming that it was.

In the confused and ill-documented story of northern Africa, of the Sahara and the countries to the north and south, there runs a golden thread. From the Nile valley in the east to the Atlantic in the west there was trafficking in gold with the interior of Africa at all times in recorded history. Slaves and gold, gold and slaves, provided the life-blood of the trade of the Maghrib with the Sudan. The gold flowed north in two main streams, the Garamantian road, from the Fezzan to Tripoli, and the Taghaza road from the Niger to Sijilmasa in Morocco; the one in the east and the other in the west. The flow seems to have been steady but not spectacular. There were occasions, however, when the world caught a fleeting glimpse of gold in quantities which clearly betrayed fabulous wealth hidden far away in the interior. Early in the fourteenth century Mansa Musa emerged dramatically from the desert to astonish Egypt and the western world by his prodigal display of gold. Two centuries and a half later the Moors of Morocco so enriched themselves with gold by conquering the countries of the middle Niger that an obsequious Christendom competed with the Turks for the favours of their sultan. Where the gold came from was a problem which Christian and Muslim tried unceasingly to solve, and a quest which inspired some of the great exploits in the history of geographical discovery. But so secretive were all those engaged in the trade that the solution was not found till very recent times.

In the days of Herodotus there were Ethiopians far up the Nile so rich, he tells us, that they bound their prisoners in fetters of gold:[12] and the Greeks of the Homeric period once shipped a whole cargo of gold from Egypt. Far away to the west, too, there had long been trading in gold with Africans on the Atlantic coast. Neither Herodotus nor any other of the ancient chroniclers mentions trading in gold anywhere between these two geographical extremes. That the trans-Saharan gold trade had not yet been born is possible; if it had the Carthaginians would not have told anyone about it. But there is no certainty in the matter.

Thucydides tells us the Carthaginians were rich in gold and this is to some extent confirmed by the amount of gold found in Punic cemeteries.[13] Pliny was surprised that the fine imposed by Rome on Carthage was payable in silver instead of gold, not because of the scarcity of gold in Carthage, but in the world.[14] Scipio's triumph was graced with a fine display of gold which was presumably Punic, but there is no evidence of the Carthaginians having traded in gold in the Mediterranean. So the grounds for assuming that the gold trade was the reason for the importance they attached to the Garamantian road is exceedingly slender. Nevertheless the illustrious Stéphane Gsell thought it might have been.[15] In any case it is difficult to accept his suggestion that the gold the Carthaginians may have got from Fezzan came from so far afield as the upper reaches of the Niger. There were, as we shall see in a later chapter, much more probable sources of supply, including the Fezzan itself.

Slaves and gold, then, are possible explanations of Punic interest in the Garamantian road, but the grounds for including gold are the weaker. They become weaker still when we consider that the Carthaginians' wealth in gold does not appear to have been in excess of what they could have got from the west coast of Africa where we know they obtained anyway some of their supply.

In his account of the peoples of the west coast of Africa Herodotus tells us that

off their coast, as the Carthaginians report, lies an island, by name Cyraunis . . . and there is in the island a lake, from which the young maidens of the country draw up gold-dust, by dipping into the mud birds' feathers smeared with pitch. If this be true, I know not; I but write what is said.[16]

Herodotus continues,

the Carthaginians also relate the following:—There is a country in Libya, and a nation, beyond the Pillars of Hercules, which they are wont to visit, where they no sooner arrive but forthwith they unlade their wares, and, having disposed them after an orderly fashion along the beach, leave them, and, returning aboard their ships, raise a great smoke. The natives, when they see the smoke, come down to the shore, and, laying out to view so much gold as they think the worth of the wares, withdraw to a distance. The Carthaginians upon this come ashore and look. If they think the gold enough, they take it and go their way; but if it does not seem to them sufficient, they go aboard ship once more, and wait patiently. Then the others approach and add to their gold, till the Carthaginians are content. Neither party deals unfairly by the other: for they themselves never touch the gold till it comes up to the worth of their goods, nor do the natives ever carry off the goods till the gold is taken away.[17]

It would be pertinent to ask how it was that if the Carthaginians were so secretive about their trade in the east they allowed so much to be known of what they were doing in the west. The answer is that geographical and political circumstances made secrecy impossible. In Herodotus's time the Carthaginians may already have occupied Gades (Cadiz), but they were not yet the complete masters of the southern extremity of the Iberian Peninsula that they later became, and therefore could not control the passage of the Straits. Not until they did were they able to keep secret from Europe what was going on at the point where Africa approached so closely to it that there was unceasing traffic between the two, and, as Strabo tells us, the poor men of Spain went fishing in their frail craft 'around the coast of Maurusia as far as the river Lixus'.[18] The rest of their African empire was lapped by a sea which they could and did control. There, says Strabo, they 'used to throw into the sea any foreigners who sailed past their country to Sardinia or the Pillars'.[19]

We now come to one of the most controversial documents in ancient history. In the temple of Chronos at Carthage there is said to have existed a lengthy inscription describing a voyage down the coast of West Africa made under the command of the suffete Hanno. This inscription was destroyed after the Roman capture of Carthage, but not before a copy had allegedly been made by some Greek or Roman writer.[20]

Hanno was commissioned by the Carthaginians 'to sail past the Pillars of Heracles' and 'to found cities of the Libyphoenicians' (the Phoenicians residing in Africa). 'He set sail with sixty vessels of fifty oars and a multitude of men and women to the number of 30,000, and provisions of other equipment'. After establishing a number of settlements along the Atlantic coast of Morocco, the expedition reached a big river, the Lixus. A nomadic tribe, the Lixitae, dwelt on the banks of the river. Having obtained interpreters from this tribe, the Carthaginians continued southwards along the desert coast until they reached an island, Cerne, where they founded another colony.

From Cerne they sailed on 'through the delta of a big river named Chretes' and on to 'another deep and wide river, which was infested with crocodiles and hippopotami'. Then they turned back to Cerne, but set out again and sailed south for twelve days until they reached 'a high wooded range, with varied and fragrant trees'. After doubling this cape, they found themselves 'in an immense recess of the sea fringed with low-lying land'. Here they saw 'fires flaring up by night in every quarter at intervals, some greater, some less'. Sailing on for another five days, they came to a 'great gulf'. In the gulf lay an island with a lake in the middle of it, and an island in the middle of the lake. 'Landing on the smaller island we could see nothing but forest, and by night many fires being kindled, and we heard the noise of pipes and cymbals and a din of tom-toms and the shouts of a multitude.' Hastily leaving the island, the Carthaginians 'coasted along a country with a fragrant smoke of blazing timber, from which streams of fire plunged into the sea'. Further on they came to the highest mountain they had yet seen, known as the Chariot of the Gods; 'in the centre a leaping flame towered above the others and appeared to reach the stars. . . . Following the rivers of five for three further days', they came to another gulf, which also contained an island, and in the island a lake, and in the lake a smaller island. This second island was 'full of wild people', for the most part 'women with hairy bodies', whom the interpreters called Gorillas. The Carthaginians were unable to catch any of the men, but 'secured three women, who bit and scratched and resisted their captors'. 'But we killed and flayed them, and brought the hides to Carthage. This was the end of our journey, owing to lack of provisions.' So ends the story of Hanno's expedition, an expedition which is generally thought to have taken place about 480 B.C.

Until recently, scholars have tended to accept the inscription as genuine, and have concentrated on trying to identify the places mentioned in it. Many different interpretations have been put forward. Some scholars have suggested that the great mountain seen by the explorers and described by them as 'the Chariot of the Gods' must have been a volcano and pointed out that the only volcano on the coast of West Africa is Cameroon Mountain. Others have found it impossible to believe that the Carthaginians could have reached so far along the coast, and have identified the mountain with Kakulima in Sierra Leone, the flames on its flanks being caused in their opinion by grass or forest fires.[21]

Within the last ten years, however, the work of two French scholars, G. Germain and R. Mauny, has tended to show that Hanno's Periplus may not be a genuine document at all. Germain, a classical philologist, has subjected the text to careful scrutiny and come to the conclusion that 'at least three quarters of it is nothing more than a mediocre literary exercise, whose sources, many of them of literary origin, can sometimes be identified'.[22] Mauny has approached the text in a different way. He has pointed to the difficulties of navigation along the Saharan coast, and in particular to the fact that it is almost impossible to follow the coast northwards in the face of contrary winds. He has worked out the distance covered by galleys in a day—not more than fifteen miles, so that a journey from the Wadi Nun in Morocco to the mouth of the Senegal, a distance of about 1,250 miles, would have taken close on three months, and this journey would have to be made along a particularly barren stretch of coast. Finally, he has shown that in the middle ages no record exists of any ship propelled by oars making a successful journey beyond Cape Bogador.[23]

So far no Carthaginian remains have been discovered by archaeologists south of Mogador on the Atlantic coast of Morocco. Given the absence of reliable archaeological evidence, any speculation about the Carthaginian presence in West Africa during the first millenium B.C. can only remain in the realm of fantasy or of guesswork.

In the Sahara, also, there is an absence of the sort of archaeological evidence that might help to throw new light on the Carthaginians' relations with the tribes of the interior. But one theory put forward by the great Saharan scholar, E. F. Gautier, is worth noting.[24] Gautier attempted to identify the mysterious, highly valued and now rare aggrey bead of the West Coast with the Carthaginian carbuncle. There is great division of opinion over what an aggrey bead really is, partly owing to its having been much copied all through the centuries by enterprising Venetian glass-makers. It appears, however, often to have been made from chalcedony, a name derived from the Greek word for Carthage. In classical times, as we have seen, the carbuncle was known as the Carthaginian stone. From this Gautier seemingly argues: aggrey beads were chalcedony, chalcedony was the Carthaginian stone, the Carthaginian stone was the carbuncle, therefore the Punic carbuncle, which came from the Garamantes, and the aggrey bead are the same thing. The argument is not a difficult one to assail and, its weaknesses apart, circumstances are wholly against it.

Although, as Gautier points out, aggrey beads are now associated only with the Guinea coast it is evident from the frequency with which they have been found in Saharan tombs that they were once very widely distributed throughout northern Africa. Gautier's assumption, following the argument outlined above, that these beads were made and distributed by the Carthaginians seems over-bold. Why not by the Garamantes themselves? To a people capable of building four-horse chariots bead-making from chalcedony ought to have been child's play. Alternatively, there might well have been others, besides the Carthaginians, who bought chalcedony from the Garamantes to make into beads.* There is an old indigenous bead industry at Bida in Nigeria which got its stone from Kano, but, according to tradition, the stone originated in Egypt or the Atlas mountains. The one is possible,† the other highly improbable. The source might well have been the Fezzan, the country of the Garamantes.

But one day the Carthaginian carbuncle may, after all, turn out to have been the aggrey bead, and Gautier proved right. If that happens we shall be much nearer to knowing why the Carthaginians clustered so closely round the head of the Garamantian road.

* Although chalcedony has not yet been recorded in the Fezzan, it has been found in both Algeria and the Libyan Desert. (Mr. J. D. H. Wiseman, British Museum [Natural History], in a letter to the author.) It is probable, therefore, that the Garamantes were able to obtain it from within their own territory. Pliny (v. 5), moreover, as we have seen, mentions a Mount Gyri, in their country, 'where precious stones were produced'.

† Raw material recently obtained from Kano by the Bida bead-makers has been found to be pieces of worked carnelian and agate that must have come from Cambay. (Letter from Mr. A. J. Arkell to the author.)

3

Romans and Garamantes

'The Romans, *carefull Relaters of their great victories, doe speake little of the interior parts of* Affrica.'—RICHARD JOBSON.

THE elation of the Romans at the destruction of Carthage was tempered by misgivings. The commitments their triumph might involve were unpredictable. What particularly disturbed them was the prospect of having to administer a host of barbarous and warlike tribes. Yet the need for the military occupation of Africa was inescapable, for only thus could there be protection against a Carthaginian resurgence, fostered and nourished by the tribes. Long experience of administering conquered territories had taught the Romans that one commitment leads to another, that no sooner is a frontier established than another is needed farther afield to protect the first. They resolved, however, to confine themselves to occupying a small province round Carthage, the Provincia Africa,* and to leave the government of the rest of the country to the native rulers.

Initially this policy was successful, but eventually it foundered on the impossibility of curbing the jealousies and aspirations of Libyan potentates, the long arm of whose machinations reached even into the domestic politics of Rome. After Caesar's victory over Juba at Thapsus in 46 B.C. Numidia was taken over, and on the death of Ptolemy, the son of Juba II, in A.D. 40 so was Mauretania. By the time of the emperors the whole of the North African littoral, from Lepcis to the Atlantic, had come under Roman rule.

It was not long before circumstances similar to those which had forced this lateral expansion compelled extension in depth and brought full realization of the worst apprehensions voiced at the fall of Carthage. So long as their occupation was limited to a narrow coastal zone the Romans had to deal only with tribes anchored fairly closely to the soil, who are notably easier to control

---

* From this the name spread to the whole continent. The Regency of Tunis long remained officially the Royaume d'Afrique and was so called in the treaty made by the Bey, Husain Pasha, with the French in 1830.

than pastoral nomads. The plateaux behind the coastal belt, extending inland to a long ridge of highlands, the Aures mountains and, in Tripolitania, the Gebel, were then, as they are today, the home of semi-nomadic tribes such as the Nasamones in the east and the Mauri in the west, troublemakers whose countries had to be occupied. So the defensive zone of the Roman *limes* was advanced to the foothills of what must have appeared to be an admirable natural line of defence. It was perhaps only then that it became evident to the Romans that there was no apparent limit to their commitments. They had brought within their jurisdiction arid but grassy uplands, the High Plateaux in the west, the Tell in the centre, and the Gefara in the extreme east, all of which were the summer grazing grounds of wholly untamed desert tribes. In the dry summer months, when there was no pasture left in the desert, these grazing grounds were essential to the survival of the flocks and herds on which the desert tribes depended for their existence. They used them in exercise of long-established rights. In no sense were these seasonal migrations predatory, and they were accepted as a normal feature of tribal life by the semi-nomadic and sedentary upland tribes. But the desert breeds predatory instincts and compels man to live permanently on a war footing. The desert nomad, therefore, has both the inclination and the power to prey upon his neighbours, and not infrequently he does. In early Roman times, however, the nomads of the Sahara had not acquired the camel which in later times gave them great mobility and made them far more formidable neighbours.

To the Romans these annual incursions of untamed warrior tribes, who knew no masters but their own chiefs, were certainly unwelcome. That they presented an economic rather than a political problem doubtless escaped them. They had yet to learn that the desert nomad would defend to his last breath his traditional grazing rights, whether in the desert or the uplands. The Romans therefore attempted to curb, if not stop, the annual northward surge from the desert into their territory. As a result they antagonized the tribes of the northern Sahara, and the desert became both a refuge and a recruiting ground for all who rebelled against Rome.

Early in the occupation the Numidian chieftain Jugurtha, finding himself hard pressed, 'made his way', Sallust tells us, 'through vast deserts to the Gaetuli, a wild and uncivilized tribe', amongst whom he raised an army.[1] Tacitus relates how a century and a half later Tacfarinas, in similar circumstances, successfully appealed to the Garamantes for help, an occasion to which we shall return shortly.[2]

Finding it impossible to keep the nomads from penetrating their *limes* or from joining forces with rebellious tribes, the Romans attempted to forestall their incursions and break their power for evil by garrisoning the northern oases. The chain of new outposts extended westwards from the Gulf of Gabes through Tozeur, Nefta, Negrine, and Biskra, south of Bou Saada and from there north-west along the Hodna plain. Each outpost commanded one or more routes of access from the desert to the uplands. Vescera (Biskra), guarding the approaches to the great El-Kantara gorge,* was garrisoned by a regiment from the deserts of Asia, the *numerus Palmyrenorum*, troops familiar with desert warfare being preferred for this key position. In Tripolitania the defences were pushed out to the escarpment of the Gebel. Early in the third century this new front, stretching from the Syrtes to Mauretania, had become, as was inevitable, integrated into the defensive zone and thus once more was the *limes* advanced towards the desert. Throughout its length the Romans were confronted by bitter and implacable enemies. Only in the extreme west, in Mauretania, were the desert nomads still remote, both geographically and politically. Nowhere else could the Roman troops relax their vigil. The famous third Augustan Legion, based on Lambaesis (Lambessa), to which these defences were entrusted, was now recruited locally and was soon to become a wholly African corps.

On the Syrtic coast, in the region of the three towns of the Emporia, Lepcis Magna, Oea, and Sabratha, from which Tripolitania got its name, close contact with the desert was not new. Concerned as they had been at the cost of the occupation of Africa, the Romans had wasted no time in taking over the Carthaginian trade with the Garamantes, a shadowy but, as the Romans were to learn, a formidable people. Herodotus had described them as very powerful. Their power did not wane with the passage of time. Early in the first century A.D. Tacitus called them invincible.[3] Their home-country was Phazania (Fezzan), a conglomeration of oases in the heart of the Sahara, and their capital Garama, the modern Germa; but we also hear of them close to the Syrtic coast,

---

* Previously the Romans had been content with commanding the northern head of the gorge from Lambaesis (Lambessa), the headquarters of the Legio III Augusta, which they called The Bridle of the Desert Tribes; but it soon proved to be nothing of the sort, and they had to post a garrison at the foot of the gorge, at Vescera (Biskra).

and in the south-east their range probably extended to the Nile.*
In Herodotus they appear as a sedentary people engaged in agri-
culture† and commerce. To Lucian they were nomads and dwellers
in tents who made seasonal migrations into the remote south in
the course of which, we may presume, they continued to raid the
Troglodytes for slaves as Herodotus had said.[4] It is evident that
they owed their predominant position in the east-central Sahara
to numerical strength and wide geographical range in conditions
which sometimes, as in the Fezzan, permitted a sedentary life, and
sometimes, as in the desert separating the Fezzan from the coast,
imposed nomadism. They comprised tribes which dwelt in towns
and villages, and others which were pastoral and nomadic. By the
Romans they were respected as traders but resented as disturbers
of the peace of Tripolitania.

Ethnologically the Garamantes are not easy to place, but we
may presume them to have been negroid.[5] They are variously
described as lightly clad and naked, and according to Pliny they
lived in promiscuous concubinage with their women, a practice
which the civilized are over-prone to attribute to the uncivilized.
Their use of horsed chariots, and their worship of animal-headed
gods, which are a common feature of contemporary rock-drawings,
suggest that culturally they owed something to Egypt but in circumstances which are still shrouded in the mists of remote antiquity.

No doubt the continuance of their trade with the Emporia was
welcome enough to the Garamantes, but the change of alien rulers
on the Syrtic coast was certainly repugnant. A mercantile power
with no interests outside trade, which politics were never allowed
to disturb, had given place to a formidable military power to
whom close administrative control was of first importance. The
coastal tribes, who had accepted the overlordship of the powerful
Garamantes, had now to bow to alien masters. If an actual limit
to the traditional seasonal migrations of Garamantian flocks and
herds from the desert into the uplands was not set, clearly they

---

* The Kura'an, a nomadic people of mixed Tebu and negro descent, appear to be
the modern representatives of the Garamantes. They occupy the deserts north of
Darfur and Wadai which were Garamantian country. It is significant that the
Bayuda Desert, north of Khartoum, was known as the Desert of Goran as late as
the seventeenth century, and was so called by Leo Africanus. (L. P. Kirwan,
'Christianity and the Kura'an', *Journal of Egyptian Archaeology*, XX, 1934, pp.
201-3.)

† Herodotus said they 'cover the salt with mould, and then sow their crops'. Early
in the nineteenth century G. F. Lyon, describing the Fezzan, speaks of 'gardens
. . . white with salt'. (*Travels*, p. 206.)

continued only on sufferance and depended on meek acquiescence to the will of the occupying power. The harshness of Roman rule was doubtless a constant source of complaints and solicitations for protection from the subjugated peoples of the coast to their powerful desert neighbours. The Carthaginians, immersed in trade, had never presented themselves to the Garamantes as a rival power. The Romans, on the other hand, had quickly made it clear that they were not merely a rival power but the only power. To a great people like the Garamantes, whose predominant position in the eastern Sahara none had ever dared to challenge, the change of rulers on the coast was intolerable.

How soon a rupture between Romans and Garamantes occurred is uncertain, but towards the close of the first century B.C. the Romans felt compelled to embark on what must have appeared to them a very hazardous expedition against the Fezzan. They had recently had to crush a revolt by the Gaetuli, who had probably invoked the willing aid of the Garamantes. Whether this was the *casus belli* or not, so daring an operation as the invasion of the Fezzan would hardly have been undertaken except under prolonged provocation culminating in an outright challenge to Roman authority.

The expedition was led by the proconsul Lucius Cornelius Balbus, a native of Spain. It took the Garamantes by surprise and the Fezzan was successfully subjugated. The many towns which were captured included Garama (Germa), the capital, and the important outlying oasis of Cydamus (Ghadames) which also lay in Garamantian country. Among the places mentioned by Pliny as having been captured is Mount Gyri 'where precious stones were produced', which unhappily remains unidentified.[6]

It is probable that the object of the expedition was to break the Garamantes and make impossible any further challenge to Roman supremacy. On the other hand, its intention may have been merely punitive. It certainly failed on the former score, as it was bound to, for war against desert nomads can never be pressed home: their answer to overwhelming force is wide dispersal and guerilla tactics. An army cannot break them any more than a fist can a pillow.

Nevertheless, the expedition was acclaimed as a notable achievement, which indeed it was. Never before had Rome carried war into the heart of the Sahara. To the grave difficulties inherent in desert warfare had been added the problem of an initial thirty days' march through almost waterless country before the enemy

SICILIA

CARTHAGE
PROCONSULARIS
• Cirta
Thysdrus
• Lambaesis
• Thevesta
Thapsus
NUMIDIA
Sufetula
• Vescara
SYRTIS MINOR

LOTOPHAGI
Sabratha Oea
Lepcis Magna
ASTACURES
AUSTURIANI
TRIPOLITANIA
MARMARIDAE
ARZUGES
(Garian)
SYRTIS MAJOR
LYBIA PENTAPOLIS
GAETULI
(Mizda)
MACAE
IFURACES
• Cydamus
(Ghirza)
(Bu Ngem)
Arae Philaenorum
(Gheria el-Garbia)
MAZICES
• Rapsa
(HAMMADA EL-HAMRA)
NASAMONES

Augila •

PHAZANIA
GARAMANTES

• Garama

AGISYMBA
REGIO
(TIBESTI)

(AIR)

ENGLISH MILES
50   0   100   200   300   400

Tribal names are in Italics: GAETULI

II. Roman Africa

could be hit where he was at all vulnerable, in his settlements in the Fezzan. The enemy, too, was the greatest power in the interior known to Rome. Balbus received a signal mark of honour. Although a native of Gades (Cadiz) he was given a triumph, the only foreigner ever so honoured.

The discovery that, in spite of the intervening desert, the Fezzan was assailable from the coast must have been a disagreeable shock to the Garamantes, and the devastation which Balbus left behind him a warning that Roman military strength was not to be lightly challenged. The salutary lesson was effective in preventing the direct intervention of the Garamantes in northern politics, but it encouraged them to aid the anti-Roman activities of their neighbours. For example, they championed the cause of the Marmaridae of Cyrenaica, but were defeated by the proconsul of the province, Publius Sulpicius Quirinius. In A.D. 17 a revolt, led by the brilliant Roman-trained Libyan soldier Tacfarinas, broke out and spread eventually from the Syrtes to the Atlantic. It so seriously threatened the Roman occupation that the ninth Spanish legion had to be brought in to reinforce the Legio III Augusta. For seven years Tacfarinas successfully defied the alien overlords, during which time he was twice compelled to seek refuge in the desert.[7]

On the second occasion, if not also the first, it was the Garamantes who gave him shelter, despite the efforts of the Romans based on Lepcis to prevent his reaching them. At this juncture Tiberius suddenly decided to withdraw the Legio IX Hispana from Africa. This caused deep concern to the proconsul, P. Cornelius Dolabella, for his seemingly endless campaign against Tacfarinas had reached a critical stage which demanded the use of every man on whom he could lay his hands. Tacfarinas naturally took fresh heart from this surprising withdrawal in which he saw a sign that the power of Rome was crumbling, and, persuading the Garamantes to the same view, he secured their help, though perhaps not on the scale he had hoped for. Still smarting under their defeat by Quirinius, they were cautious and unwilling to commit themselves deeply. Tacfarinas, Tacitus relates, 'had the King of the Garamantes . . . to be the partner of his raids, not indeed with a regular army, but with detachments of light troops'.[8] Dolabella with Tacfarinas still in the field and no troops to spare for the punitive expedition which in other circumstances would have followed the Garamantian intervention, had to let the wild desert people go unpunished. When, however, Tacfarinas was killed in battle, and Roman troops were disengaged, the Garamantes took alarm and sought to forestall the retribution they feared awaited them. At the close of the campaign Dolabella took home with him, Tacitus relates, 'envoys from the Garamantes, a rare spectacle in Rome. . . . The nation in its terror at the destruction of Tacfarinas . . . had sent them to crave pardon of the Roman people.'[9]

The visit of the envoys was probably welcome, for it rather surprisingly convinced the Romans that they had nothing more to fear from the Garamantes and it provided an excuse not to launch a second costly expedition against the Fezzan. Balbus, they knew, had succeeded only because he had taken the Garamantes by surprise. Since then the latter had become too vigilant for that to recur, and, as a further protection, they had resorted to the commonest and most effective method of defence against attack in the desert. 'It has been impossible', wrote Pliny, 'to open up the road to the Garamantes country, because brigands of that race fill up the wells with sand.'[10]

The Garamantes were not slow to realise that they owed their escape from punishment for helping Tacfarinas less to the good offices of their envoys than to the defensive measures they themselves had adopted. The confidence this gave them was further strengthened by the Romans' ill-advised withdrawal of the rest of their troops from Tripolitania because peace seemed to them assured. However, initially the trouble which followed was different from what they might have expected. In A.D. 69 war broke out between the neighbouring cities of Oea (Tripoli) and Lepcis. This would have mattered less if it had not brought the Garamantes into the field once more. Convinced that if worsted in battle they had only to scuttle back into the desert and fill in the wells behind them to stop pursuit, and confident in their immunity from attack in the Fezzan, they responded to an appeal for aid from the people of Oea and, together with these new allies, they laid siege to Lepcis. This brought the legate of Numidia, Valerius Festus, hurrying down the coast to restore order, which he did with surprising speed. He freed Lepcis, defeated the Garamantes, recovering much of their loot, and pursued them into the desert. In doing so he achieved something remarkable. He found, Pliny tells us, a new and shorter road across the desert, known as the *Praeter Caput Saxi*, which is not very different from its modern native name of Bab Ras al-Hammada.[11] It was probably the road running due south from Oea through Garian, Mizda, and El-Gherria el-Garbia which later on, in the reign of Caracalla, was marked with milestones. The inference is that Valerius Festus discovered a road unknown to the Garamantes. This is incredible, for he was operating in the Garamantes' own country which they must have known far better than the Romans, and at least as well as any tribe from whom the latter could have obtained guides.

But the mystery surrounding the discovery of the *Iter Praeter Caput Saxi* extends over a much wider field. Before the end of the century other odd things happened which have never been explained.

The first was a very surprising *rapprochement* between the Romans and the Garamantes, from which flowed two remarkable Roman expeditions through the Fezzan and far into the country beyond. They took place in the reign of Trajan, somewhere about A.D. 100. The first, led by Septimius Flaccus, legate of Numidia, marched for three months southward from the Fezzan, which almost certainly must have taken him into the Sudan. Perhaps that country will one day yield evidence of its having done so. Ptolemy, however, thought the story, which he had got from Marinus of Tyre, an exaggeration. The second expedition, led by Julius Maternus, is also recorded by Ptolemy and from the same source.

Julius Maternus, setting out from Leptis Magna and Garama with the King of the Garamantes, who was beginning an expedition against the Ethiopians, by bearing continuously southward came within four months to Agisymba, the country of the Ethiopians where the rhinoceros is to be found.[12]

Ptolemy was reluctant to credit this story also, but it is more circumstantial than the other and rings true to the extent that a strong case has been made for identifying Agisymba with Tibesti. Some have sought to identify it with Air, but, as F. R. Rodd (Lord Rennell) has pointed out, Air is not easily accessible from the Fezzan and would therefore not have been visited by the Romans except for some pressing need of which there is no evidence.[13] Tibesti, on the other hand, lies close to the natural road leading southward from the Fezzan to Negroland which, we believe, was then in use as a trade route and therefore would scarcely have been ignored by the Romans. When the Arabs and, after them, the Turks found themselves, like the Romans, in occupation of the Fezzan and desirous of extending their authority southward, both penetrated to Tibesti, but neither reached Air. The same writer has also pointed out that whereas in Air there are no names similar to Bardetus and Mesche, which are mentioned by Ptolemy as the names of mountains in Agisymba, there are in Tibesti a Bardai and a Miski.

The association of the Garamantes with the Romans leaves little room for doubt about the object of the joint enterprise. The Romans might of course have endeavoured to cement their new friendship by agreeing to help in an attack on formidable neighbours. There is, however, no evidence that the Garamantes had any enemies in the south whom they would not have been able to subdue long before the coming of the Romans. It is far more likely that they asked the Romans to go with them on a slave-raiding expedition and that Julius Maternus readily seized this opportunity for seeing new country. That he was himself interested in catching slaves is improbable, for the Romans do not appear to have concerned themselves with the slave-trade of central Africa. If slave-raiding was the object of the joint enterprise there can be no doubt that Agisymba was Tibesti, which is generally accepted as the home of the Troglodyte Ethiopians whom Herodotus tells us the Garamantes used to raid. In the absence of any proof of how far south Septimius Flaccus penetrated, Tibesti may be regarded as the farthest point in the interior of Africa west of the Nile valley reached by the Romans.*

Far more important than these speculations is to consider what circumstances led to the surprising *rapprochement* and made possible two military expeditions, apparently in quick succession, into remote lands which not long before must have appeared to the Romans hopelessly inaccessible. The strange discovery of the *Iter Praeter Caput Saxi* is probably part of the same problem which, by some odd inadvertence, has wholly escaped the attention of the many erudite scholars who have closely studied the history of the Roman occupation. But, despite its complexity, it is susceptible of a simple though not immediately obvious explanation.

In North Africa the art of war, and much else besides, was at about this time being revolutionized by the camel. In the history of the northern half of the continent no event had greater consequences than the introduction of this now indispensable animal. When it happened and in what circumstances are matters of great

---

* But not, of course, of things Roman. For example, in 1931 a Roman coin of the age of Constantine was dug up at Buea in British Cameroons. (Letter from the late E. J. Arnett to the author.)

uncertainty. The wide distribution throughout the region of remains of a quaternary camel for long seemed clearly to indicate
that it had been there continuously since before the dawn of history.
It is now known that the quaternary beast did not survive into
historical times. The later camel is believed to have been introduced into Egypt by the Persians in the sixth century B.C. Alexander the Great used camel transport on his expedition to the
Oracle of Jupiter Ammon, but Siwa appears to have been the most
westerly point reached by the camel at this period. When one con-
siders the great need there was for it in Cyrenaica and Tripolitania,
let alone the Sahara, this is astonishing. One of the reasons was
probably the failure of this animal to thrive in Lower Egypt, which
instead of being, as one might expect, a breeder and exporter of
camels was an importer. It still has to satisfy its requirements by
buying from Upper Egypt and Palestine. The camel reached the
present Republic of the Sudan some time before the Christian era,
but its failure to spread from there westwards seems quite un-
accountable. Its absence from the numerous early rock-drawings
which, as we have seen, so richly record the desert fauna, both
wild and domestic, clearly shows that it did not.[14]

Caesar captured twenty-two camels at Thapsus in 46 B.C. This
is the earliest record of them west of Siwa. Although the Romans
were familiar enough with the use of camels in Asia and must have
realized how valuable they could be in Africa, they seem to have
taken to their use there very slowly. Long after Thapsus they were
still using horses in military operations in which the camel would
have been of far more use. Moreover, in the history of the Roman
occupation camels are not again mentioned until 400 years later.
In A.D. 363, when the people of Lepcis appealed to the governor
of Africa for help against the Austuriani, who were ravaging their
territory, he replied that he could not come to their aid until they
sent him 4,000 camels for transport for his troops.[15]

The Romans may themselves have been responsible for the
introduction of camels, but it is significant that we first hear of
their being used in North Africa not by the Romans but by those
in rebellion against them. Moreover, as their military operations
did not normally take them farther than the fringes of the Sahara
and as nowhere west of Tripolitania did they ever attempt to
penetrate the desert their need for them can never have been at all
general or pressing.

The introduction of domestic animals is so often associated with the migration of peoples that it is perhaps more than a coincidence that the first appearance of the camel in Roman Africa closely synchronized with the first arrival of the Zenata in the same region. These nomadic Berbers, who were destined many centuries later to give the western Maghrib the powerful dynasties of the Merinids of Fez and the Abd al-Wadids of Tlemcen, came from the east by way of Cyrene. Whether this migration was inspired or fostered by the Romans we are unable to say, but it seems probable that the Zenata were responsible for bringing the camel into general use throughout Gaetulia and the steppes of the High Plateaux.

Somewhere between 46 B.C. and A.D. 363 the Roman army started using camels. It is a very wide margin of time with no data to work on. Nevertheless, that the Legio III Augusta took to camel transport during the first century A.D. seems highly probable, if only because that would explain so much that is obscure. It is significant that only a century later, as local sculptures show, the camel had become common enough in Tripolitania to be used for tillage.

The story of the discovery of the *Praeter Caput Saxi* road by Valerius Festus immediately becomes understandable. The new road was new only in the sense that it had been too waterless to be used by horses, but camels had made it practicable. The nineteenth-century explorer of this very desert, G. F. Lyon, declared that 'horses generally occasion more trouble to a caravan than anything else. The immense quantity of water necessary to be taken for them is always averaged at one camel for each horse, not including other loads of corn or dates for their food.'[16] Not only did the camel make this new road practicable, but it made desert travel much faster.

The *rapprochement* between the Romans and the Garamantes can also now be explained. The pursuit of the latter by Valerius Festus and his camelry after their defeat before Lepcis had shown the Garamantes that the Romans could go where they could not and much faster. Gone was their immunity from pursuit; the desert was no more a safe refuge nor was the Fezzan any longer secure from invasion. The emergence of this new arm of the Romans had much the same effect on the Garamantes, albeit on a trivial scale, as the atom bomb had on the Japanese in 1945, and with the same result. They at once capitulated and threw their country open to the alien invader.

Finally, we can now see clearly how the great expeditions of Septimius Flaccus and Julius Maternus into the far interior suddenly became possible. The Garamantes had not only lost the will to resist but were courting Roman favours and extending welcoming arms. The camel, too, had made the crossing of the Sahara easier than ever before.

Although, as we shall see, the Romans took full advantage of the ready access they had gained to the Fezzan, the century following their two expeditions to the remote interior was uneventful for Tripolitania. With the accession of Septimius Severus in 193 the scene changed. Lepcis emerged from provincialism and assumed the grandeur which recent excavation has so splendidly revealed. There is no more romantic spot on those 2,000 miles of historic coastline, stretching from the Altars of the Philaeni to the Atlantic, than the little harbour of the great Lepcis at the mouth of the Wadi Lebda. Here indeed is the very gateway of the Sahara, the northern terminus of the Garamantian road, which for centuries was to remain one of the great trans-Saharan caravan routes. As you stand on the quay at which the galleys of Ostia berthed and gaze southward over those superb ruins it is pleasant to recall that the great emperor they commemorate, whose birthplace Lepcis was and who spoke the Latin tongue with a Punic accent, died at York in 211.

Severus's interest in the land of his birth was not confined to Lepcis. The defensive zone, the *Limes Tripolitanus*, was reorganized, strengthened, and extended, not, one suspects, because there was greater need to protect the city the emperor chose to glorify, but to enhance the prestige of his native land.[17] Out of the desert, beyond the *limes*, two new garrisons of the Legio III Augusta were established, one at Bu Ngem and the other farther west at Cydamus, an oasis which in later times became noted as a caravan centre under its present name of Ghadames. It is probable that at this time also a garrison was established at Garama, the Garamantian capital. The period is one of which few written records have survived, but archaeological research has recently thrown a welcome beam of light into the dark shadows.

Early in the nineteenth century the explorer Dr. Oudney reported finding a Roman mausoleum at Germa which, visited a generation later by Henry Barth and described by him with astonishing accuracy,[18] became justly famous.* In 1934 an Italian

A comparison of modern photographs of the mausoleum with Barth's drawing of it (*Travels*, Vol. I, p. 157) is but one of innumerable examples of the remarkable

archæological mission brought back from Germa the rich and
varied collection of Roman things which are now in the Museo
Coloniale at Rome, some of which had been found in the mausoleum itself.[19] The objects are chiefly pottery, glass, and lamps, but
they include fragments of woollen cloth, multi-coloured but, not
surprisingly, predominantly Tyrian purple. The collection shows
that goods of Mediterranean origin, and many of them Roman,
were freely reaching the Fezzan from the end of the first century
until the fourth or later; the mausoleum itself appears to belong
to the second century. The opportunities for trade opened up by
the expeditions of Septimius Flaccus and Julius Maternus had not
been neglected. The archæologists discovered precisely what history had led us to expect. Earthworks to conserve water, of a pattern
which recalls similar measures in Tripolitania, show that Roman
interest in the Fezzan embraced development as well as trade, but
trade was predominant.

Roman trade presents so vast a field for research that the interest
of the many illustrious historians who have made it their study
has never seriously extended to the Sahara, which admittedly was
of little commercial importance. They have been content to assume
that the commodities in which the Romans traded with the Fezzan
were those which in later times flowed northwards up the Garamantian road, notably gold, slaves, ivory, and ostrich feathers.
There are no historical grounds for such an assumption. There is
in fact no record of the Romans having imported from the Fezzan
any one of these articles.

Pliny is helpfully emphatic. 'Our only intercourse', he wrote,
'is the trade in the precious stone imported from Ethiopia which
we call the carbuncle.'[20] Similarly, a century earlier Strabo had
referred to the Fezzan as the country carbuncles came from.[21] To
both writers the Garamantian road stood for the carbuncle trade.
In the face of two such definite statements it is difficult to resist the
conclusion that carbuncles were the most important commodity
in the Roman trade with the Fezzan. There is no suggestion in
later records that they did not so remain.

Gold was at one time mined in the Fezzan, but probably not so
early as the Roman occupation. It is possible, however, that the
Romans obtained some gold from there, but with so many more

---

accuracy which that truly brilliant traveller maintained throughout the five fat
volumes in which he recorded his travels in the interior of Africa.

accessible and abundant sources, from Spain to the Urals and from the Mediterranean to the Baltic, it is improbable that gold was a staple of their Saharan trade.

Ostrich feathers can certainly be ruled out as an important article, because they were still in abundant supply in the north. So can wild animals for the arena or their hides, and for the same reason. Moreover, the cost of transporting live animals or hides across the desert would have been prohibitive.

Ivory is a possibility. Elephants were still numerous in North Africa at the beginning of the Christian era but became extinct by the fourth century. On the other hand, Asia and the Red Sea, sources on which the Romans had long depended, were still supplying ivory, perhaps on an increasing scale, so there was certainly no dearth of it. That some was obtained from the Fezzan is possible, but had the quantity been important it would hardly have escaped mention by both Strabo and Pliny.

Under both the Republic and the Empire the Romans employed slave labour, but their sources of supply in Europe and Asia were almost unlimited. Prisoners of war alone provided a well-nigh inexhaustible source in republican times. A single raid on Epirus brought in some 150,000 captives; at the fall of Carthage a large proportion of its inhabitants were enslaved; for long years the flow from Asia Minor was abundant and continuous. Besides, there were the great slave markets of the Mediterranean, notably Delos where, Strabo tells us, they could handle up to 10,000 slaves a day.[22] Not only were European and Asian slaves in abundant supply, but they were far better suited to the requirements of the Romans than Africans, being better adapted to the climate and stronger physically. Apart from statuettes caricaturing negroes and a first-century mosaic in Pompeii picturing a negro slave at a banquet, there is very little evidence of negro slaves in the time of the Empire.[23]

It is therefore difficult to believe that Rome had any desire to draw on Africa for slave labour, still less any need to do so, on an important scale. We hear of Numidians and Gaetuli being used as litter-bearers and footmen. 'I should like Cato', wrote Seneca, 'to see one of our dandies with his outriders and Numidians.'[24] But these came from the African littoral which, like every other country, had its own slave markets, and their use seems to have been small and was perhaps no more than a passing fashion, like negro pages in eighteenth-century England. For negro slaves, which alone

would have come up the Garamantian road, there was little or no
room in the Roman economy. The few who were in domestic
service were easily obtained from the negro community on the
African littoral, the flotsam of the desert oases which doubtless
then, as in later times, were cultivated by slaves from the Sudan.
We may therefore confidently dismiss the possibility of slaves having played more than a very minor part in the Roman trade with
the Fezzan.

To sum up, there is no reason to doubt what Strabo and Pliny
wrote about the carbuncle trade. It must have been the staple of
the north-bound caravans. There was probably a general trade as
well in which ivory perhaps played a part and which may occasionally have included a few slaves and possibly a little gold. Civet has
so far escaped mention as a commodity the Romans may have
sought in the Fezzan; throughout recorded history it has been in
common use in the Sudan and the Sahara and, anyway in medieval
times, was in demand by the perfumers of Europe as it is today.
It would almost certainly have been known to the Romans through
their connexions with the Red Sea trade and might well have been
included in general cargo from the Fezzan. Ill-informed though
we are about the Garamantian trade it is evident that it was of
negligible account in the immense and far-flung oversea trade of
Rome. Nevertheless it was an important element in the history of
the Roman occupation of North Africa.

In the last chapter we saw that in Carthaginian times the
Garamantian trade had been important enough to attract comparatively close settlement on the Syrtic coast, and that it had
been the origin and sustenance of Lepcis, Oea, and Sabratha. In
Roman times these small trading posts grew into handsome cities,
which might well suggest that the trade which had given them
birth had also made them great. This was not so. They appear to
have owed their wealth under the emperors to agriculture, which
they did much to develop, to fisheries and the purple dye trade.
At the outset agricultural development was encouraged for political
rather than economic reasons, in order to anchor the semi-nomadic
tribes to the soil and thus help to solve acute administrative problems. But it was also directed towards satisfying the needs of Rome
itself, one of which was for olive oil. Thus Tripolitania had become
one of the principal olive-oil producing countries of the Empire,
to which the numerous ruins of oil presses scattered up and down
the country still bear witness. Grain and other crops were grown

under the elaborate systems of irrigation to which reference has
already been made. There were also vineyards, but only to satisfy
local needs. Since Carthaginian times the countryside had been
transformed and with it the economy of the Emporia. The galleys
sailing between Lepcis and Ostia were more frequently loaded
with olive oil than with the products of the Fezzan and the
Sudan.

In the Hoggar mountains, in the heart of the central Sahara,
there is a ruin which belongs to the Roman period and is linked
with the Mediterranean, although there appears to be nothing
Roman about it. Near the oasis of Abalessa stand the ruins of a
small fortress or a large fortified house, a multi-chambered building constructed in a manner unknown to the modern Tuareg but
still practised by the Tebu of Tibesti. Traditionally it was the home
of a woman named Tin Hinan who, mounted on a magnificent
white camel, mysteriously arrived in Hoggar from the far-away
oasis of Tafilelt in southern Morocco and from whom the local
Tuareg aristocracy claim descent. Excavation has revealed a tomb
in which were the bones of a woman, not of Moroccan but of
Egyptian type and strongly recalling the ruling class portrayed on
Pharaonic monuments. On the arms of the skeleton were bracelets
of silver and gold, on the breast a gold pendant and various beads,
some of chalcedony. In the tomb were quantities of other beads,
many of them the famous aggrey beads, a fertility charm, a bunch
of herbs, baskets of dates and grain, milk-bowls, a coin of Constantine and much else besides, all now exhibited in the Musée du
Bardo at Algiers. Besides the coin, the glass is Roman and together
they indicate a fourth-century date. The story of Tin Hinan—
where she came from, why she chose, and how she reached, so
remote a place to dwell in—presents one of the desert's most elusive
problems, made doubly enticing by excavation having so pleasingly
confirmed the legend.[25]

When we look back through the centuries at the Roman period
there clearly stands out an event which transcends all others in
importance, and yet it was one in which the Romans probably
played no part. This was the introduction of the camel, an event
of such far-reaching consequences that it marked the dawn of a
new era for the northern half of the continent. It widened the field
for human endeavour and affected the economic life of the whole
community. The camel gave man a freedom of movement he had
never known before and brought within his reach the remotest

pastures. The caravan routes lost half their terrors and new roads were opened for the flow of trade and culture.

With all these changes came a man new to Africa, the camel-owning nomad, turbulent, predatory, elusive, and unassailable. Thus was civilization faced with a menace from which it has never since been wholly free and one which the legionaries of Rome never knew.

4

The Tuareg and Other Peoples
of the Sahara

*'This part of the worlde is inhabited especially by the Africans or Moores,
properly so called; which last are of two kinds, namely white or tawnie Moores,
and Negros or blacke Moores.'*—JOHN PORY.

IN the seventh century A.D., before the Arab invasion of North
Africa, the Sahara was peopled by two distinct types of man, dark-
skinned or negroid, and light-skinned.

Archaeological evidence suggests that 'neolithic negroid groups
from the Sudan began to spread northwards some five thousand
years ago through the entire length of the then relatively fertile
Sahara'.[1] Classical authors from the time of Herodotus on refer to
'Ethiopians'—a Greek word which literally means the people 'with
burnt faces'—as occupying all the land to the south of Libya or
North Africa. A number of dark-skinned groups of people are still
to be found among the present population of the Sahara.

'Most of the agricultural centres of the southern half of the
Sahara are still peopled mainly by negroid folk, known as Chou-
chan, Fezzanese, or Dauada in the eastern and central desert,
and in the west as Haratin.'[2] In oasis society the Haratin occupy a
modest position, 'working as sharecroppers in the plantations of
landlords who are nearly always white and often warlike nomads',
but they are regarded as being in a different class from the *abid* or
slaves. It has often been thought that the Haratin must be the
descendants of negro slaves, brought to the oases by their Berber
masters, and it is likely that negro slaves are to be found among
their ancestors. But the Haratin are not only of slave origin:
although they possess some negro features in their dark skin and
kinky hair, the shape of their nose and face is often quite unlike
that of the negroes of the Sudan, and 'their blood-group pattern is

quite different from that of any other people of the Sahara or even the Sudan, but resembles rather that of the Pygmies of the western Congo rain forest'.[3] Tentatively it may be suggested that the Haratin contain among their ancestors people of that negroid stock which inhabited the Sahara in neolithic times.[4]

Another dark-skinned people are the Tebu who inhabit the massif of Tibesti and much of the country to the south. In skin-colour the Tebu are 'normally very dark in all respects'. Their blood-group pattern is quite different from that of the Haratin and of the negroes of the Sudan, but 'is so much like that of the Berbers' that it has been suggested that the Tebu must originally have been of Berber stock.[5] On the other hand, their language belongs to an entirely different language family from Berber. Given these contradictions they remain perhaps the most enigmatic of Saharan peoples.

The light-skinned people of North Africa were known to the Greeks as Libyans. Later, the Romans referred to them as barbarians, *barbari*, and this expression was taken over by the Arabs and later passed into European usage, so that 'Berber' came to be the word applied to the native inhabitants of *Barbary*.

People of Berber stock were to be found not only in North Africa—the modern Tunisia, Algeria, and Morocco—but also in the Western and Central Sahara. Today a distinction must be drawn among the light-skinned inhabitants of the desert between Arabic-speakers and Berber-speakers. Some of the Arabic-speakers, the Chaamba, for example, a tribe of nomads in the northern Sahara, are people of Arab descent who entered North Africa from the east in the centuries after the Arab conquest. But other Arabic-speakers represent tribes of Berber origin that have come under strong Arab influence. Many of the tribes of the Western Sahara, now collectively described as Moors, come into this category.

Among the Berber-speakers of the Sahara there are a number of different groups, among them the inhabitants of Ghadames and of the Mzab and an isolated outpost of Berber-speakers, the Ida bel Hassen, in southern Mauritania. But the dominant Berber group is formed by the Tuareg. Today the Tuareg are found in a number of tribal confederations, whose area extends from Ghadames and In Salah in the northern Sahara to the Niger and beyond, and covers the massifs of Ahaggar, Air, and Adrar of the Iforas. The confederations are 'divided politically into tribes which are subdivided into clans and the latter into fractions. Socially the nomadic population is divided into three main classes, the Tuareg "nobles" and "vassals" and the Negro slaves.' [6] Their language, Tamaheq, is a dialect of Berber, and their alphabet, Tifinagh, is partly derived from the ancient Libyan script. The most striking characteristic of the Tuareg is the curious custom of the men of covering the face with a *litham* or veil, leaving only the eyes exposed. There has been much speculation about the origin of the *litham*; Heinrich Barth, for example, thought it might have been designed to imitate the shape of the helmet of medieval knights, but no fully convincing explanation has yet been put forward. The *litham* must have been introduced sometime between 600 and 1000 A.D. Classical and Byzantine authors make no mention of a veil in their descriptions of Libyan tribes, but al-Bakri, writing in the eleventh century, mentions that all the tribes of the desert wear the veil. [7]

Classical writers provide a good deal of information on the tribes of the Central Sahara. Thus the Alexandrian geographer, Ptolemy, writing in the second century A.D., mentions along with the Garamantes the Natambes, the Makkorenes, and the Pharusii. The Natembes have been identified with the Inataben, the Makkorenes with the Imaqqoren, and the Pharusii with the Iforas, the modern names still being applied to tribes or tribal fragments among the Tuareg. Evidence such as this suggests 'that the population of the central Sahara has scarcely changed in the last 1800 years'. [8]

Classical writers are less informative on the people of the western Sahara. To obtain an impression of the population of this part of the desert before the arrival of the Arab tribes, one must turn to the works of medieval Arab geographers and historians. The leading authority on Berber history is the great fourteenth-century historian, Ibn Khaldun. According to Ibn Khaldun, the Berber-speaking population of North Africa was divided into two groups, the Botr and the Branes. One of the most important branches of the Botr was represented by the Zenata. The Zenata were nomads who had migrated from the east in historic times. They occupied the northern belt of the Sahara. 'They move their dwellings from one location to another', Ibn Khaldun wrote of them, 'they spend the summer in the Tell and the winter in the desert. They use force in carrying off the people living in cultivated areas and they resist the control of a just and regular government.' [9]

The Branes consisted of two main branches, the Masmuda and the Sanhaja. The Masmuda were primarily a sedentary people, occupying the mountainous parts of Morocco. The Sanhaja contained both sedentary people and nomads: the sedentary Sanhaja occupied Kabylia in eastern Algeria, and the nomadic Sanhaja were to be found in the western Sahara. The nomadic Sanhaja comprised a number of tribes, including the Lemta and the Lemtuna. At the same time many of the Tuareg tribes appear to have been associated with the Sanhaja. Medieval Arab writers seem themselves to be confused about the exact relationship between the Sanhaja of the western Sahara and the Tuareg who occupied the central part of the desert. Thus one of the earliest authorities, Ibn Haukal, writing in the tenth century A.D., referring to the Banu Tanamak (Kel Tamaheq, the people who speak *tamaheq*, the language of the Tuareg), states that they are rulers of Tadmekka, a town to the north of Gao, and lists the names of many of their tribes, some of which are identical with the names of tribes still living in the same area. He adds that some people say that the Bani Tanamak came originally from the Sudan, and that by their mothers they are children of Ham—a statement that could be explained by reference to the practice of intermarriage between the Tuareg and women of the dark-skinned communities living in their area. On the other hand, according to Ibn Haukal, other authorities say that the Bani Tanamak are clearly associated with the Sanhaja.[10]

In the medieval history of the Sahara, the Sanhaja of the western desert came to play a more important part than the Tuareg, for they became the founders of the great Almoravid dynasty. Conflict between the Sanhaja and the Zenata of the northern Sahara is one of the great themes of this period of history. But, beginning in the eleventh century, tribes of Arab nomads started to move across the northern Sahara and later spread into the western desert, and the Zenata Berbers were either pushed northwards or else completely arabized. Many of the Sanhaja tribes were reduced to vassal status; they accepted the language of the invaders, abandoned the veil, but retained many other Berber customs.* [11] The Tuareg, on the other hand, protected by their mountains in Air and Ahaggar and living away

---

* These vassal tribes were known as Zenaga, a corruption of Sanhaja. In the fifteenth century the Portuguese applied the name of these tribes to the river on whose banks they were living, which thus became known to Europeans as the Senegal.

from the main trade-routes were able to preserve both their language and their customs, and even possibly to assimilate certain Arab tribes.[12]

Today the Tuareg are Muslims, but they retain many beliefs belonging to an earlier religion. The Arabs sometimes called them Christians of the Desert and there is some evidence to suggest that at one period in their history they may have been influenced by Christianity. Their language contains several words which may have had a Christian origin: *Mesi*, meaning God, and *andjelous*, meaning angel, are two striking examples. The names Samuel, David, and Saul, which are rarely used by the Arabs of Africa, are common among the Tuareg. On the other hand, the prevalence of the cross-motif in many of their artifacts seems to have no special Christian significance, for the same motif is found throughout the whole Muslim world. Up to the time of the Arab conquest there were, of course, many Christian communities in North Africa. In the sixth century the Garamantes of the Fezzan were converted to Christianity; but their conversion appears to have been a purely political act, of no abiding importance. It is reasonable to assume that some Tuareg tribes had some contact with Christian communities before the Arab conquest, but there is no reason to believe that they were ever converted to Christianity.[13]

There are two other smaller groups of people—the Zaghawa and the Jews—who played some part in the early history of the Sahara and the Sudan, although there is much that is obscure about their contribution. Today the Zaghawa are a tribe of nomads living on the Chad-Sudan border to the north of Darfur. They are described as being 'largely a mixture' of Tebu and negro 'with Libyo-Berber affinities'. Their language is a dialect of Tebu.[14] The Zaghawa are mentioned by most of the medieval Arab geographers, but there is some confusion about their racial origin. According to Yaqubi, writing in the ninth century A.D., 'the first of the Sudanese [i.e. negro] kingdoms is that of the Zaghawa in Kanem'.[15] Yaqut, writing four hundred years later, agrees that the Zaghawa are a Sudanese people.[16] But Ibn Khaldun numbers the Zaghawa among 'the people of the *litham*', the Saharan Berbers.[17] Perhaps these accounts may be reconciled by assuming that the Zaghawa were a people of Tebu–negro origin, who were dominated for a time by a class of Tuareg Berbers.

In modern times the Maghrib has contained a population of up

to half a million Jews, and it is clear that a Jewish population has
been settled in North Africa for many centuries. It is possible that
some Jews accompanied the first Phoenician settlers at the beginning of the first millenium B.C., but 'the first true wave of Jewish
immigrants to North Africa seems to have arrived late in the
sixth century before Christ, in Cyrenaica', where 'it was probably
soon thoroughly submerged racially in a sea of local Berber converts
to Judaism.'[18] In 115 A.D. there was a major Jewish revolt against
Roman rule in Cyrenaica. After the revolt had been suppressed
many Jews fled westwards, and some of them probably established
themselves in the oases of the northern Sahara, where their
presence was recorded in medieval times. Some scholars have
suggested that after the Cyrenaican revolt a great wave of Jewish
immigrants crossed the Sahara and settled in West Africa, where
they became the founders of the kingdom of Ghana, whose early
rulers were said to have been white, and contributed to the
ancestry of the modern Fulani.[19] There is not enough reliable
evidence for this theory to be accepted in its entirety, but it is not
unreasonable to suppose that a limited number of Jews found their
way across the Sahara in the middle ages.* [20]

5

Peoples of the Sudan

THE great belt of country that lies between the Sahara and the
tropical forest—the area which historians are accustomed to refer
to as the Western Sudan—provides the home of a great variety of
different peoples. In the valley of the Senegal, and in the country
between the Senegal and the Gambia, the dominant people are the
Wolof and the Tucolor. Between the Senegal and the Niger, and
in the valley of the Upper Niger and its tributaries, live a number
of peoples—Soninke, Mandingo, Bambara, and Dyula are the
most prominent among them—who have many basic features in

* In the literature of the time there is only one reference to the presence of Jews south
  of the Sahara. This occurs in the work of Valentin Fernandes, writing at the beginning of the sixteenth century. Fernandes states that there were living in Walata Jews
  who were 'very rich but greatly oppressed, some of them wandering merchants,
  others gold smiths or jewellers'.[21]

common, such as language and social organization, but who have been influenced by their differing environments and historical experiences to develop along different lines. In the area of the middle Niger the dominant people are the Songhai, to whom are affiliated the Zerma and the Dendi. Within the Niger bend and in the basin of the Upper Volta live a great variety of people, among them the Mossi, the Lobi, and the Senufo, who speak related languages. People of Mandingo stock have also moved into this area. Across the Niger, in what is now the north-western corner of Nigeria, live the Hausa. Between Hausa country and Lake Chad the dominant people are the Kanuri. South of the Hausa and the Kanuri live a great variety of smaller tribes. Finally, there is one group, the Fulani (or Fula) who are to be found in most of the countries between the Senegal and Lake Chad. Within the forest area, which occupies a much smaller part of West Africa than the savannah, the main peoples are the Akan of southern Ghana (they include the Asante and the Fante), the Yoruba of Western Nigeria, and the Ibo of Eastern Nigeria.

There are no written records of any description to throw light on the history of West Africa before 900 A.D., and the earliest records—those contained, for example, in the writings of Arab geographers—are only of use for the peoples living in the northern-most part of the Sudan. But even when deprived of written records the historian has other sources to fall back on: linguistic research, archaeology, ethnology, and oral tradition.

At first sight, a map showing the main peoples of West Africa is dauntingly confusing. Linguistic research, however, has made it possible to clarify the picture by introducing a number of broad divisions. Thus most of the peoples of West Africa speak languages that have been recognized as belonging to a single family, called by some scholars, Niger-Congo.[1] This suggests that many of the peoples of West Africa, whether they live in the savannah or in the forest, may have their origin in a common stock. On the other hand, the differences between languages in the same broad family group are very great. If all the languages are derived from a common stock, it must have taken many hundreds, possibly even many thousands of years, for the differences between them to evolve. Yoruba and Idoma, for example, are closely related languages, yet linguistic research suggests that they have been growing apart from one another for a period of six thousand years.[2] Yoruba and Idoma are both Kwa languages, Kwa being the name of one of the main divisions of the Niger-Congo family. If it is estimated that it should have taken so long for languages within a single division to have become separated, one must presumably throw back to an even more remote period the separation between different divisions of the Niger-Congo family, Kwa, Mande, Voltaic, and others.

Some West African peoples speak languages that are in no way associated with the Niger-Congo family. Hausa, together with the languages of many of the smaller tribes of Northern Nigeria, represents one of the sub-groups of the Afro-Asiatic or Hamito-Semitic language family, a family that also includes Berber and Arabic. Kanuri is closely related to Tebu, the two languages together forming part of an isolated language family which has been designated Nilo-Saharan. The position of Songhai is obscure; it is certainly not a member of the Niger-Congo family but may be related to the Nilo-Saharan languages. Tentatively it may be suggested that elements in the Kanuri and Songhai people must at one time have had their home further north; elements among the Hausa, further east.

Linguistic research, at least in its present stage, suggests a broad but somewhat vague pattern. Archaeology can on occasion throw a piercing shaft of light on to a small area. This is what has happened with the remarkable Nok culture of Northern Nigeria. During the 1930s and 1940s, tin-mining operations on the edge of the Nigerian plateau led to the accidental discovery of a number of figurines modelled in baked clay, the earliest of which were found at the village of Nok in southern Zaria province. Further research has shown that the people who made the figurines were basically agriculturalists who used both iron and stone implements. Radio-carbon analysis has provided a date as early as 900 B.C. for some of the figurines; others have been dated around A.D. 900. Artifacts of the same culture have been found over a wide area straddling the Benue and Niger valleys above their confluence. It is possible that the makers of the figurines of the Nok culture were in fact the direct ancestors of the present people inhabiting the area: the hairstyle shown on one of the modelled heads is similar, it has been remarked, to that still practised by one local tribe. It appears equally possible that there is some connexion between the Nok culture and the culture that evolved in Ife and Benin, for the Nok heads are remarkably similar in style to the Ife heads, the earliest of which have been dated to the eleventh century.[3]

There are many other sites of interest to the archaeologist in West Africa: south of Lake Chad, for example, are to be found the occupation mounds of the legendary So people, who preceded the Kanuri inhabitants. Excavation has revealed 'enormous pots, probably originally used for grain or water-storage, but also used for burials' and 'a fascinating array of modelled clay objects', together with a number cast in bronze, the earliest probably belonging to the eleventh century.[4] In the Senegal and Gambia area there exists a number of megalithic sites in the form of stone circles. Other megalithic sites have been found further east, within the borders of modern Mali; the age, purpose, and origins of these megaliths have not yet been satisfactorily explained.[5] Sites such as these are immensely provocative: they force the historian to acknowledge the extent of his ignorance, and at the same time raise many questions in his mind—how did this culture come to evolve and what relation does it have to the known cultures of North Africa or the Nile valley, and to cultures in other parts of West Africa?* Undoubtedly it will take many years of patient research before archaeologists can begin to suggest definite answers. Yet one is beginning to perceive from the sites already brought to light how complex and fascinating the early history of West Africa is likely to prove.

Among the negro peoples of West Africa, the basic social and political unit appears in the past to have been the small local group, bound together by ties of kinship. When a number of such groups came together they formed a clan. The heads of local clans were usually responsible for certain religious rites connected with the land. In some parts of West Africa, in isolated areas of forest, swamp, or mountain, such small groups maintained their independence of outsiders until the establishment of European rule in the early twentieth century. Elsewhere considerable states emerged, in some cases at an early date.

Oral traditions provide the only evidence for the early history

---

* The introduction of iron-working provides one of the themes that links the history of West Africa with that of other regions. The art of smelting iron was discovered in Asia Minor in the second millenium B.C. It spread to Egypt, and from Egypt southwards to the kingdom of Meroe. From about 300 B.C. to A.D. 300 Meroe is known to have been an important centre of iron manufacture. The people of the Nok culture possessed the art of smelting iron, and this knowledge may have reached them from Meroe. Alternatively, it may have reached them from the north, brought by smiths who had had contact with the Carthaginians. (For a study of the introduction of metal working into West Africa, R. Mauny, 'Essai sur l'histoire des métaux en Afrique Occidentale', *Bulletin de l'I.F.A.N.*, Dakar, 1952, 545–595.)

of the states of West Africa. Of ancient Ghana the Timbuktu historian, as-Sadi, records that the kingdom existed before the *hijra* (A.D. 622), that there were twenty-two kings before that date and twenty-two after it, all of them being of white race, though their origin was uncertain.[6] The first king of the Songhai, according to the same source, was Za-alayaman, a stranger who came from the Yemen.[7] The founders of the Mossi-Dagomba states are regarded as 'red men', characteristically horsemen whose original home was 'on the road to Mecca'.[8] The Hausa myth of origin tells of a certain Bayajidda who came from Baghdad to Kanem, and then passed on to Daura, where he killed a great snake and married the queen. His descendants became the founders of six of the Hausa states.[9] Saif, the first name in the dynastic list of the rulers of Kanem-Bornu, is said to have lived in 'Yaman' (Arabia).[10]

Basing their theories on these legends, most of the earliest European scholars to study the history of West Africa suggested that the states of the Sudan were the creation of 'white' immigrant invaders. Thus the French scholar, Y. Urvoy, asserted that all along the Sudan the seeds of a higher civilization were introduced into the 'diffuse and inert mass' of black peasant communities by people of white race, 'small groups reduced in numbers because they have had to cross the Sahara, warlike, very mobile, bringing with them, in spite of the hereditary anarchic tendencies of the nomad, the sense of empire, a reflection of the political ideas of the Mediterranean and Near East, possessing also a certain pride of race'.[11]

To modern scholars, such theories appear too simple, tainted too by a certain, even if unconscious, racist bias. Recent thought and research suggests that the whole process of the emergence of states in West Africa was at once more complex and more obscure. Thus M. G. Smith, in his study of Hausa traditions of origin, sees 'indications of a confused period of immigration, struggle, and cultural change, the violence and duration of which probably varied over time as well as place in accordance with the differences of population structure.'[12] It is still accepted that some of the states of the Sudan may have owed their origin to immigrant invaders, some of whom may have been of 'white', probably Berber, stock. But this generalization must be made subject to two modifications.

In the first place 'it must be stressed', as Mauny and Vansina have pointed out, 'that conquerors did not necessarily belong to a so-called "superior" civilization, but simply had at their disposal either more efficient military techniques or a political organization which enabled them to mobilize and deploy more men than their enemies and in a shorter period.' Secondly, it should not be assumed that conquest by immigrant outsiders was the only way in which a state might be created. It is possible for one among many local groups to succeed in imposing its domination on its neighbours. The kingdom of Mali, for example, whose foundation owed nothing to white immigrants, may have evolved in this way. Alternatively, 'dispersed communities of an unorganized population may invite leaders of immigrant groups to organize them into a state', a theory which may provide the clue for the origins of the Songhai kingdom.[13]

The kingdoms which began to emerge in the Sudan about the end of the first millenium and the great 'empires'—Ghana, Mali, Songhai—which played so large a part in the medieval history of West Africa differed in many ways from the modern nation-state. One must not think of them as compact and homogeneous units. 'The Sudanese empire', Trimingham has pointed out, 'was an amorphous agglomeration of kin-groups having little in common except mythical recognition of a far-off suzerain.' Such empires had no precise boundaries, for 'the ruler was not interested in dominating territory as such, but in relationship with social groups upon whom he could draw to provide levies in time of war, servants for his courts and cultivators to keep his granaries full. . . . These steppe empires give the appearance of structural weakness and instability. They rose rapidly, expanded prematurely, and then either died away like Mali or suffered a catastrophic disintegration like Songhai.'[14] Beyond the confines of the great empires lay a great variety of different units: smaller states such as those of the Mossi of the Niger bend, which maintained a remarkable political stability for many centuries, city-states such as those founded by the Hausa or the So and drawing much of their wealth from trade and industry, nomadic pastoralists, independent kin-groups. The more closely one looks at the early political geography of West Africa, the more complex the pattern becomes. And yet, one may reflect, the pattern of medieval Europe—with its shadowy empires, its turbulent marches, its vigorous cities, its many isolated communities—was not in many ways so dissimilar.

6

The Arabs

'Our ancient Chroniclers of Africa, to wit, Bichri *and* Meshudi, *knew nothing of the land of Negros but only the regions of Guechet and Cano.'*
LEO AFRICANUS.

THE beginning of the third century A.D. marked the apogee of Roman rule in North Africa, yet even then signs of severe weakness could be detected. For the Romans had never succeeded, as the French were later to do, in occupying the whole of North Africa. Throughout the whole period of their rule, they had to face the possibility of conflict with the native Berber inhabitants, living either in mountainous areas like the Aures within the *limes* or in the desert beyond the bounds of the empire. From the middle of the third century, when the structure of the empire was gravely weakened by political and economic crises, Berber revolts occurred almost continuously. At the beginning of the fourth century the Emperor Diocletian decided to draw in the frontiers by abandoning most of Mauretania Tingitana (northern Morocco) and Mauretania Caesariensis (western Algeria). This was a period when some of the Berber tribes living on the edge of the desert acquired the use of the camel; their increased mobility must have made them an even greater threat to Roman rule.

During the fourth century the North African provinces were further weakened by the religious schism between the Catholics and the Donatists. The Donatists, whose name was derived from their leader Donatus, strongly criticized those Christians who had renounced their faith during the periods of persecution before the Edict of Constantine in 313. In their revolt against the established order some of the Donatists made common cause with the Circumcelliones. The movement of the Circumcelliones (those who prowl *circum cellas* round barns) was a peasants' revolt, a protest by the rural proletariat against the injustices of the age. By the beginning of the fifth century the established order emerged triumphant, but among the mass of the people in Roman Africa 'a subdued hatred smouldered on—against the Empire, the official church, and the landowning aristocracy, joint partners in oppression.' [1]

Thus, when in 428 the Vandal horde, led by their king Genseric, crossed the straits from Spain to Africa, they found no force capable of seriously checking their advance. In 439 Genseric occupied Carthage, built a fleet, and proceeded in the course of the next twenty years to occupy most of the islands of the Western Mediterranean. In Africa Genseric had little alternative but to maintain the basic structure of Roman rule. Some of the great landowners were expropriated and the Catholic Church was subject to persecution (the Vandals followed the heretical Arian faith), but for the Romanized Berbers who made up the mass of population there can have been little difference between Vandal and Roman rule. Genseric died in 477; his successors were not men of the same stature, and their followers must have felt the enervating effects of a life of ease and luxury, and so, when in 533 the Emperor Justinian despatched a Byzantine army, under the command of Count Belisarius, to the conquest of Africa, Vandal resistance collapsed within the space of a few months.

The Berbers had refrained from taking sides in the war between Vandals and Byzantines, but once the Vandals had been defeated, they broke out into revolt. From then on, the Byzantines had to face an endemic state of war with the tribes. They were only able to maintain their hold on North Africa by building an elaborate network of fortresses and by practising a skilful diplomacy to prevent the Berbers of the Aures and other parts of Numidia from joining forces with the formidable camel-nomads of Tripolitania. Byzantine rule was as harsh, if not harsher, than that of the Vandals or the Romans: Justinian, wrote the historian Procopius, 'exhausted and looted Africa at his pleasure . . . he imposed crushing taxes that had not existed at all before and awarded the better part of the land to himself.' [2] Justinian's successors did no better for North Africa: Berber revolts, renewed religious discords, maladministration, and oppression mark the years of Byzantine occupation. The province, which covered little more than the present Tunisia, was in no state to resist another invader.

The first advance of the Arabs westward from Egypt began in 642. Impelled no longer by religious zeal (for that had spent itself), but by sheer lust for conquest, they fell upon the countries of the North African littoral, to which they gave the name of the Maghrib, or the West. In 647 the Prefect Gregory, who had recently declared himself independent of Byzantium, was defeated at

Sufetula (Sbeitla) and Byzantine rule in Africa practically ended. The Arabs chose for their headquarters a site at the head of the sea-board road to Egypt and far enough from the coast to be safe from the Byzantine fleet. Here, in the heart of the Maghrib, they built the city of Kairwan.

During the next thirty years the Muslim world was chiefly occupied with schisms in its own ranks, from which sprang most of the great sects of Islam. In 678 the Arabs renewed their assault on Africa and, led by Uqba ibn Nafi, they swept the whole length and breadth of the Maghrib. They even reached the Atlantic, where the triumphant Uqba spurred his horse into the waves to show that his conquest of the country was complete. Southward they occupied the Fezzan and reached the oasis of Kawar, but they turned back as they were on the point of discovering the grasslands of the Sudan.* Some settled in the oases of the desert and probably intermarried with the Jews. The Kunta Arabs of the south-west Sahara seem to have sprung from such a union.

Just when the Arab triumph seemed complete the Berbers' passionate love of liberty gave birth to one of those supreme national efforts which, at the moment of crisis, have so often saved the conquered from extinction. With the aid of the Greeks, whose support they had secured, and led by one of their own kings, Koceila, they destroyed Uqba and his army near Biskra in 683. They razed Kairwan and drove the rest of the Arabs back into Egypt. 'The conquest of Africa', declared an Arab governor, 'is impossible; scarcely has one Berber tribe been exterminated than another takes its place.'

A few years later Hassan, the governor of Egypt, set out finally to subdue the Maghrib. He rebuilt Kairwan, destroyed Carthage, and swept the few remaining Byzantines into the sea. Once again the Berbers rallied, this time under a Zenata prophetess named Kahena who drove the Arabs back and for long held them at bay. In 703 she too was defeated and five years later the Arabs under Musa ibn Nusair again swept the country from east to west. But their aspirations were not yet satisfied. In 711 the Arabs, greatly strengthened by Berber converts, invaded Spain where they developed the remarkable civilization for which their name will always be honoured.

* Arab merchants from as far away as Khorasan were attracted to the Fezzan by the slave-trade. (H. R. Palmer, *Mai Idris Alooma of Bornu*, Lagos, 1926, p. 67.)

In the Maghrib, the Arabs were faced with a constant struggle against the Berbers. The area controlled by the Arabs was confined to their towns and cantonments. The Berbers 'apostatised twelve times before Islam gained a firm hold over them'.[3] In the eleventh and twelfth centuries much of modern Morocco and Algeria was dominated by Berber dynasties, first the Almoravids, then the Almohads. But in the middle of the eleventh century North Africa was subjected to another Arab invasion, that of the Banu Hilal and the Banu Sulaim. These Arabs were Bedawin, marauding nomads who had been driven from Arabia into Egypt. The Fatimid caliph of Cairo, anxious to rid his country of such turbulent and uncontrollable guests, urged them to seek a new home in the Maghrib, of which he had despairingly washed his hands. They eagerly responded and swarmed into the country, 200,000 strong. The Banu Sulaim remained in Cyrenaica. The Banu Hilal pushed on westwards and penetrated far into the interior, slaying and destroying wherever they went. This, the Hilalian invasion, was likened by Ibn Khaldun to a swarm of locusts devouring the whole country over which it passed. The most serious consequence of the devastation was that enormous areas went permanently out of cultivation and the desert crept in. Directly or through their herds, these wild Arabs also destroyed most of the forests, thus creating the shortage of shipbuilding timber which in later times was so serious an embarrassment to their piratical descendants.

As we had occasion to note in an earlier chapter, the Maghrib is strewn with the ruins of the cities, towns, villages, aqueducts, dams, cisterns, and bridges which went down before the savage horde, and the desert has never relaxed its grip on great areas which before the Hilalian invasion were cultivated by man. More important than the devastation these Arabs wrought was the permanence of their hold on the country. Unlike their kinsmen of the earlier invasions, they had come to stay, and their descendants still people the country, though only the lowlands. That the Berbers have so successfully preserved the purity of their race is partly due to the Arab deluge having submerged only the low country. The highlands, to which the Berbers belonged, were hardly affected.

The persistence with which the Berbers have maintained their purity of race has constantly astonished ethnologists. In spite of the introduction into their country of Phoenician, Roman, Vandal,

Jewish, and Arab blood they show few traces of alien stock. Particularly striking is the way in which Berbers and Arabs have failed to amalgamate. Although they have lived in the closest proximity for over a thousand years, during which the Arab has imposed his religion, language, dress, and many of his customs on a large part of the Berber population, the latter have preserved their distinct racial type. In the Aures mountains, for example, only about 25 per cent. of the population have dark eyes. The Arab remains primarily a herdsman, dwelling in tents, fanatical and deeply superstitious, with a feudal tribal organization. The Berber, on the other hand, is a highlander, a tiller of the soil, and a dweller in towns and villages, and he is essentially democratic; although capable of fanatical outbursts, he is rarely moved by religious enthusiasms.

Grievous though the effects of the Hilalian invasion were, the coming of the Arabs conferred immense intellectual benefits on the Maghrib. They brought with them the learning and broad outlook they had absorbed from the Hellenistic culture of the late Roman empire, which later were to blossom into the rich Muslim culture of Spain.

No branch of learning was more enriched by Muslim scholarship than geography. Inspired by the works of Ptolemy, which the Christian churches had translated into Arabic, the Arabs were quick to develop an interest in foreign lands, which the vast extent and cosmopolitan character of the Muslim world stimulated and nourished. Throughout the length and breadth of Islam the Muslim traveller was sure of a welcome wherever he went, and the same hospitality awaited him among isolated Muslim communities in infidel lands. There is no more striking example of the extraordinary breadth of the Muslim horizon than an incident in the life of that great traveller Ibn Battuta. While staying in Sijilmasa, in southern Morocco, he discovered that his host was the brother of a man he had met some years before in western China.[4]

Another incentive to foreign travel, and therefore to the study of geography, was the *Hadj* or pilgrimage to Mecca, which was obligatory to every Muslim who had the strength and means to perform it. In obedience to this pious duty men of many nations regularly gathered in the holy cities, as they still do, and there, on common ground, freely exchanged information about each other's lands.

Trade provided another great stimulus to travel. Their commercial enterprise took the Arabs as far east as China and southwards into the Indian Ocean. The remarkable extent of their trade is well illustrated by the finding of great hoards of Islamic coins on the shores of the Baltic, and the note of an Arab geographer that at one of their markets, where they were trading for furs, the night was but an hour long.

Before the coming of the Arabs, little or nothing was known of Africa south of the Maghrib. We owe practically the whole of our knowledge of the early history of the interior to a small group of Arabic authors, the chief of whom were al-Masudi, Ibn Haukal, al-Bakri, al-Idrisi, Yaqut, al-Umari, Ibn Battuta, and Ibn Khaldun. Our debt to these learned men is so great that a brief notice of each cannot be omitted from a volume largely based on translations of their works.[5]

al-Masudi's importance to us lies not in his contribution to our material, but in his influence on the later writers to whom our debt is profound. He was a native of Baghdad. We do not know when he was born, but he died in A.D. 956. He spent twenty years wandering about the Islamic world and is believed to have visited countries as far afield as China and Madagascar. He had a surprisingly accurate notion of the shape, size, and motion of the earth, and in this respect was much ahead of Christian thought. He believed the Atlantic, the Green Sea of Darkness, to be impossible to navigate, a belief which some Christians shared. His notice of the Sudan is limited to a reference to the curious silent trade in gold.

Ibn Haukal, almost a contemporary of al-Masudi, was also a native of Baghdad. He spent twenty-five years in travel, and claimed that his *Book of Ways and Provinces* contained all that had 'ever made geography of interest to either princes or peoples'. He and Ibn Battuta were the only medieval writers, whose works have survived, to visit the interior of Africa. His is the earliest account we have of the Western Sudan, of which he is the first known explorer. He visited Audoghast and Kumbi, the capital of Ghana, and saw the Niger flowing eastwards, which led him to believe it to be the Nile of Egypt. He was the first to voice the traditional contempt of Muslims for negroes, of whom he wrote:

I have not described the country of the African blacks and the other peoples of the torrid zone: because naturally loving wisdom, ingenuity, religion, justice and regular government, how could I notice such people as these, or magnify them by inserting an account of their countries? [6]

The eleventh century saw the appearance of a work of great importance to the student of North African history. Its author was Abu Ubaid al-Bakri, a member of an illustrious Arab family who had formerly enjoyed considerable power in Spain under the Ummayads. He was born in the first half of the eleventh century and spent the whole of his life in Spain. His works included a monumental one on geography, running into several volumes, which contained a remarkable description of northern Africa. His account of the Sudan is of particular interest because it represents the earliest attempt at a general survey of the country. From its accuracy, which much impressed later writers, it is evident that al-Bakri had access to documents of the first importance, doubtless in the official archives in Cordoba. He died in 1094.*

The first half of the twelfth century produced a work which was the most important contribution to geography since al-Masudi. The author was al-Idrisi, a Spanish Arab in the service of Roger II, the Norman king of Sicily. Muslim writers of the day naturally looked askance at one who had entered the service of an infidel prince, especially at a time when the crusades had engendered the bitterest hatred between Muslim and Christian. Nevertheless, the name of al-Idrisi was honoured in three continents.

Perhaps because of the disapproval with which his fellow-countrymen viewed him, very little is known of al-Idrisi's life. His grandfather was emir of Malaga, but later the family had been exiled to Africa, where they settled in Ceuta. There al-Idrisi was born in about 1100. He appears to have been educated in Cordova and to have spent his early manhood travelling in Spain, Africa, and Asia Minor.

Roger, a patron of all the sciences, was passionately interested in geography. He spent fifteen years amassing information on his favourite subject, and quickly learnt that the most fruitful source of information was the Arabs, with whose treatises he filled his library. It was therefore natural for him to look round for an Arab scholar to reduce to order the fruits of his labours, and there was

* The best copy of al-Bakri's geographical work is in the British Museum. There is another copy in the Bibliothéque Nationale in Paris.

no more obvious choice than al-Idrisi. The collection of material continued under al-Idrisi's guidance and culminated in 1154 in the production of the famous *Book of Roger* or, as it was sometimes called, the Rogerian Description of the World. al-Idris was exceptional among Arab geographers for the accuracy with which he described Europe, and for his sympathetic understanding of western thought, both products of his environment.*

The next scholar to contribute to our early knowledge of the interior was Yaqut, who was born in Byzantine territory in 1179. His parents were Greeks, but when still a child he was carried off and sold as a slave to a merchant in Baghdad, by whom he was given a good education. He travelled widely in the interests of his master and compiled a geographical dictionary of some note. He died in 1229.

The thirteenth century produced no Arabic work of interest to us, but we are adequately compensated by the rich output of the fourteenth.† We owe to the *Masalik al-Absar* of al-Umari most of what we know of the memorable pilgrimage of Mansa Musa of Mali. al-Umari was an Arab of Damascus, born in 1301, who spent his early life in the service of the sultan of Egypt. After a few years in Cairo he returned to Damascus where he devoted himself to literature.

Contemporary with al-Umari were two noted men of letters who will always be regarded as ornaments of Arab civilization. These were Ibn Battuta, one of the most remarkable travellers in history, and Ibn Khaldun, to whom we owe much of our knowledge of early Berber and Arab history.

Ibn Battuta was born in 1304 at Tangier, where his family, who were Berbers, had been settled for several generations. He was educated as a theologian and at the age of twenty-one performed the *Hadj*, which gave him a taste for travel which became a passion. After visiting the Middle East he set out for India to join the scholars from many parts of the world who were thronging the court of the sultan of Delhi. He followed a circuitous route through Asia Minor and over the steppes of central Asia to Khorasan. His reception in India, where his reputation as a

---

* A much abridged edition of al-Idrisi's *Book of Roger* was printed by the Medici in Rome in 1592, but the first complete edition was a French translation of two manuscripts in the Imperial Library in Paris which was published in 1836. The Bodleian possesses a manuscript copy written in Cairo in 1456.

† The famous *Geography* of Abu'l Fida (1273–1331) is omitted because it is of little value to the student of the history of the interior of north-west Africa.

scholar had preceded him, was satisfying to his vanity, and his subsequent appointment as Malikite qadi of Delhi scarcely less so to his purse. Seven years later the Sultan, Muhammad Tughluq, sent him on a mission to China, but soon after leaving Delhi he was set upon by his enemies and had to fly and abandon his mission.

We next hear of him on the Malabar coast whence he made his way to the Maldive Islands. There he was appointed qadi, but the zeal with which he administered the law was so little to the liking of the islanders that he had quickly to leave their shores. After visiting Ceylon and Assam he realized his ambition of seeing Peking, though without obtaining the audience of the Mongol emperor to which he had looked forward. He then set out on his homeward journey, travelling by way of Sumatra, Malabar, and Syria, and reaching Tangier in 1349. A pilgrimage to Mecca which should have been completed in six months had become a world tour lasting twenty-four years. But his passion for travel was not yet satisfied. There was still one Muslim country to be seen. This was the Sudan, to which he now made his way. It was the last journey of his life and the most noteworthy, for it enabled him to give the world the first detailed narrative of travels in the heart of western Africa. It has been estimated that by the time Ibn Battuta had returned to Fez he must have travelled about 75,000 miles. He died in 1368 or 1369.

Ibn Khaldun, a contemporary of Ibn Battuta, came of an Arab family who had fled from Spain to Africa at the time of the Almoravid invasion and settled in Tunis, where he was born in 1332. His literary attainments secured for him a court appointment at an early age, but, not satisfied with his prospects with the sultan, he moved to Fez where he also obtained a position at court. His egoism and love of intrigue landed him in prison. On his release he adopted the life of a political adventurer, for which he was admirably suited. Ibn Khaldun's reputation as an erudite scholar enabled him to dupe one royal patron after another. After serving in Granada, Bugie, Biskra, and Tlemcen he returned to Tunis, where he probably started his great work on the history of the Berbers and Arabs. His craving for political power and his abuse of it soon compelled him to seek a new field for the exercise of his talents. His choice of Egypt proved a happy one, for both himself and posterity.

He was made Malikite Mufti of Cairo, but in 1387 he retired

and settled down in a village of the Fayum to a life of study and research. Here he spent many years in quiet retirement during which he compiled the greater part of his monumental historical work. In the course of his peregrinations from one court to another he had collected an enormous mass of material which he was able to sift and digest in the seclusion of the Fayum. After fourteen years there he was called upon to assume once more the important duties of Mufti in Cairo, but owing to his severity to transgressors he was not suffered to hold office for long.

In 1400 he accompanied the sultan of Egypt on his unsuccessful attempt to save Damascus from Tamerlane. Abandoned by his master, he made his way to the Tartar camp where he hoped to obtain a safe-conduct to Egypt, and perhaps to satisfy a historian's natural desire to meet in the flesh the greatest warrior of the day. The results were wholly gratifying to the aged scholar; he obtained his safe-conduct and was granted a long audience with the Tartar conqueror.

Ibn Khaldun died in Cairo in 1406, recognized as the greatest Muslim scholar of his day. Although there was little to admire in his character, he deserved well of posterity, which owes to his erudition and industry so great a part of its knowledge of early Arab and Berber history.

There were other medieval Arabic scholars on whose works we shall have occasion to draw. Among them was the famous historian of Egypt, al-Maqrizi (1364–1442). Several we know of only through the works of others, as for example Ibn Said, the geographer who died in 1286. He wrote an account of the Sudan, which unfortunately has not survived. But, if we may judge by the frequency with which he is quoted by Abu'l Fida, Ibn Khaldun, and others, his work was of great interest and its loss a grievous blow to scholarship.

After the fourteenth century, Muslim letters began rapidly to decay. Nevertheless, we depend largely on Arabic writers for much of the later history of the Western Sudan. The most important of these was as-Sadi, the author of the *Tarikh as-Sudan*.

Abdarrahman as-Sadi was born in Timbuktu in 1596. He came of an aristocratic Sudanese family and from early youth was accustomed to moving in influential circles. He was intensely proud of his native city, and in his *Tarikh* he constantly reverts to its importance as the metropolis of Negroland. His first public appointment was that of a notary at Jenne where he afterwards became *imam*, a post he later filled at Timbuktu. He played an active part in political life and received the title of *Katib*, or Secretary to the Government, in recognition of his public services. He probably died soon after 1655, the date to which he carried his history of the Sudan.

For the first part of his *Tarikh*, covering the rise of the Songhai empire, he drew largely on chroniclers not all of whose works have come down to us. He mentions only two, the Biographical Dictionary of Ahmad Baba and a work entitled *al-Kabir*. Ahmad Baba, who died in Timbuktu in 1627 after several years captivity in Marrakech, was a member of the illustrious family of the Aqit who, like so many of the *literati* of Timbuktu, were of Jedala stock. It is noteworthy that he completed his education under a learned Mandingo, Muhammad Baghyu'u, who had been one of his father's pupils and had attained some repute as a scholar. Most of the scholars of Jenne, which was highly regarded as a seat of learning, were negroes; those of Timbuktu were mostly of Berber blood. At least eleven of Ahmad Baba's works are still in existence and he is remembered to this day as a great scholar.[7] As-Sadi had been too young to come under his direct influence, but he benefited greatly from the cultured society of which Ahmad Baba had long been the leader.*

---

* We owe the discovery of the *Tarikh as-Sudan* to Henry Barth,[8] who found a copy in Gwandu in 1853. He had the manuscript in his hand only for a few days, which left him time to make no more than a few short extracts. He was wrongly told that the book had been written by Ahmad Baba. Of the three surviving manuscript copies of the *Tarikh* two are in the Bibliothéque Nationale in Paris.

MEDIEVAL EMPIRES

7

The Almoravids

'That same plain of Morocco is a fine place to dwell in, compared with our glorious Seville! What if these barbarians have encamped there? Between us and them there lie deserts and great armies, and the waves of the sea.'
A SPANISH VIZIER.

As the Arabs spread westwards the focus of interest travelled with them into the Maghrib al-Aqsa, the Farthest West, the country now called Morocco. Here great rolling plains and a vast expanse of upland pastures, all blessed with a generous rainfall and countless perennial streams, separated the Mediterranean from the Sahara instead of the narrow arid corridor which had so closely confined the invaders on their westward migration from the Nile. The conditions, though less favourable, were not dissimilar from those they were later to turn to so remarkable an account in Spain. The Arabs were at last able to form permanent settlements to which their conquest of Spain and the remarkable growth of Muslim scholarship and wealth which followed it brought all the benefits of propinquity to seats of learning and cultured ease.

The constant passage of men and ideas across the Straits kept the Arabs of Africa abreast of the great achievements of their brothers in Europe and made Morocco a vital link in the chain which bound eastern and western Islam. From the east came scholars, merchants, and craftsmen seeking a share in the wealth and culture of the west. From Spain there was a ceaseless flow of the oppressed, victims of political and religious persecution, and fugitives from justice; most of them were skilled agriculturalists, but many erudite scholars were of their number. Thus was the Maghrib al-Aqsa nourished by two converging streams of fresh and invigorating blood. How richly their confluence blessed the country is strikingly illustrated by the city of Fez. Early in the ninth century 2,000 families from Kairwan settled on one bank of the little Wad Fez; a few years later 8,000 families expelled from Cordoba settled on the opposite bank. Although for centuries they held aloof, each regarding the other with jealousy and mistrust, from these two communities, the Kairwanis and the Andalusians, sprang the city which became, and still remains, the intellectual centre of the Maghrib.

Morocco was also drawing great benefit from the rise of a powerful kingdom far away in the south, on the fringes of the Sahara and the Sudan. In spite of its remoteness and the barrier of an immense desert, this shadowy kingdom of Ghana was carrying on with Morocco a trade on which both countries were growing rich. The northern *entrepôt* of this trade was Sijilmasa, in the oasis of Tafilelt, just south of the Atlas mountains. Extensive ruins clothed in rank vegetation are all that remain of this once famous city, which was founded in the eighth century A.D.*

One of the earliest references to Sijilmasa occurs in Ibn Haukal who, writing in the tenth century, tells us that

it is a town of middling size . . . one cannot enter Sijilmasa but by way of the desert, which the sand renders difficult. The town is situated near the gold mines, between them and the land of the Blacks, and the land of Zuilah. These mines are said to be of the most pure and excellent gold; but it is difficult to work them, and the way to them is dangerous and troublesome.[1]

In the following century al-Bakri described Sijilmasa as a city of imposing buildings, and remarkable for the excellence of its climate.[2] Early writers are unanimous in attributing the city's wealth to the gold trade with Ghana, but it was common knowledge that the gold did not originate in Ghana but in a mysterious country beyond it called Wangara.

Closely linked with the gold trade was the salt trade in which also the merchants of Sijilmasa were deeply interested. The salt came from the mines at Taghaza, twenty days' march down the road to Ghana. Although well endowed by Nature in many

---

* Sijilmasa was not the only town in North Africa which maintained a trade with the Sudan. To the east of Sijilmasa lay the kingdom founded at the end of the eighth century by Ibn Rustem, one of the leaders of the heretical Ibadite sect, with its capital at Tahert (modern Tiaret). According to the chronicles of Tahert, the rulers of the city were in contact both with Ghana and with Gao during the ninth century. (Tadeusz Lewicki, 'L'État nord-africain de Tahert et ses relations avec le Soudan occidental à la fin du VIIIe et an IXe Siècle', *Cahiers d'Études Africaines*, 8, 1962).

respects, the Sudan has always suffered from lack of salt, an essential which the Sudanese had to obtain from elsewhere. Taghaza, far away in the north and buried deep in the desert, was their chief source of supply, but they never got enough for their needs. Consequently some of the remoter and more backward peoples had an insatiable, or anyway unsatisfied, craving for salt. Amongst them were the gold diggers of the mysterious Wangara, who sometimes would not part with their gold for anything but salt. The salt of Taghaza, therefore, was essential to the gold trade of Sijilmasa.

The gold trade with Ghana was probably well established before the coming of the Arabs.* That their keen commercial sense did much to develop it cannot be doubted any more than can the cupidity it engendered in their breasts. Some time between A.D. 734 and 750, within a few decades of their occupation of Morocco, they sent an expedition across the desert to attack Ghana.[3] This was a far more perilous undertaking than the expeditions led by Septimius Flaccus and Julius Maternus along the much easier Fezzan road. The discovery and capture of the source of the gold pouring into Morocco was undoubtedly the inducement for so ambitious an enterprise. Like a similar expedition sent down the same road and for the same purpose some centuries later, it reached the Sudan and obtained a lot of gold, but it failed in its purpose. All the Arab expedition achieved was an apparently ineffective attack on Ghana, from which anyway some of their troops never returned, for al-Bakri speaks of their descendants, the al-Honeihin, being still there in the eleventh century.

French archaeologists have now established beyond reasonable doubt that extensive ruins about 300 miles west-south-west of Timbuktu mark the site of the ancient capital of Ghana, the city of Kumbi, which is mentioned only once in recorded history, in the *Tarikh al-Fattash*, an earlier work than the *Tarikh as-Sudan* and equally important.[4] According to as-Sadi, the kingdom of Ghana was of considerable age, having had twenty-two kings before the Hijra and as many after.[5] The ruling dynasty was white, but the people were black Mandingo. As Mahmud al-Kati, on the other hand, pointed out in the *Tarikh-al-Fattash*, there was some disagreement about the origin of the ruling dynasty, some saying it

* Recent research has shown that there was an ancient caravan route running north and south across the Sahara farther west than the Sijilmasa–Taghaza road. Possibly the Arabs used the former. (R. Mauny, *Bull. IFAN*, IX, 1947, pp. 341–57.)

was of Soninke origin, others that it was derived from the Mandingo—an improbable theory in al-Kati's opinion; yet others said that it was derived from the Sanhaja Berbers, which seemed to him the more likely explanation.[6] But whatever its origin, it is clear that to the Arabs of the eighth and ninth centuries Ghana was the greatest of the negro kingdoms of the Sudan. The approximate frontiers of Ghana were the Niger on the east, and the Senegal and its tributary the Faleme on the south; north and west was the desert.[7]

That desert nomads make bad neighbours was as true south of the Sahara as it was north of it. At this time, when Ghana had achieved a commercial and territorial importance which no other negro kingdom had ever approached, dark and menacing clouds were gathering in the desert to the north-west. The kingdom was threatened by a confederation of Sanhaja tribes led by Tilutan, chief of the Lemtuna. At the head of an army of 100,000 Sanhaja camelry, Tilutan had already imposed his authority over nearly all the Berber tribes of the western Sahara and begun to raid southwards, harrying the vassals of the king of Ghana. The latter, overawed by the immense strength of his warlike neighbour, dared not resist these encroachments. Tilutan, however, was equally anxious to avoid a trial of strength, and as he was content with merely raiding the outlying portions of Ghana a direct conflict between these powerful neighbours was averted.[8]

The Lemtuna capital was Audoghast, the modern Tegdaoust, which lay only fifteen days' march westward from Kumbi, in eastern Tagant, and one month from Arguin on the coast. It was a large town with fine buildings, surrounded by groves of date palms beyond which lay the desert. The inhabitants were Berbers, who owned great numbers of negro slaves, and a large Arab community engaged in the caravan trade.[9]

Water was abundant in Audoghast and made possible the raising of a wide variety of crops, including dates, wheat (a luxury reserved for the rich), millet, figs, vines, gourds, and henna. Cattle and sheep were abundant and cheap. It was an important *entrepôt* for gold, which it imported from the Sudan and re-exported to the Maghrib, notably to Sijilmasa. Imports included wheat, dried fruit, brass, and clothing from the north, ambergris and salt from the coast, and gold and honey from the Sudan. In describing the constant passage of caravans between Audoghast and the Maghrib, Ibn Haukal cites as an example of the large scale on which trade was done the indebtedness of a native of Sijilmasa to a merchant of Audoghast for a sum of 40,000 gold *dinars*.* [10]

The people had amassed great wealth which enabled them to lead lives of ease and luxury, and to cultivate the arts of civilization. Audoghast was famed for the skill of its cooks and for the beauty of its white-skinned damsels, on whose charms al-Bakri dwells with enthusiasm. To such lengths would these young women go to preserve their looks that they preferred to recline rather than sit lest they should distort the elegant symmetry of their posteriors.

Although Audoghast managed outwardly to preserve friendly relations with Ghana, there was constant friction between the Lemtuna and Soninke. The latter waylaid caravans from the north as they approached Audoghast, and the Lemtuna retaliated by intervening in the internal affairs of Ghana and by taking part in private feuds between vassal chiefs. The Soninke, however, gradually became the dominant power, but although they recovered the outlying districts which had been filched from them they made no attempt to occupy Audoghast.

Early in the eleventh century the Sanhaja tribes combined, as in the time of Tilutan, to resist the encroachments of the Soninke and possibly even to break the power of Ghana. Nothing came of this resolve because an unexpected chain of events diverted Sanhaja aspirations into a different channel.

As a result of their intercourse with the Muslim traders who had settled in their midst, some of the Sanhaja had been converted to Islam, and their chiefs customarily performed the *Hadj*. When their paramount chief, Yahia ibn Ibrahim, was passing through Kairwan on his return from one such pilgrimage he fell under the influence of the learned Abu Amran, whom he astonished by his doctrinal ignorance and his assurance that his Saharan subjects were even less instructed than their emir. When he saw how deeply he had shocked the doctor from Fez shame moved him to seek his aid in finding a theologian to instruct him and his people in the orthodox religion. Thus it came about that Yahia was accompanied home by the preacher Abdullah ibn Yasin, a disciple of a certain Wajjaj of Sijilmasa. The consequences were destined to disturb the peace of two continents. [11]

Ibn Yasin began his ministrations among Yahia's own tribesmen, the Jedala, who found the austere doctrine of the ascetic

* A *dinar* was the weight of seventy-two grains of barley.

from the north and the restrictions that he tried to place upon them so repugnant that they burnt his house and drove him from their country. Accompanied by two faithful Lemtuna, he sought seclusion at a place surrounded by water, either an island in the Senegal or a promontory on the coast, where he founded a *ribat*, a monastery organized on military lines.* This strange behaviour aroused interest, and the curious began to seek instruction in the mysterious rites practised by the holy man. Many found inspiration in the new teaching and became fervent disciples of the preacher. When his followers numbered about a thousand Ibn Yasin called them together and bid them go forth and compel the world to accept the reformed faith. They were known as *al-Murabitun*, the people of the *ribat*, a word which was changed in Spanish usage into Almoravid.[12]

In 1042 the Almoravids, with Ibn Yasin at their head, started a *jihad* against the Jedala and the Lemtuna, who till then had rejected the new doctrine. The alternatives of death or conversion resulted in a triumph for the Almoravids, but victory was robbed of its sweetness. Their austere leader denied them the pleasures of pillage and rape, and thus damped the enthusiasm with which they had espoused his cause. When he followed this up with even more tyrannical restrictions they turned on him and he had to fly.

The prophet now made his way back to his old master, Wajjaj, in Sijilmasa. Here he found both sympathy and followers anxious to avenge the wrongs he had suffered in the desert. Wajjaj, threatening expulsion from Islam to all who refused to obey Ibn Yasin, sent his disciple and his new adherents back into the desert with orders to destroy whoever opposed them. Ibn Yasin carried out his master's instructions to such effect that before long, either through the fervour of his preaching but more probably through the weight of support he had secured in the north, most of the tribes of the western desert had accepted the new doctrine and were united under his banner.

Ibn Yasin now set about turning to account the predominant position he had secured for himself in the western Sahara. A capable, perhaps brilliant, organizer and undoubtedly an inspiring leader, he now formed an army of 30,000 men made doubly

---

* '*Ribats* were fortified frontier posts whose guards were often effective propagators of Islam . . . Later these *ribats* changed their character from centres of proselytization to centres of Sufi teaching'. (J. S. Trimingham, *A History of Islam in West Africa*, 23, n2.)

formidable by the fanatical fervour with which their leader had inspired them.* Some were mounted, on camels or horses, but most were on foot. They were armed with pikes and spears which they used to deadly effect, fighting with fanatical fury and cheerfully courting death. Although they had never before known any form of restraint they now obeyed a discipline as rigid as that of a modern army. Their ranks never broke, nor did they ever pursue a beaten enemy.

Ibn Yasin, already master of the western desert, now prepared to employ this redoubtable army in spreading the orthodox religion amongst the heretical tribes of the north. The project seemed to be divinely inspired, for no sooner had this decision been taken than Ibn Yasin received an appeal from his old master Wajjaj to hurry north to rescue the people of Dra'a, in southern Morocco, from the oppressions of the emir of Sijilmasa. Ibn Yasin at once marched north. He defeated the Sijilmasa army, slew its emir and seized the city. Leaving behind him a garrison for the protection of the citizens against further abuses of power, he marched back into the desert to counter a new threat to his cause.[13]

Although Ibn Yasin could command the allegiance of most of the tribes of the western desert, the people of Audoghast, who had fallen under the tutelage of the hated Soninke of Ghana, had become defiant. The great market was divided by the mutual hatreds of its Berber and Arab communities, a circumstance which enabled Ibn Yasin to capture it in 1054. As a warning to others who might be tempted to challenge his authority, he lifted all restraint on his troops, with the result that the citizens were massacred and their women raped.[14]

Meanwhile the people of Sijilmasa, finding that their new masters were not such an improvement on the old as they had hoped, had determined to regain their freedom. Undeterred by, or perhaps in ignorance of, the fate of Audoghast they rose and massacred the Almoravid garrison; but aghast at their own handiwork, they attempted to lay the blame on the Zenata and besought Ibn Yasin to come north and drive them from their country. His response was to re-occupy Sijilmasa. This was easy enough, but, being himself a native of the place, he well knew that

* Other scholars have suggested that the religious motive, though it provided 'the initial impulse, a new unity, and the will to conquer', was only subsidiary. The Sanhaja Berbers felt themselves hemmed in between the Zenata, who controlled Sijilmasa, and the Soninke, who had occupied Audoghast. (J. S. Trimingham, *A History of Islam in West Africa*, 25).

his sojourn there with a formidable horde of Sanhaja at his back
was unlikely to continue long undisturbed. Sijilmasa was an outpost of another world, the Arab world of the Maghrib al-Aqsa, to
which he himself belonged, and to which the Almoravid occupation was a menace and a challenge. Sooner or later powerful
forces would be sent to drive him back into the western desert,
his uncertain mastery of which fell far short of his mounting
ambitions. He now took a decision worthy of a great leader. He
decided to assail the Atlas and conquer the Maghrib al-Aqsa.
Before the north had time to suspect that he was contemplating so
bold a project the Almoravids came pouring over the Glawi and
Kundafi passes into the plains of Morocco. But a little later, in
1057, Ibn Yasin was killed in battle.

With his death there passed one of the most remarkable char-
acters in African history. The great movement which he had
fathered and directed had, by the time of his death, united into one
kingdom practically the whole of the western Sahara as well as the
fertile northern districts of Sus, Aghmat, and Sijilmasa and its
dependencies. The foundations, too, had been laid for a yet
greater empire, extending even beyond the shores of Africa. Only
a man of heroic qualities could have achieved so much.

The Almoravids elected a spiritual leader to succeed Ibn Yasin,
but he died very shortly afterwards, and complete control passed
into the hands of their emir, Abu Bakr. Establishing his headquarters at Aghmat, close to where the city of Marrakech was
shortly to rise, he continued the northern campaign on which Ibn
Yasin had been engaged at the time of his death.[15]

But these operations now received a check, not from the front
but from the rear, from the desert. The chief weakness of the
Almoravids was their inability to control their adherents. They
had no state but an empire consisting of a loosely knit confederation of nomadic tribes held tenuously together by a common creed
and a common fear, the fear of the consequences of secession.
Although they had accepted the reformed religion they were not
deeply inspired, and fear of Ibn Yasin diminished in proportion to
his distance from them. Their inherent love of independence was
not weakened and the old inter-tribal jealousies were unabated.
That the tribes hung together at all is surprising.

The people who had caused most anxiety were the Jedala, in the
extreme south-west quarter of the desert. When Ibn Yasin had
gone north to re-occupy Sijilmasa he had left behind him a force to

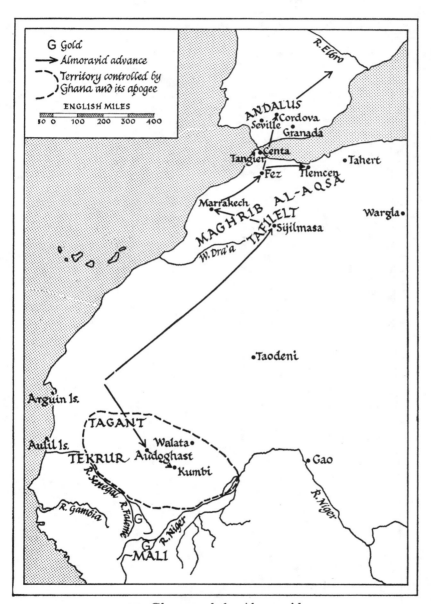

III. Ghana and the Almoravids

watch these people, but they had nevertheless rebelled and had never been subdued. Now, following on the death of Ibn Yasin, came news of trouble between the Lemtuna and the Mesufa. Both were loyal adherents of the sect, but the quarrel might well lead to the defection of one or the other. With the Jedala still in open rebellion there was grave danger of a complete breakdown of Almoravid control in the desert. Abu Bakr therefore decided that he must himself go south to restore order. Before setting out he handed over the command of the northern army to his cousin Yusuf ibn Tachfin.

The personal intervention of Abu Bakr quickly restored order, but he saw that unless an outlet could be found for the turbulent spirit of these desert nomads they would soon be at each other's throats again. So, placing himself at their head, he led them against the pagan Soninke negroes who were subject to the king of Ghana.

Meanwhile, in the north the Almoravids were going from strength to strength. Yusuf, abounding in energy and enterprise, had led his victorious army into the heart of the Maghrib al-Aqsa, committed apparently to a career of conquest with almost limitless possibilities. When Abu Bakr returned unexpectedly from the south he found that his lieutenant had no intention of handing back the command of the army. With no alternative but to acquiesce, Abu Bakr formally relinquished the Maghrib to his cousin and discreetly withdrew into the desert.

Yusuf, with none to dispute his authority, now settled down to a career of conquest which was destined to bring him power and fame transcending his most ambitious dreams. As he moved northwards district after district submitted to him. Wherever he went he proclaimed himself the champion of the masses, the liberator of the people from the cruel tyranny of corrupt princes. The peasantry rallied to him, eagerly joining in the overthrow of the local tyrants and swelling the ranks of his army. In 1062 he founded Marrakech at the foot of the passes by which he had entered the country. A year later he entered Fez without meeting resistance and soon he was standing on the heights above Tangier which, like the neighbouring port of Ceuta, was strongly held by Andalusian troops. Not feeling himself yet powerful enough to provoke a trial of strength with his formidable neighbours across the Straits, he turned eastwards where many small principalities offered an easy prey. He first captured Tlemcen, the Zenata capital, made it his base for further operations and before long obtained the mastery of all the country up to Algiers.

Although Yusuf had hesitated to challenge the power of Andalusia, he had in fact nothing to fear from that quarter. The triumph of the Almoravids was in marked contrast with the sorry plight of their co-religionists the other side of the Straits. There the Christians under Alfonso VI, king of Leon, Castile, Galicia, and Navarre, were threatening the continued existence of Muslim rule. The Muslim emirs, bitterly jealous of each other, instead of uniting against the common foe were ever courting Alfonso's help in their disputes. One by one they were falling under his sway, paying for his costly protection with tribute which they squeezed out of their own starving peasantry. The more abject their abasement the greater grew the arrogance of Alfonso, who now called himself 'Lord of the Two Faiths'. The steady advance of his army was scarcely interrupted by the feeble efforts of the Muslims to resist him. Despairing of ever stemming the increasing vigour of Christian aggression, they became paralysed by blank despondency. Either they must submit to Alfonso or abandon their homes and eke out their miserable lives in the penurious wastes of Africa. In their desperation they began to look for succour beyond the Straits where lay Yusuf and his victorious host, masters of the Maghrib.

Mu'tadid, king of Seville, the most powerful of the Andalusian sovereigns, had been watching with increasing apprehension the triumphant advance of the Almoravids. From the moment he had heard of the wild Berber tribesmen pouring over the Atlas passes into the plain of Morocco he had been obsessed with the conviction that they were destined to conquer Andalusia. 'Why should this news cause you uneasiness, my lord?' asked one of his viziers. 'Truly that same plain of Morocco is a fine place to dwell in, compared with our glorious Seville! What if these barbarians have camped there? Between us and them there lie deserts and great armies, and the waves of the sea!'

Few shared Mu'tadid's alarm, and when in a very dark hour someone suggested seeking Almoravid aid against the Christian aggressors the proposal was rejected as too desperate a measure. Such formidable and uncouth barbarians might well prove awkward guests if once admitted to so fair a land as Andalusia. What if they refused to leave? Or, worse still, what if Yusuf preferred the role of master to that of ally? Might it not be wiser to submit to

Alfonso, the measure of whose tyranny was more easily gauged than that of Yusuf ibn Tachfin? But the proposal had the support of the theologians, who had heard good reports of the simplicity and piety of the Almoravids, and was favoured by the masses who could not imagine any tyranny worse than they were already enduring at the hands of their own emirs. Mu'tamid, who had succeeded his father Mu'tadid as king of Seville, resolved their doubts. 'I have no desire', he declared, 'to be branded by my descendants as the man who delivered Andalusia a prey to the infidels; I am loath to have my name cursed in every pulpit; and, for my part, I would rather be a camel-driver in Africa than a swineherd in Castile.'[16]

Negotiations were accordingly opened with Yusuf. He was invited to come to the assistance of the Spanish Muslims, but certain safeguards were required of him. He sent the envoys back with an evasive and ambiguous reply. While the emirs were debating the next step their perplexity was turned to consternation by the news that Yusuf had already crossed the Straits and seized Algeciras, which he was fortifying and provisioning, evidently as a base for further operations. The implications of a horde of desert nomads from beyond the Sahara establishing a bridgehead in Europe were indeed alarming, but although Yusuf quickly made it clear that his career of conquest was not ended, events took a better course than many feared. Advancing inland, hailed as a deliverer by the people and with obsequious gifts by the emirs, he joined forces with Mu'tamid and marched against the Christians. They opposed him with overwhelming numbers, but by superior strategy he defeated them, in October 1086, at Zallaqa, near Badajoz. Alfonso, wounded by a negro guard, barely escaped with his life.

Yusuf belied the apprehensions of the Spanish emirs by immediately returning to Africa, and taking with him all his army except for 3,000 men he had generously left at Mu'tamid's disposal. His gallantry and piety had won the hearts of the people who, as they bade him farewell, acclaimed him as the saviour of Islam.

With the departure of Yusuf, the Castilians took fresh heart and began again to harry Muslim lands. Once more the emirs appealed to Yusuf to come to their aid. He came back, but this time with the firm resolve to make himself master of Muslim Spain. It was not a difficult task. The people saw that their only hope of relief from the cruel exactions of their emirs lay in one who, they well knew, had in Africa abolished all taxes not sanctioned by the Quran. Yusuf was equally welcome to the theologians who likened the frugal lives of the Almoravids to the simplicity of the early followers of the Prophet. Only by the emirs and their minions and the privileged classes, who regarded Yusuf as an uncouth barbarian seeking to usurp their power, were they regarded with mistrust. But no one was capable of resistance. First Granada and then Seville fell, to be quickly followed by the rest of Muslim Spain. By 1102 the Almoravids ruled from the Senegal to the Ebro.

Yusuf ibn Tachfin did not long survive this final triumph. He died in 1106 and was buried in a simple tomb at Marrakech, a city which was itself to become a worthy monument to its founder and, under the Almoravids, the southern capital of the Maghrib al-Aqsa.* In spite of his immense conquests and the boundless power they placed in his hands, throughout his career Yusuf remained true to the lofty ideals preached by Ibn Yasin far away on that obscure island in the Senegal. Few conquerors can have so fully justified the confidence reposed in them by the people conquered. He gave them, both in Africa and Andalusia, the blessings of tranquillity and, in more modest measure, prosperity. But these blessings ended with his death.

He was succeeded by his son Ali ibn Yusuf, a young man of twenty-three, who had grown to manhood in the enervating surroundings of the Andalusian court and had never known the austere life of the desert. He was noted for his piety, but religious zeal did not make up for his inexperience and an upbringing which ill-fitted him for his responsibilities, nor excuse his unfortunate choice of advisers. His favourites, in their efforts to ape the refinements of the Andalusians, had assimilated only the worst features of Hispano-Muslim culture. The old Berber chiefs were not prepared to grant the spineless youth the devoted allegiance they had so readily given to his rugged father, who had been bred in the same hard school as themselves. So slight and grudging was the recognition they accorded him that very soon his Christian militia became his principal support. This unfortunate dependence on infidels naturally only diminished the slight respect in which he was held.[17] But decadence was not confined to the court. The Almoravids were no exception to the rule of the transience of

* The name Morocco is a corrupt form of Marrakech.

shepherd kings. Ease and culture are the enemies of the simple virtues of the desert nomad, engendered by the frugal life and daily dependence on sword and spear for survival, and they destroyed the Almoravids as surely as they did the Hyksos and the Ottoman Turks.

As the new emir's authority weakened and his subjects became more enervated and increasingly divided by sectarian disputes, Almoravid rule grew harsh and tyrannical. To the sorrows of the oppressed peasantry was added a revival of raids by the Christians, to whom the growing effeteness of the conquerors had given fresh heart.

The Andalusians thus quickly lost the benefits they had at first enjoyed from the change of rulers, and before long they were regretting the days of their own emirs whose passing had been so welcome to them. Driven at last to desperation, they rose and massacred their oppressors. But this revulsion of feeling against the Almoravids was not confined to Andalusia. In the Maghrib a new Berber sect, the Almohads or Traditionists, arose and drove them out. Under the brilliant leadership of Abd al-Mumin,* the Almohads established a kingdom which stretched from the Atlantic to the Syrtes, and under their enlightened administration the country prospered. But this new Berber kingdom did not last long; within a hundred years it had fallen into ruins, and from the chaos that followed its fall there emerged the dynasties of the Hafsids of Tunis, the Abd al-Wadids of Tlemcen, and the Merinids of Fez.

8

The Gold of Ghana

'At this towne the Caravan from Barbary doth stay and abide, we know their whole trade is for gold.'—RICHARD JOBSON.

IN the middle of the eleventh century, when al-Bakri was engaged upon his memorable description of Africa, the western Sahara was in a ferment of political excitement over the triumphant progress

---

* Abd al-Mumin was the builder of the Kutubia at Marrakech. The architect was also the designer of the Giralda at Seville, but the Kutubia came first.

of the Almoravids. In the north the Maghrib al-Aqsa was already half paralysed by the grip of Yusuf. But in the south pagan Ghana, an object of the bitterest hatred to every member of the sect, remained proudly independent and in full enjoyment of commercial liberty, its thriving trade with the Maghrib seemingly undisturbed by the political upheaval created by the Almoravids. The divorcement of trade from politics is not unusual, but it was particularly characteristic of northern Africa. Leo Africanus relates how certain tribes of the Atlas, who were constantly at war with each other, held a regular truce to ensure the continuance of their inter-tribal markets.[1] Even during the long centuries of conflict between Christian Europe and the Barbary states, trade between the opposite shores of the Mediterranean was so little disturbed that Christians and Muslims continued fearlessly to frequent each other's markets.

Al-Bakri has left us an account of Kumbi, the capital of Ghana, based on information he obtained from Barbary merchants who knew the negro city well. It is almost confined to accounts of the magnificence of the court and of commercial activity, the two aspects of life most likely to impress a foreign merchant.[2]*

The capital consisted of two separate towns, about six miles apart: one was reserved for the Muslim population and contained a dozen mosques where distinguished jurists gathered; the other, known as al-Ghaba or The Forest, was pagan and the seat of the court. Most of the houses of Ghana were clay huts thatched with straw, but there were also some buildings of stone.

Al-Ghaba took its name from the groves with which it was surrounded. These groves, which were probably little more than thickets of thorn, were jealously guarded against intruders, for they were the centre of the spiritual life of the nation. Here dwelt the fetish priests who tended the national gods and doubtless practised the gruesome rites which have always characterized West African fetishism. Here too were the burial places of the kings, and the prisons from which none was ever known to return.

The king was the centre of a court where elaborate ceremonial and gorgeous pageantry combined to present a scene which probably did not give a greatly exaggerated impression of the wealth

---

* The first Arab writer to mention Ghana is al-Fazari, in 773. He refers briefly to 'the territory of Ghana, the land of gold'. Al-Yaqubi, writing in 872, regarded Kawkaw (Gao) as the greatest kingdom in the Sudan, but mentioned Ghana as being 'also powerful'. (J. S. Trimingham, *History of Islam in West Africa*, 48, 51.)

and resources of the kingdom. At an audience the king, adorned in jewellery and a golden head-dress, sat in a pavilion around which stood ten horses in gold trappings. Behind the throne were ten pages holding shields and gold-hilted swords. To the right stood the sons of vassal princes, magnificently attired and with ornaments plaited into their hair. Before the king sat the viziers, and at his feet the governor of the city. The pavilion was guarded by hounds, wearing collars and bells of silver and gold, which were the constant companions of the monarch.

Muslims held many of the court appointments, including those of treasurer and interpreter, and the viziers were usually Muslim. Before the ceremonies began, the royal drums, the *deba*,* were beaten. As they knelt before him the king's pagan countrymen poured dust on their heads. The Muslims showed their respect by clapping their hands.

The royal treasure included a gold nugget, a symbol of majesty, of so great a size that it became famous throughout a great part of the civilized world. Al-Idrisi said it weighed thirty pounds† and that the king used to tether his horse to it.[3] Popular rumour raised it to fabulous proportions, and when, in the fourteenth century, Ibn Khaldun reported its sale by a spendthrift prince to some merchants of Egypt it was said to weigh a ton.[4]

When the king died his body, resting on rugs and cushions, was laid in a sort of wooden dome. Near it they put robes, food, and drink. Servants whose duty it had been to prepare the king's food were buried with him. The tomb was then covered with mats, over which the assembled multitude threw earth so as to form a great mound surrounded by a ditch.

We are told very little about the people. They grew millet and other crops and they fished. They were frequently required by the king to take up arms against troublesome neighbours or for slave raids. Al-Bakri says the king could place in the field as many as 200,000 men, of whom 40,000 were armed with bows and arrows (the rest presumably with spears only).

According to al-Idrisi the capital, Kumbi, was the largest market in the Sudan, where merchants from all over the Maghrib used to gather. As we have seen, the wealth of Ghana was derived from the trade in gold which was in such abundant supply that the quantity coming on to the market had to be controlled lest the

* These drums are still known as *daba* or *taba* by the Soninke.
† A nugget twice this size was found in Bambuk in about 1900.

price fell too low. This was done by making all nuggets crown property, leaving only the *tibar* or dust for the trade.[5]

Yaqut, writing a little later than al-Idrisi, describes the gold traders of Sijilmasa and Dra'a going to the Sudan with cheap goods, notably beads,* which they supplemented with salt as they passed through Taghaza. In Kumbi they found awaiting them their agents, local people familiar with the curious customs of the trade. The merchants and their agents travelled on southwards together for twenty more days to the Senegal. The scene that followed resembled closely that described by Herodotus in his account of the Carthaginian gold trade in the same part of Africa.

When they reached the river the merchants beat great drums to summon the local natives, who were naked and lived in holes in the ground. From these holes, which were doubtless the pits from which they dug the gold, they refused to emerge in the presence of the foreign merchants. The latter, therefore, used to arrange their trade goods in piles on the river bank and retire out of sight. The local natives then came and placed a heap of gold beside each pile and withdrew. If the merchants were satisfied they took the gold and retreated, beating their drums to signify that the market was over.

The merchants once tried to discover the source of the gold by treacherously capturing one of the timid negroes. He pined to death without saying a word, and it was three years before the negroes would resume the trade, and then only because they had no other way of satisfying their craving for salt.[6]

al-Masudi, writing in the tenth century, tells us that in his day this silent trade in gold was well known in Sijilmasa.[7] Late in the fifteenth century Cadamosto was informed by Arab and Sanhaja merchants that it was still the custom.[8] It was also described, as we shall see, by much later travellers. Silent trade or dumb barter was a feature of the Wangara gold traffic for many centuries.†

* The making of beads for the Sudan trade was an important industry in Ceuta, where there were coral fisheries.

† But this curious method of trading was far from being peculiar to the gold trade of West Africa. In the first century A.D. it was a feature of the silk trade carried on by the Romans with the Chinese on the banks of a river in Parthia. Fa-Hein, the fifth-century Chinese explorer, found it in Ceylon. A century later it was reported as a custom of the Abyssinian gold trade. Examples from other parts of the world could be quoted. Till recently it was practised by the Pygmies of the Congo, and may be still.

The curious way in which Ghana obtained its gold added to the mystery surrounding the situation of Wangara, the search for which was to tax to their utmost the resources of the Moors and later to become one of the chief objectives of a score or more of European adventurers and explorers. Where this mysterious country lay will be considered in a later chapter.

Ghana's foreign trade was not confined to gold. Merchants from the Maghrib al-Aqsa and Wargla, the capital of Mzab, made the long and perilous journey across the Sahara to buy also negro slaves, for which there was always a ready sale in the north. Kumbi was noted for its slave market, which was kept well supplied by raids on the more primitive bush tribes on the southern frontier, the common practice of the Sudanese all the way from the Atlantic to the Red Sea. Ghana got its slaves mostly from cannibal tribes who were known to the Arabs as Lemlem or Demdem.*

To the west of Ghana, athwart the Senegal, lay the kingdom of Takrur of which we know very little, although for a long time its name was better known in foreign lands than that of any other Sudanese region, which implies that it may have been more important than its modest records suggest.† The early Arab geographers sometimes applied the name to the whole of the Western Sudan. The kings of Mali, the heirs to the greatness of Ghana, were known in Egypt as the kings of Takrur. It is, too, the name by which people from the west are today often known in the Eastern Sudan.

In the eleventh century Takrur was the home of the Tucolor who later settled in Futa, where they are still known as Tekarir. Like the Soninke of Ghana, the Tucolor were very active traders. They too were sending gold and slaves to the Maghrib, but they seem to have been interested also in more local trade. They imported salt from Aulil, at the mouth of the Senegal, for distribution over a large part of the Western Sudan. Their chief industry was the weaving of a coarse cloth called by al-Bakri 'chigguiya', which must have been the *alchezeli* mentioned as a

* Nyam-Nyam, which appears to be another variant, is today a common name for cannibals in the Western Sudan. The Fulani emirs of Kano and Zaria used to employ Nyam-Nyam as executioners; one of them was still a member of the emir of Kano's household as late as 1925.

† 'The first dynasty [of Takrur] of which tradition has preserved the memory is that of Dya'ogo, probably of foreign origin, who founded a chieftaincy about A.D. 850. This was overthrown (c. 980) by the Manna . . . a Soninke chieftaincy. According to al-Bakri, this ruling family of Takrur was the first Negro family to join Islam.' (Trimingham, 45).

local product by Cadamosto in the fifteenth century and the *shigge* which Barth purchased in Timbuktu in the nineteenth.[9]

Amongst the tribes the Tucolor raided for slaves were the Ferawi who, according to al-Bakri, were in such dire need of salt that they would exchange it for an equal weight of gold, in which their country was very rich.[10]

There was no more love lost between the Tucolor and the Soninke of Ghana than between the latter and the Almoravids. Although many of the Soninke were Muslims and their religion was no bar to their occupying high offices, Ghana remained predominantly pagan and therefore a menace to Almoravid supremacy in the western Sahara. The overthrow of Ghana was an ambition cherished by every member of the sect and a project which Abu Bakr must have had in mind when in 1062 he handed over the northern army to Yusuf and returned to the desert. But it was not till fourteen years later that he captured Kumbi, massacred its inhabitants, and successfully imposed Islam on the whole country which, with its goldfields, became an apanage of the Almoravids.

The consequences of the fall of Ghana were not as far-reaching as might have been expected, because the collapse of the Almoravids in the south was even more rapid than in the north. With the destruction of the common enemy the old inter-tribal feuds which had so weakened the Almoravids in their early days broke out once more. Some tribes, among them the Mesufa and the Lemta, refused to serve under any chief of the Lemtuna, who were, as they had always been, the backbone of the sect. The Jedala, aloof as ever, still remained outside the fold. On the death of Abu Bakr in 1087 the crumbling structure of Almoravid hegemony in the desert disintegrated altogether.

Thus, in little more than a decade, did the Soninke of Ghana recover their independence, but, like the Almoravids, they were too divided by tribal jealousies to take advantage of it. Each of the tribes which, united, had given the kingdom its strength now wanted complete independence and would make no sacrifice for the common good.

In 1203 the most powerful tribe, the Susu, seized Kumbi. The consequences for this great market were disastrous; and very soon the Arab merchants and some of the richer Soninke traders marched out into the desert and built themselves a new town a hundred miles to the north on a camping ground of caravans called Walata. The new market prospered and became one of the most important in the whole of the western Sahara. Kumbi, meanwhile, disappeared from history.[11]*

9

Mansa Musa of Mali

'The people of this region excell all other Negros in witte, ciuilitie, and industry.'
LEO AFRICANUS.

WHEN the Susu seized Kumbi their horizon was clouded by the growing power of another branch of their race, the Mandingo of Mali, an as yet unimportant kingdom extending from the upper Bakhoy eastwards across the Niger. Unlike the pagan Susu, the Mandingo had been converted to Islam in the early days of the Almoravid movement.[1] This may have had something to do with there being little love lost between the two tribes. The Susu, flushed with their capture of Kumbi, were probably cherishing ambitions with which Mali might interfere. They sought to check these potential rivals by contriving the death of the eleven brothers who were heirs to the throne of Mali. There was a twelfth, Sundiata, whom they spared, probably because he was a sickly child and unlikely to survive in any case. This omission was as fortunate for Mali as it was disastrous for the Susu. Sundiata thrived, and on growing to manhood turned his unusual abilities to such good account that he became the founder of a great empire. In spite of the lapse of seven centuries without any written records, Sundiata, or Mari Jata as he came to be called, is still regarded by the Mandingo as their national hero.[2]

On his accession, Sundiata's position was precarious, not because of the Susu, but because his own people did not like him.

---

* In the fourteenth century Kumbi was referred to by both Abu'l-Fida and Ibn Khaldun as if it still existed in their time. They were probably confusing it with Walata which Marmol, two centuries later, described as 'Gualata quo otros llaman Ganata'. (Abu'l Fida and Ibn Khaldun, quoted by C. Montiel, 'Les Empires du Mali', *Bulletin du Comité d'Études Historiques et Scientifiques de l'Afrique Occidentale Française*, Paris, 1930, 90; Marmol, quoted by M. Delafosse, *Haut-Sénégal-Niger*, II 59). It is possible that the decline of Kumbi was also caused by increasing desiccation, probably as a result of over grazing.

He therefore surrounded himself with a band of desperadoes, who enabled him first to keep his own people in order and then to embark on a series of aggressive wars against his less powerful neighbours. He was victorious in every campaign, and with each success came a fresh accession of strength to his private army. His position with his own people was now unassailable, but in making it so he had incurred the bitter hostility of the Susu, on whose territory he had encroached during his campaigns. The Susu decided to take the field against him before Mali became any more powerful; but it was already too late. In 1235 he destroyed their army at Kirina, which was probably just north of Kulikoro. He was now able to claim tribute from people covering a vast expanse of territory, far larger than ancient Ghana, for Mali's influence reached northwards to the Sahara, westwards to the upper Senegal and eastwards to the Niger.

Until that time the Mali capital had been Jeriba (upstream from modern Bamako), but Sundiata now moved it to the neighbouring town of Niani, which was usually referred to as Mali and sometimes as Mande.* Sundiata himself never took the field again, but his armies continued to extend the frontiers, especially in the west where they reached the Gambia river and the marches of Takrur. Mali had already become the most powerful kingdom in the Western Sudan, but it owed its subsequent fame in Europe less to its territorial extent than to the vast wealth it drew from the Wangara goldfields. Nevertheless, at the mines the Mandingo were not quite masters in their own house, for in the timorous pagan diggers they found their match. The latter's invariable response to the repeated efforts of their conquerors to impose Islam on them was to stop producing. Only by leaving these queer people quite alone could the Mandingo ensure the continuous flow of gold on which their thriving trade depended.

Sundiata's dynasty proved worthy of its founder. In the reign of his grandson Mansa Musa, who came to the throne in 1307, half a century after Sundiata's death, the fame of Mali spread through Europe and the Middle East. This was almost wholly due to Mansa Musa's pilgrimage to Mecca. The spectacular scale on which it was conducted caused such a sensation in Cairo and other places which witnessed the passage of his splendid caravan, that the name of the Mandingo monarch quickly became familiar throughout a large part of the civilized world.

* *Mali* is in fact the Fulfulde term for *Mande*. Fulfulde is the language of the Fulani.

Mansa Musa set out on the *Hadj* in 1324, the seventeenth year of his reign, accompanied by a host of followers. We know he passed through Walata and Tuat, but which road he took from there to Cairo is uncertain. It was probably through Wargla and thence along the coast of the Syrtes, which would have given merchants from many parts of Europe trading with Africa an opportunity to witness the splendour in which he travelled before he reached Cairo. Mansa Musa, mounted on horseback, was preceded by 500 slaves, each carrying a staff of gold weighing 500 *mithqal*.* In Cairo it was not the splendour with which the negro potentate surrounded himself so much as his piety and open-handed generosity that made him popular. His pale complexion, variously described as red or yellow, was unexpected and contributed to the sensation he caused. In spite of its pomp, his pilgrimage appears to have been without any political motive. He at first refused to pay the customary compliments to the Mamluk Sultan, al-Malik an-Nisian, because of the need to kiss the ground in his presence. The elaborate arrangements made by the sultan for the comfort of his guest on his onward journey make it clear that no pains were spared to honour him. There was no trace of the traditional contempt of sophisticated orientals for the negro.[3]

Al-Umari, who was in Cairo twelve years after Mansa Musa, found the townspeople still singing his praises. The hordes of petty officials who habitually sponged on the wealthy recalled his gifts of gold, of which he had brought with him 80 to 100 camel loads, each weighing three *kantar* (or about 300 pounds). Others had benefited from the profitable trade they had done with his gullible followers, simple but well-mannered folk who would readily pay five *dinar* for a garment worth only one. Fine clothes and women slaves were what interested them most. As a result of the extravagance of the Sudanese and the lavish generosity of their monarch, so much gold was suddenly put into circulation in Egypt that its market value fell sharply and had not recovered in al-Umari's time.

Mansa Musa's prodigal display of wealth was not confined to Cairo. He showered gold wherever he went, and in the holy cities his charitable gifts were particularly lavish. It is, therefore, hardly surprising that by the time he got back to Cairo on his homeward journey he had nearly come to the end of his immediate resources. This caused him little embarrassment, for there was no difficulty

* A *mithqal* or *mitkal* was about ⅛ oz. of gold.

in finding temporary accommodation for the monarch of a country which produced gold on a scale which had dazzled so many eyes. One of those who came to his assistance, a merchant of Alexandria, followed him all the way back to the Sudan to recover his loan. The man died in Timbuktu but Mansa Musa repaid his heirs in full.[4]

Before he had completed his homeward journey, Mansa Musa heard of the capture of Gao, the Songhai capital, by one of his generals. Songhai was an important riverain kingdom, extending along the middle Niger for a thousand miles downstream from the frontier of Mali. The news of this enormous extension to his dominions decided Mansa Musa to turn aside and visit Gao. There he received the personal submission of the Songhai king, but to ensure the fidelity of his new vassal he took back to Mali with him as hostages two of the latter's sons, Ali Kolen and Sulaiman Nar.

Mansa Musa's entourage included an Andalusian poet, to whom he had become attached in Mecca and whom he had persuaded to enter his service. The poet, whose name was as-Sahili, was also an architect, and the first task given him by his new master was to replace the mean structure which in Gao passed for a mosque with something better suited to the worship of Allah. The new mosque, which was still standing three hundred years later and whose foundations still survive, was built of burnt bricks the use of which was till then unknown in the Sudan.

There was another Songhai town which almost rivalled Gao in importance and which lay on Mansa Musa's quickest way home up the Niger. This was Timbuktu, a town which owed its importance to its geographical position, for it served as the meeting place of those who travelled by land and those who travelled by water, the nomads of the desert and the riverain peoples of the Niger. Here they met to exchange salt and dates and the merchandise of the Maghrib for the grain, kola nuts, and gold dust of the Sudan. In about 1100 the tents of the traders began to give place to grass huts, and these in turn to more permanent dwellings of sun-dried bricks, such as are found there today. Two centuries later it had become an *entrepôt* for the trade passing between Jenne and Walata, and the neighbouring fishing village of Kabara had become its port. Its situation, close to a navigable waterway tapping so great a part of the Western Sudan, gave Timbuktu a great advantage over neighbouring markets whose trade it gradually absorbed.[5]

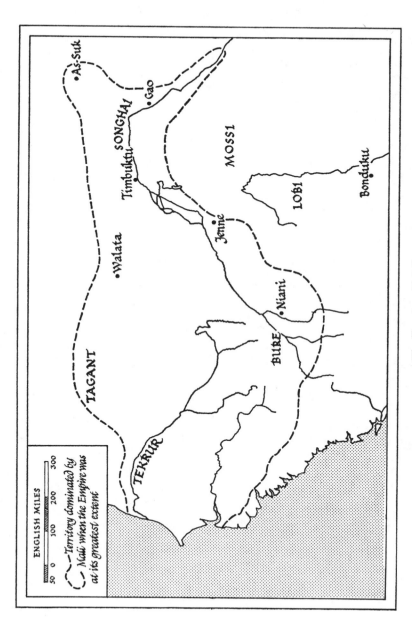

iv. The Empire of Mali

Commercial prosperity brought with it both wealth and culture. Timbuktu captured Walata's trade and then its culture, both of which had been in the hands of the Jedala, the intelligentsia of the desert. These people, always ready to adapt themselves to changing circumstances, came originally from Adrar, in Mauritania, whence they had migrated to Kumbi on its becoming an important market. When, at the beginning of the thirteenth century, the Susu seized Kumbi, the Jedala joined the exodus to the new settlement at Walata which they made a seat of learning. When Walata began to lose its trade to Timbuktu the Jedala followed. There they long remained, a scholarly as well as a mercantile people, who were the first to give the city its reputation as a seat of learning and who regularly provided the learned *imams* for the principal mosque. The greatest Jedala scholar was Ahmad Baba, the historian whom as-Sadi so frequently quotes.*

By Mansa Musa's time, trade and letters were well established in Timbuktu, and both were to benefit from the change of ruler. As-Sahili was at once set to work to build a new mosque as well as a palace for the monarch. The town very soon became the most important market of the interior, and its fame as the chief *entrepôt* for *tibar* or gold dust attracted trade from all quarters—from Dra'a, Sus, Sijilmasa, and Fez in the Maghrib al-Aqsa, from Tuat, Ghadames, the Fezzan, and Augila in the desert, and also from Egypt, to whose trade with the Sudan Mansa Musa's pilgrimage had been a great stimulus. With the merchants came the *literati* and divines of many lands to gather round the noted Jedala scholars of the Sankore mosque.

Mansa Musa died in 1332. He left behind him an empire which, in the history of purely African states, was remarkable both for its extent and its wealth, and as a striking example of the capacity of the negro for political organization. From Takrur in the west it spread eastwards to Gao and beyond, and included much of the Sahara. Southwards the empire extended as far as the forests. Curiously enough, however, the little town of Jenne, small though

---

* But Jedala trade and scholarship were not confined to the western desert. The Jedala established themselves in Morocco and then in Portugal, probably through intermarriage in Africa with Portuguese Jews. In the fifteenth century King Duarte of Portugal's doctor was a certain Master Guedalha, who was also the astronomer royal and is thought to have cast the horoscope of Prince Henry the Navigator quoted in *The Chronicle of Guinea*. As late as the nineteenth century the principal merchant house in Marrakech was Guedalla & Company.

commercially and culturally important, situated only a few days'
march from Niani, but admirably protected by a network of
waterways, still preserved its independence.

Mansa Musa's reign had seen a great expansion in the trade
of Mali, largely due to the assiduity with which he cultivated
foreign relations. Apart from the friendships with Egypt and
Arabia which his famous pilgrimage had established, he was on
cordial terms with the Merinid sultan of Fez. He was, in fact,
the first to penetrate the iron curtain of colour prejudice which
shut off the negro from the civilized world, and to win for the
true African a small measure of the respect which, even today,
is often grudgingly granted him.

Abundant evidence of the prestige and fame attaching to Mali
and its great ruler is to be found in the *mappae-mundi* of the
European cartographers who at this time were making the first
serious attempts to represent the interior of Africa. One of the
earliest references to Mali and its king is in a *mappa-mundi* of
Angelino Dulcert of Majorca, dated 1339—only seven years after
Mansa Musa's death. There, in the middle of the western Sahara,
seated on a throne, in royal robes and a crown, sceptre in hand, is
Rex Melly.[6] With the cartographers' curiosity about Mansa Musa
went an interest in how to reach his country. Dulcert shows the
Atlas mountains cut by the 'Valley of Sus where there is a road
that goes to the land of the Negroes'. European concern with the
interior, however, was purely commercial. The early fifteenth
century Catalan portulan of Florence shows the Atlas broken by
the same road and states that 'it is by this passage that the merchants travel who are going to the King Melli'.[7] The well-known
Catalan atlas of Charles V, drawn by Abraham Cresques of
Majorca in about 1375, shows in the middle of the desert a veiled
man on a camel riding towards a monarch seated on a throne.[8]
The latter, in royal robes and a crown, holds a sceptre in one hand
and in the other a nugget of gold which he is offering to the rider.
'This negro lord', reads the inscription, 'is called Musa Mali,
Lord of the Negroes of Guinea. So abundant is the gold which is
found in his country that he is the richest and most noble king
in all the land.'* The fame of the great negro ruler long persisted,
and many believed him to be no less a personage than the
mythical Prester John. One of the last maps in which Mansa

* Similar wording is found on the Majorcan planisphere of Mercia de Viladestes of
  1413 and a Venetian *portolano* of 1433.

Musa's name appears is that of Waldseemüller of 1516,[9] and it seems to have faded from the maps only as a result of the flood of light cast on to the interior of Africa by Leo Africanus.*[10]

10

Ibn Battuta: A Fourteenth Century Traveller in the Sudan

'He who does not travel will not know the value of men.'
MOORISH PROVERB.

AFTER the death of Mansa Musa the fortunes of Mali declined through the profligacy and incompetence of his successors. The throne first passed to his son Maghan who, in a reign of only four years, permitted his splendid heritage to suffer two major reverses, one of which was disastrous. Shortly after his accession the warlike Mossi of Yatenga on the upper Volta raided Timbuktu, routed the Mandingo garrison and burnt the city.[1] By an unhappy chance, an embassy from Abu'l Hassan, the greatest of the Merinid sultans of Fez (whose trade mattered much to the Mandingos), happened to be in Timbuktu at the time.

An event of more far-reaching consequences followed. Maghan had incautiously permitted complete freedom to the two Songhai princes, Ali Kolen and Sulaiman Nar, whom his father had kept as hostages after the capture of Gao. The young men had been quick to see that the change of ruler might prove an opportunity for their country to regain its freedom. They managed to slip away to Gao and evict the Mandingo from the capital. Ali Kolen

* The cartographers had some difficulty in reconciling certain attributes of the negro, notably his short hair and his nakedness, with their ideas of what a great monarch ought to look like. In their view, a beard was essential to kingship. Dulcert cautiously gave Mansa Musa a very short scrubby beard. This was not dignified enough for later draftsmen, so they gave him a flowing beard. As time went on a feeling grew that Mansa Musa, in spite of the black skin he was always given, looked too European. He then began to appear (for example on the planisphere of Jayme Bertrand of 1482)[40] still seated on a throne, crowned and robed, but with the royal robe cut down to a brief cloak, and otherwise stark naked. The cartographers did not neglect the opportunity which this afforded for emphasizing an alleged physical attribute of the negro.

was proclaimed king of the Songhai and established himself so firmly in his father's old capital that none could turn him out.

Maghan was succeeded by his uncle Sulaiman, a brother of Mansa Musa, who did much to repair the damage done by his nephew. Although he failed to recover Gao, he restored control over most of his dominions. Sulaiman did much to encourage the establishment of Islam, building mosques, instituting the practice of weekly prayers and inviting learned jurists to his country. He maintained cordial relations with the Merinids of Morocco and compelled many of the communities of the Southern Sahara to recognize his suzerainty.[2]

Of these the most important to Mali was the town of Takedda, a thriving centre of the caravan trade. The site of Takedda—the name itself is derived from the Tuareg word *Teguidda*, meaning 'spring'—has been provisionally identified with the extensive ruins found at Azelik, lying about a hundred and fifty miles south west of Agades. According to Ibn Khaldun, it was seventy days' march south-west of Wargla, with which it had close commercial ties. Once a year a caravan of 12,000 camels used to pass through Takedda on its way from Niani to Cairo; even allowing for probable exaggeration, this shows that trade between Mali and Egypt was considerable. Takedda, however, did not owe its prosperity to its transit trade but to its copper mines from which the Maghrib, Egypt, Mali, Hausa, and Bornu drew their supplies of the precious metal. Mansa Musa once said that these mines were his most important source of revenue; ancient copper-mine workings have been found a few miles to the east of Azelik, and at other sites in the same area.[3]

The event of Sulaiman's reign of most interest to us is the visit to Mali of the renowned traveller, Ibn Battuta, to whose narrative we owe much of our knowledge of the Muslim world in the first half of the fourteenth century. He was sent to the Sudan by Abu Inan, who had seized the Moroccan throne from his father Abu'l Hassan. Setting out in 1352, he took the road through Sijilmasa, where he fitted out his caravan, Taghaza, and a place called Tasarahla, which was evidently then a desert stopping place of importance. Here his caravan rested for a few days in order to mend and refill their water-skins. Here, too, they sent out the *takshif*, the Mesufa messenger who customarily went ahead of a caravan to Walata to announce its approach and to get water sent out to meet it in the desert If, as sometimes happened, the *takshif* failed to arrive and no water was sent out, there was danger of the caravan perishing in the desert.

On this occasion, the *takshif*, who was paid a hundred gold *mithqal* for his services, was almost blind. The point is not without interest. Leo Africanus, who travelled this same road a century and a half later, mentions a caravan losing its way and being saved by a blind guide who 'riding foremost on his camel, commanded some sand to be given him at every mile's end, by the smell whereof he declared the situation of the place'.*[4] Happily, all went well for Ibn Battuta who records the pleasure with which, on the seventh day out from Tasarahla, he and his companions saw the fires of those who had come out to meet them.

Two months after leaving Sijilmasa the caravan reached Walata, the most northerly outpost of Mali and the threshold of the Sudan, where Ibn Battuta had a friend, a merchant of Salee, to whom he had written to hire a house for him. So we may be sure that no pains were spared to honour so distinguished a visitor. Nevertheless, he proved an odious guest. He had hardly arrived before he was regretting having come, merely because he was disgusted at finding negroes, whom hitherto he had known only as slaves, behaving as masters in their own country. He was obviously

* In recent years a blind guide used to pilot caravans across the 90 waterless miles between Umm Qubur in the Red Sea Hills and the Nile valley (W. G. Murray, *Sons of Ishmael*, p. 69). In the present writer's experience, Africans are no better than Europeans at finding their way in unknown country. But those who, like most nomads, are accustomed to travelling very long distances, seem to retain a sense of direction which renders them largely independent of sight. That civilized man does not necessarily lose the same sense was shown in the Second World War when a trawler captain, far out in the North Sea, surprised the Royal Navy by finding his way back to port in dense fog without instruments. In certain circumstances, as the quotation from Leo shows, the senses of touch and smell can be more valuable to a guide than his sight. For example, Mildred Cable (*The Gobi Desert*, p. 11) relates how, in the Gobi Desert, 'pebbles picked up on the wide expanse could be located to the actual spot where they were collected'. Similarly, as W. B. K. Shaw once pointed out to the author, the shingle on the Chesil Beach is so perfectly graded that fishermen landing there in the dark can tell where on the beach they are by feeling it. The explorer Denham (*J. of R. African Society*, XXXV, 1936, p. 159) relates how, in the desert south of Fezzan, 'sometimes the Arabs know by smelling the earth where the springs lay and are never known to mistake the spot'.

The use in the western Sahara of blind guides who found their way by their sense of smell is also recorded by Thomas Pellow (*Adventures*, 1890, pp. 195-9) and J. G. Jackson (*An Account of Morocco*, 1809, p. 240, and *An Account of Timbuctoo*, 1820, p. 5).

That blind guides, who one might have thought there was never any need to use, are several times mentioned in the sparse annals of Saharan travel suggests that they offered certain advantages over guides who could see.

at pains to emphasize how condescending it was for one who knew every Muslim country from Morocco to China, to visit a black country at all. When a Mandingo official invited him and his companions to his house, he refused. His friends persuaded him to go, but the party was not a success.

The repast [he tells us] was served—some pounded millet mixed with a little honey and milk, put in a half calabash shaped like a large bowl. The guests drank and retired. I said to them 'Was it for this that the black invited us?' They answered 'Yes; and it is in their opinion the highest form of hospitality.' This convinced me that there was no good to be hoped for from these people.[5]

So he decided to return forthwith to Morocco, with a pilgrim caravan that was just setting out. Happily he decided that, having come so far, he had better first go and see what the capital was like.

Before continuing his journey, he spent a few more days in Walata. The people, he tells us, were mostly Mesufa, whose clothes were made of fine Egyptian cloth. Mutton was plentiful and the women were of surpassing beauty, but he thought the important social position and liberty accorded to them very extraordinary, and the local custom of uterine descent most odd.

Ibn Battuta left for Niani with only three companions and a guide, the country being so settled and peaceful that there was no longer any need to travel in company. Although it was twenty-four days' march to Niani, they carried neither food nor gold nor silver. With salt, beads, and aromatic goods for barter, they were able to obtain food in variety at each village they came to. When he crossed the Niger Ibn Battuta assumed it to be the Nile of Egypt. He described it flowing past Timbuktu, Gao, and 'Muli in the land of the Limis', and thence to Yufi which may well have been Nupe in Nigeria. His conviction that he was describing the Nile then led him sadly astray. 'From Yufi', he went on, 'the Nile descends to the land of Nuba, who profess the Christian faith, and thence to Dunqula (Dongola), which is their chief town.'[6]

In Niani Ibn Battuta found himself amongst fellow-countrymen, by whom he was hospitably entertained. He had the misfortune to fall ill directly he arrived and was looked after by an Egyptian doctor. When he was well enough to attend Sulaiman's court, he found the ceremonies interesting enough to be recorded in some detail. In their pageantry they closely resembled what

took place at Kumbi. People seeking audience presented themselves in rags and poured dust on their heads. Applause was
signified by the twanging of bow-strings, and two goats were
there to ward off the evil eye. Among those visiting the court
when Ibn Battuta was there, were some cannibals from Wangara
whose entertainment he describes:

> The sultan received them without honour, and gave them as his
> hospitality-gift a servant, a negress. They killed and ate her, and having
> smeared their faces and hands with her blood came to the sultan to
> thank him. I was informed that this is their regular custom whenever
> they visit his court.[7]

Although Sulaiman's way of welcoming his Wangara subjects
must have confirmed Ibn Battuta's worst apprehensions, as he
grew better acquainted with the Sudanese he came to recognize
some of their good qualities, especially their love of justice and
the security of their roads. He was, in fact, no more proof against
their charm and kindliness than, as we shall see, his fellow-
countryman Leo Africanus and the great European explorers of
later times.

> The negroes [he wrote] possess some admirable qualities. They are
> seldom unjust, and have a greater abhorrence of injustice than any
> other people. Their sultan shows no mercy to any one guilty of the
> least act of it. There is complete security in their country. Neither
> traveller nor inhabitant in it has anything to fear from robbers or men
> of violence. They do not confiscate the property of any white man who
> dies in their country, even if it be uncounted wealth. On the contrary,
> they give it into the charge of some trustworthy person among the
> whites, until the rightful heir takes possession of it. They are careful to
> observe the hours of prayer, and assiduous in attending them in con-
> gregations, and in bringing up their children to them. . . . Among
> their bad qualities are the following: The women servants, slave-girls,
> and young girls go about in front of every one naked, without a stitch
> of clothing on them. Women go into the sultan's presence naked and
> without coverings, and his daughters also go about naked. Then there
> is their custom of putting dust and ashes on their heads as a mark of
> respect. . . . Another reprehensible practice among many of them is
> the eating of carrion, dogs, and asses.[8]

Ibn Battuta seems to have enjoyed himself in Niani, for he
stayed there eight months. At the end of February 1353, he set
out for Timbuktu, riding a camel because he could not afford the
100 gold *mitkal* which a horse would have cost. He obviously did

not think much of Timbuktu, for he tells us little more than that
the people, like those of Walata, were Mesufa Berbers and he
mentions the tomb of as-Sahili, the poet-architect of Andalusia.
From there he continued his journey by water, following the
Niger downstream in a dug-out canoe and stopping at Songhai
villages where he obtained meat and butter in exchange for salt,
spices, and glass beads. At one of these villages he was given a
slave boy, who was with him years afterwards when he was writing
the story of his travels.

He considered Gao one of the finest towns in the Sudan, but
had nothing of interest to say about it. After a month there he
left for Takedda with a large caravan of merchants from Ghadames.

The inhabitants of Takedda [he tells us] have no occupation except
trade. They travel to Egypt every year, and import quantities of all
the fine fabrics to be had there and of other Egyptian wares. They live
in luxury and ease, and vie with one another in regard to the number
of their slaves and serving-women. The people of Mali and Walata do
the same. They never sell the educated female slaves, or but rarely
and at a high price. . . . The copper mine is in the outskirts of Takedda.
They dig the ore out of the ground, bring it to the town, and cast it in
their houses. . . . The copper is exported from Takedda to the town of
Gobir, in the regions of the heathens, to Zaghay,* and to the country
of Bornu which is forty days' journey from Takedda.[9]

While he was here, he was summoned back to Fez, for which he
set out with a caravan of 600 women slaves, travelling by way of
Air, Tuat, and Sijilmasa.

It is impossible to read Ibn Battuta's account of the Western
Sudan without being impressed by the extent of its commercial
activity. At this time the trans-Saharan caravan traffic seems to
have been very heavy and the ties between the Maghrib and the
Sudan close and strong. We know something of how the Sudan
trade was organized from an account of the way in which an
important merchant house of Tlemcen managed their affairs.
The firm consisted of five brothers named al-Makkari, who were
co-equal partners. Two of them were established in Walata,
where they collected ivory and gold, and occasionally they visited
the important markets farther south. They were kept supplied
with European trade goods by two other brothers in Tlemcen.

* Possibly to be identified with Zaghari, a place mentioned by Ibn Battuta as lying
to the south-west of Lake Debo on the Niger. The area is also known as Dyaga.
(Trimingham, 54, n2.)

The fifth brother, the head of the firm, had settled in Sijilmasa, still the most important northern centre of the caravan trade, where he was able to watch the markets closely and keep his brothers advised about price fluctuations. It must have been people such as the al-Makkari brothers that Abu Hammen, king of Tlemcen, had in mind when, early in the century, he said he would gladly banish all merchants except those who traded with the Sudan. The latter brought great wealth to his kingdom, but the others only impoverished it.[10]

By the beginning of the fifteenth century the power of Mali was but a pale shadow of what it had been in the time of Mansa Musa. The Mandingoes had probably lost control of Takrur and perhaps also of the greater part of Songhai, though they still had a tight hold on Timbuktu. The extent of Mandingo influence in the Sahara has always been doubtful. According to Ibn Khaldun, some of the nomadic Berber tribes still paid tribute to the king of Mali, whom he calls the Malik as-Sudan or King of the Land of the Negroes,* and he says they furnished troops for the Mandingo army. From what we know of the proud desert people, we may be permitted to doubt whether this correctly represented the true relationship between them and their negro neighbours.

The end of the fourteenth century marks the beginning of Mali's decline. With the government at the centre gravely weakened by dynastic quarrels, the tributary states either asserted their independence or found themselves forced to submit to new overlords, Tuareg, Songhai, or Mossi. But while the empire was crumbling in the north and east, its supremacy was still recognized in the west. When the Portuguese reached the Gambia in the 1450s, they found that the local Mandingo recognized the ruler of Mali as their overlord. Later in the 1490s and again in the 1530s the rulers of Mali appealed to the Portuguese for aid against their enemies. But nothing could arrest the empire's decline. The process of fragmentation continued apace, until by the end of the seventeenth century the heartland of Mali was 'filled with hundreds of village states of which the descendants of Sun Dyata ruled only one.'[11]

---

* One of the hereditary titles of the emir of Kontagora in Nigeria is Sarkin Sudan, which is Hausa for Malik as-Sudan.

11

The Crescent and the Cross

'Thou shalt surely find the most violent of all men in enmity against the true believers to be the Jews, and the idolaters: and thou shalt surely find those among them to be the most inclinable to entertain friendship for the true believers, who say, We are Christians.'—QURAN, *Sura* v. 82.

THE conquest of North Africa by the Muslim Arabs did not lead to the immediate disappearance of Christianity. Christian Berbers were allowed, as long as they paid tribute to their conquerors, to enjoy civil and religious liberty. They never lost touch with Rome, and the Popes used to send priests to minister among them without fear of molestation by Muslims. How strangely the toleration of the Arabs compares with the fanatical fury of Charlemagne, who at this very time was offering the alternatives of death or baptism to the barbarous Saxons of the Elbe and Weser! At the end of the ninth century there were nearly forty episcopal towns in the Arab provinces, Carthage still being the seat of the Primate of All Africa. Sometimes distress or famine would drive uncouth African clergy across to Italy, where their strange ways, not the least of which was their refusal to regard celibacy as a virtue, caused considerable embarrassment to the Popes.[1]

Circumstances, however, were against the survival of these scattered Christian communities. Deprived of any opportunity of recruiting their numbers from outside, it was inevitable that they should ultimately be absorbed in the great mass of the Muslim population which surrounded them. Tolerated but ignored, they gradually became a depressed class to whom apostasy, affording as it did the only hope of worldly advancement, made a strong appeal.

As a result of war and piracy numbers of Christian captives were constantly brought to the shores of Africa where they were sold as slaves. Some succeeded in purchasing their freedom, and most of these returned to their own country. A few, however, were content to remain in Africa, where they either found employment in the ports or, very occasionally, banded together to form agricultural settlements in the interior. One such colony was established near Kairwan by some natives of Sardinia.[2] These colonies eventually adopted the language and religion of the country and became absorbed in the Muslim population.

But these scattered communities of Christians, whether of pre-Arab or later origin, played a negligible part in the life of the Maghrib. Gradually, however, two other classes of Christians began to make their influence felt. These were the mercenaries and the merchants, both of whom were destined to become very powerful factors in the political and economic life of the country.

No feature of the relationship between Europe and Africa in the Middle Ages is so striking as the extent to which Christian mercenaries were employed in the Maghrib. The custom apparently began in the twelfth century, when both the Almoravids and Almohads used Christian troops. But their worth was soon more widely recognized. Before long the Frankish militia or *Frendji*, as they were called, became an established institution throughout the length and breadth of Barbary.

The first care of nearly every Sultan was to provide himself with a personal bodyguard of *Frendji*. They were everywhere regarded as a *corps d'élite*, and there was never any question of their being required to apostatize. On the contrary, churches and priests were provided for them, and they were usually led by officers of their own race and creed.* The Popes constantly interested themselves in the welfare of these mercenaries, and sometimes made themselves ridiculous by the extravagance of their demands for special privileges for them.

Far from being the rabble of renegades and fugitives from justice we might expect, these Christian corps were highly disciplined and well-organized bodies of troops in the ranks of which were to be found many honourable men of noble birth. It will be recalled that the Knight in Chaucer's *Canterbury Tales* had once served in Barbary. Many were disappointed men, who had come to Africa as soldiers of fortune, or disgruntled princes and knights who,

---

* It should be noted, however, that Leo, writing early in the sixteenth century, mentions that 'The King of Tunis hath fifteene hundred most choise soldiers, the greatest part of whom are Renegadoes or backsliders from the Christian faith'. (Leo Africanus, 1896, III, 724).

together with their followers, had left their ungrateful countries to seek more congenial service under the African Sultans. Such were Frederick of Castile and Frederick Lanza, whom St. Louis found fighting against him with many other Christians when he landed in Tunis in 1270.[3]

Italians, French, Castilians, English, and Germans were to be found serving in the armies of the various African Sultans, notably at Marrakech, Tlemcen, Bugie, and Tunis. They were regularly recruited in Europe by arrangements with the Christian monarchs concerned and with the full approval of the Holy See. In 1128 Abd al-Mumin, the Almohad, obtained 12,000 Castilian horsemen from Ferdinand III for service against the Almoravids. But it was understood that he should give in exchange ten fortified towns near the Castilian frontier, and that on the capture of Marrakech, for which these troops were especially required, a church should be built for them with the exceptional privilege of being allowed to ring its bells at the hours of prayer.[4] So large a body of Christian troops was probably quite exceptional, but the kings of Tlemcen and Tunis regularly maintained forces of 2,000 to 3,000 *Frendji*. At Tlemcen they eventually acquired so much political power that they had to be disbanded.

In courage and discipline the Christian militia were greatly superior to the native troops, but they were chiefly valued for their unfailing loyalty to their masters. Like foreign mercenaries in Europe, they were much used as personal body-guards by rulers whose lives were constantly endangered through political jealousies and tribal disputes, which were of no interest to foreigners. The conduct of the Christian militia was usually in happy contrast to that of the undisciplined mob of Arabs and Berbers, who formed the greater part of the armies, and they could be depended upon to stand fast long after the other ranks had broken.

The importance of the *Frendji* to the political life of Barbary greatly strengthened the ties which linked Europe and Africa. They helped to ensure the observance of the numerous commercial treaties which from the twelfth century onwards were constantly being negotiated between Christians and Muslims for the advancement of their mutual commercial interests. In this connexion the officers of the militia were often required to act as interpreters and as witnesses to the signatures of the plenipotentiaries.

During the long struggle between Berbers and Arabs large areas of the Maghrib had gone out of cultivation, and this caused disastrous famines, especially in years of drought. Europe being the only quarter which had corn available for export to Africa, the Arabs found themselves under the necessity of reopening the ancient trade which had for so long been carried on between the opposite shores of the Mediterranean. Another consequence of the devastation they had wrought was a shortage of timber suitable for shipbuilding. As soon as the Arabs began to take to a seafaring life they were forced to turn to the richly wooded hills of the northern shores of the Mediterranean for the supplies they needed. But the confidence of Christian merchants was not easily restored. In the seventh and eighth centuries maritime trade in the Mediterranean was almost at a standstill.

A marked change took place in the reign of Charlemagne, whose friendship with the Caliphate of the east was as cordial as his hatred for that of the west was bitter. This served to increase the rift in the Muslim world and to hearten Christian seamen, who again ventured forth and, by their superior seamanship, made the Mediterranean once more a Christian sea. When Harun al Raschid's ambassador to Charlemagne arrived in Pisa from Africa he was accompanied by an officer representing the governor of Ifrikiya, whose presence cannot have been without a political significance. Later the governor of Carthage sent Charlemagne the bones of St. Cyprian. Africa next gave him an elephant, which had come from Baghdad.[5] These gestures could scarcely be ignored. Gradually confidence was restored and Christian merchants discovered that they were again welcome in Barbary ports.

The tenth century was a period of great prosperity in the Maghrib. Large areas which had fallen derelict were, thanks to the introduction of elaborate systems of irrigation, once more under cultivation. The olive was again cultivated on a very large scale. Kairwan was producing sugar, Msila cotton, Sebab indigo, Gabes silk. The manufacture of cotton and woollen cloths and pottery was restoring to Tripoli, Sfax, and Tunis their former prosperity. In the west the coral fisheries of Ceuta and Tenes were again active. But probably the most profitable trade was that which the Maghrib was carrying on with the Sudan, whence slaves, ivory, ebony, and gold dust were imported.

Ibn Haukal, describing the country at this time, tells us that 'the Maghrib is chiefly remarkable for black slaves . . . (the white slaves come from the quarter of Andalus) . . . and coral, and ambergris, and gold, and honey, and silk, and seal-skins'.[6] In the east there was an enormous demand for slaves—Christian, negro, and mulatto—and for eunuchs, which were chiefly supplied from Constantinople and the Maghrib. Most of the African trade in slaves passed through Kairwan, the richest city in the land.

So much prosperity inevitably attracted Christian merchants, who soon discovered that great profits were to be derived from the African trade. The galleys of Naples, Venice, Genoa, Pisa, Marseilles, and Castile were regularly to be found in the ports of Barbary, especially at Bona, Tunis, Sfax, and Tripoli, where they bartered their manufactured goods for slaves, olive oil, coral, and other produce. But the Italians were by far the most active. The great commercial prosperity of the Arabs of Barbary at this period has been attributed largely to the traffic with Italy on the one hand and with the Sudan on the other.[7]

The Crusades which greatly embittered the relationship between Christians and Muslims in Syria and Spain, had a stimulating effect on the Barbary trade. The Arabs of the Maghrib, now thoroughly Berberized, had no interest in the political affairs of their co-religionists in Syria, Egypt, or Spain, and took little heed of the repeated demands of Damascus and Cairo for reinforcements and subsidies. This greatly strengthened the confidence of European merchants carrying on business with Barbary. Even when the Popes found it necessary to forbid Christians to trade with Muslims, or to serve in their fleets and armies, an exception was made in favour of the Arabs of Barbary. The trade now became sufficiently advanced to be based largely on mutual trust. Credit was readily given, and every nation maintained permanent establishments in Africa, and many also had their own Consuls. The protection of the interests of foreign merchants was one of the chief duties of the head of the Arab Customs in each port.

In the second half of the twelfth century the Almohads completed their conquest of the Maghrib. All the country from al-Mahdiya in the east to the Atlantic in the west became subject to Abd al-Mumin, their warrior Sultan, who had always disapproved of the presence of so many Christian galleys in African harbours. As the result of his measures Christian trade with Barbary received another check. Although generally hostile to Christians, whose ships his seamen always attacked, Abd al Mumin was not ill disposed towards the Genoese, to whom, to their very great advantage, he granted a treaty of peace.

But Genoa did not long enjoy her privileged position. The death of Abd al-Mumin in 1163 gave the Pisans an opportunity of re-entering the field in which they had formerly been predominant, and of competing with their hated enemies the Genoese. Some years later the Normans of Sicily, between whom and the Almohads there had been bitter war for twenty years, recovered their old privileges in Africa, and soon afterwards the Barbary ports were again thrown open to practically all Christians.

When Christian trade with Africa first became general and the numbers of Europeans engaged in it greatly increased, those who had been first in the field sought to secure the advantageous positions, which they had won for themselves by their own enterprise, by negotiating treaties with the African Sultans. Most of the concessions granted them had been mere verbal arrangements. Among the first Christians to enter into formal treaties with the Muslims of Africa were the Norman kings of Sicily. At the end of the eleventh century they strengthened their commercial ties with the Maghrib by entering into binding contracts with the Sultans of al-Mahdiya and Kairwan. The Pisans and Genoese, quickly perceiving the advantage which had been gained by the Normans, set about negotiating similar treaties in order to safeguard their own privileges.

Such treaties, which always guaranteed the personal safety of the nationals of the contracting parties in each other's ports, were as much to the advantage of Muslims as of Christians, and they were often initiated by the former. In 1133 the Almoravids sent two galleys to Pisa seeking a treaty, which was readily granted. Pisa, at this time enjoying the predominant position at sea which had formerly been held by her rivals of Amalfi and Naples, was carrying on a very large trade with Tunis. She also had over a hundred vessels trading with Morocco, where her merchants had been allowed to establish their own trading factories. Similar privileges were granted to the Genoese and later to the Marseillais. Gradually the whole of the African trade became regularized by a vast number of commercial treaties between the European and African trading ports.

The increased sense of security which these treaties inevitably gave permitted a very much more elaborate organization of Christian interests on the African coast. Practically every nation had its own Consul in each of the African ports with which it traded, and most had also their own *fonduks*, not unlike the trading factories established by Europeans on the coast of West Africa several centuries later. The Consul's duties were to settle disputes between his nationals, to see that they were fairly treated by the Arab Customs, to act as an intermediary between them and the Sultan, to safeguard the estates of deceased merchants, and to protect the interests of those who were absent. The Consul, who held office for a limited term, was required to maintain an establishment worthy of the nation he represented, and his household always included a chaplain.

Apart from liability to frequent interruption by political disturbances, to which North Africa has been subject throughout its troubled history, Christian trade with Barbary was carried on with singularly little difficulty. Piracy was the chief cause of friction. Always an intensely popular form of lawlessness among the maritime peoples of southern Europe and irresistible to the predatory instincts of the Arabs, it was a force which none could control. Not till the coming of strong central governments and powerful navies centuries later did the evil begin to abate.

Arab pirates enjoyed certain advantages over their Christian rivals. In Africa great prestige attached to piracy, which was encouraged by the Sultans (who were deeply interested in its success) and, as long as it was directed against Christians, by religion. It was a popular and well-organized industry and, directly and indirectly, engaged the activities of a large part of the population. In Europe, speaking generally and leaving out of account the wicked little Italian republics who were always a law unto themselves, Church and State and public opinion were against piracy. The Christian corsairs, however, had better vessels and were better seamen than their rivals, and were fully able to hold their own.

If Christians seem more often to have been the victims than the authors of piracy, it is because their coasts were less easily defended, because their trade was greater and therefore more vulnerable, and because their history is better known than that of the Arabs. The superior seamanship of the Christian corsairs, moreover, made them more formidable than their Muslim rivals, who did not gain the ascendancy till the Turks came and organized them on a national basis.

The Genoese, Pisans, and Provençals were all inveterate pirates. But none of these attained to the rapacity of the Greeks of the Ægean islands who for centuries were the scourge of the eastern Mediterranean and who taught the dreaded Turkish corsairs of later times the mysteries of their nefarious trade. Although the activities of Christian pirates were usually directed against Muslims, they frequently attacked Christian vessels. In very early times certain Italian republics, notably Amalfi, were even known to join forces with Arab corsairs in raids on other Christians. The profits were very considerable, and in times of trade depression it was no unusual thing for an otherwise perfectly respectable Christian merchant to have an occasional 'flutter' in piracy.

As trade increased during the thirteenth century, Europe sent to Africa a wide range of goods many of which were required for the trans-Saharan caravan trade. Of the metals, copper was especially required for re-export to the Sudan, where its bright colour made it popular. The principal glassmakers of Venice had their representatives in Barbary where, till recent times, there was always an enormous demand for glass beads for the Sudan trade. European cloth also commanded a ready sale south of the Sahara. Wine from France, Spain, and Greece was sold publicly throughout Barbary, where its use was not by any means restricted to the Christian communities. The Almohads reproached the Almoravids with being wine-drinkers, but that they themselves were open to the same reproach is proved by the surviving records of the medieval wine-shippers of Marseilles. In spite of numerous laws which made it illegal for Christians to sell ships or ship-building materials to Muslims the great shipyards of Venice and Genoa regularly built vessels for the African market. These craft were very superior to those of Arab build, and so anxious were the Sultans to encourage their use that sales of Christian vessels in African ports were exempt from duty.

The goods received by Europe in exchange were equally varied. In spite of the ban of the Holy See and the proscription of captives under the terms of innumerable treaties, slaves, both white and black, continued to be imported into Christian Europe, where Pisa and Genoa were the chief centres of the iniquitous trade. In the fourteenth century we first hear of malaguetta pepper, which was then being imported into Nimes and Montpellier from the Sudan through Barbary.* The Sudan also supplied ivory, ebony, and 'Morocco' leather, all required for sale to the Christian merchants, the gaily-coloured leather being particularly popular

---

*The Italians, puzzled by the mysterious origin of this strange product, called it Grains of Paradise, by which it later became widely known and from which the Grain Coast of Guinea derived its name.

in the markets of England and Normandy. But undoubtedly the most significant of North Africa's exports was gold from the Sudan.

The significance of this gold trade to the countries of Latin Christendom requires some explanation. Europe's own native sources of gold were extremely limited, being confined to a few alluvial deposits. In Roman times the Emperors had maintained a gold coinage and this had been continued by the rulers of the barbarian successor states. But during the latter half of the first millenium A.D. there was a steady loss of gold. Some was looted by Scandinavian pirates, some buried in times of trouble, but the greater part appears to have been sent eastwards, especially to Byzantium, to pay for the luxury goods of the Orient. As a result of this steady drain in specie, gold coinages disappeared from the currency of the kingdoms of Western Europe by the eleventh century, their place being taken by silver coinages which were cumbersome and inconvenient. The first sign of a return to gold occurred in 1254 when the Florentines produced a gold coinage; they were followed by most of the other states of Latin Christendom.

These gold coinages were 'the heralds', as R. W. Southern has pointed out, 'of a new economic situation in which Europe was established as an important export area. The position of two centuries earlier had been reversed: instead of the European consumer scraping the bottom of the till to pay for the spices and luxuries of the east, the Italian merchant was seeking new markets for the ever-increasing flow of goods from beyond the Alps. Venice in the first place, but increasingly in the twelfth century Genoa and Pisa, were the great agents in effecting this change in the commercial position of Europe. . . . As the activities of the Latin merchants were extended in area to the Black Sea, and to the markets of Syria and North Africa, so the towns on which these merchants were based developed new and aggressive commercial policies. With commercial power came plans for—or rather an instinctive drive towards—conquest and colonization!'[8]

As to the actual amount of gold imported into Europe from North Africa, there is need for much more intensive research in the commercial archives of the Mediterranean states. Clearly West African gold production was increasing steadily from the eighth century onwards, until the sixteenth century when the average annual production has been estimated by Raymond Mauny to have been about 9 metric tons.* About two-thirds of this amount, Mauny suggests, was exported. To carry this weight of gold no more than fifty camels would have been required. The gold was brought from the mining areas of the Sudan, usually in the form of dust. It was refined and made into ingots at the great commercial centres on the northern or southern borders of the Sahara, Sijilmasa or Audoghast, Wargla or Timbuktu. From there it passed to Fez and Marrakech, Tunis and Cairo, and to the ports where Europeans offered their wares.[9]

Their vigorous trade familiarized the Christian galleys with every inch of the Barbary coast. It kept busy a score of African ports, in nearly all of which the Christian merchants maintained permanent establishments. But the interior was closed to all but a very few, and Europe for long remained in profound ignorance of what lay beyond the greater part of the coast. Individual merchants occasionally penetrated to Marrakech, Tlemcen, Constantine, and Kairwan, but it was very rare during the Middle Ages for European traders to secure a permanent footing in these or in any other of the important markets of the interior. An early fourteenth-century Italian cartographer, Giovanni da Carignano, mentions on one of his maps that the source of certain information was a Genoese doing business at Sijilmasa with merchants trading with Walata and Guinea.[10] Christian merchants also probably maintained establishments at Tlemcen, which was always an important *entrepôt* for the Sudan trade, but very near to the coast.[11] Generally speaking the activities of Christian merchants were restricted to the maritime towns.

From Leo we gather that the native merchants of the ports had little to do with the trade of the interior, which was in the hands of middlemen who naturally resented intruders, whether Muslim or Christian. Consequently any enterprising European merchant who attempted to extend his activities to the interior was likely to find his treaty rights of little avail among people who regarded him as an unwelcome intruder. Trade was made impossible for him, and he very soon wished himself safely back in the neighbourhood of his own *fonduk* on the coast. Early in the thirteenth century a Venetian ambassador obtained permission for his countrymen to travel with their caravans wherever they liked throughout the

---

* In 1937 West African gold production was 21.4 metric tons. 80% of this amount came from the Gold Coast, where modern mining equipment made possible the exploitation of deep underground seams.

dominions of the Sultan of Tunis, but there is no evidence that they derived much benefit from the privilege. It was a great deal easier to secure the good will of a Sultan than that of jealous native traders.

The failure of Europeans to penetrate Africa during the Middle Ages was in striking contrast with the extraordinary journeys which they were then making into the remotest parts of Asia. Merchants and ecclesiastics brought back a certain amount of vague information about the nearer *hinterland*, but the far interior, where immensely rich countries were known to exist, remained wrapped in an alluring atmosphere of mystery.

12

The Quest for Gold

'Beating and laying open the way where and how this Golden Trade should rise.'—RICHARD JOBSON.

DURING the greater part of the Middle Ages it was, as we have seen in the previous chapter, practically impossible for Christians to obtain any first-hand knowledge of the interior of Africa, but they found in the Jews a valuable source of information.

From very early times the Jews have formed an important element in the population of the Maghrib. Like other foreigners they were regarded with contempt and were frequently treated with contumely. But they played a very active part in the trade of the country and they sometimes rose to occupy high official positions, especially in Morocco. From the Maghrib they spread, as we have already seen, into the oases of the Sahara and into the Sudan. The *mellahs* of Barbary consequently became the repository of a great deal of information about the interior of the continent, but it was long before any of this became available to the outside world.

Late in the fourteenth century Majorca produced a valuable series of maps of Africa which represented a modest but definite advance in geographical knowledge. These maps were the product of a colony of Jews who, originally noted as makers of clocks, astrolabes, quadrants, and other instruments, were now acquiring considerable fame as cartographers. Their maps were commercial rather than political, from which it is evident that they were based upon information supplied by their co-religionists in Africa. The African trade of Majorca was at this time very prosperous owing to the friendly relations, cemented by various commercial treaties, which existed between Aragon and Barbary. The Jewish carto-grahpers of Majorca, therefore, were very well placed to obtain first-hand information about the trade routes leading to the Sudan.

These Jewish maps were too crude and inaccurate to have much topographical value, but they lit up, if only dimly, what had hitherto been impenetrable darkness. They gave positions to places like Timbuktu, Gao, and Mali which were already known in Europe as great and infinitely remote markets, and this gave some shape and form to a region hitherto visualized only as a repository of untold wealth. The most important of these maps was the so-called Cata-lan Atlas of Abraham Cresques which, it will be recalled, did so much to spread through Europe the fame of Mansa Musa.

But the interest of Jewish cartographers in Africa was not allowed to continue for long. The persecutions of the Jews by Ferdinand and Isabella spread from Spain into Africa and, as already related, through the Sahara into the Sudan. Consequently the later Majorcan maps betray a gradual loss of knowledge.[1]

The Majorcan school, however, had brought about a consider-able advance in European cartography, especially in Italy. The keen interest in Africa, which we see in the Italian maps of the time, sprang from close commercial ties between the Barbary states and the petty Italian republics. Nevertheless, European knowledge of the interior was still superficial and second-hand, although it had been gained at a critical time when Christians were beginning to look towards Africa for a solution to their economic problems.

By the beginning of the fifteenth century, the demands of a greatly increased foreign trade and a series of disastrous wars had left Europe's reserves of precious metals severely reduced. Because the trade goods of the West were too bulky and heavy for camel transport, gold was needed to pay for the valuable produce of India, China, and the Spice Islands, all of which came overland and were in ever-increasing demand. The depletion of Europe's gold reserves was therefore becoming a grave embarrassment to her bankers. Men's minds naturally turned to Africa and to the problem of where the Barbary gold came from.

The boundless sea, which beat with such turbulence on the

rugged western shores of the known world, had not yet been explored. Some years had still to pass before Christian seamen were
to challenge the current belief that certain doom awaited the
mariner so rash as to round Cape Bojador. There was therefore
no question of seeking Africa's hidden goldfields by way of the sea,
a possibility which few had seriously contemplated since the days
of Herodotus. But the Majorcan maps set men thinking about the
overland routes, the jealously guarded secret of the Moors of
Barbary. They not only proclaimed the wealth of the interior, but
they showed a road leading to the hidden goldfields. A gap in the
Atlas mountains in the Catalan map was marked: 'Through this
place pass the merchants who travel to the land of the negroes of
Guinea.' Here, as well as in earlier *mappae-mundi* which were
similarly marked, was a clear invitation to Christian adventurers
to elude, if it were possible the vigilance of the Moors and penetrate
their continent from the north.

However, it was not until the middle of the fifteenth century
that the first recorded attempt was made to penetrate Africa overland from the north for commercial purposes.* It was not surprising that the attempt should have been made by a Genoese merchant, Antonio Malfante, for Genoa had long been active in the
North African trade and the rulers of the city were gravely concerned about the need to obtain gold as the basis of their currency.
Malfante landed at Honein and got as far as the centre of the
Sahara in an endeavour to discover the source of the African gold.
He sent back from Tuat a report which gave useful geographical
information about the interior, but nothing helpful about the
object of his journey. He had repeatedly asked an old sheikh, who
knew the Sudan well, where the gold came from, but always got
the same answer: 'I spent fourteen years in the negro country and
never heard of, or saw, a man who could say of certain knowledge

* In 1283, an unknown European—one of a group of twelve sent out by a certain
cardinal to report on all the countries of the world—travelled with a salt caravan
across the desert to a country, possibly ancient Ghana, where the negroes worshipped
a dragon that lived on an island in the middle of a lake (De la Roncière, *La Découverte
de l'Afrique au Moyen Age*, I, 108–12.)

In the early fifteenth century, a certain knight of Toulouse, Anselm d'Ysalguier,
was said to have visited Gao on the Niger, married an African lady of noble lineage,
and returned home accompanied by his wife, three African women, and three
eunuchs, one of whom became a famous doctor. The story is so engaging that one
would like it to be true. Unfortunately, a local historian in Toulouse has found
convincing reasons for doubting its authenticity (De la Roncière, III, 1–5, quotes the
documents on which the story is based; Mauny, *Tableau Géographique*, 463, refers
to the article by Fr. Galabert in which the story is criticized).

"This is what I saw, this is how they find and collect the gold."
Also it is to be presumed that it comes from afar, and, in my
opinion, from a very circumscribed area.' Everyone else he had
questioned had been similarly unhelpful, either deliberately or
through ignorance. Nothing more was ever heard of Malfante.[2]

Malfante made his journey at a time when the Florentines were
beginning to interest themselves in Africa. By her geographical
position Florence had long been precluded from competing with
Venice and Genoa for sea-borne trade. She had probably felt little
need for such expansion, for the astuteness of her great banking
houses had won for their city a position in European affairs with
which they could well afford to be content. Although hampered
by the aggressive domination, first of Pisa and then of Siena, and
constantly rent with civil strife, the city nevertheless maintained
its predominant position in the financial world.

In 1407 Florence seized the port of her Pisan rivals and from
this new base her merchants vigorously applied themselves to
overseas expansion. They were particularly successful in North
Africa where they negotiated several very advantageous commercial treaties by which they acquired monopolies in Tunis,
Bona, Bugie, Algiers, and Oran, to the exclusion of all other
Christians. In Tunis, they gained the exceptional concession of
being allowed to trade in the hinterland.

The Florentines, succeeding where others had failed, profited
from the opportunity of exploring the interior of Africa which their
new privileges afforded them. We know little of their activities in
this sphere, the only record being a passing allusion to what today
would be considered a noteworthy journey performed by a great
Florentine traveller. This man was Benedetto Dei, who travelled
widely in the interests of Florentine trade. He was the agent of
the Portinari, a great merchant house which in its wide foreign
interests may be compared with the Centurioni of Genoa.

Dei's mission appears to have been to establish trade with the
east by outflanking the Turks, but his thoughts were not all of
trade. In Beirut he collected a serpent with a hundred teeth and
four legs. From Jerusalem, which moved him to loftier thoughts, he
sent home a mass of holy relics. In Carthage he secured a chame-
leon 'which lived on air'. Tunis he found remarkable for its
crickets. Sfax roused him to meditation on the Punic wars, but he
was brought back to earth in Archudia, where his interest was
aroused by the sight of monkeys being sold like chickens with their

legs tied together. He subsequently went to Paris, and then, in 1470, to Timbuktu, a visit which he lightly dismissed as a mere incident of travel. 'I have been', he wrote, 'to Timbuktu, a place situated beyond Barbary in very arid country. Much business is done there in selling coarse cloth, serge, and fabrics like those made in Lombardy.'[3]

To one with so strong, if somewhat eccentric, a bent for zoology, Timbuktu must have been disappointing, but it is to be regretted that the first recorded visit of a European to that remote city should be passed over so lightly. It has been suggested, and with reason, that by 1470 there was nothing very remarkable in this journey and that Dei had been preceded by others of his country-men. We know that only a few years after Dei's journey the Portuguese established a factory at Wadan whence they sent a mission to Timbuktu, but these incidents belong to the romantic story of the maritime exploration of the western coasts of the continent.

13

The Discovery of Guinea

'You cannot find a peril so great that the hope of reward will not be greater. . . . Go forth, then, and . . . make your voyage straightway.'—PRINCE HENRY THE NAVIGATOR.

IN classical times no feature of the known world conveyed so perfect an impression of infinity as the boundless ocean of the west. In all other directions great land masses held promise of discovery and expansion. Neither the frozen *tundra* of the north nor the un-inhabitable deserts of the south inspired the same degree of terror as that with which men contemplated the boundless ocean which beat incessantly upon the rugged western shores of their world. The Arab geographers had long called it the Green Sea of Dark-ness and their notions persisted till the close of the Middle Ages. Ibn Khaldun described it as a vast and boundless ocean on which sailors dared not venture for fear of being lost in mist and vapour.[1]

Until 1434 no sailor, neither Christian nor Muslim, knew any-thing of the coast of Africa beyond Cape Bojador, the promontory which lay some two hundred miles beyond the southern borders of Morocco. Their ignorance was not surprising. The Saharan coast was in itself particularly uninviting; it could offer the voyager little or nothing in the way of food and water. But even more serious to the sailors of an age of sail were the difficulties caused by wind and current. For on the long stretch of coast between Cape Bojador and Cape Blanco the wind blows almost continuously throughout the year from the north-east, and the current flows from north to south. To sail south around the bulge of Africa presented no especial difficulty; but medieval sailors knew that in the face of such winds and currents it would be virtually impossible for them to sail north again along the coast.[2]

For the Muslims of North Africa, to whom the caravan routes of the Sahara presented no secrets, there was really no incentive to try and find another way round the desert. Arab geographers record three occasions when Muslim sailors found themselves on the coast beyond southern Morocco; but on each of these occasions the journey ended in shipwreck and in two of the three episodes it is clear that the incident relates to a ship accidentally blown off course, while the third—al-Idrisi's story of the eight Muslim adventurers who set sail from Lisbon (the town did not fall to the Christians until 1147) and reached two hitherto unknown islands— may represent either the garbled narrative of an early voyage to the Canaries or a fabulous yarn strongly influenced by reminiscences of Sindbab.[3]

The first authentic Christian voyage down the coast of Morocco took place in 1291. It was financed by a group of Genoese businessmen who sent out two galleys, captained by the brothers Vivaldi, in the hope that they would be able to find a sea-route to the Indies. Nothing was ever heard of the Vivaldis and their ships after they had passed Cape Nun. In the fourteenth and early fifteenth centuries a number of European sailors—men not only from Portugal but also from Genoa, Castile, Aragon and even from distant Normandy—reached and explored the archipelago of the Canaries and the island of Madeira. To European adventurers in an age when 'land and the labour of those who worked it' provided 'the principal source of wealth' the Canaries with their Guanche inhabitants presented a particularly tempting field for colonization.[4] But there were other reasons for their interest. Thus Jean de Béthencourt, the leader of the Norman expedition of 1402, was moved partly by the hope of discovering that 'River of Gold' that was so enticingly marked south of Cape Bojador on some of the fourteenth-century maps.[5]

Of all the maritime nations of Europe it was, of course, the Portuguese who were to play the leading part in exploring the sea route down the coast of Africa. Portuguese contact with Africa dates back to the twelfth century. The raids then launched against the coast of Morocco represent the first stage in what has been called 'the inversion of the Muslim conquest of the Iberian peninsula'.[6] By the fourteenth century the Portuguese were established as a considerable naval power. Then in 1415 occurred the decisive event that marks the opening of the great phase of Portuguese expansion, the capture of the Moroccan port of Ceuta.

Among those who had taken a leading part in the Ceuta expedition was the twenty-one-year-old Prince Henry, third son of John I of Portugal. During the campaign he had heard much of the gold-laden caravans of the Sahara about which he had read when a boy. He returned to Portugal determined to seek the golden land of Guinea by way of the sea, and to divert to the coast the rich desert trade which kept so many Barbary ports filled with Christian galleys. Later the opening of a sea route to India, the discovery of the mysterious priest-king Prester John, and the conversion of the heathen became declared objects of the voyages he so brilliantly directed, but the discovery of the gold of Guinea was their primary object.[7]

Gathering round him men skilled in the arts of the sea, and assisted by his brother Don Pedro, a much-travelled man,* Prince Henry planned and organized the voyages which made his name famous and which, by laying the foundations of scientific exploration, made possible the great discoveries in the Old World and the New later in the century.

Owing to the difficulties of navigation and to terror of the supernatural, the work of exploration went foward slowly. But in 1434 Gil Eannes, one of Henry's squires, returned to his master with a sprig of rosemary gathered on the mainland south of Cape Bojador. This was a turning point in the history of geographical discovery. Gil Eannes had proved for all time the absurdity of the superstitious terror with which mariners regarded the unknown. The impenetrable mists from which the sailor brave enough to round the cape could not escape, the devils which lurked behind

---

* Recent research points to Don Pedro as possibly the predominant partner in the enterprise and as deserving more credit than has been accorded him.

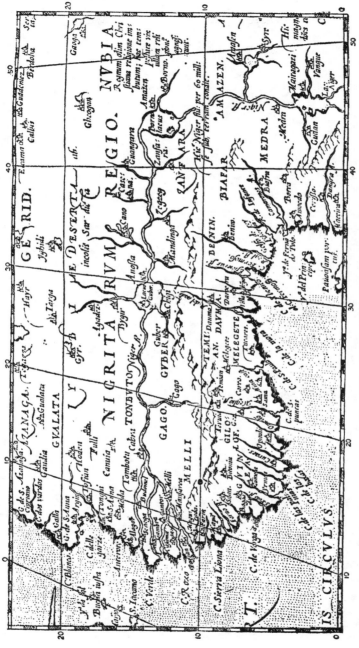

v. The *Africae Tabula Nova* of Ortelius (1570)

the headland waiting to destroy him, and the liquid fire by which his body would be consumed, had all been proved to have no reality, as Henry in his wisdom had repeatedly declared.

Discovery now went ahead with greater speed, especially after 1440 when the Portuguese began to use the newly-designed caravel. Compared with earlier vessels, caravels were much more manoeuvrable; the Venetian Cadamosto called them the best sailing vessels afloat.* It seems likely that the use of caravels enabled the Portuguese to make one momentous discovery: that it was possible to return from the coast of West Africa not by sailing northwards along the coast, battling against contrary winds, but by striking boldly westwards for several hundred miles into the Atlantic to reach a part of the ocean where winds blew favourably from the south and west. It is not known exactly when the Portuguese made this discovery, for no contemporary chronicler mentions it—their silence is in no way surprising: information about the new route was clearly regarded as 'top secret' —but the discovery is most likely to have taken place about 1440.[8]

So the caravels gradually worked their way farther and farther down the coast. Footprints of men and camels showed that even the desert was inhabited. Then some Sanhaja nomads were captured and brought home, together with a little gold-dust which encouraged the hope that the long-sought land of gold might not be far off. Later a whole cargo of captives was shipped to Lisbon where they were sold into slavery, with profoundly tragic consequences, for it taught Europeans how rapidly money could be made by the enslavement of Africans. The character of the voyages then began quickly to change.

From the start public opinion in Portugal had been so hostile to Henry that he had found it difficult to man his ships; all that was now changed. The press of volunteers was so great that many had to be turned away. This led to buccaneering voyages, which quickly proved that slave-raiding was far more profitable than geographical discovery. Henry did not let opportunities for personal gain distract his captains from the work in hand, and he kept the interests of his own country much in mind. Pleading that the salvation of the souls of the heathen was one of the main

* In his voyage of 1434 Gil Eannes used a *barca*, a cumbersome boat of twenty-five tons (the equivalent of 50 modern tons) with a square sail. Caravels were ships of fifty tons and upwards; they had three masts and lateen sails. (E. Prestage, *The Portuguese Pioneers*, 1933, 332–3).

objects of the work of exploration, he secured from the Pope for the Crown of Portugal whatever new discoveries might be made between Bojador and the Indies, with consequences which were profoundly to affect the partition of Africa and much besides in centuries to come.

In 1445 Nuno Tristam sailed south beyond the desert and discovered a rich and fertile land where negroes, hitherto known to Christendom only as the slaves of others, led a free life. Many had doubted whether there was a limit to the desert, so the discovery that beyond it there lay a well-favoured land, perhaps offering rich rewards to the explorer, was sensational. The next important discovery was the mouth of the Senegal, at first thought to be the Niger, which Herodotus and others had said was a western branch of the Nile of Egypt. So its discoverers called it the Nile, and carved there on a tree Henry's arms and his motto, *Talent de bien faire*. 'Of a surety I doubt', comments the contemporary chronicler Zurara, 'if since the great power of Alexander and of Caesar, there hath been any prince in the world that ever had the marks of his conquest set up so far from his own land.'[9]

With the discovery of the Senegal the Portuguese had reached the Sudan, the land of the Black Moors as opposed to the brown-skinned Tawny Moors of the Sahara, and they gave it the name of Guinea.* The finding of this apparently certain gateway to

---

* The name Guinea is usually said to have been a corrupt form of the name Ghana, picked up by the Portuguese in the Maghrib. The present writer finds this unacceptable. The name Guinea has been in use both in the Maghrib and in Europe long before Prince Henry's time. For example, on a map dated about 1320 by the Genoese cartographer Giovanni di Carignano, who got his information about Africa from a fellow-countryman in Sijilmasa, we find Gunuia, and in the Catalan atlas of 1375 Ginyia. A passage in Leo (1896, III, 822) points to Guinea having been a corrupt form of Jenne, less famous than Ghana but nevertheless for many centuries famed in the Maghrib as a great market and a seat of learning. The relevant passage reads: 'The kingdom of Ghinea . . . called by the merchants of our nation Gheneoa, by the natural inhabitants thereof Genni and by the Portugals and other people of Europe Ghinea.' But it seems more probable that Guinea derives from *aguinaou*, the Berber for negro. Marrakech has a gate, built in the twelfth century, called the Bab Aguinaou, the Gate of the Negro. (Delafosse, *Haut-Senégal-Niger*, II, 277–8).

The modern application of the name Guinea to the coast dates only from 1481. In that year the Portuguese built a fort, São Jorge da Mina (the Elmina of today) on the Gold Coast, and their king, John II, was permitted by the Pope to style himself Lord of Guinea, a title which survived until the recent extinction of the monarchy.

The English golden guinea coin is so called because it was first minted, in 1662, from gold imported from West Africa by the African Company of London merchants. (The Chief Clerk, Royal Mint, in a letter to the author.)

the interior inspired great hopes of the capture of the overland trade.

So far little had been learnt about the trade of the interior. This was partly due to the irreparable harm done by raiding for slaves, which had almost prohibited friendly intercourse with the natives. The Mandingoes, wrote Jobson, an English sea-captain who visited the Gambia in 1620, were 'very fearefull to speake with any shipping except they have perfect knowledge of them, in regard they have been many times, by severall nations surprized, taken and carried away.'[10] Some progress had been made at the settlement established by the Portuguese on the island of Arguin, close to Cape Blanco, to which a modest trickle of caravan traffic had been diverted. Little commercial information was obtained until the Venetian seaman, Alvise Cadamosto, was sent by Prince Henry to discover the Gambia river, which was believed to be very rich in gold. He found the river, but not the gold. Unlike the Portuguese captains, Cadamosto appreciated the importance of securing the confidence of the natives, and this enabled him to obtain information denied to his predecessors. He learnt that the old silent trade in gold was still carried on somewhere in the interior and that gold was being bartered for salt as in the past. This suggested the need to get into touch with a known centre of the salt trade, such as Timbuktu, but where the goldfields lay no man could say.

The Portuguese then sought to make contact with various countries in the interior, including Takrur, Mali, and Timbuktu. Nothing came of their efforts. Only one member of the mission to Timbuktu succeeded in returning to the coast; the report on his journey has never been discovered.

By this time, however, the Portuguese had succeeded in tapping another source of West African gold. In the 1470s they made contact with that part of the coast of Guinea that came to be known as the Gold Coast. Here in 1482 they built a massive fortress, São Jorge da Mina (later known as Elmina). The Portuguese appear to have thought that the gold that was brought to them by the local people came from one large mine; in fact it was produced in innumerable alluvial deposits. There is evidence to suggest that gold from this part of West Africa had begun to be exported northwards towards the end of the thirteenth century.[11] But it was clearly more convenient for local producers to sell their gold to the Portuguese who were near at hand rather

than face the long journey to Jenne and Timbuktu. By the beginning of the sixteenth century, gold from the Gold Coast was
accounting for an amount that has been estimated at about one-
tenth of the total world supply at that time. This was a fact of
immense significance. Gold from the Costa da Mina provided,
as J. D. Fage has suggested, both 'the incentive for renewed royal
interest and participation in Portuguese overseas expansion' and
'the source of capital to enable it to be brought so swiftly to so
triumphant a conclusion'.[12] Nor may the consequences of this
discovery have been limited only to Portugal. The Portuguese
posts on the coast began to attract Mandingo traders from the
interior, and this in turn affected the flow of gold across the
Sahara. The decline in the flow of gold from the Sudan appears
to have had a very serious effect on the economy of the states of
North Africa in the late fifteenth and early sixteenth centuries.[13]

But though the Portuguese occupied a position of strength on the
coast, they were never able to make a successful penetration of the
interior. Their position was described in a striking passage by the
great chronicler, Joao de Barros, who himself had served at Mina.

It [Guinea] is so peaceful, meek and obedient an estate, that, without
our having one hand holding a lighted lunt on the touch-hole of a
gun and the other hand holding a lance, it gives us gold, ivory, wax,
hides, sugar, pepper, malaguetta; and it would give us more things if
we would only penetrate into the hinterland . . . But it seems that for
our sins, or for some inscrutable judgment of God, in all the entrances
of this great Ethiopia that we navigate along, He has placed a striking
angel with a flaming sword of deadly fevers, who prevents us from
penetrating into the interior to the springs of this garden, whence
proceed these rivers of gold that flow to the sea in so many parts of our
conquest.[14]

The Portuguese lost their posts on the Gold Coast to the Dutch
in the 1630s. In the early eighteenth century the Gold Coast was
providing Europeans—not only Dutch and Portuguese, but also
Englishmen, Frenchmen, Brandenbergers, and Danes—with about
3,500 pounds of gold in a good year, 'a quantity not notably
different from that obtained in the sixteenth century'.[15] And yet
Europeans were never able to discover the actual source of the
gold. 'The Natives', an Englishman wrote in 1758, 'have ever
expressed great Jealousy at every attempt made by Europeans
to discover the Nature and Produce of their Country and particu-

larly their Gold.'[16] It was not until late in the nineteenth century
that many of the gold-producing areas of the Gold Coast and
neighbouring countries were first visited by European travellers.

14

Wangara

*'And yet may Africa have a Prerogative in Rarities, and some seeming
incredibilities be true.'*—SAMUEL PURCHAS.

THE source of West African gold was a remarkably well kept
secret. It puzzled almost all outsiders for over two thousand years,
and for half that time their efforts to discover where the gold
came from were as unremitting as they were unsuccessful. The
Arabs were aware of the existence of gold in West Africa at an
early date, for their first reported expedition to the Sudan,
launched in 734, brought back a considerable quantity of the
precious metal. al-Fazari, writing before the end of the eighth
century, mentions Ghana as a land of gold.[1] A century later, Ibn
al-Faqih came out with the statement that in Ghana gold grew
in the ground like carrots.[2] al-Bakri, in the eleventh century, was
more precise: the best gold in Ghana, he stated, came from the
town of Ghiarou. Ghiarou lay twelve miles from the 'Nile',* it
could be reached in eighteen days from the capital of Ghana, and
it contained a great number of Muslims.[3] al-Bakri also mentions
another source of gold, Iresni, a town lying on the 'Nile' and
opposite the country of Malel (Mali). 'The pagan known as
Nounghamarta, are traders', al-Bakri added, 'and carry Iresni
gold into all the countries'.[4] Then, in the twelfth century, al-Idrisi
stated that West African gold came from two sources, Takrur to
the west, and Wangara, further east, a country 'renowned on
account of the quantity and quality of gold that it produces'.[5]

Later, medieval Arab geographers made frequent mention of
the wealth in gold possessed by the great rulers of West Africa,
but they could be no more precise about its source than al-Idrisi

* The designation 'Nile' tended to be applied by Muslim geographers to any large
river in West Africa and not only to the Niger.

had been. In the fifteenth century, it will be recalled, the Italian traveller Malfante had been told by an old sheikh of Tuat that though he had lived fourteen years in the Sudan, he had never met anyone who could describe from personal experience the source of Sudanese gold.[6] Undoubtedly there must have been a considerable number of privileged middlemen who knew exactly where Wangara was, but they were always on their guard against interlopers. The search for Wangara, in which, as we have seen, both Christian ships and Muslim armies were engaged, cost kings their thrones, peoples their freedom, and thousands their lives. At the end of it all no-one was any the wiser.

Although the earliest references to the trade, those of Herodotus about the maidens of Cyraunis and the silent trafficking of the Carthaginians, have no direct bearing on the problem of Wangara, they are relevant because they show that from the earliest times the trade had two distinctive features, its silence and the important part played in it by women. They also show how unwise it is to dismiss as wholly imaginary even the most improbable stories about the trade. What could appear more fanciful than the charming story about the maidens drawing up gold on birds' feathers smeared with pitch? The implication that even in those remote days the women packed their gold-dust in quills, as they still do, is as irresistible as it is stirring to the imagination.

When, fifteen hundred years later, the source of the West African gold began to engage inquiring Arab minds, the trade had changed in one important respect. To Herodotus it had been a sea-borne trade; to the Arabs it was an overland trade between the Sudan and the Maghrib al-Aqsa. Dumb barter, however, was still its chief characteristic, and its dependence on women remained. That the oversea and overland trades, in spite of the lapse of 1,500 years, had these two points in common suggests that they had also a common origin, that each derived its gold from the same goldfields. We are unlikely ever to know whether this was so, for though it seems that the Carthaginians were trading somewhere on the coast of southern Morocco, we have no idea how the gold came to be brought to the coast. Nor does it matter to our present purpose, which is to discover where the overland trade had its origin. As everyone said it was in Wangara, our first need is to establish where this mysterious country was.

Gold has been found in many parts of West Africa, but our search for Wangara, which yielded gold in great quantities for a number of centuries, can be confined to the four gold-bearing districts which we know to have been exceptionally productive over long periods. These are Bambuk, which lies between the upper Senegal and the Faleme rivers; Bure, at the junction of the upper Niger with its tributary the Tinkisso; Lobi on the upper Volta; and Ashanti in the hinterland of the Gold Coast.[7]

A study of the early records of the trade enables us to narrow our choice still further. According to the anonymous author of the twelfth-century *Tohfut-al-Alabi*,

in the sands of that country [Ghana] is gold, treasure inexpressible. They have much gold, and merchants trade with salt for it, taking the salt on camels from the salt mines. They start from a town called Sijilmasa . . . and travel in the desert as it were upon the sea, having guides to pilot them by the stars or rocks in the deserts. They take provisions for six months, and when they reach Ghana they weigh their salt and sell it against a certain unit of weight of gold, and sometimes against double or more of the gold unit, according to the market and the supply.[8]

Writer after writer emphasizes the essentiality of salt to the trade. 'The business done at Taghaza', wrote Ibn Battuta in the fourteenth century, 'for all its meanness, amounts to an enormous figure in terms of hundredweights of gold-dust.'[9] Wangara was a country in which the lack of salt was chronic and it remained so for many centuries.

It was also not as remote a country as the mystery surrounding it suggested. That it was ever part of the kingdom of Ghana is uncertain, but probable. It was certainly at one time subject to Mali, because Sundiata conquered it and when he tried to convert the pagan gold-diggers to Islam they downed tools and the Mandingo got no gold.[10] It is evident, therefore, that Wangara did not lie south of the savannahs of the Sudan, for while Ghana and Mali expanded northwards into the desert and westwards towards the Atlantic, neither attempted to penetrate the belt of thick bush which separated the savannahs from the coastal rain forest in the south. Moreover, according to al-Bakri the goldfields were only eighteen days' march from Kumbi, the Ghana capital.

The lack of salt in Wangara and the country's comparative accessibility from the great markets of the Sudan clearly show that it cannot have been Ashanti. The goldfields there are too near to the coast for their supply of salt ever to have become a

serious problem* and, sunk in the forest belt, they were too far
from the Sudan to have been accessible from the north. Nevertheless, in 1819 Joseph Dupuis, who visited Kumasi on a diplomatic
mission, thought otherwise. He believed Ashanti, together with a
long coastal strip to the east of it, to be 'the true and only Wangara
known to the nations of North Africa; wonderful as it may seem,
that we should have actually colonized the country for many
ages past, without ever having known it even by name'.[12] He was
undoubtedly wrong.

So we have now only to consider the rival claims of Bambuk,
Bure and Lobi. At the beginning of the twentieth century, before
any of these countries had been touched by the European coastal
trade, they had to obtain their salt from far away in the desert,
from Taghaza and Idjil. Moreover, all three were within reach
of the principal Sudanese gold markets where in former times
the Barbary merchants used to gather. But the advantage lay
with Bambuk and Bure which were nearer to the ancient Kumbi
and, thanks to the Niger, more accessible than Lobi from Jenne
and Timbuktu. At one time, probably, both Bambuk and Bure
had been subject to Ghana, and they certainly had been to Mali:
Lobi can never have belonged to either. That Bambuk and Bure,
unlike Lobi, were almost embedded in Mandingo country is
especially significant. Besides being the name of a country, Wangara was also the name by which the Mandingo people, especially
the Soninke and Dyula branches, have long been widely known in
the Western Sudan. In the Maghrib and in Europe the gold trade
was particularly associated with the Mandingo whose wealth was
proverbial. 'There are no countries in the world richer in gold
and silver than the kingdoms of Mandinga', wrote Purchas.[13]
Long before that, in the fourteenth century, a map by Abraham
Cresques mentioned a voyage by Jaime Ferrer in quest of the
Rio do Ouro and the kingdom of Mandinga and its gold.[14]

The only early account we have of Wangara is al-Idrisi's brief
description. He said it was an island, 300 miles long and 150

---

* But not so near that the jealous middlemen could not deny access to the mines to
the European traders on the coast. 'There is no small numbers of men in Europe',
wrote William Bosman at the end of the seventeenth century, 'who believe that the
goldmines are in our power; that we, like the Spaniards in the West Indies, have
no more to do but to work them by our slaves: Though you perfectly know we have
no means of access to these treasures; nor do I believe that any of our people have
ever seen one of them: Which you will easily credit when you are informed that the
negroes esteem them sacred, and consequently take all possible care to keep us
from them.'[11]

broad, surrounded by the waters of the 'Nile'. The island was
flooded during much of the year, but when the water receded the
local negroes moved in to collect the gold it left behind, and
remained there until the water rose again.[15]

al-Idrisi did not write with the same authority as Ibn Battuta
and Leo Africanus because he had not seen the countries he described. Nevertheless, he was well informed and seldom more so
than when describing Wangara. For his description almost exactly
fits the goldfields of Bure. These goldfields, which are still
regularly exploited by the local people, are not in fact on an
island, but lie in a country so hemmed in by rivers—the Niger
and its tributaries—that it could easily be mistaken for one. The
gold is still regularly worked between the fall and rise of the floods,
from January to May, exactly as described by al-Idrisi.* Yaqut,
the twelfth-century geographer, adds another convincing detail.
The goldfields lay near a river. When the merchants from Barbary arrived at the river, they beat on big drums to summon the
local natives, who were completely naked and lived in 'holes in
the ground'.[17] These holes must have been the pits which are
still dug by the local people in their search for gold. Finally there
is the fact that a small part of the gold-bearing area is today
variously called Gbangara, Gwangara, Gangara, or Gangaran.[18]

The goldfields in Bambuk are very similar to those in Bure.
Bambuk is also a country of rivers, being bounded by the Senegal
and the Faleme, and the gold is mined in much the same way as
in Bure. But both al-Idrisi and al-Bakri mention, it will be recalled,
two gold-bearing areas, Takrur and Wangara for al-Idrisi,
Iresni and Ghiarou for al-Bakri. It would seem, then, that Wangara and Iresni, which lie more to the east, should be identified
with Bure, Takrur and Ghiarou with Bambuk.[19] But as the distance between Bambuk and Bure is not much more than a hundred and fifty miles, and as the two regions were very similar
there may well have been some confusion between the two.

Bambuk and Bure were not the only gold-producing areas in

---

* The seasonal working of this alluvial gold, which was naturally more abundant at
the beginning of the season than at the end of the previous one, gave rise to some
very odd beliefs. One, according to Yaqut, was that gold grew in the sands of
Wangara like carrots, another that it grew like coral, a third that it travelled
mysteriously underground, and a fourth was the familiar legend of gold being found
in the nests of ants which, to quote the anonymous author of the *Libro del Conosci-
miento*, were as big as cats. These ants appear on the famous thirteenth-century
Hereford Map.[16]

West Africa. The claims of Lobi also have to be considered. It will be recalled that Cadamosto, the fifteenth-century Venetian sea-captain in Portuguese service, has been remarkably successful in obtaining information from the natives. There is no better example of this than his informative account of the gold trade. Salt caravans from Taghaza, he tells us, travelled south through Timbuktu to Mali where the salt had to be transferred from the camels' backs to men's heads, the pasturage being 'very unsuitable for four-footed animals. . . . There are no quadrupeds in this country because they all die.' At Mali the great slabs of salt were broken into small pieces

so that each man carries one piece, and thus they form a great army of men on foot, who transport it a great distance . . . until they reach certain waters. . . . Having reached these waters with the salt, they proceed in this fashion: all those who have the salt pile it in rows, each marking his own. Having made these piles, the whole caravan retires half a day's journey. Then there come another race of blacks who do not wish to be seen or to speak. They arrive in large boats, from which it appears that they come from islands, and disembark. Seeing the salt, they place a quantity of gold opposite each pile, and then turn back, leaving salt and gold . . .

and so on, exactly as described by Herodotus and later authorities.

In this way [he concludes], by long and ancient custom, they carry on their trade without seeing or speaking to each other. Although it is difficult to believe this, I can testify that I have had this information from many merchants, Arab as well as Azanaghi [Sanhaja], and also from persons in whom faith can be placed.[20]

Cadamosto's account differs from others in one respect. The silent trafficking did not take place at the goldfields but at some point to which the gold was brought in boats and which lay in tsetse-fly country. But this is not material because both Bambuk-Bure and Lobi lie in 'fly' country and gold from either might have been brought in boats.

Cadamosto goes on to describe the appearance of these shy gold-diggers according to an account given by some Mandingoes who had treacherously ambushed four of them:

They were very black in colour, with well-formed bodies, a span higher than they themselves. The lower lip, more than a span in width, hung down, huge and red, over the breast, displaying the inner part glistening like blood. . . . It was thought that their lips became putrid, being in a warmer country than ours: . . .[21]

Nearly two hundred years later another European, Richard
Jobson, returned from West Africa with a similar story. He had
travelled some way up the Gambia river without discovering anything of importance, but he had returned with a new theory about
the silent trade with an invisible people.

The reason why these people will not be seene [he wrote] is for
that they are naturally borne with their lower lippe of that greatnesse it
turnes againe, and covers the greater part of their bosome, and remains
with that rawnesse on the side that hangs downe that through occasion
of the extreame heate it is still subject to putrifaction so as they have
no meanes to preserve themselves but by continuall casting salt upon
it, and this is the reason, salt is so pretious amongst them: their
countrye beeing so farre up in the land naturally yeeldes none.[22]

The similarity of the two passages is so close that the possibility
of the Englishman having plagiarized the Venetian cannot be
excluded. Both obviously refer to the use of lip discs, one of the
various forms of labret widely worn by women in Africa. The lip
disc is sometimes so big that when, for domestic or ceremonial
reasons, it is removed, the lip hangs down below the chin as
described by Cadamosto and Jobson.* Today the lip disc is not
found in Bambuk or Bure but it is still used in Lobi where it is
worn by the women of the Birifor and Lobi tribes.[23] This has led
some to conclude that the goldfields described by Cadamosto and
Jobson were in Lobi and that Lobi must therefore be the Wangara
of history.[24]

This argument is not easy to sustain. Before the tribal pattern
of Africa was stabilized by European administration it was fluid,
and migrations in obedience to political or economic needs were
frequent. It is therefore dangerous to attempt to interpret the past
in terms of the present, and unwise to assume that what is local
practice today has long been local custom. In Lobi, for example,
while the Lobi themselves seem to have been in their present
country since the fourteenth century, their neighbours the Birifor
did not arrive until the nineteenth. It is as unwise to assume that
the lip disc has always been used in Lobi as that it has never been
used in Bambuk and Bure, especially as it is frequently found in a
zone stretching right across Africa from the Atlantic to the Indian

* The British Museum has a pair of lip discs taken from the upper and lower lips
of a woman of the Sara tribe of the Territory of Chad which measure 5·1 and
6·9 inches in diameter respectively. (Mr. W. B. Fagg of the British Museum in a
letter to the author.)

Ocean, and is used by tribes as far removed as the Lobi of western Guinea and the Mawia of Mozambique.

As Cadamosto sailed no farther than the Rio Grande and Jobson only to the Gambia, it is as unlikely that either of them heard of Lobi, as it is probable that both heard of the goldfields of Bambuk and Bure. That lip discs were worn in the latter countries in their days seems a fair inference to draw from what they wrote.

Nevertheless, there are good reasons for thinking that the trans-Saharan trade drew on Lobi for some of its gold, which is far more to the point than the identify of Wangara.

Closely associated with the ancient gold workings of Lobi are numerous stone buildings, unlike anything found elsewhere in West Africa, and obviously the work of people much less primitive than the present inhabitants of the country. Who the builders were remains a problem, the solution to which could hardly fail to throw fresh light on the early days of the gold trade. Whoever they were, they were obviously important producers of gold which they were much more likely to have sold in the markets of the Sudan than on the coast. Between them and the sea lay the impenetrable forest belt and, in the heart of the forest, the Ashanti goldfields to satisfy coastal needs.[25]

It will be recalled that Leo said that gold was sometimes so abundant in Gao that traders had to return home with a third or a half of what they had brought to market. Had this gold come from Bambuk or Bure, it would inevitably have been brought down the Niger by merchants from Timbuktu or Jenne, important markets it could not by-pass. Such sophisticated traders would have known their business better than to flood the Gao market to their own detriment. Traders ignorant enough to do that must have come from elsewhere, presumably from Lobi which, so far as we know, was the only alternative source of supply available to Gao.

Clearly then, the trans-Saharan trade drew its gold from both the Bambuk-Bure and the Lobi goldfields. Which were the more important we do not know, and it does not greatly matter. While there is little room for doubt that the former were the Wangara of the Arab geographers, it may well be that Lobi was a Wangara of later times.

But in their search for the true Wangara the geographers cast much farther afield than the upper waters of the Senegal, Niger,

and Volta. To the confusion of several generations of cartographers Leo Africanus, the early sixteenth-century Moorish
traveller in the Sudan, placed Wangara in Hausa. 'Guangara',
he wrote, 'adjoineth south-easterly upon Zamfara, being very
populous, and having a king reigning over it, which maintaineth
a garrison of seven thousand archers and five hundred horsemen,
and receiveth yearly great tributes.'[26] This might mean that
Wangara was south-east of Zamfara or that Zamfara was south-
east of Wangara. The ambiguity perplexed the cartographers,
some of whom read it one way and some the other. But all, until
the end of the eighteenth century, placed Wangara in Hausa,
many hundreds of miles to the east of where it belonged, thus
greatly deepening the fog of mystery in which its identity was
wrapped.*

But Leo had more than that to say about Wangara.

> The inhabitants [he wrote] are very rich and have continual traffic
> with the nations adjoining. Southward thereof lieth a region greatly
> abounding with gold. . . . So often as the merchants of Guangara
> travel unto the aforesaid region abounding with gold, because the
> ways are so rough and difficult that their camels cannot go upon
> them, they carry their wares upon slaves' backs.

Leo's emphasis on the wealth of his Wangara shows that he
thought he was describing the Wangara of al-Idrisi: but there was
a difference. Whereas the latter was a producer of gold, Leo's
Wangara obtained it from farther south, in (as others had said)
'fly' country.

As Leo had only just come from the west, where he had seen
a good deal of the gold trade, his placing Wangara where he did
is very surprising. It is probable that the mistake arose from the
dual meaning of the name Wangara, from its application to both
a country and a people. In Hausa there have long been settlements of Mandingo who are known locally as Wangara or Wangarawa. In the nineteenth century, according to Barth,[27] they
were the principal merchants of Katsina, which is not far from
Zamfara, and they may have been important people locally in
Leo's time. While Leo was in Zamfara he probably heard of a
settlement of Wangara or Mandingo somewhere to the south.

---

* When planning his last journey down the Niger, Mungo Park expected to pass
through Nupe and Katsina before reaching Wangara.

C. Ritter and F. A. Oetzel, in their map of 1822, placed Wangara where the
Niger delta was later found to be.

This settlement may have been in the Gwari country or on the Zamfara river, where alluvial gold can still be found. Indeed, until well into the twentieth century local chiefs used to make their women wash gold in the river-beds.* Alternatively, Leo's Wangara may have been much further to the south-west in the gold-bearing areas of Ashanti or Lobi.[28] In the nineteenth century the trade-route between Hausa and Ashanti was greatly frequented, but kolanuts provided the main article of trade. This trade-route was probably established in the fifteenth century, for the Kano chronicle mentions that in the reign of Yakubu, 1452–1463, 'salt became common in Hausaland' and 'merchants from Gwanja [Gonja in northern Ghana] began coming to Katsina.'[29] But whatever the exact location of Leo's Wangara, it seems to have been confused in Leo's mind with the Wangara described by al-Idrisi.

In the middle of the sixteenth century, the problem of the identity of Wangara came near to being solved once and for all. The Portuguese sent a number of missions into the interior, to Timbuktu and to the capital of the kingdom of Mali. No detailed account of these missions has ever been found, beyond the brief reference made to them by the contemporary historian, de Barros, but it is by no means improbable that the Portuguese were able to gather a considerable amount of information about the gold trade of the interior. For the Portuguese, however, the gold-deposits of the Gold Coast provided an excellent source of supply, and there was less incentive for them to attempt to develop trade with the interior.[30]

In the seventeenth century, both the English on the Gambia and the French on the Senegal picked up information about the gold in the interior. In the 1660s a certain Colonel Vermuyden, member of an expedition financed by a group of Englishmen including James, Duke of York, went up the Gambia and claimed to have discovered a 'vast Proportion of Gold'. Twenty years later Cornelius Hodges, an English sea captain, succeeded in reaching the gold areas of Bambuk, only to find that famine in the surrounding country had led to the temporary abandonment of the mines. A more extensive exploration of Bambuk was made by a

* On the other hand, Gangara, which in Hausa means a declivity, is a common place-name in north-west Hausa. Both Sir Richmond Palmer and Mr. F. de F. Daniel have suggested to the author that Leo's Guangara was possibly a Gangara in the district of Katsina Laka, north-west of Zaria.

Frenchman, Sieur Compagnon, in 1714. At this time the French, moving up the Senegal, had succeeded in establishing a trading post, Fort St. Joseph, on the borders of Bambuk. But though the French maintained this post for forty years, the amount of gold which they acquired was disappointingly meagre.[31]

Mungo Park, in the course of his first expedition to West Africa (1795–7), was able to obtain a considerable amount of information on the production of gold in the country between the Faleme and the Niger.[32] Thirty years later René Caillié came near to reaching the country of Bure. He learnt that Bure contained 'many very abundant gold mines' but gathered that the natives who worked them were 'ignorant of the extent of these riches'.[33] It seems to have occurred to neither Park nor Caillié that the gold-bearing areas they had seen or heard about represented the Wangara of history for which men had searched so diligently for centuries past. This was probably because by the beginning of the nineteenth century the goldfields were approaching exhaustion and production was of small account.* The silent trade, too, which would certainly have arrested their attention, was no longer practised in the area.†

Meanwhile explorers and geographers still speculated on the identity and position of Wangara. Lyon, who got no further than Fezzan in his attempt to reach the Sudan from Tripoli, inquired about it. What he learnt shows how easy it was for Leo to be misled by the wide application of the name, and how closely people in the heart of the Sahara as late as the nineteenth century associated Wangara with the silent trade in gold.

Wangara [he tells us] is a place of which we cannot obtain any decided account; it is, however, generally supposed to be a low country, and sometimes inundated. One person states it to be twenty days south of Tembuctoo; another places it south of Kashna [Katsina];

---

* At the beginning of the nineteenth century J. G. Jackson found gold still flowing fairly freely into Morocco, and it was still known as Wangara gold. He mentions 'twisted gold rings of Wangara' (*An Account of the Empire of Morocco*, London, 1814, p. 290). Later he quoted an invoice dated 1790 and sent from Timbuktu to a merchant of Fez which included '500 skins Tibber Wangaree, or gold-dust of Wangara' and '100 Sibikat deheb Wangaree, Wangara gold in bars' (*An Account of Timbuctoo and Housa*, London, 1820, p. 347). According to Rohlfs, however, by the middle of the century the trade was of little importance.

† In fact it seems likely that the silent trade in Bambuk and Bure, both areas comparatively easily accessible to Muslim traders, was not practised after the beginning of the eleventh century. The silent trade described by Portuguese writers was carried on in the more remote gold-bearing areas.[34]

and many even assert, that it is beyond Waday: but it is quite impossible from the varied accounts given of it, to form any idea as to its actual situation, or even existence.

Should there really be three places so called, may it not be probable that it is a general name for marshes and swamps? In the one spoken of behind Tembuctoo, the capital is said to be Battagoo, and is a large town, near which much gold is reported to be found. An invisible nation, according to our informant, inhabit near this place, and are said to trade by night. Those who come to traffic for their gold lay their merchandise in heaps and retire. In the morning, they find a great quantity of gold dust placed against every heap, which, if they think sufficient, they leave the goods; if not, they let both remain until more of the precious ore is added. These traders in gold dust are by many supposed to be devils who are very fond of red cloth, the favourite article of exchange.[35]

A few years later similar inquiries led the explorer Major Dixon Denham to what was clearly the right conclusion. 'All gold countries', he wrote, 'as well as any people coming from the gold country . . . are called Wangara.'[36]

*   *   *   *   *

To this historical account of the search for Wangara one must add a modern epilogue, for gold still plays a part in the economy of West Africa. Today, however, the only country to export gold is Ghana, and most of the Ghanaian gold is mined 'from shafts of up to 3,700 feet in depth'.[37] But gold-mining is still carried on in Bure, the ancient Wangara, and plays an important part in the local economy of the area. There are between twelve and fifteen thousand full-time gold workers, and every year another hundred thousand come into the area from the outside. Production is estimated at 30,000 ounces a year, compared with exports from Ghana of 851,000 ounces (1958).[38]

In 1960, two members of the University of Ghana undertook an 'expedition to Wangara'. They visited a gold-mining area near the Guinea–Mali frontier. The vivid and precise description they have given of the methods employed by the local miners helps to amplify the accounts that have come down from medieval writers.

Parallel rows of holes about two and a half feet in diameter, up to about forty feet in depth and three to five feet apart, are cut through the hard lateritic crust to the alluvium below. Once underground, the miners join up each hole with its neighbours until the entire area is undermined by a grid of tunnels. The soft gold-bearing alluvium, which is recognized by the presence of quartz pebbles resulting from the breakdown of the original gold-bearing quartzite, is removed by the miners with a sharp, short-handled pick. The pick is of necessity short-handled since the galleries which connect the various shafts are only about three feet high. In these galleries the miner works in a crouched position with water up to his waist. After removal, the pay-dirt is placed in a large calabash and floated along the gallery to the bottom of the shaft where another miner carries out the preliminary washing. After this preliminary washing the pay-dirt is transferred to a second calabash (the first being returned to the face worker) and hauled to the surface, where it is heaped in piles to await the arrival of the women in the afternoon. It is the women who carry out the final wash, standing knee-deep in pools of water close to the mining shafts. From each calabash of pay-dirt, swirled swiftly and dexterously around, emerge perhaps a few grains of gold dust. Each group of miners seems to be a fairly stable and well-balanced team made up of those who cut and mine, those who haul the pay dirt to the surface, the wives and daughters who 'wash', a smith who maintains the picks, the *chef du mine* who directs operations, collects the daily yield of gold and sells it to the itinerant merchants who in turn supply the gold-smiths of nearby towns.

This is apparently as it has always been. This was how the gold was mined that flowed through the medieval empires of Mali and Ghana, across the Sahara to, say, Sijilmassa; from Sijilmassa to, say, Ceuta; from Ceuta to, say, Genoa; from Genoa to Heaven knows where.[39]

THE RISE AND FALL OF THE
SONGHAI EMPIRE

15

The Songhai

*'The language of this region is called Sungai, and the inhabitants are black
people, and most friendly unto strangers.'*—LEO AFRICANUS.

THE middle course of the Niger is interrupted at two points by
rapids, at Kénié (below Bamako) and at Bussa, where Mungo
Park was drowned. Between these two points there lie a thousand
miles of navigable waterway, which include the great northward
bend of the Niger. The river here is generally fringed with a
luxuriant growth of *borgu*, a nutritious aquatic grass, to which the
people bring their cattle from great distances. The banks are much
broken by creeks and inlets, and the course of the river is studded
with islands. North and south is an immense area of desert, the
south being just as much the home of predatory Tuareg as the
north. Throughout the turbulent history of the Western Sudan
the middle Niger has always been the resort of the oppressed.
The countless hidden creeks and inaccessible islets provided security for fugitives, and the *borgu* food and shelter for their herds.

The Songhai were made up of a number of different groups,
sedentary cultivators, some of whom appear to have been related
to the Mossi, hunters (Gow), and fishermen (Sorko) who moved
up the Niger from somewhere further to the east and eventually
spread to Timbuktu and the great lakes beyond it. Sometime
before A.D. 900 an alien dynasty, known as Za and of uncertain
origin, was established among the Songhai. As-Sadi, the Timbuktu historian, records how the first Za, Alayaman, slew the
Songhai river-god.[1]*

* The French historian, Delafosse, stated that the Za were of Lemta Berber origin.
This was only a conjecture. As-Sadi states that Za-alayman came from Yemen and
adds that his descendants were tall, strong, well-built men but makes no mention
of the colour of their skin.[2]

The Songhai capital was originally at Kukiya (modern Bentia), which lies at the easternmost end of the navigable stretch of the middle Niger. Later the capital was moved to Gao, a town known to Arab geographers from the ninth century. Gao was situated on the left bank of the Niger, where it is joined by the Tilemsi valley coming down from the heart of the Sahara.

A few days' march up the Tilemsi valley, in the mountainous district of Adrar of the Iforas, was Tadmekka, an old and important desert market. The Arabs called it as-Suk, The Market, the name by which its extensive ruins are still known. In the eleventh century it was trading with Kairwan and Ghadames in the north, and with the Sudan in the south, and its currency was unstamped gold. To the east of Gao, and also out in the desert, lay the third important market of this part of the interior, the copper-mining town of Takedda. Situated on a great navigable highway* and within easy reach of such important markets as Tadmekka and Takedda, Gao was doubly assured of a commanding position in the trade of the Western Sudan.[3]

Gao, as described by al-Bakri in the eleventh century, consisted of two towns, 'that of the King and that of the Muslims', a fact that has been confirmed by recent archaeological research. The mass of the people were pagans, but the ruler was a Muslim; according to as-Sadi, the ruling dynasty had been converted to Islam in A.D. 1009. The rulers were in touch with the larger world of Islam; on their accession, so al-Bakri was informed, they received a Quran from the Ummayad Caliph of Cordoba.[4]

We know very little of the fortunes of the Songhai between the eleventh and fourteenth centuries, but it is evident from the importance which Mansa Musa attached to the capture of Gao that they must have prospered. For a century after the liberation of the city by Ali Kolen and his brother, the Songhai of Gao had to content themselves with defending their freedom against the Mandingo of Mali. The power of the latter, however, was steadily waning, and the Tuareg, led by Akil ag Malwal, drove them out of Timbuktu. This opened the way for the Songhai to recover the

* Had the middle Niger been better supplied with timber the river would have been more valuable to the Songhai. Most of the way from Timbuktu to Gao the desert impinges on both banks of the river, and there are few trees except the fan palm, very poor material of which perforce nearly all the canoes of the middle Niger are built. On occasions, as when Askia Daud was building a mosque in Timbuktu timber was imported from downstream.

city which traditionally was theirs, but only Tuareg avarice and treachery made it possible.

When the Tuareg drove out the Mandingo, they appointed a Sanhaja named Umar to govern the city. His chief emolument was to be one-third of the taxes he collected, the rest going to his retainers and supporters. However, his desert overlord, Akil, took to descending on the city just as the taxes were coming in, and carrying off for himself the governor's share. When, to make matters worse, Akil and his followers started forcing their way into the houses of the people and violating their women, Umar sent a message secretly to the Songhai offering to hand the city over to them if they would come to its deliverance.

The king of Songhai at this time was Sonni Ali, an able and ambitious ruler, who was not slow to seize the opportunity Umar had offered him. Placing himself at the head of his cavalry, he at once marched on Timbuktu. When Akil and Umar saw the Songhai host approaching, the former immediately fled to Walata, closely followed by the timorous scholars of the Sankore mosque. Umar, who had expected a rich reward for his treachery, suddenly panicked and also fled. Sonni Ali entered Timbuktu in January 1468 and put a great number of its citizens to the sword.

The people of Timbuktu had black skins, but much Berber blood flowed in their veins, and so proud were they of it that they scorned the negroid Songhai as uncouth savages, although their rulers may have been of Berber origin. Sonni Ali, in whose features there was probably little trace of northern blood, was passionately hated by as-Sadi, the historian of the Western Sudan, who calls him such names as master-tyrant, libertine, and scoundrel, and presents him as one who gloried in the massacre of the learned and pious.[5] It may be that Sonni Ali merited the opprobrium which as-Sadi heaped upon him, and it is certain that he was a Muslim in name only. But he could excuse his ruthlessness to the people of Timbuktu on the grounds of their friendship with the Tuareg, the traditional enemies of the Songhai. From the earliest times, the riverain villages had been a constant prey to the nomads, against whose incursions they were defenceless and whose desert haunts they could not assail.

Sonni Ali's next success was the capture of Jenne, which, according to tradition, had successfully withstood ninety-nine assaults by the kings of Mali. Jenne had been founded in the thirteenth century by the Soninke, who built it on the site of an earlier settle-

ment on a backwater of the Bani river. It was the metropolis of
the fertile and populous region of rivers, lakes, and swamps above
Timbuktu through which the waters of the Niger and the Bani
percolate before uniting to make their great sweep to the east.
According to as-Sadi, it was one of the principal markets of
Africa where one met merchants from the Maghrib bartering salt
of Taghaza for the gold of the south. 'It is because of this blessed
town', he wrote, 'that caravans come to Timbuktu from all points
of the horizon.' It is a convincing tribute, for as-Sadi was intensely
jealous of the reputation of his own city of Timbuktu, of which
Jenne was a rival in both trade and culture.[6]

The fame of Timbuktu and the glamour surrounding it—the
one attributable to the rather highly coloured picture painted by
Leo Africanus in the sixteenth century, and the other to the
hysterical outpourings of certain writers in the twentieth—have
obscured the claims of Jenne to recognition as a commercial and
intellectual centre of the first importance. Whereas Timbuktu
was devoid of natural defences and at the mercy of any invader,
Jenne was surrounded by a network of waterways which, besides
making it easily accessible, gave it the security which for 800 years
attracted the merchants and men of letters of the Maghrib. In
Timbuktu trade and learning were constantly interrupted by
desert politics; in Jenne, on the other hand, they took deep root,
and formed a nucleus from which the culture of the Mediterranean
littoral was constantly being spread into the surrounding
country.

Sonni Ali prevailed over Jenne only at the cost of a siege lasting
several years. The rise and fall of the waters probably made complete investment impossible, for we know that the besiegers had
constantly to change their positions. Famine afflicted besieged and
besiegers alike, but just as the latter reached the limit of their
endurance and were about to withdraw the town capitulated. On
this occasion Sonni Ali's treatment of the vanquished, who were
not friends of the hated Tuareg, was as merciful as it had been
harsh at Timbuktu. There is doubt about the date of the fall of
Jenne, but it was probably 1473.

The success of Sonni Ali's western campaign had excited the
jealousy of the Mossi of Yatenga, whose raid on Timbuktu shortly
after Mansa Musa's death will be recalled. In 1480, with even
greater daring, they marched north-west into the desert and captured Walata after a month's siege. After sacking the town they

withdrew, carrying off with them a great number of women and children, and an immense quantity of booty.

Meanwhile Sonni Ali, still obsessed with his hatred of the Tuareg, was planning vengeance on Akil and the rest of those who had eluded him at the fall of Timbuktu and were still in Walata, having survived the Mossi raid. He planned to destroy Akil and to add Walata to his empire. To accomplish this, he conceived the astonishing project of digging a canal all the way from Lake Fagbine to Walata, a distance of about 200 miles. In the fifteenth century the lake may have extended as far west as Bassikunu, which would have reduced the distance somewhat, but even so one can but marvel at a man of Sonni Ali's calibre planning so fantastic a project. We can only suppose that his experiences during the siege of Jenne had so convinced him of the military advantages of a navigable waterway that he thought the building of a canal the surest way of making Walata an integral part of his empire. Whatever the reasons, the gigantic task was put in hand. The threat of an attack by the Mossi provided a timely excuse for its early abandonment.

The Mossi threat was no idle one, and they had to be driven back. Finding Sonni Ali too strong for them, they next directed their inexhaustible martial ardour against the Mandingo of Mali who, hard pressed by the Songhai in the north and by the Fulani of Futa in the west, appealed to some new and powerful neighbours for help. These were the Portuguese who, as the result of the remarkable series of voyages inspired and directed by Prince Henry, had now established trading settlements on the west coast of Africa. The most northerly of these settlements was at Arguin, whence the Portuguese had penetrated inland as far as Wadan and established a trading post there. They wisely refused to go to the help of the Mandingo.[7]

We next hear of Sonni Ali back in Timbuktu, once more tormenting its people and provoking another exodus into the desert. But they had not long to wait for relief from the tyranny which had so long oppressed them. It came with Sonni Ali's death in 1492.

During a reign of twenty-seven years Sonni Ali had transformed a petty kingdom into a formidable empire which dominated a great part of the Western Sudan. Apart from his energy, enterprise, and administrative ability, without which he could not have achieved so much in the political field, there was nothing in his

character to endear him to his people. By most of his subjects
he was held in the deepest awe, because of his skill as a magician;
he was said to have been able to transform himself into a vulture,
and to possess a charm which could render his soldiers invisible.[8]
He was long remembered for his cruelty, but his worst crimes
were usually followed by deep remorse, and he was sometimes
capable of a generous action as, for example, at the fall of Jenne.
On another occasion, he astonished the notables of Timbuktu,
whom he usually treated with the utmost brutality, by giving
them a number of beautiful Fulani girls, some of whom became
the legal wives of their masters; as-Sadi was descended from one
such union.

The successor to the throne was Sonni Ali's son, who quickly
lost it to one of his father's lieutenants, with whose accession the
ancient dynasty came to an end. The usurper was Muhammed
Ture, a negro Soninke who took the title of Askia, by which the
dynasty he established became known, he himself being Askia
Muhammed I. The new ruler was endowed with fine qualities
which made him worthy of the position he had usurped. He had
a genius for political organization and a profound respect for
religion and learning. Under Askia there was at once a Muslim
revival, and the *literati* were accorded a status they had never
before enjoyed. In Sonni Ali's time they had been the most
oppressed section of the community, but now they were the most
favoured. With the revival in learning went, as always in the
Sudan, a great stimulus to foreign trade which brought added
wealth to Gao and Timbuktu.

Soon after his accession, Askia set out on a pilgrimage to Mecca.
His caravan included an escort of 500 cavalry and 1,000 infantry,
and with him he carried 300,000 pieces of gold from the treasure
left by Sonni Ali. Of this sum a third was set aside for the charitable foundations of the holy cities. In spite of Askia's pilgrimage
being conducted on a scale comparable with that of Mansa Musa'
a century and a half before, it did not attract the same attention
in the Middle East (for all we know it attracted none). This was
most likely due to Askia being less arrogant and more orthodox
than Mansa Musa, whose disregard for the conventions probably
attracted as much public comment as his ostentatious display of
wealth. Whereas Mansa Musa could hardly be persuaded to pay
the customary courtesies to the sultan of Egypt, Askia asked the
Abbassid caliph of Egypt to invest him with the 'Caliphate of the

lands of the Blacks', a move designed to extend his prestige among the Muslims of his empire.[9]

Askia quickly turned his mind to extending the frontiers of his dominions, which comprised the whole of the great territory Sonni Ali had ruled over. His early campaigns were mostly undertaken, as might have been expected of one just returned from the *Hadj*, in the name of Islam and were directed against his pagan neighbours to the west and south. In the west he seized much territory belonging to Mali, the greatness of which was now no more than a dim memory, and he reached nearly to the Atlantic. But the most important of Askia's campaigns came some years later when he conquered Hausa, which lay beyond his eastern frontier.

The Hausa States extended eastwards from the Niger towards Lake Chad, and were well-watered and fertile. They were the home of a negroid people of varied origins who were, and still are, distinguished for great qualities. Industrious farmers and enterprising traders, they were particularly noted for the skill of their craftsmen, especially their weavers, dyers, smiths, and leather-workers. They lived in walled towns and villages. Of their towns Kano at least was of sufficient importance to have attracted Barbary merchants to settle there. But Hausa lacked natural defences, and its peace-loving inhabitants were too individualistic to be capable of united action. The country, therefore, fell an easy prey to the invading Songhai, who met serious resistance only at Kano.

With the conquest of Hausa, Askia added a rich and populous country to his already vast dominions, but it brought the Songhai into fresh conflict with their traditional enemies, the Tuareg, whose habit it was to raid the Hausa peasantry in the same way that their kinsmen in the west raided the Niger villages. Tuareg aggressiveness had always presented the Songhai with an apparently insoluble problem. No way had yet been devised for stopping or even curbing, their incursions, because effective retaliation was impossible. It was useless to pursue across the desert people too mobile to be caught and able to live where all others must die of hunger and thirst. The conquest of Hausa aggravated the Tuareg problem, but, as Askia was quick to see, it opened the way to a partial solution. As, in Roman times, the Garamantes had been vulnerable only in Fezzan, where they had permanent settlements, so were the Tuareg assailable only in their settlements in Air or Asben, especially in their town of Agades which was within striking distance of Hausa.* So Askia next conquered Air and, to make doubly sure trouble should not recur, he drove the Tuareg out into the surrounding desert. But, like the French in the early twentieth century, Askia had yet to learn that the surest way to lay up trouble for the future is to deprive nomads of their precious grazing grounds.

On his two eastern campaigns, against Hausa and Air, Askia had been accompanied by Kanta, king of Kebbi,† a small kingdom lying between Hausa and the Niger, and a vassal state of Songhai. After the Air campaign Kanta, dissatisfied with his share of the spoils (so it was said), rebelled against Askia and declared Kebbi independent. For the ruler of so small a kingdom to defy so formidable an overloard demanded great courage, but Kanta was taking a calculated risk. None knew better the weaknesses of the Songhai army and the improbability of its being able to assail him successfully in the great Kebbi marshes. Added to this strategic advantage was his confidence in the unswerving support of his brave and resolute people, who were blindly devoted to him. His confidence proved justified. From behind the seven stone walls of Surame, his capital, the ruins of which still stand as an impressive memorial to its founder, Kanta successfully defied the Songhai whose only attempt to destroy him resulted in their utter defeat.

Kanta's real danger lay not in the west, where his native marshes protected him, but in the east, where a formidable neighbour, Mai Ali of Bornu, was viewing with alarm the rise of a kingdom capable of defying the Songhai. Between Kebbi and Bornu there was no natural barrier, only the rolling plains of Hausa, across which Mai Ali now led his army to break the growing power of Kebbi. Like Askia, he was defeated before the walls of Surame and had to retreat hurriedly with the Kebbawa at his

---

* The first Tuareg to establish themselves in Air were the Lemta who had come from Bornu. Their predecessors in Air had been the negroid Gobirawa whose capital was T'in Shaman, near where Agades was subsequently built. The Lemta and Gobirawa lived peacefully together until the arrival of other Tuareg, Kel Geres and Sanhaja, who drove out the Gobirawa or absorbed them. That was early in the fifteenth century. Air then became an independent Tuareg kingdom with an amenokal or sultan of its own. If, as the Tuareg of Air allege, their first amenokal was appointed from Stambul he must have been a Christian Byzantine and not a Muslim Turk. As his name was Yunis or John and his wife's Ibuzahil or Izubahil, which are very like Isabel, this is less improbable than it might otherwise appear.[10]

† In his *Infaq al-Maisur*, Muhammad Bello of Sokoto describes Kanta as a slave of the Fulani. (E. J. Arnett, *The Rise of the Sokoto Fulani*, Kano, 1929, p. 13.)

heels. Kanta is remembered less for his defeat of the Bornu army than for his successful defiance of the Songhai, which remains the most cherished tradition of his people.*

When he drove the Tuareg out of Air, Askia planted there a colony of Songhai who settled mostly in and around Agades. In spite of their isolation and the turmoil and upheavals of the coming centuries, the Songhai influence in Agades proved remarkably persistent. In the 1850s the language of the town was still Songhai, though, as Barth noted, it had been 'greatly influenced by inter-course with the Berbers'. As late as the 1920s there were still a few old men living in Agades who could speak a dialect of Songhai.[11]

In the closing years of his life, Askia was overwhelmed by tragedy. Three of his sons, led by the eldest, Musa, rebelled against him. Now an old man and worn out in the service of his country, he summoned his brother Yahia to his aid. But the sons killed Yahia, marched into Gao and forced Askia to abdicate in favour of Musa. Thus ended in 1528 the reign of perhaps the greatest monarch that ever ruled in the Western Sudan. His people were less indebted to him for the vast empire he gave them, than for his teaching them organized government by which alone could security and prosperity be achieved. These two conditions of life were found wherever he ruled. In a later chapter we shall turn to Leo's graphic description of the Sudan under Askia the Great, as he came to be called. But all did not end with his abdication. Unhappily for this truly great man, there lay before him years of misery, degradation, and despair.

Musa, a bloodthirsty tyrant, was assassinated by his outraged subjects. He was succeeded by Askia Bengan Korei, the leader of the disastrous attack on Kebbi, who evicted the old Askia from the royal palace, where Musa had allowed his father to stay, and banished him to an island in the Niger. He was released six years later, when another palace revolution brought another of his sons, Ismail, to the throne, but died shortly afterwards in 1538.

In extent at least, the Songhai empire was greater than either Ghana or Mali. But it suffered from grave weaknesses. The ruling dynasty was unable to establish a peaceful system of succession, consequently its history, from the time of Askia Muhammad's

* The Kebbawa claim that Kanta's brazen canoe still lies in the marsh below Birnin Kebbi. Kanta had a worthy descendant in the gallant old Sarkin Kebbi Samma of Argungu whom the British, after their conquest of Sokoto, found sturdily holding his own against the repeated aggressions of the Fulani whose twin capitals, Sokoto and Gwandu, were only a few miles from his own.

deposition, is made up of fratricidal struggles, palace revolutions, and *coups-d'état*. Then again, Songhai rule must have been heartily detested by many of the subject people who had to bear the weight of its oppression. Finally, as Jean Rouch has suggested, the rulers' support and encouragement of Islam may have been a source of weakness, for it tended only to accentuate the gulf between the favoured townspeople and the farmers in the bush.[12] But there can be no doubt that the tribute which flowed into the treasury at Gao as a result of the Askia's conquests gave a great stimulus to trade, brought merchants and occasional men of learning to the Sudan, and so increased the stimulating intercourse with the world of the Maghrib.

Among the learned men who came to Gao in the reign of Askia Muhammad was a certain Muhammad al-Maghili, a native of Tlemcen. In his youth al-Maghili lived in Tuat, in the north-central Sahara, where he quickly won renown as a preacher. He is said to have been the apostle of Islam to the Tuareg, by whom his name is still honoured. The massacre of a colony of Jews in Tuat was attributed to the fervour of his preaching which may also have been the cause of similar massacres of Jews in Gorarin and Tuggurt at about the same time. But the austerity of the code which al-Maghili preached was as unacceptable to the desert people as that of Ibn Yasin had been five centuries before. He was driven out of Tuat and fled southward through Air to Hausa, preaching on the way and adding to his reputation.[13]

A copy of a work by al-Maghili was discovered in the 1930s in Katsina. A treatise on government, appropriately named *The Obligations of Princes*, it was written for the king of Kano and reveals high ideals and the writer's keen appreciation of the practical difficulties of government. 'The veiling of the king from his subjects is the source of all mischief' is a refrain it often repeats. By contrast, a notable passage reads:

> The sojourn of a prince in the city breeds all manner of trouble and harm. The bird of prey abides in open and wild places. Vigorous is the cock as he struts round his domains. The eagle can only win his realm by firm resolve, and the cock's voice is strong as he masters the hens. Ride, then, the horses of resolution upon the saddles of prudence.[14]

In 1502 al-Maghili left Kano for Gao, where news reached him that Jews who had survived the massacre in Tuat had avenged themselves by murdering his son. In his grief and rage, he endeavoured to persuade Askia to expel the Jews from Gao, but anyway for a time, he failed. A few years later, however, Askia closed Timbuktu to Jewish traders and forbade his subjects to traffic with them. We know little more of al-Maghili. He died in 1532 and his influence endured long after his death. Indeed, there are still places in the Western Sudan which men hold sacred because he worshipped there four centuries ago.

al-Maghili was followed to the Sudan by a better known visitor from the north. This was Leo Africanus, on whose account of the country geographers and cartographers remained dependent for almost all they knew of the interior of Africa for the next 300 years.

16

Leo Africanus: an Early Sixteenth-Century Traveller in the Sudan

'Moreouer as touching his exceeding great Trauels *. . . I maruell much how euer he should haue escaped so manie thousands of imminent dangers. . . . How often was he in hazard to haue beene captiued, or to haue had his throte cut by the prouling Arabians, and wilde Mores? And how hardly manie times escaped he the Lyons greedie mouth, and the deuouring iawes of the Crocodile?'—* JOHN PORY.

IN 1518 an Arab galley was captured by Christian corsairs off Jerba, the Island of the Lotus Eaters, just as it was approaching the Tunisian shore. Among those on board was an unusually intelligent Moor who, although still in his twenties, had travelled widely in countries then unknown to Europe. So, instead of selling the young man into slavery, which was then the common fate of captives, the corsairs carried him to Rome and presented him to Pope Leo X, hoping thereby to turn him to better account than they would be able to do in the great slave markets of Pisa and Genoa.

Leo X was a Medici, a son of Lorenzo the Magnificent. He won the praise of his contemporaries for his munificence to men of letters, and the respect of posterity for his patronage of the arts, if for nothing else. All with claims to intellectual distinction were warmly welcomed to his court. Nevertheless, nothing could have seemed less probable than that a young Moor taken from a galley should become an honoured member of the papal court, and his 'discovery' the Pope's chief contribution to letters and science. The young man's name was al-Hassan ibn Muhammad al-Wazzani, but he probably preferred to be called al-Fasi, the man of Fez, the great seat of learning to which he owed his education. As he spoke Spanish it was not difficult for the Pope to discover his literary attainments and, much more important, his astonishing knowledge of remote and inaccessible African kingdoms.* The Pope immediately freed the young man, granted him a pension and secured his conversion to Christianity. At his baptism he gave him his own names, Giovanni Leone, from which he became commonly known as Leo Africanus.

When he was captured, Leo Africanus had with him a rough draft in Arabic of the work which made him famous, *The History and Description of Africa and the Notable Things therein contained*. He completed this work in the Italian language in 1526, three years after his patron's death. In 1550 the manuscript fell into the hands of Ramusio who published it in his collection of *Voyages and Travels*. It was translated into English by John Pory, a scholarly friend of Richard Hakluyt, and was published in London in 1600.

Apart from his African travels and the circumstances of his arrival in Rome, we know little of the life of Leo. Here and there in his published work we find a clue to his early history and his travels outside Africa, but these are not always very helpful. 'For mine owne part,' he tells us, 'when I heare the Africans evile spoken of, I wile affirme my selfe to be one of Granada, and when I perceive the nation of Granada to be discommended, then will I professe my selfe to be an African.'[1] Such candour is certainly engaging, but it is sadly provoking to the student wanting to know where he was born.

It has, however, now been established beyond reasonable doubt that Leo was born in Granada in 1493 or 1494 of well-to-do

---

* At this time, little or nothing appears to have been known in Europe of the work of Arab geographers. A Latin translation of al-Idrisi was published in Paris in 1619, but translations of the works of other medieval Arab geographers did not appear until the nineteenth century. Cadamosto's account of his voyage to West Africa, which contained some information on the interior, was first published in Vicenza in 1507 in the collection *Paesi novamente retrovati*. The maps of the fourteenth-century Majorcan cartographers can only have been known to a very small circle of scholars.

Moorish parents.[2] For a short time before his birth the family had
been subjects of Ferdinand and Isabella and had therefore experienced Christian rule in its most benevolent form. The day had
not arrived when Cardinal Ximenes would poison Isabella's mind
with the foul heresy that to keep faith with heretics was to break
faith with God. Before then, the infant and his parents had joined
the stream of cultured emigrants who were continually drifting
from Granada to Fez and other African centres of Muslim culture.
Arrived in Fez, they found themselves part of a large community
of recent exiles from Spain who were settling in large numbers
in the city and its neighbourhood.

Morocco was in a state of political disintegration. The Portuguese were in occupation of much of the coast and endeavouring
to extend their influence inland. The south was in the hands of
the Saʿadian Sharifs, under whose dominion Fez was shortly
to fall. At the end of the fifteenth century, however, Fez was still
enjoying great commercial prosperity and was at the peak of its
fame as a seat of learning, its mosques and libraries being the
resort of students from many parts of the Muslim world. It was
therefore the most natural haven for the exiles from Granada.

Leo's father, a man of wealth and consequence, was accorded
in Fez the same honour that he had enjoyed in Granada, together
with unusual facilities for educating his son under some of the
most distinguished scholars of the Muslim world. Of these opportunities the child took full advantage, soon proving himself to
be exceptionally intelligent. He started earning his own living at
a very early age as a notary in the Moristane, the Hospital for
Aliens in Fez. But it was not long before he began the wanderings
which brought him fame. As he travelled from town to town in
the Maghrib, his knowledge of the law brought him plenty of
work. Sometimes he acted as a *qadi* or judge, but more usually as
a clerk or notary to merchants and government officials. Occasionally he traded on his own account. At times he served the sultan
on diplomatic missions; at others he lived by hawking verses of
his own composition. This varied life brought him adventures
and took him far afield, even as far as Constantinople and Tartary.
His many coastal voyages and inland journeys in the company of
merchants familiarized him with the length and breadth of Barbary and gave him an intimate knowledge of its trade.

His account of his travels in North Africa clearly shows that
the Sudan trade played a predominant part in the economic life

of the Maghrib. There is frequent mention of merchants doing 'great traffic into the land of the Negroes' and Leo mentions a score or more of towns covering the whole length of Barbary, from the Atlantic in the west to Tripoli in the east, which were engaged in the trans-Saharan trade. It is noteworthy that the most important, such as Fez, Sijilmasa, Tlemcen, Wargla, and Ghadames, were inland towns, the trade being in the hands of middlemen who prevented the coast merchants, with whom the Christians traded, from direct participation in the trans-Saharan traffic.

The principal goods exported to the Western Sudan were European trade goods (especially cloth), sugar from Sus in southern Morocco, wearing apparel, brass vessels, horses, and books. The principal commodities for which these goods were exchanged were gold, slaves, and civet. Leo mentions a present given by the sultan of Fez which consisted almost entirely of produce of the Sudan:

> Fiftie men slaves and fiftie women slaves brought out of the land of the Negros, tenne eunuchs, twelve camels, one Giraffa, sixteene civet-cats, one pound of civet, a pound of amber [ambergris], and almost six hundreth skins of a certaine beast called by them Elamt [addax gazelle] whereof they make their shieldes, everie skin being worth at Fez eight ducates;* twentie of the men slaves cost twentye ducates a peece, and so did fifteene of the women slaves; every eunuch was valued at fortie, every camel at fiftie, and every civet-cat at two hundreth ducats; and a pound of civet and amber is solde at Fez for threescore ducates.[3]

Happily for posterity, Leo was to see for himself the countries from which the slaves, the eunuchs, the gold, and the civet all came.

The most important events in Leo's life in the eyes of his European contemporaries, though probably not in his own, were his journeys to the Western Sudan, for they enabled him to give to Europe the first detailed account of the interior of Africa, of which men's conception was so blurred that they could not distinguish fact from legend.

His narrative was particularly valuable because it described the country just when Songhai had been raised to its political and economic zenith by the conquests of Askia the Great, in the wake

---

* The Tuareg make their shields of addax skins. The horns are said to have been used by the Greeks to make their lyres.

of whose triumphant armies Leo travelled. He was thus able to add to a narrative of great geographical value a picture of one of the greatest political organizations which the negro has ever achieved.

The occasion of his first journey was a mission, of which Leo was a member and his uncle the leader, sent to Songhai by the Sharif of Fez, Mulai Muhammad al-Kaim, the founder of the Sa'adian dynasty. The date appears to have been about 1510, when Leo was still under twenty years of age. His second journey was made three years later, possibly in the capacity of a merchant. On both occasions he took the Sijilmasa-Taghaza road to Timbuktu.

After crossing the Atlas and passing through Sijilmasa, which by this time was in decay, the mission plunged into the desert. Their first stopping place of any consequence was Taghaza, Leo's description of which we will come to later. Suffice it to say here that he found it exceedingly disagreeable, and that he and his companions were thankful to reach Walata in safety and with the worst perils of the journey behind them. In Walata, which was the most northerly outpost of Songhai, Leo and his uncle met Sudanese in their own country for the first time. Most of the early travellers in the Sahara, Christian and Muslim alike, recorded their relief at finding themselves amongst friendly negroes whose kindly welcome to strangers was in such pleasant contrast to the surly arrogance of the desert nomads. Leo was of their number. 'The language of this region is called Sungai [Songhai]', Leo noted, 'and the inhabitants are blacke people and most friendly unto strangers'.[4]

The route the mission followed after leaving Walata is uncertain, but they probably went straight to Timbuktu. At this time Timbuktu is estimated to have had a population of 25,000. It was a considerably smaller town than Gao, the capital of the Songhai empire, but its drier climate made it a more congenial centre for Maghribi traders in the Sudan.[5]

To the sophisticated travellers from the north Timbuktu presented a mean appearance, the houses being mere 'cottages built of chalk and covered with thatch' to which the buildings put up by as-Sahili for Mansa Musa were in striking contrast:

howbeit there is a most stately temple to be seene, the wals whereof are made of stone and lime; and a princely palace also built by a most excellent workeman of Granada.

Here are many shops of artificers and merchants, and especially of such as weave linnen and cotton cloth. And hither do the Barbarie merchants bring cloth of Europe. All the women of this region except maid-servants go with their faces covered, and sell all necessarie victuals. The inhabitants, and especially strangers there residing, are exceeding rich, insomuch that the king that now is, married both his daughters unto two rich merchants. Here are many wels containing most sweete water; and so often as the river Niger overfloweth they conveigh the water thereof by certain sluces into the towne. Corne, cattle, milke and butter this region yeeldeth in great abundance: but salt is verie scarce heere, for it is brought hither by land from Tegaza which is five hundred miles distant. When I myself was here, I saw one camells loade of salt sold for 80 ducates. . . .

The inhabitants are people of a gentle and cheerful disposition, and spend a great part of the night in singing and dancing through all the streets of the citie: they keep great store of men and women-slaves, and their town is much in danger of fire: at my second being there halfe the town almost was burnt in fivee howers' space. Without the suburbs there are no gardens nor orchards at all.

The mission's business was not with the common people, but with the Timbuktu-koi, the governor of the city, who, we may be sure, spared no effort to impress the envoys of the Sharif with his wealth and power.* [6] Leo, however, was not unduly dazzled by the splendour of the court:

The rich king of Tombuto (as he called the governor) hath many plates and scepters of gold, some whereof weigh 1,300 poundes: and he keepes a magnificent and well furnished court. When he travelleth any whither he rideth upon a camell which is led by some of his noblemen; and so he doth likewise when hee goeth to warfar, and all his souldiers ride upon horses. Whosoever will speak unto this king must first fal down before his feete, and then taking up earth must sprinkle it upon his owne head and shoulders: which custom is ordinarily observed by them that never saluted the king before, or come as ambassadors from other princes. He hath always three thousand horsemen, and a great number of footmen that shoot poysoned arrows, attending upon him. They have often skirmishes with those that refuse to pay tribute, and so many as they take they sell unto the merchants of Tombuto. Here are verie few horses bred, and the merchants and courtiers keepe certain little nags which they use to travel upon: but their best horses are brought out of Barbarie. And the king so soone

* One cannot be absolutely certain that Leo ever met the great Askia. But on one of his journeys he met the Askia's brother at the port of Kabara on the Niger and described him as 'blacke in colour, but most beautifull in mind and conditions'.

as he heareth that any merchants are come to town with horses, he commandeth a certain number to be brought before him, and chusing the best horse for himselfe he payeth a most liberal price for him.

Here [continues Leo] are great store of doctors, judges, priests, and other learned men, that are bountifully maintained at the king's cost and charges. And hither are brought divers manuscripts or written books out of Barbarie, which are sold for more money than any other merchandise. The coine of Tombuto is of gold without any stampe or superscription: but in matters of smal value they use certain shels brought hither out of the kingdome of Persia, four hundred of which shels are worth a ducate* and six pieces of their gold coine with two third parts weight an ounce.[7]

Leo was describing Timbuktu at the peak of its prosperity. Nevertheless, it is difficult to find in Leo's words any justification for the insistence of posterity on reading into them a picture of romantic splendour. It was permissible to share Leo's evident surprise at finding so much commercial and intellectual activity—always the first aspects of life to engage his attention—but not to deduce, as so many did, that Timbuktu was a magnificent city. The glamour with which Europe so long and so erroneously invested the city was also partly due to its remoteness and its close association with the gold trade. Disillusionment awaited René Caillié on his arrival in the city three centuries later. 'I had formed', he wrote, 'a totally different idea of the grandeur and wealth of Timbuktu. The city presented, at first view, nothing but a mass of ill-looking houses, built of earth.'[8] There are still those who cannot write of Timbuktu without a hysterical sob.

In his account of the Sudan, Leo wrote a description of the towns of Mali (Niani) and Jenne, but he stated that he had reached them by navigating 'with the current' from Timbuktu. This remark implied, as there will be cause to stress, that the Niger flowed in a westerly direction. If Leo had really taken a boat up the river, he could hardly have made such a mistake. But if he never saw Mali and Jenne with his own eyes, he must have met many of his compatriots who knew both places well.

At the time of Leo's visit to the Sudan, Jenne had been a Songhai town for some years, but its importance as a market and

---

* Cowry shells, which were imported into Africa from the East through Cairo, have been in continuous use as a currency in the Western Sudan since the eleventh century, and probably much longer. In Ibn Battuta's time their local value was 1,150 cowries to the gold *dinar*. For the cowry-*mithqal* exchange rate see p. 161 below.

a centre of learning had probably suffered little. A century later as-Sadi was still able to describe it as one of the great markets of the Muslim world, where one met salt merchants from Taghaza and those who brought gold from the mines of Bitu (another name for Bonduku, a district north of Ashanti).[9]

Leo found Jenne abounding in barley, rice, cattle, fish, and cotton. 'Their cotton', he tells us, 'they sell unto the merchants of Barbarie, for cloth of Europe, for brazen vessels, for armour, and other such commodities. Their coin is of gold without any stamp or inscription at all.'[10]

Leo found that although Askia had so oppressed the king of Mali that 'he was scarce able to maintain his family'; there was, nevertheless, a

large and ample village containing to the number of sixe thousand or mo families, and called Mali, whereof the whole kingdom is so named. And here the king hath his place of residence. The region it selfe yeeldeth great abundance of corne, flesh, and cotton. Heere are many artificers and merchants in all places: and yet the king honourably entertaineth all strangers. The inhabitants are rich, and have plenty of wares. Heere are great store of temples, priests, and professours, which professors read their lectures only in the temples, because they have no colleges at all. The people of this region excell all other Negroes in witte, civilitie, and industry.[11]

Like all other explorers of the Sudan, Muslim or Christian, and whether they reached it by way of the Sahara or by the equally hazardous routes from the Guinea coast, Leo gradually succumbed to the charm of the Sudanese.

On his first visit to the Sudan, Leo appears to have returned direct from Timbuktu to Morocco. But on his second journey he seems to have travelled east, probably on the overland route, from Timbuktu to Gao, Askia's capital. He found Gao a great unwalled town:

The houses thereof are but meane, except those wherein the king and his courtiers remain. Here are exceeding rich merchants: and hither continually resort great store of Negros which buy cloth here brought out of Barbarie and Europe. . . . Here is likewise a certain place where slaves are to be sold, especially upon such days as the merchants use to assemble; and a yoong slave of fifteene yeeres age is sold for six ducats, and so are children sold also. The king of this region hath a certain private palace wherein he maintaineth a great number of concubines and slaves, which are kept by eunuches: and for the guard of his owne person he keepeth a sufficient troupe of horsemen and footmen. . . . It is a wonder to see what plentie of merchandise is daily brought hither, and how costly and sumptuous all things be. Horses bought in Europe for ten ducates, are sold again for fortie and sometimes for fiftie ducates a piece. There is not any cloth of Europe so coarse, which will not here be sold for fower ducates an ell, and if it be anything fine they will give fifteen ducats for an ell: and an ell of the scarlet of Venice or of Turkie-cloath is here worth thirtie ducates. A sword is here valued at three or four crownes, and so likewise are spurs, bridles, with other like commodities, and spices also are sold at a high rate: but of al other commodities salt is most extremelie deare.[12]

Leo found that gold was so abundant in Gao that the natives could not always sell all they brought to market and had to return with much of it.[13]

Continuing his journey eastwards, Leo probably next came to Agades, a town which paid tribute to the Songhai. As with Jenne and Mali, one cannot be absolutely certain that he visited Hausa. His brief but useful description of it could easily have been based on second-hand information. Of Gobir he wrote: 'Heere are also great store of artificers and linnen weavers: and here are such shooes made as the ancient Romans were woont to weare, the greatest part whereof be carried to Tombuto and Gago.' The next passage, describing the sowing of rice exactly as practised today on the Gulbin Sokoto and the Gulbin Kebbi, we will consider later when we come to the influence of Leo's work on the map of Africa.[14]

The Hausa kingdoms of Zamfara, Katsina, Kano, and Zaria had all, Leo learnt, been desolated by the recent Songhai invasion and crushed by the heavy burden of tribute imposed on them. To enforce payment Askia had 'sent governours hither who mightily oppressed and impoverished the people that were before rich'.[15] Indeed, Hausa has always been rich, but more on account of the extraordinary industry of the Hausa peasantry, craftsmen, and traders than of the fertility of its soil, though that is not inconsiderable.

'In my time', Leo wrote, the Hausa king of Gobir, 'was slaine by Askia the king of Tombuto, and his sonnes were gelt, and accounted among the number of the king's eunuchs . . . and most part of the inhabitants were carried and kept for slaves by the said Askia'. The rulers of Katsina, Zaria, and Zamfara had all been slain, but the ruler of Kano had been more fortunate. He had surrendered only after a long and gallant resistance which had secured for him the respect of his conqueror and the generous terms he was granted. He was allowed to retain his kingdom subject to his paying a third of his tribute to Askia, and, as what we may assume to have been a compliment, he was required to marry one of Askia's daughters.

Pursuing his eastward journey, Leo next came to Bornu which the Songhai armies had not reached. Bornu lay at the southern end of the least arduous of all the desert crossings; from the ninth century onwards it had been regularly in touch with the markets of the north. In Leo's time its trade with Barbary was mostly in horses, and although gold was so abundant that even the royal hounds wore chains of gold, the Bornuese insisted on paying for the horses with slaves, of which, owing to constant wars with their weaker neighbours, they had far more than they needed. They would give as many as fifteen or twenty slaves for a single horse, but the Barbary merchants would have much preferred gold. In later times they came for slaves only and would not trade for anything else.[16]

From Bornu Leo appears to have travelled on eastwards through 'the kingdome of Gaoga', a state formed by the Bulala people between lakes Chad and Fitri. Gaoga was regularly visited by merchants from Egypt; it was probably in their company that Leo travelled on until he reached Nubia and the city of Dongola on the Nile.

*   *   *   *   *

In the first half of the sixteenth century men's minds were too occupied with stirring events much farther afield to be greatly concerned with Africa. The old century had closed with the discoveries of a new world by Columbus, and of a sea route to India and the Far East by Vasco da Gama. The former suggested possibilities so vast that they could not be assessed; the latter presented the certainty of immense gain. In the space of five years the horizon of European man had been broadened to an extent which he found impossible to comprehend. But that was not all. The new century had opened with the discovery of Brazil, the first sighting of the Pacific, the founding of a Portuguese empire in India, and the first circumnavigation of the globe.

All this had happened between Leo's birth and his writing

about his travels in Africa which, compared with the great geographical events through which he had lived, must have seemed to him and to others of comparatively small account. It is, therefore, not altogether surprising that his story remained almost, if not quite, unknown until its publication by Ramusio in the middle of the century. Before the end of the century Ramusio's *Voyages and Travels* had run through several editions, and Leo's work had been translated into Latin, French, and English.

Meanwhile, the cartographers had been redrawing the map of Africa in the light of Leo's glowing narrative, their dependence on which remained almost complete until the coming of Mungo Park and the other great African explorers of more than two centuries later. Unfortunately, the work on which the cartographers drew so heavily was marred by a blunder as great as it was inexcusable, a blunder of almost incredible magnitude.

Herodotus had said that a great river flowing from west to east divided Africa as the Danube divided Europe. This was believed to be the Niger of Pliny and Ptolemy. In the tenth century Ibn Haukal, the first of the Arab geographers to visit the Sudan, confirmed Herodotus's statement that the Niger flowed to the east. Two centuries later, however, the great al-Idrisi, who never set eyes on the Niger and seems to have confused it with the Senegal, said that it flowed to the west. In the fourteenth century Ibn Battuta was able to declare that he had seen the Niger flowing to the east. But so greatly was al-Idrisi respected that many preferred what he related at second hand to what lesser men reported from personal experience. Consequently there was much doubt in men's minds about who was right. To Leo was given the opportunity of resolving that doubt, and with it one of the oldest mysteries of the geographical world. Alas, he more than failed.

The river Niger passes through the middle of the country of the Blacks. The river begins in a desert called Seu, where it emerges from a great lake * In the opinion of our geographers the Niger is a branch of the Nile, which disappears underground and emerges to form this lake. Some people say that the river rises in the mountains in the west and flows eastward to form a lake. This is not exact; we ourselves have navigated the river from Timbuktu in the east and followed the current to the kingdoms of Jenne and Mali, both of which lie to the west of Timbuktu.[17]

---

* Seu is possibly a variant of Sao or So, the name given to the original inhabitants of Bornu. In this case the lake would be Lake Chad.

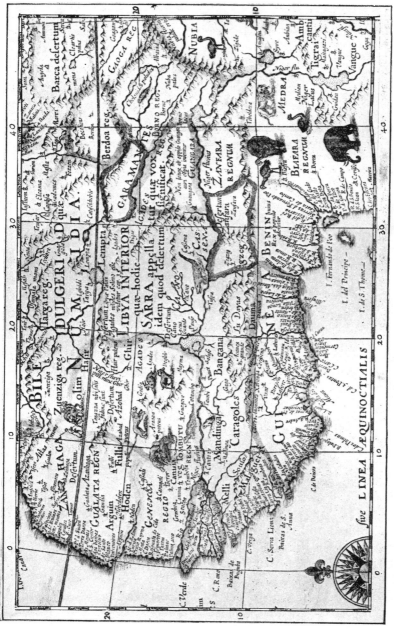

VI. The *Africae Nova Descriptio* of Blaeu (1665)

This passage makes it clear that Leo was concerned to give the impression that the Niger flowed not eastwards, but westwards. How did he come to make this extraordinary blunder? If he had actually sailed on the river for several hundred miles, he could hardly have got the course wrong. But even if he had never been on the river, he must have seen it at Kabara. Quite possibly he paid little attention to the river's course at this time, and came away with only a vague recollection of its direction. The geographers of Rome, we may presume, were not going to allow their faith in al-Idrisi to be shaken by a young Moorish captive. Under their insistent questioning Leo may well have come to believe that they were right and his own vague notion that the river flowed eastwards was wrong. To cover his confusion he may have invented the story that he had actually sailed the Niger. But this is speculation. What is certain is that almost all European cartographers, basing themselves on al-Idrisi and Leo, gave the Niger a westerly course so that on their maps it merged with the Senegal and the Gambia, and poured its waters into the Atlantic. Leo was not proved decisively wrong until that great day in 1796 when Mungo Park reached Segu and saw the river flowing to the east.

Leo's *History and Description of Africa* was not a gazetteer, but, as the title says, a description of African countries through most of which the author had travelled. He was writing for readers seeking information about Africa, not for makers of maps. Inevitably, when the latter started work on the text they did not always find its interpretation for their purpose very easy. Sometimes passages were read in different ways by different cartographers. Lack of clarity in the text contributed to the mistakes, but the blame for an important one rests wholly with the mapmakers.

Leo said that in the Hausa kingdom of Gobir there was 'abundance of rice. . . . At the inundation of Niger all the fields of this region are overflowed, and then the inhabitants cast their seede into the water only.' To begin with, the cartographers quite reasonably took this to mean that in Gobir there was a vast marsh, which in 1554 Tramezino, for example, showed on his map as *Nigritis Palus*. They then, it seems, began to suspect that this passage in Leo referred to the great lake which in the previous century Diego Gomez, one of Prince Henry's captains, had reported to be somewhere in the interior of West Africa, his informant probably having in mind the great lakes, Debo and Fagbine, above Timbuktu.[18] Starting with Giacomo di Gastaldi's map of 1564 a big lake, which he called *Lago de Guber*, begins to appear on the maps and there it remained until nearly the end of the eighteenth century.*

Nothing could be less fair to Leo than to judge him by what the map-makers made of his text. His *History and Description of Africa* was a mine of new and long-sought information, and for two and a half centuries as indispensable to all who were concerned with Africa as it is today in the narrower field of historical study. If we close a kindly eye to his amazing blunder about the course of the Niger, no comment on his work is more apt than his own condescending reference to Pliny: 'He erred a little in some matters concerning Africa: howbeit a little blemish ought not quite to disgrace all the beautie of a fair and amiable body.'[19]

17

Mulai Ahmad al-Mansur

'By divers ways he got excessive store of gold.'—RO. C.

LEO did not owe his fame to his travels which, for a Moor, were not particularly unusual, but to the remarkable account he gave of the countries he visited. His vivid narrative, however, would not have interested his countrymen for, unlike the Christians, they knew all about the remote countries he described, and they were never better informed than at the time of Leo's visit when the trans-Saharan trade was booming as never before.

The conquests of Askia the Great had endowed the Songhai with immense surplus wealth. Their vast dominions, stretching from the rain forests in the south far into the Sahara in the north, and from Hausa in the east almost to the Atlantic in the west, had

---

* The lake was also sometimes called *Sigismes* and sometimes *Guarde*, but why has never been explained in either case. I. Blaeu in 1659 and J. Senex in about 1700 named one half of the lake *Sigismes* and the other *Guarde*. N. de Fer in 1698 and H. Moll in about 1710, having a more critical sense than their predecessors, thought it better to stick more closely to Leo. The one gave *Marais de Guarde*, and the other *Bogs and Morasses de Garde*. D'Anville and Robert in their map of 1770 showed the lake but gave it no name.

natural resources which more than sufficed for their needs. A fertile soil cultivated by an industrious peasantry under a wide range of climatic conditions, rolling savannahs supporting great herds of cattle, goats, and sheep, and countless rivers and lakes teeming with fish, provided an inexhaustible and varied food supply. To satisfy the rest of their essential needs they had highly skilled craftsmen to convert to their use their great mineral wealth —notably in iron and copper—and the inedible products of the soil. Not only did they lack for nothing, but they had a great surplus of gold and slaves, for which there was an insatiable foreign demand. They could provide both in almost unlimited quantities; gold because they controlled the chief sources of supply, slaves because they had only to raid their weaker neighbours to get all they wanted.

The principal use for this surplus wealth was the purchase of luxuries, which to the Songhai meant the trade goods of the Mediterranean. With tribute pouring constantly into Gao and Timbuktu, the Songhai were now able to trade with the Maghrib on a scale which had not previously been possible to a Sudanese people, not even to the Mandingo of Mali in the days of Mansa Musa. Never before had the gold and slaves so much needed in the north been in such abundant supply. Consequently the caravan routes of the Sahara were carrying more traffic than ever before. All along the North African littoral there were, as Leo tells us, merchants trading with the Sudan, and in every Sudanese town there were expatriate Moors and Jews engaged in the same trade.

At the end of the sixteenth century, when gold was still pouring freely into the Maghrib and when Leo's account of the rich countries in the heart of Africa was being widely read in Europe, Morocco suddenly received a new and wholly unexpected accession to wealth.

*　　*　　*　　*　　*

History offers few parallels to the disaster which befell the Portuguese in 1578 on the field of al-Ksar al-Kabir. They had been reluctantly dragged into war with the Moors of Morocco by their young and half-witted king, Don Sebastian. No circumstance within the king's contriving which could ensure defeat had been lacking. But the magnitude of the disaster which followed exceeded the worst apprehensions of those who had so reluctantly followed him into battle. In the space of six hours on a hot August day, a force of 26,000 Portuguese had been annihilated: less than a hundred had escaped death or capture. But that was not the full measure of Portugal's disaster. To the loss of the flower of her manhood were added the forfeiture of her sovereignty to Spain and the passing of her great colonial empire into the hands of the cruel and fanatical Philip. These were direct results of the battle which Edward Creasy so strangely overlooked. But the battle of Alcazar did not change the course of history only in Europe: its consequences to Africa spanned the Sahara, stretching a bloody hand from Fez to the Niger and beyond.[1]

Numbered among the dead on the field were the commanders of both armies, Don Sebastian and Abd al-Malik, the Sharif of Fez. Not the least dramatic circumstance of the battle had been the mortal sickness of the Sharif, who could barely sit his horse and knew himself to be a dying man. He expired in the moment of victory, having prudently nominated as his successor his younger brother, the twenty-nine-year-old Mulai Ahmad. The new Sharif now added al-Mansur, the Victorious, to his name.

The battle had won for the Moors a prestige in both the Christian and Muslim worlds which far exceeded anything they had ever before enjoyed and to which they were never again to rise. Nevertheless, al-Mansur began his reign loaded with cares. The country was divided, as it always had been, into factions which might at any moment rally to the support of any one of three or four pretenders who considered they had better claims to the throne than al-Mansur himself. His accession, indeed, was not generally popular, and as the whole of the credit for the overwhelming defeat of the Christians had rightly gone to his dead brother, he was denied the support which a popular hero would have enjoyed. It very soon became apparent that the unrest, which under the firm rule of his brother had only smouldered, might at any moment burst into flame. There were few he could trust, least of all the people of the capital, for the Fezzis detested the ruling house.[2]

Other perils weighed no less heavily on al-Mansur's mind. Europe was unlikely to allow so great a defeat to go unavenged, and the most probable instrument of Christian vengeance was his formidable neighbour, Philip of Spain, from whom he was separated by only a few miles of sea. Still closer at hand, at Algiers, were the Turks who had long resented the stubborn resistance of the Moors to absorption into the Ottoman empire, and were bitterly jealous that it had fallen to so contemptible a people to avenge their own crushing defeat at Lepanto only seven years before. There was none to applaud the triumph of al-Ksar al-Kabir, and on every hand danger threatened.

Nevertheless, before long a procession of congratulatory envoys began to arrive, bearing costly gifts, but usually with an axe to grind. The first was from the pasha of Algiers, the next from Portugal bent on the ransoming of captives, as was also the ambassador of William of Orange, some of whose subjects had served under Don Sebastian. Elizabeth of England, anxious to continue her illicit exchange of arms for Moroccan saltpetre, sent an ambassador, but, not altogether surprisingly, without a present of sufficient consequence to be recorded. Nevertheless, at court there were advocates for an alliance between her and al-Mansur. The ambassador of France brought a magnificent present in the hope of securing a Moorish alliance for the treacherous Henry III, who always sought to ally himself with any enemy of Christian Europe. The most honoured of the envoys was the ambassador from Spain, whose sumptuous present of a ruby the size of a man's hand, an emerald as big as an apple, and a casket of immense pearls al-Mansur found both gratifying and reassuring. The least welcome was the Turk, who was deliberately kept waiting for his audience so long that Murad did not forget the affront.

Meanwhile, al-Mansur was proving himself a capable ruler. A happy combination of firmness and restraint enabled him gradually to strengthen his position, and before long his hold on his throne was secure enough to cause him little concern. Foreign affairs also assumed a more reassuring aspect. As time passed without any attack, apart from an abortive Turkish expedition which Murad recalled before it could reach Morocco, it became apparent that the danger of foreign aggression was less than he had supposed.

With his worst cares lifted from his mind, al-Mansur was able to enjoy some of the fruits of victory. The chief of these were the ransoms of the thousands of Christian captives, which none knew better how to turn to account than the Moors with their unrivalled experience of corsair raiding. It is not possible to compute what the ransoms amounted to, but for several years after the battle they kept the Sharifian treasury overflowing with foreign gold. After allowing for the utmost extravagance at home, there was sufficient left to provide financial accommodation for needy Christian princes. Numbered among the latter were the king of France and Don Antonio, the Pretender to the throne of Portugal, whose needs were granted at the urgent request of Queen Elizabeth.

al-Mansur's personal extravagance was chiefly concentrated on building a vast and splendid palace in Marrakech on which he employed thousands of Christians. Many ship-loads of the most precious materials of the East were imported from India for its decoration. Italy and Ireland supplied the marble for its thousands of columns.* It was surrounded with elaborate gardens in keeping with the magnificence of its interior, and on its completion six years after the battle, al-Badi, as it was called, presented a picture of unrivalled splendour.†

Although the Sharif's relations with his neighbours remained outwardly friendly, preparedness for war continued to be a compelling need. At heart the Turks were undoubtedly as hostile as ever, and the Christian Powers, except for France implacable enemies of Islam, could never be trusted. Philip was pressing for the cession of the little Atlantic port of Larache, so convenient for the guarding of the western approaches to the Straits; the Turks also coveted it and even France and the Netherlands were showing an unwelcome interest in its future. There was, moreover, a rumour that the English had designs on the more southerly port of Mogador whence they got the sugar which was a staple of their trade with the Moors.

In all these circumstances the maintenance of his armed forces on a war footing continued to be one of al-Mansur's principal cares. Abd al-Malik had got all the timber for his galleys and the arms he needed for his army from Elizabeth, the only Christian sovereign prepared to defy the papal ban on trafficking with Muslims in war material. She had only done so because of her pressing need for saltpetre for making gunpowder, which she could get only from the Moors. Although she had gone to infinite pains to conceal her part in the illicit trade, Philip knew all about it, and the destruction of a Christian army at al-Ksar with arms supplied by England had greatly aggravated the bitterness of his resentment. So, when he learnt of Elizabeth's wish to resume the trade with al-Mansur, he objected so strongly that the Sharif felt compelled to refuse her. But the resumption of the trade was as necessary to al-Mansur for his supply of munitions as it was to Elizabeth for

* According to al-Ifrani the Irish were bartering marble in Morocco for an equal weight of sugar.
† al-Badi or the Dar al-Bideea, was destroyed by Mulai Ismail in 1707.

her saltpetre. Before long Spain and the rest of the Catholic world became aware that the Moors were obtaining from England not only ship timber, cannon balls, and oars, but also shipwrights which they had never done before.[3]

Meanwhile the likelihood that all this war material would be needed for the defence of Morocco was steadily growing less. Their interminable Persian campaign and grave domestic problems were so sapping the strength of the Turks that it was quite clear that there was no danger of their embarking on any new foreign enterprise. Nearer home the union of the crowns of Spain and Portugal had not had the fell consequences the rest of the world had foreseen. Revolt in the Netherlands was proving only less exhausting to Philip than the Persian campaign to the Turks, and on top of that he was faced with the probability of war with Elizabeth. The Spaniard, therefore, was no more to be feared than the Turk. Yet instead of al-Mansur's demands on Elizabeth diminishing they continued to mount.

The reason for this was a well-kept secret. With his throne secure and the danger of foreign aggression lifted from his mind, the Sharif was planning to use his army in an astonishing enterprise. He had resolved to invade the Sudan and wrest from the ignorant Songhai the source of the gold which was pouring into the Maghrib in such abundant streams. The possibility of doing so had doubtless crossed Moorish minds before this, as it had Prince Henry's in the previous century. After long years of carefully planned and fruitless endeavour, the Portuguese had shown that the goldfields could not be reached by way of the sea. al-Mansur had determined that they were accessible by land. To most minds the hazarding of an army on desert routes already strewn with the bones of men and animals left behind by small trading caravans would have seemed madness. But al-Mansur thought the risks more than justified.

18

Taghaza

'Mankind can live without gold but not without salt.'—CASSIODORUS.
'The price of a negro is salt.'—MOORISH PROVERB.

DUMB barter with an invisible people and the invisible people's reluctance to part with their gold for anything but salt were the most striking characteristics of the West African gold trade. These fundamental principles, dictated by an unknown and very primitive people, had to be accepted without question by all who entered this peculiar trade. They were restrictions which confined the business to privileged Sudanese middlemen who knew where to go for the gold and how to behave when they got there, and to Barbary merchants who could produce the necessary salt. The principal source of this was Taghaza, which lay in the middle of the desert on the main caravan route between Morocco and Timbuktu.* In spite of Taghaza's predominant position in a trade in which many grew rich and many more aspired to share, so far as we know it had no political history, at least until the sixteenth century. It just went on producing salt, undisturbed by desert or more distant politics. One would have looked for a troubled history in a place so fundamentally important to a trade which excited the cupidity of so many nations. But al-Mansur's aspirations were to put an end to the traditional tranquillity of Taghaza. Before considering the political importance so rudely and unexpectedly thrust upon it, we shall do well first to see what manner of place it was. Fortunately it was visited and described by both Ibn Battuta and Leo Africanus.

In the middle of the fourteenth century, according to Ibn Battuta, Taghaza was

an unattractive village, with the curious feature that its houses and mosques are built of blocks of salt, roofed with camel skins. There are no trees there, nothing but sand. In the sand is a salt mine; they dig for the salt, and find it in thick slabs. . . . No one lives at Taghaza except the slaves of the Mesufa tribe, who dig for the salt: they subsist

* There were a number of other salt deposits in the Western Sahara, notably at Idjil and Nterert (Awlil). Salt from both these deposits was carried to the countries of the Western Sudan. The trade in marine salt appears to have been mainly local.[1]

on dates imported from Dra'a and Sijilmasa, camel's flesh, and millet imported from the Negrolands. The negroes come up from their country and take away the salt from there. At Walata a load of salt brings eight to ten *mithqals*;* in the town of Mali it sells for twenty to thirty, and sometimes as much as forty. The negroes use salt as a medium of exchange, just as gold and silver is used (elsewhere); they cut it up into pieces and buy and sell with it. The business done at Taghaza, for all its meanness, amounts to an enormous figure in terms of hundredweights of gold-dust.[2]

Leo Africanus, who passed through Taghaza on his way to the Sudan, draws a more graphic picture of this desolate district and of the misery of its inhabitants:

In this region [he wrote] is great store of salt digged, being whiter than any marble. This salt is taken out of certain caves or pits, at the entrance whereof stand their cottages that work in the salt-mines. And as these workmen are all strangers, who sell the salt which they dig unto certain merchants that carry the same upon camels to the kingdom of Timbuktu, where there would otherwise be extreme scarcity of salt. Neither have the said diggers of salt any victuals but such as the merchants bring unto them; for they are distant from all inhabited places almost twenty days' journey, insomuch that oftentimes they perish for lack of food, whenas the merchants come not in due time unto them. Moreover, the south-east wind doth so often blind them, that they cannot live here without great peril. I myself continued three days amongst them, all which time I was constrained to drink salt-water drawn out of certain wells not far from the salt-pits.[3]

In this sixteenth century the mines were still being worked for the Mesufa nomads by negro slaves.

In spite of the remoteness of Taghaza from the Sudan and its proximity to Morocco, the mines appear never to have been controlled by the rulers of Marrakech or Fez. This probably mattered little because the Mesufa had every reason to foster a trade from which they benefited so much. To their profits on the sale of the salt were added the tolls and other forms of blackmail customarily levied by desert tribes on caravans passing through their country.†
At this time, however, the Mesufa were vassals of the Songhai

---

* At the end of the sixteenth century a *mithqal* or *mitkal*, approximately ⅛ oz. of gold, was worth 3,000 cowries in Timbuktu; by 1912 its value had risen to about 12,000 cowries.
† In Leo's time the Sanhaja levied a toll of one ducat's worth of cloth on every camel-load passing through their country between Taghaza and Walata.

within whose dominions, therefore, the salt-mines lay, and they were jealous of their control of them.

Although the Moors had no reason to fear the cessation of their trade with the Sudan, the possession of Taghaza would in one respect have been very valuable to them. It would have given them a great measure of control over the gold market. That they never seized the salt-mines was probably due to fear of meddling in desert politics and provoking retaliatory raids on Morocco. In 1546, however, al-Mansur's father, Muhammad al-Shaykh,* endeavoured to persuade Askia Ishak, who then ruled Songhai, to cede the mines to him. Ishak replied that the suggestion came strangely from so great a ruler as the Sharif and that 'the Ishak who will listen to it is not I. That Ishak has yet to be born.' But the Askia did not content himself with this snub. He sent two thousand Tuareg to raid the Moorish province of Dra'a which lay in the foothills of the Atlas and due west from Sijilmasa. Their orders were to pillage as much of the country as they could, right up to the walls of Marrakech if possible. The raiders did not get beyond Dra'a, but although they wrought much damage they were careful not to kill anyone. Ishak appears to have enjoined this unusual restraint because he did not want to provoke a war with the Sharif.[4] In this he succeeded, but ten years later Muhammad had his revenge. He sent a raiding party down to Taghaza which killed the Songhai governor and a number of Tuareg whom they caught loading salt on to their camels. The Tuareg who escaped the massacre told the Askia that they knew of another salt-deposit in the desert. They called the place Taghaza al-Ghizlan, but it seems likely that this was in fact Taodeni.[5]

When al-Mansur came to the throne, Askia Ishak was still alive, but Askia Daud succeeded him soon afterwards. It was so long since there had been any trouble over Taghaza, and Moorish prestige stood so high on account of the victory at al-Ksar, that it seemed to al-Mansur worth attempting a profitable arrangement with the Askia. He suggested to Daud that he should lease the mines to him for a year. The Askia, probably recognizing that the Sharif was now powerful enough to seize and hold Taghaza should he so wish, agreed and thereby established friendly relations between the two countries.[6]

Daud's successor, Muhammad al-Hadj, had been on his throne

* as-Sadi wrongly says that the Sharif was Ahmad al-Aaredj. The latter had been succeeded by his brother Muhammad in 1540, the year after Askia Ishak's accession.

only a few months when an ambassador from the Sharif arrived in Gao with a handsome gift for the new Askia. The ambassador was warmly welcomed and sent back to the Sharif with a gift of slaves (including eighty eunuchs), civet, and other rare products. The visit, far from being the innocent act of courtesy the Songhai believed it to be, was nothing less than a military reconnaissance.[7]

al-Mansur probably began to plan an invasion of the Sudan very soon after the punitive expedition he had had to send against the oases of Tuat and Gorarin had shown the practicability of moving large numbers of troops about the desert.[8] An attack on Songhai would involve an infinitely longer desert march, but al-Mansur believed it could be done. al-Ifrani, the Moorish historian, is silent about this part of al-Mansur's reign, so we know little about the preparations for the invasion. One cannot doubt, however, that the three thousand yards of English cloth which reached Marrakech in February 1584 and which were required 'for lining the tents of the arquebusiers of the victorious army' had been especially ordered for the great enterprise al-Mansur had in hand.[9]

According to as-Sadi, it was not long after al-Mansur's ambassador had returned from Songhai that news reached Gao of a Sharifian army of 20,000 men having already set out for the Sudan. Its commander had been ordered to follow a circuitous route through Wadan in south-eastern Mauretania (which the Portuguese had once occupied) from where he was to go to the upper Senegal, seize all the towns he could, and then attack Timbuktu.[10] Although there is no mention of the expedition in al-Ifrani, some confirmation of as-Sadi's story is provided, as C. A. Julien has pointed out, by a strange passage in the *Chronique anonyme de la dynastie sa'dienne*. According to this document, a mutiny took place in the Moroccan army, and al-Mansur punished the mutineers by sending them on an expedition to the Sudan, at the same time instructing their guide to abandon them in mid-desert. Of their troops one man alone managed to make a miraculous escape. 'Is this not the official or semi-official version,' Julien asks, 'of a disaster, the result of a badly-prepared expedition?'[11]

al-Mansur then sent one of his kaids with two hundred arquebusiers to seize Taghaza. The expedition arrived to find that nearly all the inhabitants, who were mostly negro slaves, had already fled. It was a hollow victory because without any negroes the mines could not be worked and there was no advantage in their capture. Askia Daud made sure of this by forbidding any of his people to return to Taghaza. So al-Mansur had to abandon the mines which, as the Songhai dared not return to them, remained closed.[12]

The closing of Taghaza was a serious matter for the people of the upper Niger, but it led to the development of the salt-mines at Taodeni. Taodeni had two advantages over Taghaza: it lay a hundred miles nearer Timbuktu and its deposits were, as yet, untouched, whereas Taghaza had been worked for more than six hundred years. Consequently Taghaza was completely abandoned, but the deposits at Taodeni are worked to this day.[13]

For the time being the Sharif was too occupied with foreign affairs to spare much time for his Songhai plans. Spain and the Turks continued to covet Larache, but he skillfully played one off against the other. He went so far as to promise Larache to Philip as a condition of a twenty years' truce, but he repudiated the agreement directly it had been signed by Spain. He showed the same lack of faith in his dealings with Elizabeth by failing to implement his promise of further assistance to Don Antonio. But in spite of these and many other cares, al-Mansur never weakened in his determination to invade the Sudan and conquer Songhai.

19

The Desert Army

'To give water is better than to give bread.'—MOORISH PROVERB.

IN 1589, when al-Mansur was in Fez vainly trying to stamp out sedition in the northern capital, a courier arrived from Marrakech with a letter for him. The writer, Uld Kirinfil, was a negro from the Sudan whom the reigning Askia, Ishak II, had banished to Taghaza. From there he had escaped to Marrakech where, disappointed in his hope of finding the Sharif, he had written representing himself to be the elder brother of the Askia who, he alleged, had usurped his throne. He begged al-Mansur to champion his cause and promised that he would be richly rewarded.*[1]

* There are four main sources for the Moroccan invasion of the Sudan. On the Moroccan side there is the brief account given by the eighteenth-century historian, al-Ifrani. This can be supplemented by the interesting account of the opening phase of the campaign, written by an anonymous Spaniard who was in Morocco

Although Uld Kirinfil was an impostor, his letter furnished al-Mansur with a pretext and an excuse not to delay any longer the invasion of the Sudan. But he had to move cautiously. There was a limit to the demands he could make on his people who set immense store by their trade with the Sudan which the campaign would certainly disturb and perhaps destroy. According to as-Sadi, this unpopular enterprise had already cost them one army lost in the desert and to attempt to send another might provoke an outburst of rebellious spirit which, as Fez had recently shown, still smouldered under the surface. The Sharif, therefore, called together the wise men of his kingdom—the viziers, governors, and important tribal chiefs—in order to secure their support for the campaign he was so eager to launch. He told them that he had decided to attack the prince of Gao, the master of the Sudan, in order to unite the forces of Islam and bring them under a single commander. The conquest of the Sudan, which was a very rich country, would greatly strengthen the armies of Islam and be an inspiration to all true believers. Finally, he declared, Askia Ishak not only lacked the qualities essential to kingship but he was not even of the tribe of the Quraysh and therefore had no right to rule at all.

The counsellors were appalled. They unanimously declared themselves opposed to the project, and gave their reasons. Between their country and the Sudan lay an immense desert without water or pasture whose roads were entirely unsuitable for the passage of an army. In addition, there were the other 'perils and terrors which haunted the desert', the chief of which was the Tuareg. None of the three previous dynasties, illustrious and powerful though they had been, had ever thought for one moment of embarking on such a hazardous project; they had recognized the inevitability of failure. 'We therefore hope', they concluded, 'that you will be guided by those dynasties, for we of today are no wiser than our forefathers.'

al-Mansur poured scorn on their fears.

You talk of the dangerous desert we have to cross [he declared], of the fatal solitudes, barren of water and pasture, but you forget the defenceless and ill-equipped merchants who, mounted or on foot,

---

at the time. On the Sudanese side there are two chronicles: the *Tarikh as-Sudan* of Abdarrahman as-Sadi, and the *Tarikh al-Fattash* of Mahmud Kati. as-Sadi was born in Timbuktu in 1596; Mahmud al-Kati died in Timbuktu in 1593, at the incredible but apparently authentic age of one hundred and twenty-five years. as-Sadi's chronicle ends in 1653; Mahmud al-Kati's, which was carried on by other hands, in 1599.

regularly cross these wastes which caravans have never ceased to traverse. I, who am so much better equipped than they, can surely do the same with an army which inspires terror wherever it goes. As for former dynasties which, you say, never contemplated such a project as mine, you know well that the Almoravids were fully occupied with the conquest of Andalusia and struggles with the Christians; the Almohads were similarly engaged and had also to fight the Sanhaja nomads; finally the Merinids had to fight the Abd al-Wadid of Tlemcen. But today the road to Andalusia is closed to us by the conquest of the whole of the country by our enemies the infidels, and we are no longer at war with Tlemcen or the rest of the kingdom of Algiers because it is all in the hands of the Turks. Moreover, our predecessors would have found great difficulty if they had tried to do what I now propose, for their armies were composed only of horsemen armed with spears and of bowmen; gunpowder was unknown to them, and so were fire-arms and their terrifying effect. Today the Sudanese have only spears and swords, weapons which will be useless against modern arms. It will therefore be easy for us to wage a successful war against these people and prevail over them. Finally, the Sudan being richer than the Maghrib its conquest would be more profitable than to drive out the Turks which would call for great efforts with very little to gain. Do not let the inaction of our predecessors lead you to regard as distant that which is within reach, and as difficult that which is easy.

The Sharif's speech had a remarkable effect on his audience. Completely won over and even enthusiastic, they dispersed, obsequiously murmuring—to quote M. Houdas's translation—'Les esprits des princes sont les princes des esprits.' The Sharif was now able to put in hand energetic preparations for the great expedition to the Sudan.[2]

In their campaigns the Moors, like most orientals, had always relied for victory on overwhelming superiority of numbers rather than on the quality of their troops and equipment. This had been notably successful at al-Ksar, but the invasion of Songhai demanded a very different technique. Before Songhai could be reached the Sahara had to be crossed. This, the most difficult part of the undertaking, prohibited the employment of overwhelming numbers. Obviously the smaller the force the greater the likelihood of its reaching Songhai. The need therefore was for a small and highly efficient expedition with the best equipment and transport that could be provided. Once Songhai was reached, numerical superiority would lie wholly with the enemy. Nevertheless, it was reasonable to expect that the superior weapons of the Moors, above all their firearms, would correct the balance. But if the first encounter with the enemy went against the Moors, their situation might quickly become desperate. They would have no reserves to call up and no base to retire on. All would therefore depend upon an early and decisive victory, probably in the face of tremendous numerical odds. This could only be achieved by sending the staunchest and best disciplined troops. With the hazards of the desert march and the risk of the first encounter with the enemy very much in mind, al-Mansur resolved that everything he sent to the Sudan, be it man or beast, arms or stores, would be of the best.

Much would hang on finding a suitable commander. al-Mansur's choice for this important post was a young kaid, a eunuch named Judar. He was a blue-eyed Spaniard from Las Cuevas in Granada who had been captured as an infant (no doubt in a corsair raid on the Spanish shore), and had grown to manhood in the royal palace at Marrakech. It was a surprising choice, because Judar had had, so far as we know, little or no campaigning experience. He had distinguished himself as a collector of taxes, presumably on account of his integrity and organizing ability, very desirable qualities in a commander who would of necessity be beyond the Sharif's control once he had taken the field. Contemporary comment, rather surprisingly, suggests that he was chosen chiefly on account of his youth.

Judar was at once promoted to the rank of pasha. Under him were ten kaids, four of whom also were renegades, Europeans who, voluntarily or under compulsion, had apostatized. The force entrusted to Judar was only 4,000 strong, but they were picked troops specially chosen for their discipline, hardiness, and courage. There were 2,000 infantry armed with the arquebus, half of them Andalusians (Spanish Moors who had migrated to Morocco) and half renegades, most of whom would have been prisoners of war too poor to redeem themselves. There were 500 mounted arquebusiers or *spahis* who were nearly all renegades, the rest probably being Turks from Algiers who were frequent deserters to the Sharifian army. There were 1,500 light cavalry armed with lances who were all Moors. The artillery comprised six large cannon and several quite small pieces, two of which made a camel-load. The gunners, we may be sure, were mostly of European birth, the master-gunners probably being free Christians, for whom there had long been well-paid employment with the Sharifian army.

Half a century earlier, French renegades were reported to be casting cannon for the Moors.[3] There were also seventy Christian musketeers, chosen from among prisoners of war—doubtless survivors from al-Ksar—who, still hopeful of one day being ransomed, had not apostatized. Judar had attached much importance to having some Christian troops, probably as a bodyguard, and was disappointed at the Sharif's refusal to let him have all the two hundred he had asked for.

The composition of Judar's army clearly shows how little faith al-Mansur had in his countrymen as soldiers. Of the 4,000 men only 1,500 light cavalry were natives of Morocco. The rest were mostly Andalusians or renegade Europeans, who together had long formed the backbone of the army.* It is significant that the official language of Judar's force was Spanish.

The non-combatants accompanying the army were 600 sappers and 1,000 camel drivers. The transport animals were 8,000 camels and 1,000 pack-horses. According to al-Ifrani, as much care was taken in choosing the animals as the men. The cavalry were mounted on the finest chargers procurable, the pack-horses were chosen for their breeding and the camels for their strength and speed.[5]

Nine thousand transport animals may seem an excessive provision for 4,000 troops, but it must be remembered that they had before them a march of nearly 1,500 miles, during which there were several long stages when they would be entirely dependent for water, food, and forage on what they carried with them.† This included, besides bullock-skins for water, 180 tents, 31,000 pounds of gunpowder, a similar weight of lead, quantities of morions, shot, tow, pitch, rosin, ropes, spades, picks, and many other implements. There was, besides, the food for man and beast—wheat, oats, and huge quantities of pressed dates.

Our principal source of information about the desert army and

---

* Europeans serving in the Sharifian army at this time were not necessarily renegades. According to John Harrison, al-Mansur's predecessor, Mulai Abd al-Malik, 'did cause come English boyes perforce to turn Moores, cutting them and making them *capadoes* or eunuches; but afterwards (as they say) repented, saying he would never more force Englishmen to turne Moores, for he found them better servants to him being Christians than Moores, for that being Christians they would stand by him and stay with him, but being Moores run away from him, having more libertie and opportunity'.[4]

† In 1821 the Pasha of Tripoli sent a military expedition of 2,000 cavalry and 500 infantry across the Sahara to Bornu. Their transport allowance was one camel to two infantrymen and two camels to one cavalryman and his horse.[6]

its equipment is a Spaniard who was then living in Marrakech, and who was probably one of Philip's agents at the Sharifian court. From what he tells us, it is evident that great pains were taken to ensure that the force was the best, in both men and equipment, that the country could provide.

But al-Mansur had also to think of contingencies which might arise nearer home after the expedition had set out for its remote destination. There was the danger of one or other of his formidable neighbours, Spain and Turkey, turning on him directly they saw that he was committed to another campaign and one from which quick withdrawal would be impossible. The Turks appeared to have abandoned their hopes of further territorial gains in Africa, but they could not be trusted. The relations between al-Mansur and Murad were more strained than ever. The insistence of the Moors that their caliph was not the Ottoman sultan but their own Sharif had always been bitterly resented in Stambul. Nevertheless, it had been al-Mansur's custom to send an annual present to Murad. The latter always made it clear that he regarded it as tribute, which had annoyed al-Mansur so much that he had given up sending the customary gift, thus farther aggravating the antipathy, not to say hatred, with which the Turks regarded the Sharif.

al-Mansur's relations with Spain, on the other hand, had improved. This was partly because, since the defeat of the Armada by the English, Philip was no longer feared as he had been. But as he was known to be secretly harbouring in Lisbon two pretenders to al-Mansur's throne he could not be trusted any more than Murad. An invasion of the Sudan might well provoke an attack by either. A sea-borne assault on Larache, still coveted by both Philip and Murad, seemed the most imminent danger. This was probably the reason for the request of the Sharif's ambassador in London for permission to hire English carpenters and shipwrights, 'for the building of certain foysts and fregates in tymes of war . . .' This was in March 1589.[7]

A month later followed the abortive attack on Lisbon by Drake and Norris for which Elizabeth held al-Mansur partly to blame. He had promised to send supplies to the English fleet but had failed to do so.[8] Nevertheless, Elizabeth sent a special envoy to Marrakech, to solicit his aid in a second attack on Portugal which she was planning for the following winter. Her envoy was coldly received and her request refused.[9] In spite of this rebuff the Queen

now renewed her demands on the Sharif for aid for her protégé
Don Antonio. On 23 June 1590, al-Mansur wrote to her excusing
his neglect of her importunate ambassador on the grounds of his
pre-occupation with the expedition which would be leaving for
the Sudan in a few days' time.[10]

But it was not till 16 October, at the season most favourable for
the desert crossing, that Judar Pasha marched out of Marrakech
at the head of the desert army. It was a spectacle which filled the
Sharif with pride. Instead of the disorderly rabble which a
Moorish army on the march customarily presented, al-Mansur
beheld an orderly column of trained and disciplined men (albeit
most of them Europeans), better equipped than any army the
Moors had ever placed in the field, and resolute and confident of
victory in the great enterprise which for years past had constantly
occupied his mind.

Judar led his force due south over the Atlas into the province
of Dra'a and camped at Lektawa, where al-Mansur had a mint
for coining gold from the Sudan. The troops found awaiting them
here the stores and transport animals assembled from a countryside which abounded in corn, dates, and lush pastures. Here, too,
on the threshold of the Sahara, the final preparations for the desert
march had to be completed. When all was ready the bullock-skins
were filled with water and loaded in pairs on to the camels. The
great march then began and the army vanished into the desert.

After months had passed without any news of Judar, there
suddenly emerged from the desert an indignant owner of camels,
doubtless a Targui, with a grievance to lay before the Sharif. He
had been peacefully grazing his camels near Arawan, only a few
days' march north of Timbuktu, when Judar and his army had
suddenly appeared over the horizon and driven off his beasts.
Few complainants could ever have been more welcome at a royal
court. The man's story clearly showed that Judar had crossed the
desert.

*   *   *   *   *

Unfortunately no account of Judar's desert march has come
down to us. There is no doubt about his route, but we know
nothing of what happened on the march nor of the toll it took in
human life, though it is permissible, as we shall see, to infer that
his losses were very heavy.

The survival of the army, let alone the success of its under-

taking, depended upon always finding water to supplement adequately what was carried in the bullock-skins. Purely military
considerations, such as secrecy of movement and the element of
surprise, had therefore to be subordinated to this one compelling
need. There was no hope of a secret approach because Judar's
dependence on wells forced him to follow a popular trade route
at the very season of the year when caravans of merchants were
most numerous. The only road was the old gold traders' trail running south from Lektawa through Taghaza, and Taodeni to
Walata. Judar had no choice but to follow this road for the greater
part of his way to the Niger. At Taodeni or thereabouts, the main
road turned south-west to Walata. Judar continued due south,
following the less important road to Timbuktu which ran through
Arawan, where, as we have seen, he seized somebody's camels.
Arrived at Arawan, which had probably taken at least two months
to reach, the worst of the desert perils were behind him, for from
there southward water and pasturage became easier as the Niger
is approached.

In what condition the army reached Arawan we do not know.
A force 5,000 to 6,000 strong with nearly twice as many transport
animals, they had set out as a single body on a march of 700 miles
over really appalling country. So meagre were the resources of
the road, that they were not even adequate for the minimum
needs of the few hundreds of traders who travelled it at intervals
during the winter months. Between Taghaza and Arawan there
was no single place with sufficient water or pasturage to afford
rest to a column of this size. Taodeni was no better than Taghaza:
both were barely capable of supporting human life.* In between
these miserable stopping places were long stages of howling wilder-
ness across which small parties of traders hurried in constant terror
of finding the next wells dry and themselves too exhausted to go
farther.

Ibn Battuta's account of the perils of travel on this road has
already been quoted. Leo's account of the same road, which he
travelled less than a century before Judar, is still more graphic:

> In the way which leadeth from Fez to Timbuktu are certain pits
> environed either with the hides or bones of camels. Neither do the
> merchants in summer time pass that way without great danger of their
> lives: for oftentimes it falleth out, when the south wind bloweth, that

* As recently as 1910 over fifty people died at Taodeni owing to the delayed arrival
of the caravan on which they depended for the necessities of life.[11]

all those pits are stopped up with sand. And so the merchants, when they can find neither those pits, nor any mention thereof, must needs perish with extreme thirst: whose carcases are afterwards found lying scattered here and there, and scorched with the heat of the sun. One remedy they have in this case, which is very strange: for when they are so grievously oppressed with thirst, they kill forthwith some one of their camels, out of whose bowels they wring and express some quantity of water, which water they drink and carry about with them, till they have either found some pit of water, or till they pine away for thirst. In the desert which they call Azaoad there are as yet extant two monuments built of marble, upon which marble is an epitaph engraven, signifying that one of the said monuments represented a most rich merchant, and the other a carrier or transporter of wares. Which wealthy merchant bought of the carrier a cup of water for ten thousand ducats, and yet this precious water could suffice neither of them; for both of them were consumed with thirst . . . For some time being sore athirst, we could not find one drop of water, partly because our guide strayed out of the direct course, and partly because our enemies had cut off the springs and channels of the foresaid pits and wells. Insomuch that the small quantity of water which we found, was sparingly to be kept: for that which would scarce suffice us for five days, we were constrained to keep for ten.[12]

We have only one direct pointer—and that not a very clear one—that Judar's losses were probably very heavy. It is Mahmud al-Kati's statement in the *Tarikh al-Fattash* that out of the original force, which he estimated fairly accurately at 3,000 to 4,000 fighting men, only 1,000 took part in the first clash with the Songhai forces.[13] Although in the circumstances Judar probably used every man he could lay hands on, al-Kati's statement does not justify the assumption of some commentators that all the rest had perished in the desert. It is significant, however, that in 1594 Laurence Madoc, an English merchant living in Morocco, reported that a column of 1,700 men lost a third of its strength on the way to the Sudan. It is not clear whether he was referring to Judar's original expedition or to a column of reinforcements sent out later. But knowing what we do of the great perils of this road and what an appalling toll of human life they took of much smaller bodies of merchants and troops on other occasions, it is difficult to believe that Judar did not suffer grievous losses in the desert.

20

The Invasion of the Sudan

'A boat is a certaine retreate, and the River a constant friend, to trust unto.'
RICHARD JOBSON.

AT the end of February, twenty weeks after leaving Marrakech, Judar reached the Niger at Karabara, near the present town of Bamba. He had chosen well, for strategically he could not have been better placed. Here the Niger was more easily crossed than anywhere else on the bend. This made it an important junction of caravan routes which Judar now commanded. Still more valuable to him was Karabara's situation midway between Gao and Timbuktu, and out of striking distance of either, for it enabled him to satisfy his army's pressing need for rest and reorganization before having to fight a major engagement.[1]

The Songhai had been fully aware of the Sharif's hostile intentions, but so confident were they of the impregnability of their Saharan frontier that the possibility of a Moorish army reaching their country never crossed their minds. They were therefore caught wholly unprepared.

Askia Ishak had of course heard of the approach of the Moors some time before they reached the Niger, but the route they had chosen suggested that they intended to invade from the west. He therefore prepared to ward off an attack from that quarter. Later he learnt that the Moors had left the Walata road at Arawan and were moving due south; this made it clear that they certainly would not attack from the west. He therefore withdrew his forces to Gao and summoned a council of war. All was confusion. Some thought the enemy's immediate objective was Timbuktu, others insisted that it must be Gao. The assembly of the fighting men from every part of the kingdom was ordered but the council broke up without deciding what their dispositions were to be.

Ishak himself took one important decision, but too late for it to be effective. He sent orders to the desert chiefs to fill in the wells the Moors were likely to use and to harry them relentlessly as they dispersed in search of water. The orders did not reach the chiefs, because the messengers were captured by a band of marauders.

Nor did the country respond to the call to arms as Ishak had hoped, because the people, like their rulers, refused to believe that an attack from the north was possible and could not conceive that the situation was as grave as it was represented. Only when the dread news spread through the country that the Moors had actually been seen at Karabara by the scared riverain peasantry did the fighting men begin to assemble.

After resting his army for a few days, Judar took the road again, marching downstream towards Gao. Before they had gone far the Moors were attacked by Tuareg, whom they drove off without difficulty. A little further on they found some victims of these same marauding Tuareg, four wounded negroes. These were the Askia's messengers on whom the Moors found the orders to fill in the desert wells. Had these messengers been sent out directly Ishak heard of the approach of the Moors, every one of the invaders might have perished in the desert. They had had a narrow escape.

The Moors now began to be harried by the local fighting men who, coming up the river in their canoes, attacked them at night. For the sake of security from Tuareg raiders, the traditional enemies of the Songhai, most of the villages in these parts were built on islands in the river. As the Moors had no boats and there was no timber in this arid region with which to build any, they could not counter-attack their attackers, nor, what was of much greater consequence, could they replenish their fast dwindling supplies of food, of which they had hoped to find themselves independent once they had reached the river. They could only ease the position a little by making rafts of water-skins and raiding some of the small island granaries.

When Judar was about four days' march from Gao he learnt that Askia Ishak was barring the way and preparing to give battle. He appealed to Ishak to surrender and thus save unnecessary waste of life, but his appeal was rejected and, being taken as a sign of weakness, it gave increased confidence to the Songhai. The following day Judar sighted the negro army at Tondibi, about thirty-five miles from Gao, and decided to engage them the next day.

Mahmud al-Kati, more conservative than other chroniclers of these events, estimated the Songhai army at 18,000 cavalry and 9,700 infantry.[2] as-Sadi says the army was composed mostly of bowmen but that the cavalry, who were armed with spears, numbered several thousand.[3] Although the Songhai professed themselves Muslims, they had great faith in the black arts and went into battle accompanied by a band of witch-doctors. According to al-Kati, the Moorish force was only 1,000 *spahis* or cavalry, half of them being Andalusians and half renegades.[4] Before the battle began the Songhai endeavoured to throw the invaders into confusion by driving a mob of cattle at them, but the Moors opened their ranks and the herds passed harmlessly through.

The Moors began the battle, as was their custom, by charging the enemy from both flanks. From the first the issue was never in doubt. In spite of their numerical superiority the ill-armed negro rabble had no chance against the firearms and superior discipline of the Moors. The only attempt at serious resistance was made by a band of fanatics who formed the advance guard. Kneeling on one leg, with shin lashed to thigh so that they could not move, they fired arrows into the advancing Moors until they themselves were annihilated. The rout of the main body quickly followed and the survivors fled, leaving behind many dead to be stripped of their gold ornaments by the Moors.*

The remnants of the Songhai army made good their escape by crossing the Niger into Gurma where, owing to the Moors having no boats, they were safe from pursuit. On Ishak's orders the townspeople followed the example of the army, but in the panic many were drowned crossing the river.

The Moors were warmly welcomed into Gao by the foreign merchants and *literati*, many of whom were fellow-countrymen of the invaders. But the warmth of their welcome was poor consolation for the bitterness of their disappointment at finding Gao so very different from what they had been led to expect.

The trans-Saharan trade in gold and slaves being the life-blood of a score or more of the Barbary ports and the source of wealth of thousands of prosperous merchants, the Western Sudan was regarded in the Maghrib as an Eldorado and the famous Songhai capital as the chief repository of its wealth. Judar and his army had therefore been confident that they would find Gao a city of imposing buildings and dazzling opulence, the capture of which would more than reward them for all they had suffered on the terrible desert march. Instead, they found only the mud-and-

---

* The various translations by Houdas have caused some confusion regarding the date of the battle of Tondibi. as-Sadi gives 17 Djomada which Houdas in 1900 translated as 12 April; al-Ifrani gives the 16th of the same month, translated by Houdas in 1889 as 16 February. The *Tarikh al-Fattash* gives 2 Djomada which Houdas translated in 1913 as 1 March.

thatch huts typical of the Sudan and no signs of the great wealth
they had expected. Even the Askia's dwelling had little to distinguish it from the prevailing squalor of the place. The townspeople had carried off with them everything that might have been
of value to the Moors and not a trace of gold was to be found. Of
more interest to posterity than to themselves was their discovery
of a cannon bearing the arms of Portugal, which the Songhai did
not know how to use, a statue of the Holy Virgin, and a crucifix.*
These were the only rewards which Gao had to offer these men for
all they had endured, for their rout of the Songhai army and for
the many perils which separated them from their homes. Their
disillusionment was grievous.

That Judar and his army were so ill-informed about a city
which was so well known to great numbers of their countrymen
was due to the secrecy which had always enveloped the Sudan
trade. Owing to their fears of interlopers cutting into their business,
Barbary merchants had always been very reticent about the remote
countries of the interior from which they derived their wealth.
Moreover, so opposed were the commercial community of Morocco to al-Mansur's Sudan campaign, that advice from such a prejudiced quarter would certainly have been ignored. The Sharif
should, of course, have known from the envoy he had sent to re-
connoitre the Sudan what manner of town Gao was, but the latter
may have feared to disillusion his master: conversely, his master
may equally well have refused to believe him.

Askia Ishak, having lost his capital and with it all desire to
resist, now opened negotiations with Judar. He offered to swear
allegiance to the Sharif and to concede to the Moors the right to
import salt and cowry shells into the Sudan. It will be recalled
that the Moors had for long past sought to get control of the salt
trade with the Sudan, on account of its being so closely linked
with the gold trade. There is no record of their having coveted
also the cowry trade, but as cowries were the principal currency of
the Sudan they may well have done so. The concessions offered by
Ishak, therefore, were important ones. Their acceptance would
have given the Moors a strangle-hold on the economic life of the
whole of the Western Sudan.

---

* These articles had probably reached Gao in the ordinary course of trade from
the Guinea coast, with which the Portuguese, Dutch, and English had for some
time been trading. A similar discovery was made in 1900 when a war fetish of the
Ashantis proved to be a fourteenth-century bronze tripod of English workmanship.[5]

Ishak's chief care was to avoid a permanent military occupation which would place an intolerable burden on his people and probably make a later repudiation of Moorish suzerainty impossible. He therefore offered Judar 100,000 *mithqal*, or 12,500 oz., of gold and 1,000 slaves if he and his army would return at once to Morocco.

The Pasha, had he had the necessary authority, would have readily accepted the offer, for, like his men, he was despondent. Not only had his illusions about the wealth of the Sudan been shattered, but disease was spreading through the ranks of the army and already many of his soldiers were dead. His only wish was to get home as quickly as he could. But he had not been authorized to make terms with the enemy. He therefore submitted Ishak's proposals to the Sharif in a despatch which stressed the sufferings of his men in the desert, their present sorry plight, and the poverty of the country they had conquered at such cost. No argument which might induce the Sharif to accept Ishak's terms was omitted. Judar had before him a long and anxious wait for the reply.

The condition of the Moorish army continued to deteriorate. In a fortnight there were 400 deaths and the Pasha himself fell ill. The transport animals, without which the Moors could not move, were also stricken and dying fast. Ishak, perceiving the plight of the invaders and eager to rid his capital of them, advised Judar to withdraw to the healthier climate of Timbuktu and offered to facilitate his departure by providing a large number of horses. Judar accepted this offer, and after a march of twenty-nine days he made a peaceful entry into Timbuktu. Many of the townspeople had fled into the desert but a number still remained, including their venerable *qadi*, Abu Hafs Umar.

Timbuktu was slightly less disappointing than Gao. The buildings were better but still of mud and therefore squalid by Moorish standards. The only relief to the pitiful scene was the Sankore mosque which still towered impressively above everything else. But to Judar and his men, who knew so well the graceful splendour of the Kutubia of Marrakech, the clumsy mud-built tower of Sankore can have appeared impressive only in comparison with the squalor of Gao. Timbuktu had, however, an air of sophistication. It was the intellectual capital of the Sudan, the resort of students from distant lands, and its scholars, like its merchants, were well-to-do. Feeling they had nothing to fear from the Moors, the merchants and the *literati* had remained in the city instead of joining in the exodus into the desert. The Moors therefore found the commercial and intellectual life of the city comparatively undisturbed, and signs of wealth were not lacking. It was probably only because his troops were too worn out to risk a renewal of hostilities that Judar did not sack the city. It was certainly not out of any regard for those who had failed to fly before him. Their sullen faces and the dignified refusal of their *qadi* to entertain him and his kaids clearly showed the resentment with which the invasion was viewed, even by those who were the least likely to be affected by it. The only people who were made to suffer for Timbuktu's cold reception were the rich Ghadamsi merchants, many of whose warehouses were pulled down to make room for a fort Judar ordered to be built.*

The arrival of Judar's envoy in Marrakech with the news of the victory at Tondibi caused great excitement throughout Morocco. Apart from the report of the army's having successfully crossed the Sahara, there had been no news of any kind since its departure for the Sudan eight months before. The Sharif, however, was far from pleased with the Pasha's despatch. He scorned the terms offered by Askia Ishak and bitterly resented Judar's having neither left a garrison in Gao nor obtained hostages from Ishak. But he was enraged by the Pasha's incredible account of the poverty of Songhai. For centuries past, gold had been pouring northwards across the Sahara in such quantities that there could be no doubt about there being vast stores of it somewhere in the Western Sudan. al-Mansur decided to replace Judar with a less complacent and more determined commander, who would wring from the negroes their hoarded wealth and the golden source from which it sprang.

It was evident, however, that the wastage of men and materials in the Sudan might greatly strain the resources of the kingdom before the gold was secured. If his subjects were to respond as the Sharif wished to the heavy demands which he expected to have

---

* The Arab merchants of Ghadames, in the hinterland of Tripolitania, for many centuries occupied a predominant position in the trade of the Western Sudan, where they still have settlements. The extent and ramifications of their business are well illustrated by the very old *turkudi* trade. *Turkudi*, a cloth woven in the Hausa city of Kano, was much used as a currency in Timbuktu. Ghadamsi merchants in Kano exported it to Ghat, a desert market in the north-central Sahara, whence it was forwarded due west to In Salah and from there south again to Timbuktu. The cloth thus made two nearly complete crossings of the Sahara instead of following the much shorter, but less safe, route up the Niger.

to make on them, no shadow could be allowed to cloud the jubila-
tions with which they were hailing the victory at Tondibi. He
therefore issued a grandiloquent and mendacious manifesto extol-
ling the achievements of the army and proclaiming the unbounded
wealth it had laid bare.[6] There was of course no mention of what
the cost had been in human life. The renewed enthusiasm which
the manifesto awakened was tempered by a measure of mis-
giving at the appointment of a new commander. The lack of any
reason for the removal of so successful a leader as Judar was dis-
quieting, and the edict, which quickly followed, for the raising
of more troops even more so.

In his anxiety to conceal the bitterness of his own disappointment, the Sharif carried deception to extraordinary lengths.
According to a report which found currency as far away as
England, he showed the Turkish ambassador a severed human
head which he declared was none other than Askia Ishak's.[7] The
knowledge that the incident would further exasperate the jealous
Murad must have added greatly to the zest with which al-Mansur
played this simple trick on the gullible Turk.

In Morocco, opinion on the merits of the Sudan campaign was
sharply divided. The masses saw in the victory at Tondibi the
promise of great wealth and of a glorious future for the country.
The better educated did not share their confidence. They were
probably influenced by merchants engaged in the Sudan trade
who had more accurate sources of information about the fortunes
of the expedition than suited al-Mansur. They felt that he had
entered into commitments which the country could not afford.
They knew that the mere holding of the territory already conquered, which was little more than the line of the Niger between
Gao and Timbuktu, would require a substantial garrison and
constant reinforcements to make good the inevitable losses from
disease and the other hazards of war. Experience had already
shown how heavy those losses were likely to be. The Tuareg
would continue to take heavy toll of troops crossing the desert,
waylaying them as they arrived exhausted at the wells and cutting
them to pieces. Moreover, the principal need would be for arquebusiers, who were mostly Andalusians on whom the Sharif
depended for the security of his throne. It was thought that far too
many of these important troops had already been sent to the Sudan.

What alarmed the merchants more than anything else was al-
Mansur's determination to secure the gold of the Sudan regardless

of cost. Being familiar with the gold trade, they knew that the goldfields must still be far off and they doubted whether he would ever be able to reach them. For centuries past the mines had been the constant and fruitless goal of Moorish merchants who were still ignorant of their whereabouts. They feared that the Sharif's determination to reach them would result in the ruin of the realm or, at best, the absorption of the whole of the Songhai tribute.

The chief concern of the merchants was, of course, for their own trade. In the past the negroes had been ready enough to barter their gold for salt and the trade goods of the Mediterranean, but if the reward of their labour was to be confiscation by the invader, very soon they would stop producing the gold. Thus the Moors would lose their most important market which, they argued rather acidly, would be very damaging to the Sharif because, like all his line, he habitually helped himself to the fortunes of his subjects whenever he felt the need.

The officer appointed to succeed Judar was Mahmud ibn-Zarqun, the kaid of all the renegades in the kingdom. He was the son of a renegade, probably Spanish or Portuguese, and, like Judar, a eunuch brought up in the royal palace. In spite of its being the worst time of year for the desert crossing, Mahmud was told to leave at once. So much concern was felt for his safety that he was ordered to march only at night. The heat was intense, the levanter was blowing and water was unusually scarce in the desert. Nevertheless, he and his escort of forty renegades reached Timbuktu safely in the very short space of seven weeks.

Mahmud Pasha, as he had now become, soon proved himself an energetic and resolute leader. As soon as he had taken over from Judar he set about ridding the army of the handicap of having to fight a riverain campaign without any boats. He felled and sawed into planks what few trees there were in and around Timbuktu, and had all the wooden doors and door-frames wrenched out of the buildings. This enabled him to build two boats which were launched within a few days of his arrival. Leaving a small garrison behind him in Timbuktu, Mahmud now set off with the rest of the army down the left bank of the Niger in search of Askia Ishak. He encountered and defeated the Songhai army at Bamba. The enemy, as usual, fled across the river into Gurma but, thanks to the boats which had followed him downstream. Mahmud was able to pursue them. So complete was the rout and dispersal of the Songhai forces, that Ishak got cut off from his followers and was murdered by tribesmen who were doubtless marauding Tuareg. After this there were so many desertions to the Moors that the Askia who succeeded Ishak quickly lost heart and offered to submit to the Sharif.

It was a famine year, and Mahmud found it so difficult to feed his troops that he was reduced to eating his transport animals. The Askia, in response to an appeal from the Pasha and in order to prove his own good faith, sent him food. He was then summoned to the Moorish camp to swear allegiance to al-Mansur, but when he and his companions arrived they were treacherously murdered. Mahmud afterwards excused his perfidy as a just reprisal for the massacre of 400 of his troops in the desert while on their way to the Sudan.

Mahmud quickly recognized the futility of trying to control the Songhai by direct military rule. He therefore appointed a puppet Askia to govern from Timbuktu in the Sharif's name. But he was disappointed in his hope that the Songhai would accept this semblance of traditional authority. They refused to obey the puppet of the Moors, with the result that the administrative chaos became rapidly worse. Meanwhile the southern Songhai, far downstream, and as yet unsubdued, appointed an Askia of their own. Thenceforward there was a puppet Askia of the north and a free Askia of the south.

Then, at the nadir of their country's fortunes, the Songhai produced a leader of great brilliance, Askia Nuh, who succeeded in rallying the demoralized forces of the kingdom and opposing Mahmud with a resolute army. This was a notable achievement, for the Songhai, having been routed in every encounter with the invaders, must have known that they had little chance against the enemy's firearms. Nuh, besides being an inspiring commander was a born guerrilla leader, who knew full well how to turn to account the natural advantages of his country and how never to miss any opportunity for inflicting loss on the enemy. This enabled him to keep the field against greatly superior forces for the next four years.

Mahmud wasted no time in striking at the new leader. Nuh was waiting for him in Dendi, orchard bush country south of Gurma. In the ensuing battle Nuh scored a moral victory. He held the enemy for a whole day and then made an orderly withdrawal. The battle had taught him that the more open the country the greater the advantage to the Moors who, given a field of fire, could prevent their ill-armed opponents closing with them. Having learnt this important lesson, Nuh withdrew far south into the forests of Borgu.

Mahmud pursued resolutely and came up with Nuh on the Mekon river, in a region of heavy rainfall, malarial swamps, and dense vegetation varying from thick bush to tropical forest. To the advantages which these conditions gave to Nuh was added the invaluable support he received from the local people. The Borgawa were warlike pagans with long experience of the great defensive possibilities of their country. They had never lost their independence, in spite of having had to withstand assaults on it by such formidable warrior kings as Sonni Ali and Askia the Great.* They hated the Songhai as they did the rest of their northern slave-raiding neighbours, but in the face of the common enemy from across the desert they now readily joined forces with them.

In these circumstances it is not surprising that before long Mahmud was regretting having allowed himself to be lured into Borgu. The Moors, having no experience of bush fighting, fell an easy prey to the guerrilla tactics of their opponents. Whether in camp or on the march, they were given no respite. An interminable and relentless succession of sudden attacks from any and every quarter, by both day and night, drained away their strength and broke their spirit. To add to their misery, the humid climate, strange food, and bad water combined to take as heavy toll of the men as the tsetse fly did of their horses.† Their afflictions were precisely those which had always prevented the effective occupation of the forests by the slave-raiding tribes of the Sudan, and which for centuries closed the interior of West Africa to the European trading settlements on the Guinea coast. The forests were as impenetrable from the north as they were from the south.

Yet two years elapsed before the utter exhaustion of his army and lack of adequate reinforcements from Morocco compelled Mahmud to admit the futility of continuing the struggle. He drafted a despatch to the Sharif not very different from that which had brought discredit on Judar. Happily for him al-Mansur had begun to realize that campaigning in the heart of Africa was less

---

* Lord Lugard, who had personal encounters with the Borgawa, attributed their military successes first to their knowledge of witchcraft and the deadliness of the poisons they dressed their arrows with; secondly to their tactics, especially their mastery of the art of ambush and their love of a night attack.[8]

† In recent years the Mekon river district was completely depopulated by sleeping sickness carried by the tsetse fly.

easy than he had thought. Moreover, Mahmud's tenacity and endurance had won his respect. He therefore read the Pasha's account of the woeful condition of his troops and the dismal record of reverses with more sympathy and understanding than he had shown to Judar in similar circumstances. He at once sent Mahmud substantial reinforcements, 1,500 cavalry, 1,500 infantry, and 500 remounts. These were followed soon afterwards by two small columns, 400 strong altogether.

But by the time these fresh troops had arrived Mahmud had made up his mind not to waste any more time campaigning in Borgu. At the end of 1593 he withdrew up the right bank of the Niger to Timbuktu, leaving behind him a garrison in Gao.

21

The Fall of Songhai

'. . . to discover some way to those rich mines of Gago or Tumbatu . . . which daily the more they are sought into, the more they are corrected.'

CAPT. JOHN SMITH

THE successful despatch of an army across the desert seems to have exhausted the Moors' capacity for organization. In the Sudan sheer incompetence quickly lost them the initial advantage their firearms had given them. Instead of turning to account the many racial, tribal, and sectarian differences which divided their opponents, they antagonized everyone they met by their brutality and treachery. As the result of these weaknesses and the ill-judged dispersal of the army over a number of small isolated garrisons the campaign gradually degenerated into a series of savage massacres followed by vicious reprisals.

The population of the Western Sudan comprised many subversive elements. The number of mutually hostile tribes springing from many different stocks, the varying degrees of civilization, a diversity of religious beliefs, and an almost total absence of natural geographical boundaries were some of the factors which combined to throw the country into turmoil directly the restraining hand of a powerful central authority was removed.

The natural sequel to the defeat of the Songhai army at Tondibi

had been an outbreak of anarchy and brigandage on a grand
scale. The news of the flight of Askia Ishak and his shattered forces
had been a signal for all the turbulent elements to break loose and
reduce to chaos these parts of the tottering kingdom which had not
yet felt the direct impact of the invader. The tribes who had been
under the tutelage of Songhai, flushed with the excitement of their
unexpected liberation, had abandoned themselves to orgies of
licence and excess. The Fulani and the Zagrana flung themselves
upon the Songhai peasants of the lacustrine region above Timbuktu. The rich province of Jenne was ravaged from end to end
by hordes of pagan Bambara. The Tuareg grew ever bolder in
their raids on the riverain peasantry.

> Security gave place to danger [wrote as-Sadi], wealth to poverty,
> distress and calamities and violence succeeded tranquillity. Every-
> where men destroyed each other; in every place and in every direction
> there was plundering, and war spared neither life nor property nor
> persons. Disorder was general and spread everywhere, rising to the
> highest degree of intensity.[1]

Throughout recorded history the Tuareg had always been a
menace to the sedentary peoples of the middle Niger, but more
especially to the people of Timbuktu whose wealth had an irresistible attraction for the desert warriors. Lying on the threshold
of the desert, Timbuktu was an easy and constant prey to their
raids, which were so sudden and unexpected that it had become
customary for all the city's business to be conducted indoors instead of in the open market.

The Tuareg had not been slow to take advantage of the chaos
which had followed the Moorish invasion. While Mahmud had
been engaged in his fruitless Borgu campaign they had raided
Timbuktu, first attacking the Moorish garrison and then, with
characteristic treachery, suddenly siding with the Moors against
the townspeople. The latter, accustomed to taking up arms in their
own defence, then rose in formidable strength against the Moorish
garrison who were only saved from annihilation by the arrival of a
relieving force of 300 arquebusiers under Kaid Mami ibn-Barun
whom Mahmud had sent back up the Niger to save Timbuktu.[2]
Mami, whose origin we do not know but may presume to have
been European, was one of the very few men al-Mansur sent to
the Sudan who showed any sympathy for the negroes or who
recognized the need to win their confidence. Although he had been

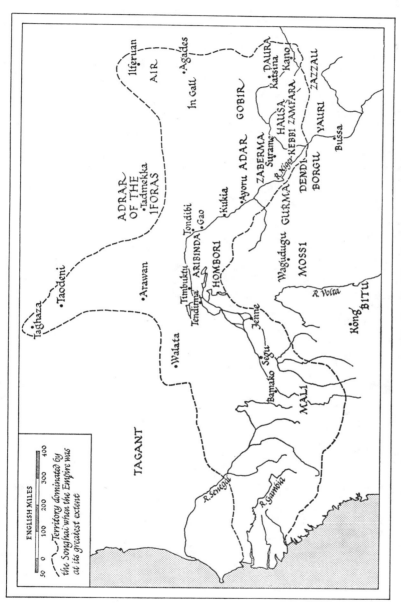

VII. The Songhai Empire

ENGLISH MILES

50 0 100 200 300 400

Territory dominated by
the Songhai when the Empire was
at its greatest extent

Taghaza
•Taodeni
•Arawan
TAGANT
•Walata
R. Senegal
R. Gambia
Bamako
Segu
Jenne
Timbuktu
Tendirma
ARIBINDA
HOMBORI
MALI
MOSSI
Wagudugu
R. Volta
Kong
BITU
GURMA
DENDI
BORGU
YAURI
Bussa
ZABERMA
Suyame
HAUSA
KEBBI
ZAMFARA
ZAZZAU
YAURI
Niger
Ayoru ADAR GOBIR
Kukia
Gao
Tonditi
Iladmekka
ADRAR OF THE IFORAS
In Gall
Ilferuan
AIR
•Agades
•Katsina
DAURA
Kano

told he might slay every living soul in the city, he showed such moderation that his sympathies appear to have lain rather with the townspeople than his countrymen. He killed with his own hand a soldier he found robbing a native, and he insisted on paying in cash for everything supplied to his troops. He even apologized to the venerable Abu Hafs Umar for the inexcusable excesses of the Moorish army. All this was so completely different from what the unfortunate natives had hitherto experienced at the hands of the invaders, that the bitterness which had divided them almost disappeared. Public confidence was restored, the people swore allegiance to the Sharif, the fugitives returned from the desert, the trade routes were re-opened, and life in the city again became normal.

The timorous scholars and merchants of Jenne had been anxiously watching events in Timbuktu, for they knew that the protection which their rivers and swamps had so far afforded them could not long continue. Taking heart at Mami's unexpectedly generous treatment of the Timbuktu rebels, they now hastened to tender their submission. This was accepted and the city's tribute was fixed at 60,000 *mithqal* of gold.*

Mami, recognizing that there was no hope of lasting peace in Timbuktu or anywhere else on the middle Niger so long as the Tuareg were unsubdued, sent a punitive expedition against the tribes who had caused the recent trouble. Assisted, one must presume, by friendly nomads who were a match for the elusive rebels, he caught them, massacred all the men, and sold their women and children into slavery. This caused such a slump in the market that slaves changed hands at the equivalent of a few pence apiece. However, other nomads, this time the powerful Sanhaja, then rose against Mami and massacred one of his outlying garrisons. The situation was only saved by the timely arrival of 2,000 reinforcements from Morocco, and it was not till Mahmud returned from the south, at the end of 1593, that the Moors were able to avenge themselves by almost annihilating the guilty Sanhaja.

Order being restored, Mahmud was free to carry out a carefully laid plan to plunder Timbuktu. So far he had got nothing out of the campaign. What little loot Gao had yielded had all gone

---

*In later years al-Mansur's son, Mulai Zaydan, took the title of King of Gao, Timbuktu, and Jenne, which clearly shows that Jenne was far more important than its modest role in the history of the Western Sudan suggests.

to Judar, and nothing at all had been found in the poverty-stricken villages of Borgu. But now came an opportunity for Mahmud to squeeze all he could out of Timbuktu. He first sent a crier through the streets announcing that on the morrow there would be a house-to-house search for arms, but that houses belonging to descendants of the sainted Sidi Mahmud, a former *qadi* of Timbuktu, would not be searched. Every man who could claim acquaintanceship with a descendant of the holy man rushed to deposit with him his valuables which certainly would be stolen if left in his own house. After their homes had been searched the townspeople were summoned to the Sankore mosque to swear allegiance to the Sharif, and were then dismissed. The descendants of Sidi Mahmud were next summoned. The doors of the mosque were closed behind them, their houses containing all the wealth of Timbuktu were plundered, their women were violated, and many of the prisoners in the mosque were massacred. Of the loot, 100,000 *mithqal* of gold were set aside for the Sharif.

Even before Mahmud pillaged Timbuktu the people, despairing of a return of the liberal treatment they had received under Mami, had abandoned hope of relief from the cruel persecutions they were enduring. At the end of 1592 Abu Hafs Umar courageously sent envoys to Marrakech to lay before al-Mansur the plight of his sorely afflicted people and to seek for mercy. The envoys were given, to their surprise, a kindly welcome at the Sharifian court and sent back with a promise that their wrongs would be immediately redressed. They were accompanied on their homeward journey by a kaid named Bu-Ikhtiyar,* described as the renegade son of a Christian prince, who carried with him orders for the better treatment of Umar and his people. But when they reached Taghaza they learnt that they had been cruelly deceived. al-Mansur had sent ahead of them a messenger with very different orders. These were for the arrest of Umar and some of the leading *literati* of Timbuktu who were, the envoys were now told, already in chains.† A few months later it was decided to

* Bu-Ikhtiyar had under him 1,200 reinforcements. Experience having shown the folly of attempting to send so large a body of troops together across the desert, they marched in two separate columns so as to make the most of what little water and pasture were available in the desert.

† All those arrested (their number may not have been more than half a dozen) seem to have been members of the Aqit family. The family had provided *qadis* for Timbuktu for many generations and were held in high esteem by the Askias. Ahmad Baba the distinguished historian, was a member of this family and was one of those arrested.[3]

send the prisoners, together with their families and their books and other possessions, across the desert to Marrakech. Belonging to the cultured and wealthiest class, they were the least suited to endure the hardships inseparable from the journey they were now compelled to undertake. Moreover, when they set out they had been further enfeebled by the months they had spent as prisoners loaded with chains. The aged Umar, too, was now a sick man.

We have no record of what the exiles suffered as they were herded and driven across the desert, nor of how many survived. One cannot doubt that the deaths, at least among the women and children, were very heavy. Despite his age and ill health Umar completed the journey, as did the illustrious Ahmad Baba.

The captives from Timbuktu were held in confinement for two years, during which time Umar died. In 1596 the captives were released, but al-Mansur refused to allow them to leave Marrakech. Ahmad Baba settled down as a teacher, and was soon attracting pious Muslims from many different parts of Morocco. Shortly after his release he was granted an interview with al-Mansur, and 'at once showed that talent for plain speaking before the mighty that had characterized his ancestors. On being brought before the Sultan he found him concealed from the public gaze by a curtain and refused to converse with him until he showed himself, remarking that, by speaking from behind a veil the Sultan was imitating God'. Face to face with al-Mansur, Ahmad Baba reproached the Sultan for treating him as he had done. al-Mansur justified himself by explaining it was part of his policy to unify the world of Islam. 'Then why', Ahmad Baba replied, 'did you not start with the Turks at Tlemcen, who are very much nearer to you?' Outwitted in this debate, al-Mansur terminated the interview forthwith. After al-Mansur's death, Ahmad Baba was allowed by his successor, Mulai Zaydan, to return to Timbuktu. He died in 1627, twenty years after his return.[4]

Meanwhile in the Sudan Mahmud Pasha's treatment of the Songhai had even disgusted some of his own officers, among whom was Ahmad ibn al-Haddad, one of the kaids who had accompanied Judar to the Sudan. Soon after the arrest of Umar and his companions, this courageous officer slipped secretly away to Marrakech in order to report to the Sharif the infamous conduct of the Pasha. al-Mansur was greatly incensed at hearing of the extent to which Mahmud abused his power, of his rapacity and cruelty, and of his habit of declaring that his sword was his sultan.

But he does not seem to have decided to replace Mahmud until the arrival of Umar and his companions, when he learnt from the commander of the escort that his share of the loot of Timbuktu was a paltry 100,000 *mithqal* of gold. On hearing this, he at once despatched to the Sudan Kaid Mansur ibn Abdarrahman with orders to take over from Mahmud and put him to an ignominious death.

Mahmud was at any rate a resolute and gallant commander in the field. During the time when his fate was under discussion in Morocco, he had been carrying on his campaign against Nuh with characteristic energy. All the way from Jenne to Gao the river was in Moorish hands. Gao was strongly held by Judar who, since his removal from the supreme command, had continued to show himself a capable leader. Nuh, unable to make headway against him, had left the valley of the Niger and retired into the mountainous Hombori district, the home of the Tombo, a warrior tribe who were redoubtable defenders of their independence until well into the twentieth century. This move did not suit Mahmud because Hombori was easy to defend and within striking distance of Timbuktu. While the Pasha was trying to dislodge Nuh from his mountain fastness he received a kindly warning from Mulai Abu Fares, a son of the Sharif, of the fate which would befall him directly Mansur arrived. Seeing that escape was impossible, Mahmud launched a reckless attack on the enemy in which he met the honourable death he deliberately sought. His great opponent, Nuh, followed him to the grave soon afterwards, killed in an attack on the Hombori stronghold by Mansur.

In the history of the Moorish campaign no leaders served their respective countries with such distinction as Mahmud and Nuh. During the four years they were at the head of the opposing armies the campaign was carried on with a determination on both sides which was strikingly absent in its earlier and later stages. Although disgrace and death deprived Mahmud of the final victory, he was the most successful of the Moorish commanders. He failed as an administrator because of his rapacity and cruelty, but, like those who preceded and most of those who followed him, tyranny was the only rule he had ever known. By Moorish standards he was a good general and one of the few loyal soldiers in al-Mansur's service. His death was only less serious to the Moors than that of Nuh to the Songhai.

On Nuh's death organized resistance collapsed and the overthrow of the great negro kingdom was virtually complete. But the Songhai people would have been the last to admit it. Their spirit was unbroken and their hatred of the conqueror implacable. The Moors, indeed, had little cause for satisfaction. Their firearms had not compensated for either the fewness of their numbers, their lack of resistance to tropical diseases, their incompetence as administrators or, above all, for the vastness of the country they were trying to subdue. Although Songhai lay prostrate, the Moors were in no sense masters of the country. Their writ did not run beyond the banks of the middle Niger, and even along its course military occupation had not resulted in administrative control, without which conquest was little more than a pretence.

The heavy demands which the campaign made on Morocco did not end with the death of Askia Nuh. Owing to some unexplained omission by the Sharif, Mansur and Judar quarrelled over which of them was to succeed Mahmud as pasha. When the dispute was referred to al-Mansur he made matters worse by appointing Mansur commander-in-chief and Judar civil governor, which merely intensified their hatred and rivalry. The resulting chaos only ended with the death of Mansur, almost certainly poisoned by Judar. A similar fate befell the kaid whom the Sharif sent out to take Mansur's place. Meanwhile Judar was exercising supreme command in the Sudan. Near at hand, however, he had a rival with whom he could not settle as easily as he had with others, namely Kaid al-Mustapha who for some years had governed Timbuktu and whose incompetence had been largely responsible for the endless trouble the city had given. His final act of folly was to try to supplant Judar. The latter, unable to dispose of his rival, agreed with him that the matter had best be left to the troops to settle. They pronounced for Judar, but more important than this decision was their sudden realization that they had now become their own masters. This eventually cost Morocco the Sudan.

Judar strangled al-Mustapha and nothing seemed more likely than that he would now defy the Sharif and declare himself an independent ruler; in fact, he had no such ambition. His only wish was to be left alone to govern the country in what he believed to be the best interests of the Sharif. The latter, realizing the futility of sending out more kaids to be liquidated by Judar, appears not only to have acquiesced but to have accepted Judar back into the same high favour as he had accorded him on his first appointment

to the command of the desert army. So complete was his recon-
ciliation with the Spanish eunuch that he summoned him back to
Morocco to quell a rebellion which was causing him much
anxiety. But Judar, whose self-assurance was now unbounded, refused to abandon the Sudan until a competent governor had been
appointed to take over from him. al-Mansur then sent out two
civilian kaids, one of them a Portuguese, but as Judar did not
think they would prove capable of repelling an attack which he
believed the Mandingo of Mali were preparing to launch against
the country he refused to hand over to them. al-Mansur next sent
out Ammar Pasha, a young Portuguese eunuch who had previously been to the Sudan as the commander of a column of 1,000
reinforcements. These he had divided into two bodies, one of 500
elches and the other of 500 Andalusians, each following a different
route, as had become customary when moving large numbers of
troops across the desert. The *elches* had reached Timbuktu safely,
but the Andalusians had perished to a man. In spite of this un-
impressive record, Judar was sufficiently satisfied with Ammar to
hand over to him and return home.

Jasper Tomson, an English merchant living in Marrakech at
the time, sent a relative in London an interesting account of
Judar Pasha's homecoming.

Six Dayes past [he wrote on 4 July 1599] here aryved a nobleman
from Gago [Gao], called Judar Basha, whoe was sent by this King
10 yeares paste to conquere the said contrye, wherein many people of
this contrye have lost there lives. He brought with him thirtie camels
laden with *tybar*, which ys unrefyned gold (yet the difference ys but six
shillinges in an ownce weight betwene yt and duccattees); also great
store of pepper, unicornes hornes and a certaine kynde of wood for
diers, to some 120 camel loades; all which he presented unto the Kinge,
with 50 horse, and great quantitye of eanuches, duarfes, and weomen
and men slaves, besydes 15 virgins, the Kinge's daughters of Gago,
which he sendeth to be the kinge's concubines. Yow must note all these
be of the cole black heyre, for that contry yeldeth noe other.*[5]

Tomson valued the thirty camel-loads of gold at £604,800.
No sooner had Judar left the Sudan than the Mandingo in-

---

* The pepper was Malaguetta pepper or chillies, then sometimes called grains of
paradise whence the Grain Coast of Guinea got its name. The unicorn's horns were
probably rhinoceros horns; the alternative suggestion of oryx horns is unacceptable
because the oryx was too common in the Sahara for its horns to have been much
valued in Morocco.

vasion he had foretold burst upon the country. The invaders were repelled, but only with difficulty, and a general rising of the tribes was narrowly averted. Nevertheless, the situation had been so mishandled by Ammar that he was at once recalled and replaced by Sulaiman Pasha, the last and certainly the best appointment to the post made by al-Mansur. Unlike his predecessors, Sulaiman was an enlightened administrator who recognized the need to win the confidence of the Sudanese. He moved the Timbuktu garrison to a camp outside the city, thus ridding its inhabitants of the spoliation and petty tyrannies of which they had long been the victims. With the same object he subjected the whole army to a severity of discipline they had not known since Mahmud's time. In consequence, the Sudan became less discontented and more peaceful than the Moors had ever known it. Unfortunately for both Songhai and Moors, this spell of ordered government was brief. It ended with the death of al-Mansur in August 1603.

Each of al-Mansur's three sons tried to seize his throne and his kingdom. Marrakech fell to the youngest, Zaydan, who ultimately prevailed over his brothers, but only after years of civil strife. He was, however, at once accepted by the army in the Sudan as the rightful successor of his father, not that this benefited him or the army in any way. He was far too occupied with anarchy at home and the precariousness of his own position to give much thought to what went on beyond the Sahara, nor could his loyal troops there be of service to him in his domestic troubles.

As the result of the recall of Sulaiman Pasha immediately after al-Mansur's death, the situation in the Sudan had deteriorated to a point where it was doubtful whether Sharifian authority could ever be restored. There had been rebellions of Tuareg, Songhai, and Fulani, not one of which had been decisively crushed, owing to the lamentable state into which the army had fallen. The troops, quarrelling among themselves, were more concerned with faction fights than with resisting enemies of their country. In 1610 Sulaiman's successor, Mahmud Lonko, was driven out by one of his own kaids, Ali at-Tlemcani, who had himself proclaimed pasha in open defiance of the Sharif.

When at last Mulai Zaydan felt himself secure enough at home to attempt to set matters right in the Sudan, he sent Ammar Pasha back there to see what he could do.* Ammar found the Sudan

---

* Ammar Pasha was accompanied to the Sudan by a French slave, the mariner Paul Imbert, to whose presence we shall have occasion to refer later.

seething with rebellion and the army so out of control that even the execution of Ali at-Tlemcani did nothing to restore even a semblance of discipline. In 1618, when Ammar arrived home to report, Mulai Zaydan wisely decided to abandon the costly enterprise to which al-Mansur had committed his country twenty-eight years previously.*

The Moors on the Niger were now their own masters. They chose their pashas and kaids for themselves, obeyed them or not as they felt inclined, and removed them at the slightest whim. For a time they chose their officers from among the soldiers who had been sent out from Morocco, but as these gradually dwindled vacancies were filled with mulattoes who were called Arma. As it was always the object of each of the three divisions which composed the army to secure the pashalik for one of its own officers, appointments frequently provoked violent dissensions. The disappointed divisions would refuse to serve under pashas of whom they did not approve and whose removal they sought to contrive with all speed. Pashas rose and fell almost overnight.[6]

The first care of every pasha was to satisfy, at all costs, the avarice of the factions to whom he owed his promotion and the opportunities it gave for personal gain. The unfortunate Sudanese became the perpetual victims of every kind of extortion from which there was no escape. When a pasha began to feel himself insecure he did not hesitate to summon to his aid the Tuareg, whose usual reward was liberty to plunder the Songhai peasantry. Anarchy and general insecurity inevitably led to reduced cultivation and devastating famines.

Timbuktu remained the Moorish capital and the seat of the puppet Askias, who rose and fell almost as frequently as the pashas. Garrisons commanded by kaids were maintained in Gao, which was in a constant state of mutiny, and in Bamba and Jenne. For purely religious reasons, one must presume, the suzerainty of the Sharif was at least formally recognized, and the Friday prayer continued to be said in his name. They seem even to have sent him tribute. As late as the middle of the century a Frenchman, who had lived many years in Morocco, reported that 'the king of Gao', doubtless meaning the puppet Askia, 'hath so great a veneration [for the Sharif] that some have assured us he pays tribute to the king of Morocco: But I cannot credit it, only this is certain, that he

---

* Nevertheless, in 1958, King Muhammed V of Morocco claimed that the frontier of his country extended to the Senegal and included Timbuktu.

sends him presents.' [7] In 1660, however, the ruling pasha, Muhammad as-Shaytaki finally repudiated the Sharif and had the Friday prayer said in his own name. A few years later the Arma, as the Moors had all become, had grown so weak that they allowed Timbuktu to fall into the hands of the pagan Bambara of Segu. This was the first step towards their fast-approaching political extinction.

By this time the Sa'adian dynasty in Morocco had given place to the Hassanids or Filalians. Mulai ar-Rachid, the third ruler of the new house, was compelled to spend the whole of his reign struggling with formidable adversaries who sought the restoration of the Sa'adians. One of the most dangerous of these was a certain Ali ibn Haidar, whom the Sharif eventually compelled to flee the country. Accompanied by a handful of followers, he sought refuge in the Sudan where, at the price of two Andalusian virgins, he secured the protection of the Bambara king of Segu, the new master of Timbuktu. He at once set about collecting a private army with which, in 1672, he set out for Morocco to avenge himself on ar-Rachid. He arrived, however, to find that the Sharif was dead. There being no ill will between Ali ibn Haidar and Mulai Ismail, the new ruler, the former retired from politics and the latter took over his army which he formed into a sort of praetorian guard. Thus came into being the famous negro Abid or Bokhari who, like the Mamluks in Egypt, were destined in later years to become so baneful an influence in the political life of Morocco.[8]

Ismail soon found that his negro troops, on account of their aloofness from local politics, were, like the white *frendji* of former times, the most dependable part of his army. So well pleased was he with them that he increased their strength by drafting into their ranks all the Haratin he could find and all the descendants of the negroes whom Judar and the other early pashas had sent as captives to al-Mansur. He also encouraged his black army to beget children, who from infancy were trained for a military life. Perceiving, however, that further means would have to be devised to keep it up to strength, he sent his nephew Abulabbas Ahmad to the Sudan to secure recruits and arrange for a regular supply of drafts.

Ahmad arrived in Timbuktu at a time when life had been made unendurable for the townspeople by Berabish raiders from the western desert, against whom their Bambara masters provided no protection. Ahmad, who evidently had with him a considerable escort, was welcomed as a saviour and, after driving out the Bambara officials, he assumed control of the city in the name of the Sharif. He spent some years there, during which time he is said to have reconquered some of the lost provinces. He seems, nevertheless, to have occupied himself chiefly with the recruitment of black troops for the Sharif. On his return to Morocco he left behind him a garrison to uphold the authority of his master, but they failed to prevent the re-entry of the Bambara into Timbuktu and were quickly absorbed into the ranks of the Arma.

By this time the Arma had degenerated into an effete military aristocracy who, so long as they paid tribute to Segu, were left alone by the Bambara. They lived chiefly by blackmailing, and selling their services to the commercial community. Trade was still prosperous, and in spite of a state of chronic anarchy there was still a large colony of foreign merchants in Timbuktu, representing the business houses of the Maghrib. If the foreign merchants failed to meet the dues levied on them by the Arma they were thrown into gaol. But when they met their obligations they received so little in return that they had to make private arrangements with the troops for any protection they needed for themselves and their caravans. Their need under both heads was, of course, constant. Each of the three divisions of the army had its regular clients to whom they hired out guards.

While the Arma of Timbuktu were battening on the rich foreign merchants, those of Gao were leading a precarious existence in the face of a new peril. Since the closing years of the sixteenth century the tribal pattern of the central Sahara had been much altered. The Kel Owi Tuareg, aided by their overlord Mai Idris Alooma of Bornu, had driven the Kel Geres out of Air and got control of the important caravan route linking Hausa with Ghat. The Kel Geres had moved westwards into Adrar of the Iforas, driving before them the Aulimmiden and the Kel Tadmekket, closely related but hostile tribes. The latter settled peacefully near Timbuktu, but the more powerful Aulimmiden seized and occupied the lush pastures around Gao in defiance of the Arma garrison whom they overcame. Although the Arma recovered the old Songhai capital, their powers of resistance were dwindling. All the way from Gao to Jenne their grip on the Niger was gradually slipping from them. By the end of the seventeenth century Gao had again been lost to the Aulimmiden and was never recovered,

and the kaids of Jenne had fallen into permanent tutelage, at times
to the Bambara, at others to the Fulani. For a time the Arma in
Timbuktu contrived to preserve a measure of independence in the
face of unremitting aggression, not by the Bambara who seem to
have lost interest in the city, but by the Tuareg. They were
assailed first by the Aulimmiden and then by the Kel Tadmekket,
at whose hands, in the middle of the following century, they
suffered a defeat from which they never recovered.

As time passed the Arma were gradually absorbed into the
indigenous population. They long survived as an aristocratic clan
whose appearance was often a reminder that the Moorish invaders of the Sudan were predominantly Europeans. They are still
to be found in Timbuktu and Jenne, but they are barely distin-
guishable from the rest of the people.

On the middle Niger, Moorish influence is still descernible in
the pottery, dress, and diet of the people; but its most enduring
effect was on the architecture of the country, notably in Jenne
where the builder's art was developed as nowhere else in the
Western Sudan.[9] The price paid for these paltry gains was the loss
to several generations of a peace-loving people of almost everything which made for human happiness. When all else of the
Spanish speech of the invaders had been forgotten, the Sudanese,
as-Sadi tells us, could still recall the dread order 'Cut off his head!'
The story of the Moorish conquest remains one of the darkest
chapters in the history of the continent.

22

Adh-Dhahabi

*'The King of Morocco is like to be the greatest prince in the world for money,
if he keep this country.'*—ANTHONY DASSEL.

AL-MANSUR'S son and successor, Mulai Zaydan, disappointed at
the little he found in his father's treasury, complained bitterly
of the drain the Sudan campaign had been on the kingdom. It had
consumed, he declared, 23,000 troops, and most of those who came
back had died of the diseases they had contracted in the tropics,

His father's empty coffers showed what a waste it all had been. as-Sadi, the author of the *Tarikh as-Sudan*, who had grown to manhood in his native Timbuktu under the heel of the conqueror, was equally convinced that the vast expenditure of men and material had been in vain.[1]

Both these men, the Sharif and the Sudanese, were prejudiced, though for different reasons. And both were wrong. The Sudan campaign had certainly failed in its purpose of obtaining control of the sources of the gold, but it had enriched the already wealthy al-Mansur on a scale which cannot have left him with many regrets even if few could share his satisfaction. Nevertheless, they called him adh-Dhahabi, 'the Golden'.

Even in al-Ifrani's day, more than fifty years after the Sudan had been abandoned, the Moors still recalled with pride the wealth which had flowed into their country as the result of the conquest.

As a result of the conquest of the states of the Sudan, the Sultan of Morocco received so much gold dust that envious men were all troubled and observers absolutely stupified. So from then on al-Mansur only paid his officials in pure metal and in dinars of proper weight. At the gate of his palace 1400 smiths were daily engaged in making pieces of gold, and there was still some of the precious metal left over, which was made into rings and other jewels. This super abundance of gold earned the sultan the surname adh-Dhahabi.[2]

al-Ifrani's estimate is confirmed by the testimony of foreigners who were living in Marrakech while the campaign was pursuing its tragic course. Among them was Laurence Madoc, an English merchant who kept his London principal, Anthony Dassel of the Barbary Company, well informed about events in Morocco. This is the report he sent to London in August 1594, ten days after the arrival of the *Qadi* of Timbuktu, Abu Hafs Umar, and the other captives whom al-Mansur had had sent in chains across the Sahara:

Your letter of late I received, and found that you would have me discover unto you the estate & quality of the countreyes of Tombuto and Gago. And that you may not thinke me to slumber in this action, wherein you would be truely and perfectly resolved, you shall understand, that not ten days past here came a Cahaia of the Andoluzes [Andalusians] home from Gago, and another principall Moore, whom the king sent thither at the first with Alcaide Hamode [Kaid Mahmud

ibn Zargun], and they brought with them thirty mules laden with
gold. I saw the same come into the Alcasava* with mine owne eies;
and these men themselves came not poore, but with such wealth,
that they came away without the kings commandement, and for that
cause the king will pay them no wages for the time they have beene
there. On the other side they dare not aske the king for any wages.
And when Alcaide Hamode saw that the Cahaia of the Andoluzes
would not stay in Gago with him, he thought good to send these thirty
mules laden with golde by him, with letters of commendations, by
which the king smelled their riches that they brought with them; and
this was the cause of the kings displeasure towards them.

So now there remaineth in Gago Alcaide Hamode, and Alcaide
Jawdara [Judar], and Alcaide Bucthare [Bu-Ikhtiyar]. And here are
in a readiness to depart in the end of this next September . . . five
thousand men most of the fettilase, that is to say of fier-mach and
muskets. . . .³

Later in the month Madoc wrote again to Dassel in response to
the latter's request for more information about al-Mansur's activities in Guinea.

The rent of Tombuto [read this second letter] is 60 quintals of gold
by the yeere, the goodnesse whereof you know. What rent Gago will
yeeld, you shall know at the Spring, for then Alcaide Hamode commeth home. The rent of Tombuto is come by the cafelow or carovan,
which is, as above is mentioned, 60 quintals.

The report is, that Mahomed [Mahmud ibn Zargun] bringeth with
him such an infinite treasure as I never heard of; it doth appeare
that they have more golde then any other part of the world beside.
The Alcaide winneth all the country where he goeth without fighting,
and is going downe towards the sea coast. This king of Morocco is like
to be the greatest prince in the world for money, if he keepe this
countrey. . . .⁴

If the thirty mules mentioned in Madoc's first letter carried no
more than the normal 70 kilos load of a Saharan donkey, the
gold on their backs would have totalled about 70,000 ounces.
The current sterling value of unrefined gold was about 50s. an
ounce, so the value of this treasure was probably in the region of
£175,000, which was a great deal of money for those days. The
annual value of the Timbuktu tribute, sixty quintals of gold, was
about £150,000: Gao was assessed at thirty mule-loads of gold,
or about £175,000. But al-Mansur's revenue from the conquered

* The Alcasava was a Sharifian palace in Marrakech.

territories was not limited to the tribute payable to him annually. For example, it will be recalled that the Englishman Jasper Tomson, who was in Marrakech when Judar arrived back from the Sudan, assessed the gold the pasha brought with him at £604,800. As late as 1607, when the anarchy in Morocco and the Sudan which followed al-Mansur's death must have checked the amount of treasure flowing northwards into Morocco, a Frenchman reported from Marrakech that treasure amounting to 4,600,000 *livres* was shortly expected from Gao and Timbuktu, 'le tout en or de tibre'.[5]

The accuracy of every one of these figures is, of course, more than suspect, but collectively the contexts from which they are taken justify the assumption that for some years at least the Sudan was paying handsome dividends.

With so much gold pouring into his treasury, al-Mansur was able to resume the extravagant expenditure which the Moorish triumph at al-Ksar al-Kabir had made possible at the beginning of his reign. But experience had taught him to spend wisely, and the new wealth was devoted more to the pressing needs of the kingdom than to personal aggrandizement. Still fearful of his powerful neighbours, al-Mansur spent a considerable sum on improving his defences against both invasion and rebellion. The fortifications of Larache, which so many seemed to covet, were considerably strengthened. At Fez he built two forts which the European slaves working on them called al Basatin, the Bastions. But perhaps his wisest expenditure was on re-equipping and developing the important sugar industry of Sus. Mindful of his obligations as the Caliph of his people, he spent lavishly on the mosques and *medersas*. But the opportunity for further enhancing the splendour of the royal palaces was not neglected, and once more he turned to Europe for skilled craftsmen.

The extent to which Englishmen were employed in Morocco seems to have impressed the famous Captain John Smith of Virginia, who happened to visit the country a few months after al-Mansur's death. In all al-Mansur's kingdom, he wrote, there

were so few good artificers that hee entertained from England Goldsmiths, Plummers, Carvers, and Polishers of stone, and Watchmakers, so much he delighted in the reformation of workmanship, hee allowed each of them ten shillings a day standing fee, linnen, woollen, silkes, and what they would for diet and apparell and customs free to transport, or import what they would; for there were scarce any of those qualities in his kingdoms but those, of which there are divers of them living at this present in London.[6]

No doubt the English watchmakers, one or two of whom we know by name, were partly employed in keeping in order the nautical and other instruments of which the Sharif was a keen buyer. His interest in them seems to have sprung from their proved value in the desert. The Moorish invasion and the misery which followed in its train so antagonized the people of the desert that guides became difficult to find. Consequently, both troops and merchants travelling to the Sudan were forced to use nautical instruments. Ammar Pasha took with him to the Sudan a French sailor, Paul Imbert, one of whose countrymen described the difficulties of Saharan travel at this time:

to steer your course [he wrote] you must make your observation from the rising and setting of the sun, and the stars and the compass must (if there be occasion) direct you. They always take care to have some or other in the caphille [caravan], who understand these matters, as Paul Imbert did, who was a mariner and well-beloved, and cherished by his master.[7]

Similarly an Englishman at about the same time said that it took six months for merchants to reach the Sudan.

of which two moneths they passe thorow the sandie deserts where no people dwell, neither any roadway, but directed by pylots, as ships at sea, observe the courses of the sunne, moone and stars, for feare of missing their way. If they lose themselves, they meete with famine and die for lacke of water, whose dead carkasses consume not, but maketh munna [mummy] or otema flesh, every way as phisicall or medicinable as that which cometh from Alexandria.[8]

In 1600 Edward Wright, the eminent English mathematician and hydrographer, was warned by a correspondent in Marrakech,* whose letter is in Purchas, that the approaching visit of a Moorish ambassador to London should prove an opportunity for making profitable sales of instruments.[9]

This King Muley Hamet [Ahmad] [the letter reads] is much delighted in the studie of astronomie and astrologie, and valueth instruments serving for the course of the sunne and moone that are of rare device, exceedingly; wherefore your sphere, your watch, your mundane dial and your sextans, your new magneticall instrument for

---

* His correspondent was his brother-in-law Thomas Bernhere.

declination, or any astrolable that hath somewhat extraordinarie in it, will be accepted; and you might sell the same at good prices. . . .

You may cause to be framed some instruments in brasse or silver, leaving the spaces for Arabique words and figures, yet drawing the pictures of them in paper exactly, and setting downe the Latine figures and the words in Latin or Spanish which is far better. There will be found here that can grave the same in Arabique upon the instruments, having some direction from you about the matter. . . . The experiments mathematicall of the load-stone will content the Ambassador much. Make no scruple to shew them what you can; for it may redound to your good. . . .

Your magnetical instrument of declination would be commodious for a yeerly voyage which some make for the King over a sandy sea (wherein they must use needle and compasse) to Gago. If you question about the matter, and shew them some instrument serving for this purpose, it will give great content.[10]

Gold was far from being the only product of the Sudan which was highly valued in Morocco. There was also a keen demand for slaves, ivory, ebony, and civet, and a ready market for much else. With all of these al-Mansur was kept well supplied by his pashas. Besides the splendid present brought him by Judar, he had previously been sent by Mahmud 1,200 slaves, half of them men and half women, also forty loads of gold, a quantity of ebony, civet, and civet cats, and a number of other rare and valuable products. In a different category was an elephant with which the Sharif was able to gratify and astonish the people of Marrakech.*

With the country's new-found wealth concentrated in the hands of the Sharif and his favourites, the common people had been denied any recompense for the heavy demands the campaign had made on them. The merchants' fears that the invasion would seriously interrupt their trade had proved justified, though business had recovered with the cessation of fighting. But all were bitterly disappointed at the failure to discover, and add to the tale of conquests, the source of the gold. The wealth of Wangara remained as remote as ever. Nevertheless, with the treasury filled to overflowing, local trade was booming, and none benefited more than the foreign merchants, for the luxuries the court most needed were almost wholly European.

The foreign mercantile communities were principally English, French, and Dutch, but English merchants predominated and

---

* The introduction of tobacco into Morocco was attributed to the elephant's negro keepers.

enjoyed a virtual monopoly of the trade passing through Santa Cruz du Cap de Ghir (Agadir) and Safi, whence the Portuguese had been driven by the Moors in 1541. The Portuguese now held only the ports of Ceuta, Tangier, and Mazaghan, and bitterly resented the loss of the valuable southern Moroccan trade. They claimed that under the famous bull of Pope Alexander VI they alone had the right to trade with Africa outside the Mediterranean. This led to a long controversy with the English which was resolved by the latter's agreeing to surrender their claims in Guinea, where they had traded since the middle of the sixteenth century; but they stubbornly refused to abandon their lucrative trade with Morocco.

The staples of the English trade were still saltpetre, and sugar from Sus, in the preparation of both of which al-Mansur had found it advantageous to employ skilled Englishmen. During the civil war following his death many of the sugar plantations were destroyed, much to England's cost. Other exports to England included gold, ostrich feathers, indigo, beeswax, dates, horses, and hawks (notably falcons and tiercels). With the gold, which was of course *tibar* from the Sudan, went quantities of Moorish sequins which Moroccan Jews were shipping to London for reminting into coin of the realm.* The chief goods shipped from England to Morocco were all kinds of munitions, ship-building materials and marine gear (both wanted for the corsair business and therefore rightly condemned by Catholic Europe as munitions of war), and great quantities of cloth.

The arms traffic, the continuance of which both Elizabeth and the Sharif wanted kept a close secret, was as much a personal link between the two sovereigns as it had been between Elizabeth and Abd al-Malik. It was a bond by which al-Mansur set great store, for England, besides being the only foreign power whose friendship he could claim, was the destroyer of the Armada of the hated Philip of Spain. In his eyes it was a friendship to be cherished and also exploited.

In 1600 a high official of the Sharifian court, the ambassador who Edward Wright had been told was a likely buyer of his instruments, arrived secretly in London. He and his *entourage* of two

* In the reign of Elizabeth and the early years of James I the main source of gold for the English coinage was foreign gold coins captured from the Spaniards or imported by merchants. After 1612 James, in order to ensure a profit from his Mint, fixed maximum prices for foreign coins and bullion, the latter being described as 'Barbary Gold'. (The Chief Clerk, Royal Mint, in a letter to the author.)

merchants, an interpreter, and twelve servants were lodged by the mystified Queen in a reluctant alderman's house in the City. On being granted an audience at Nonsuch, the ambassador astonished Elizabeth by disclosing that he had come to propose that she and al-Mansur should make a joint attack on Spain and then seize and divide between them all Philip's possessions in the Old and New Worlds. Lest the Queen should doubt the ability of the Sharifian army to play its part in so remarkable an enterprise, she was reminded of al-Mansur's recent conquest of Guinea and its 86,000 cities! [11]

Having no wish to jeopardize her supplies of saltpetre, Elizabeth returned a diplomatic answer which led the Moor to hope that means would be sought for meeting his master's wishes. The Queen found it less easy to dispose of the ambassador and his companions than the ludicrous object of their mission. In spite of the mounting resentment and undisguised hostility which the uncouth behaviour of the Moors widely excited, it took months to rid the kingdom of its unwelcome guests. As time passed a suspicion grew that the excuse for their coming was but a cloak for commercial espionage.

He of Barbary [reads a Privy Council minute] used great woordes of offer in generall of any assistance to the Queen . . . but his dryft was, under cover of their formall voyadge, to lerne here how merchandize went, and what gain we made of their sugers, that he might raise the prices accordingly. [12]

Less than three years later, in 1603, al-Mansur died and was buried in the splendid tomb which may still be seen in Marrakech. He owed much to the auspicious circumstances of his accession but he left his country greatly in his debt. In a reign of twenty-five years, during the whole of which hostile neighbours pressed menacingly on his frontiers, he had successfully preserved the independence of his kingdom and even maintained the prestige which al-Ksar had given it; he had, too, dazzled Europe with the wealth which his resolution and enterprise had won for him from the Sudan. If he had most of the faults of the oriental despot, he was exceptional in his patronage of the arts. To a love of fine craftsmanship was added a keen interest in scientific invention which, more than any other quality, distinguished him from his contemporaries.

A not unpleasing character sketch of al-Mansur by an

anonymous Englishman, the mysterious Ro. C.* of Purchas, survives:

Towards his subjects he was not too tyrannicall, but sweettned his absolute power and will with much clemencie. By divers ways he got excessive store of gold. First, by seeing his tenths truly paid from the Larbees: Secondly, by trading with the Negro, taking up the salt at Tegazza and selling it at Gago, having from thence returne in good gold. Thirdly, by husbanding his maseraws [presses] or Ingenewes [plantations], where his Sugar Canes did grow. . . . I omit his love he tooke in entertaining forraigne Artizans, the re-edifying of his house in Moruecos [Marrakech], getting Italian Marbles, the richest that could bee bought for money, and workemen hired from thence at great wages. His sumptuous provisions for the Sarraile [seraglio] and maintenance of his women, not so much delighting in the sinne, as his predecessors had done before, as to shew his glory, because the fashion of the Countrey is such to shew their riches and greatnesse upon that fraile sexe and their attendances. For his chiefest pleasures were to see the Gallantrie of his kingdome managing their good Barbarian Steeds, and the Falchons upon their winge making faire flights after the Heron.[13]

At the death of al-Mansur covetous European eyes were turning their gaze on Africa. As in the days of Prince Henry, nearly two centuries before, the sight of gold pouring freely into Morocco had directed men's minds to the possibility of capturing the trade at its source, by way of the sea. But the prospects were now far more alluring. The gold was coming in quantities never dreamed of before. The project, too, was plainly more practicable. The coast of Guinea was now well known and the interior had been probed from the trading posts which the Portuguese had established between Cape Verde and the Bight of Benin. Moreover, there was a steady, though modest, flow of gold northwards to Europe from the coast, especially from the Portuguese fort at São Jorge da Mina on the Gold Coast. The gold was brought down to the coast, but from where in the interior no one knew. Those who hoped that the Moorish and the Guinea gold had a common origin had found encouragement in Leo's narrative, and confirmation in Marmol Caravajal's *Descripcion de Africa*, a work first published in 1573 and widely read in Europe.† The world had few greater prizes to offer

* R. C. is believed to have been Captain Robert Coverte. (Mr. F. B. Maggs in a letter to the author.)

† Marmol was a Spaniard who was born in Granada and spent seven years in Africa as a slave of the Moors.

than the discovery of the hidden source of the gold, and plainly the coast of Guinea was the most likely way to it.

A proposal of this nature had been put to the Spanish court in 1591. If only Philip, wrote Melchior Petoney from Arguin on the Gum Coast (as it came to be called), would send out every year two or three caravels freighted with suitable trade goods 'his majesty might stop that passage, and keepe the king of Fez from so huge a masse of gold'. Petoney was himself trading there and finding that 'for a small trifle they will give us a great wedge of gold'.[14] But this was not the sort of project to interest Philip, weighed down with the cares of rebellion in Aragon and the interminable revolt of the Netherlands.

Owing to their predominant position in the foreign trade of Morocco, the English knew better than anyone else how immense was the quantity of gold coming into the country. Moreover, they also knew a good deal about the Guinea trade where they, together with the French, were still trafficking in gold in defiance of the Portuguese. They were thus better placed than any other nation to collect, assess, and turn to account anything that could be learnt about the gold trade. But that cannot have been very much. From Morocco came much the same story as Herodotus had told. Soon after al-Mansur's death Ro. C. described how the Moors used to carry salt from Taghaza far into the interior

to a kind of deformed Negros, who will never be seene in the commerce of trading with the Barbarian or any stranger: Wherefore they lay their Salt in the fields and leaveth it, then commeth the deformed Negro, and layeth against every man's pricell of Salt, as much of his gold as he thinketh the Salt is worth, and goeth his way, leaving his gold with the Salt: Then returneth the Moor, if he like the gold, taketh it away; if not, detracteth so much from his heap, as he will sell to the Negro for his gold. The Negro returning, if he like the quantity, putteth too more gold, or else will not barter, but departeth. Yet they seldom mislike, for the Moore maketh a rich returne, and his King a full treasure, Wherefore the deformed negro is praysed for the truest dealing man in the world.[15]

The deformed negro was new to the story, but, as we shall see, he was more than a figment of the Moorish mind.

In 1603 Henry Roberts, who had been an agent of the Barbary Company and later of Elizabeth in Marrakech, proposed to James I that he should capture the gold trade by conquering Morocco. 'Your Matie', he wrote, 'haveinge possessed this countrey, you may invade and goe as farre as you please into Genney [Guinea] which is very rich both in goulde and other great riches comodities.' [16]

But the English did nothing about the gold trade until 1618, when some London merchants formed themselves into a 'Company for the countries of Ginney and Binney [Benin]' with the purpose of 'discovering the golden trade of the Moors of Barbary'.

The Gambia river seemed to the Adventurers the most likely route to the gold-mines which were supposed to be somewhere near Gao on the Niger. As the Senegal and Gambia were thought to be the outlets through which the Niger found its way to the sea, men argued that if either of these rivers was followed from the coast into the interior it would be found to lead ultimately to the long-sought mines.

The first ship the Adventurers sent out was the *Catherine*. She was commanded by George Thompson, who was well qualified for the task in hand by long experience as a trader in Marrakech, and was probably of the same family as the Tomsons of that city. His orders were to explore the upper reaches of the Gambia in the hope of discovering the mines. But the expedition was a failure. Soon after its arrival in Africa, the Portuguese seized the ship and cut the throats of the crew. Thompson was away up the river at the time and so survived, but only to be murdered later by one of his own men.[17]

The Adventurers next sent out Richard Jobson with the *Syon* and a pinnace. As he made his way up the river, Jobson, like Thompson, was in constant expectation of meeting Moorish traders from the Maghrib. But he neither met any Moors nor found any gold-mines, and his voyage was accounted a failure. In spite of his assurances of the imminence of a great and profitable discovery, the Adventurers decided to abandon the enterprise.

But people continued to hold firmly to the belief that the Gambia was the key to the secret of the gold trade. Forty years later Peter Mundy recorded the sailing of five ships from the Downs 'towards Rio de Gamba the design concerned to discover from whence the gold commeth'.[18]

The problem was still far from being solved, and there was obviously much truth in what Jobson had said about the secrecy with which the trade was hedged. The Moors, he wrote, followed the trade 'with such great dilligence and government, that amongst themselves, none are admitted but principale persons, and by especiale order, without entertaining any other nation, what respect or familiarity so ever they have gained amongst them.'[19]

The trans-Saharan trade had naturally suffered from the long reign of anarchy in the Sudan, but it seems never to have been wholly interrupted. Slaves, in addition to gold, had become a staple of the north-bound traffic which now included also ivory.* Salt was still the principal import into the Sudan, but with it came much English cloth. The people of Sus, wrote some English merchants in 1635–6, 'have a great trade with our English comodities' to Timbuktu, Gao and other parts of Guinea, and 'from thence bring great quantitye of gould, whereof wee receive a goode parte upon the sale of our goodes'.[20] In 1638 gold was still being shipped to England but, wrote George Carteret, 'this gold may rather be accompted a treasure than a commoditie, in regard that the ancient supply from Gago which was brought in by *cafells* [caravans] in Ahmed's days, grandfather of this Kinge, is now lost by the troubles of the State'.[21] Before the end of the year the gold reserves in Morocco were running out 'for that golden trade of Gago . . . hath long since been intermitted'.[22]

* Previously the ivory traffic had been confined to the central Sahara owing to Cairo being its chief market.

23

The European Penetration of the Interior

*'For surely, those interiour parts of Affrica are little knowen to either English,
French, or Dutch, though they use much the Coast.'*—CAPT. JOHN SMITH.
'And pray what is Cape Verde? A stinking place?'—CHARLES II.

FROM the early years of the sixteenth century to the end of the
eighteenth, cartographers never lacked for new material with
which to enrich their maps. Scarcely a year passed without some
advance in geographical knowledge, and at no period did the
mapping of the world make greater strides. Yet in all that time,
throughout the three centuries following the travels of Leo
Africanus, nothing authoritative was added to the map of the
interior of northern Africa. Indeed, the greatest advance in
African cartography occurred when the French eighteenth-century cartographer D'Anville cut out the decorative details beloved
by earlier map-makers, and showed with provoking clarity how
little Europeans actually knew about the interior of Africa.* This
ignorance was a reflection of the failure of European merchants
to penetrate inland from the northern ports or from the trading
beaches of Guinea.

In North Africa, in spite of the decline of the gold trade, the
old fear of the European ousting the local middlemen continued
and he was still denied footholds in the hinterland. But the pene-

---

* In his maps of the Niger D'Anville abandoned the practice of earlier cartographers, all of whom had followed Leo Africanus and had showed the Niger flowing
westwards into the Atlantic. D'Anville re-examined the accounts of Ptolemy and
al-Idrisi, obtained new information from contemporary travellers in North Africa
and the Senegal, and came to the conclusion that the Niger and the Senegal must
be different rivers. In one of his maps the Niger is clearly shown flowing eastwards
into a lake, which is shown in the approximate position of Lake Chad. But
D'Anville's ideas were not widely accepted, and as late as the 1790s maps still
showed a westward-flowing Niger.[1]

tration of the interior had been made even more difficult for him by a material change in the political relationship between Europe and the Barbary states.

Throughout the Middle Ages, piracy, both Christian and Muslim, had been an ever-present condition of maritime life in the Mediterranean, but, as we have seen, it was never permitted to hamper trade. At the beginning of the sixteenth century this mutual tolerance was brought to an end by the unhappy synchronization of the expulsion of the Moors from Spain with the rise of Ottoman sea-power in European waters. The exiled Moors formed settlements all along the North African coast, whence they sought to avenge themselves on their hated oppressors by raiding the familiar shores of Spain and harassing Christian shipping, especially in the Straits of Gibraltar and the Malta Passage. The African coast, abounding in sheltering creeks and inlets, was admirably suited to their purpose. They succeeded, moreover, in enlisting the assistance of the Turks who, led by the famous Barbarossa brothers from Lesbos, quickly became the predominant partners in what came to be called the Scourge of Christendom. Within a few years almost every harbour from Jerba in the east to Salee in the west held its pirate fleet.

For the next three centuries the petty pirate princes were allowed to harass the whole of the carrying trade of the Mediterranean, to raid the shores of Europe, and to enslave many thousands of Christians with almost complete impunity. The European Powers, unable to compose their differences and combine to stamp out the common peril, meekly contented themselves with purchasing the safety of their vessels and the release of their nationals by paying blackmail and ransoms to the pirates. They even accredited diplomatic representatives to the African courts to arrange these matters and to secure the redemption of the more influential of the thousands of Christian slaves who endured the purgatory of the galleys or languished in the bagnios. Trade, of course, suffered, but the Moors were not denied the manufactured goods of Europe they so greatly coveted.[2]

In the seventeenth century the replacement of the galley by the square-rigged sailing ship opened to the corsairs a much wider field for their raids. They were assisted in their more distant enterprises by the numbers of English seamen who, thrown out of employment when the turbulent days of Elizabeth gave place to the peaceful reign of James I, sought service with the corsairs to save themselves from starvation. Equipped with better ships and experienced navigators, the African pirates began raiding the shores of Britain, Denmark, and Iceland. In the reign of Charles II the Salee rovers* seized and occupied Lundy island, and the people of Cork shuddered as the call of the muezzin echoed over the peaceful waters of their harbour.

With the growth of European naval power, the corsairs were once more made to confine their depredations to the Mediterranean. There they remained an intolerable menace until the close of the Napoleonic wars when, at the Congress of Vienna, the Powers at last agreed to unite against the common foe.

On the Guinea coast the situation was far more discreditable to the Europeans. Their failure to explore the interior there was due less to the formidable physical obstructions—rivers difficult to navigate, forests thought of as impenetrable, and a lethal climate—than to the unfortunate relationship which had grown up between the white traders and the coast peoples. From the first, the Portuguese had made a point of capturing local people and sending them back as slaves to Portugal. With the discovery of the New World, and the development of plantation colonies in the islands of the Caribbean and on the tropical American mainland, the demand for African slaves greatly increased.

Throughout the sixteenth century, the slave trade was almost entirely in the hands of the Portuguese. But in the first half of the seventeenth century the Portuguese lost most of their forts and factories in West Africa to the Dutch. At the same time, the English and the French began to establish colonies in the New World, and founded their own trading posts in West Africa. The growth in international demand led to a steady increase in the number of slaves exported. In the sixteenth century the average number of slaves sent across the Atlantic in a year has been estimated as 13,000; towards the close of the eighteenth century, when the infamous traffic first began to disturb the conscience of Europe, the annual export for West Africa alone was about 64,000.

By the eighteenth century, the trade carried on by Europeans in West Africa followed a pattern sanctioned by generations of

*The pre-eminence of Salee in the corsair business was due to the efficient organization created by the thousands of Moriscos who had settled there after their expulsion from Spain in 1610. Their raids into English waters were not unprovoked. In 1597 no less a man than Robert Cecil, like many of his countrymen, sent his ship the *True Love* to Morocco to engage in both trade and piracy.[3]

usage. The Gold Coast was the scene of the greatest European activity; it was here that Europeans had erected the great trading castles, Christiansborg, Elmina and others, that still stand as a memorial to this period of history. Along the coast of modern Nigeria a vigorous trade was maintained, but Europeans were not allowed to build any posts on land. On the Senegal the French had founded a few small posts deep in the interior. Wherever they were, Europeans traders were dependent on African good-will. They were accepted because of the goods—textiles, ironmongers, firearms, spirits—they brought with them. From African middlemen they obtained the goods—not only slaves, but other commodities, gum on the Senegal, gold on the Gold Coast, timber and ivory in the Niger area—they had come to purchase. African coastal traders were naturally not anxious to see European traders encroaching on the markets of the interior. But in fact, except on the Senegal where the French were drawn on by the lure of the gold of Bambuk, European traders had no desire to move into the interior. They lacked the capital to finance elaborate expeditions, they were well aware of the physical difficulties that had to be surmounted, and they were content with the return they were obtaining from the coastal trade.

That the interior of Africa remained unknown to Europeans for so long has usually been ascribed to the physical difficulties— 'burning deserts', 'impenetrable forests', 'fever-ridden swamps', 'harbourless coasts'—that had to be overcome. These physical difficulties must not be ignored, but they can easily be exaggerated. The Sahara, for example, far from being an impassable barrier, was, as we have seen, crossed by many regular trade-routes. Nor should one exaggerate the extent of African hostility. As the first generation of African explorers were to show, a shrewd and diplomatic European traveller could usually make his way through any African state. Basically, it would seem that the real reason for European ignorance lay in the simple fact that, until the late eighteenth century, Europeans had no incentive to find out more about the interior of the allegedly 'mysterious' continent.[4]

The eighteenth century was an age which saw a remarkable increase in the wealth of Western Europe. With growing wealth went an improved capacity and a more insistent desire to extend the bounds of knowledge in many different directions. In geographical exploration, the three Pacific voyages of Captain Cook were the great achievement of the age. But when men turned from these exploits to look at the map of Africa, it seemed, at least to a small group of wealthy Englishmen, a 'reproach' upon their age that the interior should still present

but a wide extended blank, on which the geographer, on the authority of Leo Africanus and of the Xeriff Edrissi has traced, with a hesitating hand, a few names of unexplored rivers and uncertain nations. The course of the Niger, the places of its rise and termination, and even its existence as a separate stream, are still undetermined. . . . Desirous of rescuing the age from a charge of ignorance, which in other respects belongs little to its character, a few individuals, strongly impressed with a conviction of the practicability and utility of thus enlarging the fund of human knowledge, have formed a plan of an Association for promoting the discovery of the interior part of Africa.[5]

The men who in the year 1788 formed this resolution were the members of a highly exclusive dining club. All of them were persons of some standing in the public life of their day. The most distinguished among them was Sir Joseph Banks. Banks had established a reputation for himself as one of the most remarkable men of science of his day when, at his own expense, he accompanied Captain Cook on his first voyage round the world. Elected President of the Royal Society at the age of thirty-five, Banks achieved an international reputation as a patron and stimulator of scientific research. Until his death in 1820, he was actively engaged in the encouragement of African exploration.[6]

The first attempts of the African Association, as the new body was commonly known, ended in failure. An American, John Ledyard, sent to Cairo with instructions to cross the continent from east to west died as a result of an accident before he could set out. An Englishman, Simon Lucas, who went to Tripoli with orders to pass from the Mediterranean to the Guinea coast, turned back when faced by a revolt of the Arab tribes of the interior. An Irishman, Daniel Houghton, who made the Gambia his starting point in an attempt to reach Timbuktu and the Hausa country died in mysterious circumstances after going several hundred miles into the interior.

At this juncture, just when it looked as though the Association would never achieve its object, a twenty-three-year-old Scottish doctor, Mungo Park, offered his services, and they were at once accepted. He was sent out to the Gambia with instructions to make his way to the Niger and ascertain its course from source to mouth. There is no need to repeat here the well-known story of how, after months of infinite peril and suffering which would quickly have broken a man cast in a less heroic mould, Mungo Park at last reached the Niger. On 20 July 1796, as he was approaching Segu, the Bambara capital, he saw, to quote his own words, 'with infinite pleasure the great object of my mission; the long sought for, majestic Niger, glittering to the morning sun, as broad as the Thames at Westminster, and flowing *to the eastward*'.[7]

Not content with this achievement, and despite broken health and the exhaustion of his resources, Park journeyed painfully on, intent on learning more about the great river he had discovered. But

worn down by sickness [he wrote], exhausted with hunger and fatigue; half naked, and without any article of value, by which I might procure provisions, clothes, or lodging . . . I was apprehensive that, in attempting to reach even Jenné . . . I should sacrifice my life to no purpose; for my discoveries would perish with me. The prospect either way was gloomy.[8]

So he turned back and made for the coast, but he was so ill that there seemed little likelihood of his reaching it. That he did so was wholly due to his having been nursed back to comparative health by a negro trader, collecting slaves for sale to Europeans on the Gambia, under whose kindly care he remained for seven months. His arrival in England where, after an absence of over three and a half years, he had long been given up for dead was sensational in itself, but the news of his discovery of the Niger awakened great enthusiasm throughout the kingdom and far beyond.

Park's eagerly awaited narrative of how he had solved one of the oldest mysteries of the geographical world was published in 1799. It was accompanied by a long memoir on the scientific results of the expedition by Major James Rennell, F.R.S., the leading geographer of the day. Besides reconstructing the geography of the Western Sudan in the light of the new discoveries, Rennell plunged boldly into the problem of the termination of the Niger. A re-reading of Idrisi and the other Arabic authors in the changed circumstances led him to declare that: 'On the whole, it can scarcely be doubted that the Joliba or Niger terminates in lakes, in the eastern quarter of Africa; and those lakes seem to be situated in Wangara and Ghana.' He regarded these two countries as the 'sink of North Africa', in which the waters of the Niger became so widely spread that they evaporated. With the great authority of Rennell to support it, this theory, which was not altogether new, found wide acceptance. Although it was so far from the truth as to appear to us almost absurd, there was considerable excuse for Rennell's mistake. It sprang primarily from Leo's blunder in placing Wangara in Hausa which, as we have seen, confused geographers for nearly three centuries. Rennell assumed that Idrisi's Wangara and Leo's were the same, and he accepted the current belief that the Hausa city of Kano was identical with the ancient Ghana.* With these two false premises it is hardly surprising that he failed in his attempt to reconcile medieval Arab geography with recent discoveries.[9]

In 1796, when Park's fate was still unknown, the African Association accepted the services of a young German, Frederick Hornemann. Hornemann went to Cairo, succeeded in passing himself off as a Muslim, and joined a caravan bound for Murzuk in the Fezzan. The last heard of him was a letter sent home from Murzuk, capital of the Fezzan, dated April 1800. But it was afterwards learnt that he had succeeded in crossing the Sahara and had made his way from Bornu through Katsina to Nupe, where he died.

In some notes sent back before he set out across the Sahara, Hornemann reported that all the people of Bornu and Hausa to whom he had spoken stated that the the Niger flowed eastwards to join the Nile. This information appeared to confirm the old theory first put forward by Herodotus.[10] Thus was lost the record of one of the outstanding journeys in this history of African exploration.

Spurred by the African Association, the British Government now decided to lend a hand by sending an expedition to the west coast to navigate the Niger to its termination. Mungo Park, who had settled down to the uncongenial life of a medical practitioner in Peebles, eagerly accepted the post of leader. He planned to make his way to Segu and there build a boat in which he would sail down the river 'through the kingdoms of Haussa, Nyffe [Nupe] and Kasna [Katsina], to the kingdom of Wangara'. If the river ended there he would return either up the Niger, or across the Sahara, or by the Nile, or through the Bight of Benin. But Park

---

* 'Of course Ghana,' he wrote, 'which in the 15th century was paramount in the centre of Africa, is now become a province of Kassina [Katsina]'. (Park, *Travels*, p. lxiv.)

himself had recently come to accept an entirely new theory, put
forward by an English merchant, George Maxwell, with trading
experience of the Congo. Maxwell had suggested that the Congo,
a great river known only at its mouth, and the Niger, known only
in its upper reaches, were in fact one and the same river. If
Maxwell was right—and Park was convinced that he was, then
it should prove comparatively simple to sail down the Niger to
the sea.[11]

Accompanied by two fellow-Scots and five naval artificers who
were to build his boat, he sailed in January 1805. On arrival at
Goree, he was joined by an escort of an officer and thirty-five men
from the British garrison, and two seamen. Except for one Mandingo guide, no natives could be induced to join the expedition.

The escort of white troops, debilitated by the appalling conditions then inseparable from garrison life in the tropics, quickly
proved a serious liability of which Park would have been glad
to rid himself. Men soon began to collapse from fever and dysen-
tery, and before long everyone had become so despondent that
only Park's resolute determination kept the expedition moving
towards its goal. By the time it had reached Bamako on the Niger,
the artificers and three-quarters of the soldiers were dead. The
survivors struggled on to Sansanding where the building of the
boat was put in hand and where, too, Park in November 1805
drafted his last dispatch.

I am sorry to say [it read] that of the forty-four Europeans who left
the Gambia in perfect health, five only are at present alive . . . but
though all the Europeans who are with me should die, and though I
were myself half dead, I would still persevere; and if I could not
suceed in the object of my journey, I would at last die on the Niger.

The dispatch and a last letter to Park's wife were carried to the
coast by the faithful Mandingo guide who, many months later,
was sent back to find out what had become of his master. He
learnt that in spite of much opposition from natives on the way,
Park and three surviving white companions had followed the
Niger for over a thousand miles and had succeeded in reaching
the Bussa rapids. Finding the banks thronged with apparently
hostile natives and not daring to land, and probably unaware
that their frail craft could not possibly survive the terrible rush
of waters ahead, they had continued downstream and perished.
Some have thought that the wild gesticulations of the armed

natives on the banks were no more than a warning to the white men of the perils towards which they were heading. Against this must be set the great reluctance of the natives in later years to discuss the incident at all.[12]

Park's second expedition had been a tragic failure in every sense. Not a single white member of the expedition had escaped death, and in spite of this heavy loss of life and the immense distance covered, no fresh light had been thrown on the riddle of the termination of the Niger. Owing to an unfortunate misapprehension that Bussa was only 80 miles below Timbuktu, instead of 800, neither the coastward direction of the river nor the magnitude of Park's achievement was recognized. Meanwhile the theory that the Niger and the Congo were one, with the weight of the great explorer's authority behind it, gained still wider acceptance. Little attention was paid to yet another theory, put forward first by a German academic geographer, C. G. Reichard, and later by a Scotsman who had lived in the West Indies, James MacQueen. Both Reichard and MacQueen argued that the Niger flowed into the Bight of Benin and that the many creeks and rivers of that coast were in fact part of the delta of the great river.[13]

In 1816, the British Government tried to test the Niger-Congo theory by sending out two expeditions; one, led by naval officers, was to attempt to travel by boat up the Congo, the other, made up of soldiers, was to strike overland from the Gambia to the Niger. Both ended in failure. The naval expedition found its passage blocked by rapids a hundred miles from the river's mouth, and lost all its officers from yellow fever. The land expedition spent six years trying to find a way into the interior, only to be blocked at each attempt by the hostility of local rulers. Meanwhile, the British Government's attention had been drawn to the possibility of using Tripoli as a gateway to the interior. In 1819, a modest expedition led by a young doctor, Joseph Ritchie, reached Murzuk in the Fezzan. Ritchie died in Murzuk, but his companion, Captain G. F. Lyon, R.N., returned safely. Though he brought back with him a mass of interesting information on the Fezzan, he could contribute nothing of any value about the course of the Niger.[14]

In 1821 the Government sent out yet another expedition from Tripoli, led by Dr. Oudney, with Major Dixon Denham and Lieutenant Hugh Clapperton, R.N., as companions. After months of delay in Murzuk, where every effort was made to prevent their going farther, they reached Lake Chad where they hoped to find at least a clue to the solution of the Niger problem. 'My heart bounded within me at the prospect,' wrote Denham, 'for I believed this lake to be the key to the great object of our search.' Clapperton and Oudney then set out to explore Hausa and search for the Niger in the west. Oudney died near Katagum, but Clapperton reached Kano where he was told that the Niger or Kworra, as it was called in its lower course, flowed into the sea at a place called Rakah, in Nupe, which was visited by the ships of the Christians. But he found the natives uncommunicative about the river because of their fear that any information would be used by foreign invaders to seize their country.

From Kano he travelled westwards to Sokoto, the capital of Muhammad Bello, the Sarkin Musulmi or spiritual overlord of the Fulani rulers of Hausa. He was warmly welcomed by Bello, whom he found sufficiently well informed about the British to want them to send their ships to Rakah to open up trade with his country. He was also anxious for them to send a consul and a physician to reside in Sokoto. He promised to help Clapperton to reach Yauri and Nupe in order to explore the Niger, but unfortunately he was persuaded to change his mind by the local Arabs, who clearly saw that opening the country to British trade, which appeared to them to be Clapperton's object, could not fail to harm their interests. Clapperton's oft-repeated insistence that the price of British friendship would be the abolition of the slave-trade, on which the Fulani were battening, did nothing to abate the difficulties which were now put in his way.

At Clapperton's request Bello had a map drawn showing the course of the lower Niger. Although the sultan had said that the river flowed into the sea at Fundah, a little below his port of Rakah, the map showed it flowing into the Nile of Egypt.* This accorded with what Denham had been told in Bornu, but Clapperton remained unshaken in his belief that the Niger would be found to end in the Gulf of Guinea. Finding further progress impossible, he rejoined Denham in Bornu and returned with him to England.[15]

No sooner had Clapperton returned to England than he volunteered to return to Sokoto to cement the good relations that he

---

* Fundah was in fact the large Igbirra town of Panda, which lay north of the Niger-Benue confluence. Rakah was the Nupe town of Raba, lying on the left bank of the Niger, a few miles to the east of the present road–rail bridge across the river.

had established with Sultan Bello. At the same time, he hoped by following a new route from the Guinea coast to the interior finally to solve the problem of the Niger. He was accompanied by four Europeans, one of whom was his servant Richard Lander. Finding, to their disappointment, that no one on the coast had ever heard of either Rakah or Fundah, which Bello had said were seaports, they landed at Badagry and set off for the north. Of Clapperton's companions, one had landed at Whydah, and was never heard of again, and two others died soon after leaving Badagry. There remained only Lander, with whom he travelled northwards through the great Yoruba town of Oyo or Katunga to the Niger which they reached at Bussa.

The journey through the forest belt had left them badly shaken in health, and even the better climate of Kano and Sokoto, which they next visited, did nothing to restore Clapperton's ebbing strength. The cold reception given him in Sokoto, where a rumour was current that the English meant to dispossess the Fulani, seems to have hastened his decline. He died there in April 1827. Although Clapperton's achievements had been less spectacular than Park's, his contributions to human knowledge were scarcely less important. In his two journeys, during both of which he had shown exceptional resolution and courage, he had traversed the continent from Tripoli to the coast of Guinea and had been the first European to reach the Western Sudan from the south.

Richard Lander, in failing health and almost destitute, made his way back to Kano. From there he set out for Fundah, at the confluence of the Niger and the Benue, where he intended to embark and follow the river to its end which he, like his master, believed to be in the Bight of Benin. When nearing the river, in full expectation of solving the greatest geographical problem of the day, his way was barred and he had to turn back. Eventually he reached the coast at Badagry, without having learnt much that was new about the Niger, and secured a passage to England.[16]

The expedition had been costly in human life and disappointing in its results. Hopes of establishing trade relations with the Fulani had vanished and little additional light had been thrown on the mystery of the Niger. There were still many who rejected the theory that it flowed into the Bight of Benin, in spite of Clapperton's conviction that it did, because of a belief that a 'deep range of granite mountains' barred its way,[17] based partly on a misleading remark contained in Mungo Park's account of his first expedition. Indeed it was in 1829 that the most fantastic theory about the Niger was put forward by a retired army officer, General Sir Rufane Donkin. Donkin, basing his argument on a wealth of quotations from the classics, declared that the Niger indubitably flowed northwards beneath the Sahara and into the Mediterranean in the Gulf of Syrtis.[18]

Richard Lander, without advantages of birth or education, was eager to return to Africa to complete the work he had commenced in the service of Clapperton. With the promise of a paltry £100 on his return and of an allowance of £25 a quarter to his wife during his absence, he entered the service of the Government and set out for Africa accompanied by his brother John, who was refused any sort of payment. Lander's orders were to make his way to Bussa and from there to follow the river down to Fundah, where he was to see whether it flowed into any lake or swamp. If he should explode the old Wangara myth he was to follow the river to the sea or, if it turned eastwards, to Lake Chad.

The two brothers reached Bussa in the middle of 1830 and from there followed the Niger down to its confluence with the Benue. Soon afterwards they were captured by Ibos, but recovered their liberty and made their way down the river to the sea. They got back to England in June 1831 and announced the solution to the problem which had puzzled the world for so long.[19]

*   *   *   *   *

Meanwhile another adventurous Scot, Major Gordon Laing, had reached Timbuktu, the precise situation and character of which were the only outstanding West African questions that interested the civilized world. Starting from Tripoli and travelling through Ghadames and In Salah, and nearly dying of wounds received in an affray with Tuareg, Laing reached Timbuktu in August 1826. At the start of his homeward journey he was treacherously murdered by his Berabish escort and his papers perished with him. Thus the world knows little of this gallant explorer and the remarkable journey which cost him his life. But people had not long to wait for their curiosity about Timbuktu to be satisfied.[20]

The year after Laing's death René Caillié, an impecunious young Frenchman of humble origin, started from the Rio Nunez to realize his long-cherished ambition of discovering the mysterious city. Disguised as an Arab, he made his way to Jenne, whence he travelled by canoe down the Niger and reached Timbuktu a year after leaving the coast. He was chagrined to find it so much less romantic than he, in common with many others, had believed it to be. 'I had formed', he tells us, 'a totally different idea of the grandeur and wealth of Timbuctoo. The city presented, at first view, nothing but a mass of ill-looking houses, built of earth.'[21] There were no signs of Leo's 'stately temple' nor of the 'princely palace also built by a most excellent workman of Granada'. Nothing was as Leo had described except the scarcity of salt. Caillié found Barbary merchants still amassing fortunes by importing salt from Taodeni and European trade goods from Morocco, Tunis, and Tripoli.

He travelled homewards across the desert, through Arawan and Taghaza, in company with a caravan of 1,400 camels taking slaves, gold, ivory, gum, ostrich feathers, and cloth to Tafilelt in southern Morocco. After enduring intense privations in the desert and more than once narrowly escaping death, he eventually reached Fez and from there returned to France, where his remarkable journey received the acclaim it deserved.

*   *   *   *   *

With the solution of the problems of the course and termination of the Niger, and the discovery that Timbuktu was after all no more than a conglomeration of mud huts, interest in West Africa evaporated. Men forgot that vast areas, including the greater part of the course of the Niger, had yet to be explored. Indeed, the remoter parts of the continent were yielding up secrets far more unexpected than anything discovered in the west. Livingstone was exploring the Zambezi and would shortly discover the Victoria Falls, J. L. Krapf and J. Rebmann were revealing to an incredulous world snow-capped peaks on the equator, and there was growing reason to believe that in the heart of the continent, which had generally been thought to be 'a scene of everlasting drought', there was a vast inland sea.

While the gaze of the civilized world was fastened on the intrepid explorers of the southern half of the continent, there arrived in England, almost unnoticed, a weary traveller who had spent five perilous years in the interior of north-western Africa. He was Dr. Henry Barth, a young German whose remarkable achievements as an explorer are only now coming to receive the recognition they merit.

Barth and a compatriot, Dr. Overweg, were members of a mission led by James Richardson which the British Government sent to Tripoli late in 1849 to negotiate commercial treaties with the chiefs of the interior.[22] Midway across the Sahara the three travellers separated, with the intention of meeting again in the Sudan. Barth's route took him to Air where he spent some time in Agades. Continuing his journey south into Hausa, he realized his long-cherished ambition of visiting Kano, 'the emporium of Central Africa', as he called it. He arrived there almost destitute, but contrived to borrow from the emir enough cowries to enable him to reach Bornu. Before he got there, he heard of Richardson's death and assumed command of the expedition, the first duty of which was to come to a trade agreement with the sultan of Bornu. Barth found, however, that the desire of the Bornuese for trade with Europe in order to obtain firearms was tempered by fear of the well-known hostility of the English to the slave-trade for which the firearms were required.

Barth then set out in search of the upper Benue, the Niger's greatest tributary, known only in its lower course. He reached it at Yola, but found the local Fulani so hostile that he had quickly to withdraw. However, his discovery of the upper Benue, which he described as one of the proudest moments of his life, was important, perhaps the most important of his many contributions to geographical knowledge.

After exploring the country round Lake Chad, where he witnessed some of the horrors of the slave-trade and the intense misery it caused, he found himself again destitute and compelled to abandon his intention of travelling eastwards to the Nile. Just as he was preparing to return to England, he received unexpectedly from Lord Palmerston dispatches and a sufficiency of dollars. The dispatches, however, suggested that instead of going east the mission should attempt to reach Timbuktu. This altogether unexpected proposal appealed strongly to the enterprising Barth who delighted in the thought of 'succeeding in the field of the glorious career of Mungo Park'. But he had to make the attempt alone for, just before he started on what was bound to be a perilous journey, Overweg died.

Barth's westward route took him through Zinder, Katsina, Kano, and Sokoto to Gwandu, where he discovered a copy of the now famous *Tarikh as-Sudan*, and thence to Say, where he crossed the Niger. He now entered a region, within the bend of the Niger, which was in turmoil owing to war between the fanatical Fulani of Massina and their Tuareg and Arab neighbours. Although he had adopted Arab dress, he had never attempted to conceal that he was a Christian. The Fulani, however, were in no mood to tolerate a Christian in their midst and Barth had therefore to adopt disguise as the only hope of reaching Timbuktu. In this he succeeded, but only after constantly imperilling his life, and when he arrived he was broken in health. Nor was he any safer, for people soon discovered that he was a Christian. Happily Timbuktu was still a city in which piety and learning counted for something, and Barth's spirited defence of his faith and his profound knowledge of the Muslim religion won him the sympathy of the more cultured and influential citizens, and also the protection of al-Baka'i to whom he owed his survival. Al-Baka'i was the sheikh of the Kunta Arabs who, with their Berabish and Tuareg allies, were for the time being in precarious ascendancy over the Fulani. The determined efforts of the latter to recover control of the city seemed likely to succeed, and opportunities for appeasing them were not to be lightly rejected. Yet when they demanded the surrender of the infidel it was refused by al-Baka'i.

Barth spent altogether about eight months in and around Timbuktu, and in spite of the ferment his presence was causing, amassed a wealth of information about the city and its history. During the whole of this time al-Baka'i, regardless of every consideration of self-interest, stubbornly refused to withdraw his protection from the Christian whom the Fulani repeatedly tried to take dead or alive. Six years later, when the victorious Tucolor warrior, al-Haji Umar, was threatening Timbuktu, al-Baka'i sent a mission across the Sahara to Tripoli to seek the aid of Queen Victoria who, Barth had told him, was the most powerful monarch in Europe.[23] Today his body lies in a tomb which the French erected to commemorate his services to civilization as the protector of the German explorer.

When he was at last able to make his escape from Timbuktu and start on his homeward journey, Barth travelled down the Niger to Hausa which, he declared, 'amongst all the tracts that I have visited in Negroland I had found the most agreeable for a foreigner to reside in'. Continuing his journey eastwards to Bornu, he recrossed the Sahara to Tripoli and arrived back in England in September 1855. During his five years' absence he had done more than any of his predecessors to reveal the secrets of the interior of northern Africa.

But the measure of Barth's achievement was little appreciated in England. On his return to London, a kindly reception by Lords Palmerston and Clarendon was the only mark of favour shown him by the Government he had served so well and which had spent little more than £1,000 on the expedition. To its lasting credit, the Royal Geographical Society awarded him its highest honour, and well he deserved it.

But Barth's name remained unknown to the public. The departure of the expedition had received some notice in the London Press, but the return of the sole survivor was not even mentioned. So slight was the interest in West Africa at this time that the publication of his remarkable *Travels and Discoveries in North and Central Africa* went almost unnoticed.* Yet those five volumes, describing in exhaustive detail every aspect of life in a vast unexplored region, are without parallel in the literature of geographical discovery. It seems almost incredible that one whose life was in constant peril could have amassed single-handed and recorded with truly marvellous accuracy such a wealth of geographical, ethnological, and historical information about countries and peoples till then almost wholly unknown.[24]

The purely geographical results of Barth's work should have ensured him lasting fame. Besides being the discoverer of the upper Benue, he was the first to describe the middle course of the Niger, which none but Park had seen. He had plotted with great accuracy rivers and mountains and scores of towns, many of which were previously unknown. But unfortunately for him, he had made no discovery spectacular enough to excite the interest of a public preoccupied with other fields. It remained for later generations to realize that it was Henry Barth who finally lifted from northwestern Africa the veil which earlier and more famous explorers had only penetrated.

---

* The publishers printed 2,250 copies of the first three volumes and only 1,000 of the last two. (Messrs. Longmans, Green & Co. in a letter to the author.)

24

Bornu, Hausa, and the Fulani Empire of Sokoto

UP to the end of the sixteenth century, the most powerful of West African states known to the people of the Mediterranean had lain in the area of the Middle and Upper Niger. After the collapse of the Songhai empire, this part of West Africa was never again to see a state that could compare in the wealth of its rulers or the extent of its territory with the three great medieval empires. Instead, the focus of political interest moved eastwards across the Niger to the area occupied by the states of the Hausa people and the empire of Kanem-Bornu.

Kanem is the name given to the country that lies north of Lake Chad and at the southern end of one of the main routes across the Sahara. Arab geographers of the ninth and tenth centuries knew of the existence of a kingdom of Kanem ruled by people of Zaghawa stock. The ruling dynasty, the Saifawa, were sprung, according to tradition, from a race of Saharan nomads. Gradually their rule was transformed from a loose overlordship over sedentary cultivators and other nomadic groups into a kingdom of a more settled nature. In the eleventh century the rulers were converted to Islam. By the thirteenth century, the influence of Kanem had spread northwards to the Fezzan and its rulers had established diplomatic relations with Tunis and Egypt. Ibn Khaldun recorded the astonishment of the people of Tunis at a giraffe sent as a present by the ruler of Kanem to the Hafsid Sultan, al-Mutansir.[1]

In the late fourteenth century, the rulers of Kanem were driven from their traditional territory by the Bulala, who came of the same stock as the Saifawa, established their power in the area east of Lake Chad, and extended their conquests westwards. The Saifawa were thus forced to retreat into the country west of Lake Chad, known as Bornu. Bornu was inhabited by a people known as the So or Sao, many of whom lived in walled cities. Gradually the Kanembu—the people of Kanem—extended their influence, partly by war, partly by peaceful infiltration, so that the Kanuri, as the present inhabitants of Bornu are called, represent a blending of So and Kanembu stocks.

The empire of Bornu appears to have been at its strongest in the late sixteenth century during the reign of Idris Alooma, a ruler whose activities are particularly well documented as they form the subject of the chronicles written by his Imam, Ahmad ibn Fartua.[2] Idris Alooma was a great warrior, and the greater part of Ahmad ibn Fartua's narrative is taken up with details of his wars. Early in his reign Idris made the pilgrimage by way of Tripoli and Egypt, and on this journey he saw for himself the value of that new weapon of war, the firearm. On his return he established a small corps of musketeers to form the nucleus of his army. These soldiers were drawn from his domestic slaves, and were drilled by Turkish instructors brought from Tripoli.*

Bornu is a country lacking any obvious natural frontiers, and so Idris found himself having to wage war on every front, against the Bulala in Kanem, against the Tuareg of Air, against Kano, against the So and other tribes living to the south. These aggressive tactics served to strengthen the core of Idris's kingdom and encouraged the gradual unification of the peoples of Bornu.

But Idris was not only a warrior. The Imam Ahmad describes him as an 'accomplished diplomatist, conversant with correct procedure and methods of negotiations'.[3] During his reign he is known to have received an envoy from the Sultan of Turkey, and detailed research into Turkish archives may well throw more light on Bornu's relations with the states of North Africa.[4] Even more important, in the eyes of his devout chronicler, was the fact that Idris proved himself a great supporter of Islam, building mosques, introducing Muslim law, and encouraging conversion. 'Truth and Right', wrote Ahmad, 'came by their own and shone in the land of Bornu. . . . All the notable people became Muslims except atheists and hypocrites and malevolent persons.'[5] When

* In 1636 one of Idris's successors, probably Umar ibn Idris, sent ambassadors to Tripoli to renew certain treaties, bearing with them magnificent gifts, including a massive bracelet of gold; in return the Pasha of Tripoli sent the Sultan of Bornu fifteen young Christians, armed with muskets. So high was the reputation gained by these slaves that twenty years later another Sultan wrote to another Pasha asking for another such present, a request that was duly granted. This story was written down by a French surgeon who spent some years in captivity in Tripoli in the late seventeenth century. (C. de la Roncière, 'Une histoire du Bornou au XVIIe siècle par un chirugien francais captif à Tripoli', *Revue de L'Histoire des Colonies Françaises*, 1919, VII.)

Idris died in 1603, Bornu was clearly established as the most powerful state between the Niger and the Nile.

To the west of Bornu lay the galaxy of Hausa states. Today Hausa-speakers number about ten million and form one of the largest linguistic groups in Africa. The Hausa represent a mingling of many different stocks; their basic culture suggests an affinity with the So of the Lake Chad area; but their traditions refer to immigrant groups coming from the north and east. Their early history is illuminated by a certain amount of material, now written down, but originally derived from oral tradition of which the Kano Chronicle represents the most detailed document.[6]

The Hausa are distinguished from many of the other people of the Western Sudan by the fact that their basic political unit— at least in the period beginning about A.D. 1000 when Hausa history first becomes known to us—was the *birni* or walled town. The town walls, examples of which may still be seen in places such as Kano, Katsina, or Zaria, enclosed a considerable extent of agricultural land. Beyond the *birni* lay smaller village communities: 'The Hausa states', Trimingham has suggested, 'were formed when one *birni* secured the acknowledgement of a widening circle of hamlets and then of other *birnis* and developed into a capital whose head (*sarki*) changed from a village to a city chief with an elaborate court and official hierarchy.'[7]

Hausa traditions speak of Daura (today a small emirate to the east of Katsina) as being the oldest of the Hausa states. To Daura there had come, according to the legend, the great hero Bayajidda, a man from the east, who killed the town's sacred snake and married the queen. From this marriage were descended the founders of the other Hausa states, Kano, Katsina, Gobir, Zazzau (Zaria), Rano, and Biram, which with Daura formed the Hausa *bakwai*, the seven Hausa states. Alongside these legitimate states, tradition sets the *Bannza bakwai*, the bastard seven (Kebbi, Zamfara, Gwari, Jukun, Yoruba, Nupe, and Yauri)—states that neighbour Hausa territory, but where Hausa is not the original language.[8]

Of all the Hausa states, Kano is the one whose history, by virtue of its chronicle, is best known to us. Much of the early history of Kano is taken up with conflict over religion between the immigrants from Daura (who about A.D. 1000 became the political rulers), and the local people. The people of Kano worshipped a god which dwelt in a tree surrounded by a wall; to this deity they made sacrifices of black fowls, black he-goats, and black dogs. The priests resolutely refused to tell the secrets of their religion to the *Sarkis*, the town's political rulers; it was not until the early fourteenth century, nearly three hundred years after the coming of the immigrants, that a *sarki* eventually succeeded in destroying the site of the traditional cult.

Until the fourteenth century, the Hausa states appear to have developed in conditions of comparative seclusion, little influenced by their more powerful neighbours to the east and to the west. They are not mentioned by any Arab geographers before Ibn Battuta, and Ibn Battuta only makes a passing reference to Gobir. This suggests that before 1350 Kano and Katsina had not yet developed into places of any commercial importance for North African traders.[9]   During the mid-fourteenth century, however, definite links were established between some of the Hausa states and Mali, then at the height of its power. The chronicles of Kano and of Katsina tell of Islam being introduced at this time by Wangarawa, who were probably Mandingo from Mali. These contacts must have drawn the northern Hausa states into the commercial network of the Sahara and the Western Sudan. It is significant that, from this time on, the Kano Chronicle makes frequent mention of slaves and slave-raiding; it is not unreasonable to assume that the Wangarawa taught the *sarkis* of Kano to recognize the commercial importance of slaves, and suggested that they could easily be obtained by raiding neighbouring peoples or by demanding tribute from them.[10]

By the mid-fifteenth century, Kano was clearly on the way to becoming a great centre of commerce. In the reign of Yakubu (1452–1463), according to the chronicle,

the Fulani came to Hausa from Mali, bringing with them books on Divinity and Etymology . . . At this time, too, the Asbenawa [the Tuareg of Air] came to Gobir, and salt became common in Hausa. In the following year merchants from Gonja began coming to Katsina; Beriberi people from Bornu came in large numbers, and a colony of Arabs arrived. Some of the Arabs settled in Kano and some in Katsina. . . . Yakubu sent ten horses to the Sarkin Nupe in order to buy eunuchs. The Sarkin Nupe gave him twelve eunuchs.[11]

Of the Hausa states, Katsina shared and possibly surpassed Kano's prosperity, for it was even better placed to keep in touch with the great currents of trade with the west and north. Gobir lay in the more arid country to the north of Katsina; much of its

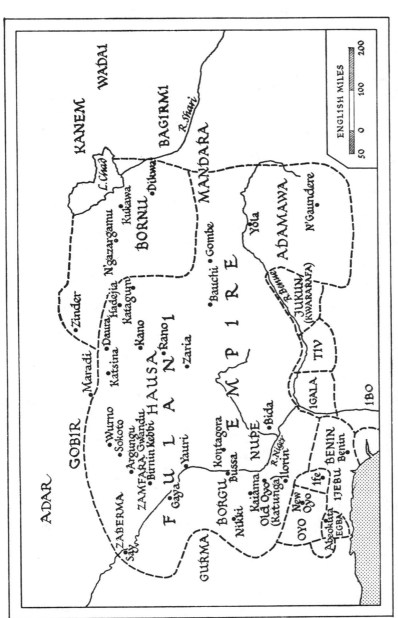

VIII. The Fulani Empire, Bornu, and other states of the Niger area in the mid-nineteenth century

history was taken up with the struggle with the Tuareg of Air. South of Katsina lay the state mentioned only by Leo Africanus under the name of Guangara; it was probably founded by Wangarawa immigrants.[12] The history of Zazzau (Zaria) is obscure: at some time in the fifteenth or sixteenth century—traditional authorities differ widely over the date—the kingdom was ruled by a great queen, Amina, whose conquests extended from the Niger to the Benue and who obtained tribute from Kano and Katsina.[13]

By the early sixteenth century, the Hausa states were under pressure from their powerful neighbours—Songhai in the west and Bornu in the east. Muhammad Askia of Songhai imposed his domination, at least for a time, over most of the Hausa states, and it was from the west that a new wave of Muslim missionaries arrived. But the influence of Bornu was even more profound. Thus Yakubu's successor as Sarkin Kano, Muhammad Rimfa (1465–1499), is recalled not only for his encouragement of Islam, but for his twelve 'innovations'. These ranged from the introduction of ostrich-feather fans and of long trumpets known as *kakaki* to the acquisition of a harem of a thousand concubines, and included the appointment of eunuchs to important offices and the establishment of a council of nine. Rimfa's model of kingship must have been drawn, as M. G. Smith has pointed out, 'from the suzerain court of Bornu'.[14]

Compared with the sixteenth century, the next two centuries are comparatively ill-documented periods. The dominant impression provided by the brief chronicles of the age is of conflict: war between the Hausa states, Zamfara against Kebbi, Gobir against Zamfara, Kano against Katsina; devastating raids by the Kwararafa or Jukun of the Benue valley against both the Hausa states and Bornu; attempts by Bornu to maintain her suzerainty over her western neighbours. At the same time there is evidence of a return to pagan practices among the ruling classes both of Bornu and of the Hausa states. In Bornu, for example, the rulers were said to have had 'great houses containing snakes and other things to which they offer sacrifices'.[15] This decline of Islam must have been associated with the anarchy that afflicted the Middle Niger after the Moroccan invasion, and which served to diminish the civilizing influence of cities such as Jenne and Timbuktu. Both the state system of the countries between the Niger and Lake Chad and the position of Islam were to be transformed by the revolutionary changes of the early nineteenth century, changes in which the Fulani, a people who had hitherto only played a modest part in the history of the Sudan, were to play the leading role.

The Fulani are the most widely dispersed of all the peoples of West Africa. They are to be found today in all the countries from Senegal to Cameroun. Some of the Fulani are pastoral nomads, roaming the bush with their great herds of cattle: these pastoralists are usually distinguished from their neighbours by their markedly lighter skin. But many of the Fulani live a settled life and are hardly to be distinguished from the people of other tribes, such as the Hausa, among whom they live and with whom they are intermarried. Fulani origins have provided a subject for debate among scholars for several generations, but recent research goes a long way towards providing a satisfactory solution to the problem.

Fulfulde, the language of the Fulani, is closely related to other languages spoken by people living in the Senegal valley. The original Fulfulde-speakers were a negroid people who probably founded the medieval state of Takrur. Throughout the centuries the fertile Senegal valley has attracted Berber pastoralists living on the edge of the desert; some of these Berber pastoralists crossed the river to reach the savannah country of the Ferlo plateau, and being isolated from their Berber kinsmen in the southern Sahara, these light-skinned pastoralists began to adopt the language of their negroid neighbours. From about the twelfth century onwards the pastoral Fulani began to spread eastwards in search of new pastures, a movement possibly set in motion by over-population or over-grazing. Their movement was a peaceful one, for their arrival in a new territory did nothing to disturb the life of the local peasant farmers: indeed their presence was often valued for they could provide farmers with milk and butter, and manure for their fields. At the same time some of the negroid Fulani also moved eastwards. They had been among the first of the people of the Sudan to be converted to Islam, and their prestige as Muslims made them welcome in the cities and in the courts of princes. The arrival of these learned Fulani divines is recorded in Kano, for example, in the fifteenth century. But while these negroid Fulfulde-speakers contained among their numbers some of the most learned Muslims in the Sudan, the light-skinned pastoralists, living away from the towns in the remote bush, were still pagan.

Between devout Muslims occupying a position of prestige and influence and nominally Muslim rulers liable to lapse into pagan practices, the possibilities of conflict were very great. In Bornu, for example, a seventeenth-century Sultan slew a Muslim teacher who cast aspersions on his rule.[16] But the first major struggle in which the Muslim Fulani were involved occurred in the Futa Jallon, a mountainous area, now forming part of the Republic of Guinea, to which Fulani pastoralists, accompanied by some Muslim teachers, had migrated in the seventeenth century. In 1725 the Muslims launched a *jihad* or Holy War against their pagan neighbours; after a struggle lasting half a century they succeeded in establishing a theocratic state, their religious leader or *imam* becoming a political ruler with the title *almamy*. Similar movements leading to the establishment of theocratic states took place at the end of the eighteenth century in Futa Toro and Bondu, in the Senegal valley.

Several centuries earlier one group of Fulfulde-speakers from Futa Toro, the Torodbe (Toronkawa in Hausa) had moved eastwards and settled eventually in the Hausa state of Gobir. The Torodbe have been described as 'something like a missionary clan', their members including many teachers and preachers.[17] To this clan belonged Uthman dan Fodio, the founder of one of the greatest States of nineteenth-century Africa, the Fulani empire of Sokoto.

Uthman dan Fodio was born in 1754. Brought up as a strict Muslim of the Maliki school, he sought to satisfy his ardent religious zeal in the career of a preacher. His piety and personal magnetism soon won him devoted disciples, especially in Gobir, where his ardent denunciation of the reversion of the Gobirawa from Islam to the paganism of their ancestors and his growing influence over the people excited the resentment of Nafata, the *sarki* or king of Gobir. Nafata decreed that none who had not been born a Muslim might practise the Islamic religion, and he forbade the wearing of turbans by men and of veils by women. But there was no open hostility, no resort to arms, until Nafata had been succeeded by his son Yunfa, a former pupil of Uthman or, as he was now commonly called, Shehu (Sheikh). Seeing in the still growing influence of his old tutor a threat to his throne, Yunfa planned to put him to death. The failure of the plot won increased sympathy for the preacher, who now became a popular hero. Thoroughly alarmed at the swelling tide of disaffection, Yunfa marched against Degel, Shehu's town, and forced him to fly. In Fulani history 21 February 1804, the date of the *Hijra* or Flight of Shehu from Degel, is memorable. He fled beyond the borders of Gobir to Gudu, where disciples rallied round him in such numbers that he found himself at the head of a great body of warriors, all burning with the religious fervour of their master and ready to lay down their lives in his cause.

In the following June the Muslims defeated Yunfa and his army on the shores of Tabkin Kwotto, and solemnly swore a *jihad* against the infidels on the field of battle. They proclaimed their leader Amir al-Mu'minin or Sarkin Musulmi, Commander of the Faithful, the title still borne by his descendant, the reigning sultan of Sokoto. 'Let no man think', declared Shehu, 'that I accept this office that I may be greater than another or that my slave may lord it over others.'

The Muslim victory served to attract many more adherents to the Shehu's cause. At first his army had consisted largely of his *jama'a*, the congregation of the faithful; now many of the pastoral Fulani joined him, inspired not by religious enthusiasm but by a simple desire for booty. Among the Hausa states, the defeat of the Gobirawa caused widespread alarm. Warned by Yunfa of their peril, the kings of Katsina, Kano, Zazzau, Daura, and Adar set upon the followers of Shehu in their own countries. The Fulani rose against the kings and the country was rent by civil war. But not all the Fulani were on the side of Shehu. Some fought for Gobir and many Hausa were to be found in the ranks of Shehu's army.

In spite of his victory over the Gobirawa, Shehu failed to capture their capital, Alkalawa, and soon afterwards he was badly defeated at Tsuntsuwa. Nevertheless, new adherents were still pouring in from the remoter parts of Hausa, and before long he had a greater army than ever at his back. Zaria fell to him in 1804. Katsina was captured after a long siege in 1805, and later in the year the Fulani forces met the Sarkin Kano in battle. The Kano army of 10,000 mounted spearmen, many of them clad in chain mail* and quilted armour, was no more than an undisciplined rabble which the resolute Fulani bowmen routed. Kano

---

* Less than thirty years ago shirts of chain mail made of wire rings pinched together were being manufactured in Omdurman and selling to local notables at £25 a suit. Chain mail of riveted links, believed to be made in India, is also sometimes found in the Eastern Sudan.

city was occupied without opposition. Later in the same year, however, Shehu's forces were severely defeated at Alwassa, near Gwandu, by a combination of Gobirawa and Kebbawa supported by Tuareg in strength. The enemy pressed their victory and for a time the situation of the Fulani was critical.

In 1806 the Fulani made another unsuccessful attempt to break the power of the Gobirawa by seizing their capital, but in 1808, after elaborate preparations, Shehu's son Bello captured the city and slew Yunfa. With the fall of Alkalawa, from which Gobir never recovered, there was none left seriously to challenge the authority of Shehu, whose prestige was further increased by the unexpected arrival of the Sarkin Air of Agades, a Targui of the Kel Owi, who had come south especially to do homage to him. That the dreaded Tuareg should confer so signal an honour on the conqueror of a country in which they had long exercised grazing rights essential to their economy, clearly showed the Hausa that further opposition would be futile.

By this time the Fulani were in conflict with Bornu, to whom some of the Hausa states had looked for assistance. In 1808 the Fulani captured and destroyed Ngazargamu, the capital of the empire. In his hour of need the Sultan Ahmad turned for support to one of the notable men of Kanem, Muhammad al-Amin or Shehu Laminu, better known to history as al-Kanemi. al-Kanemi, who enjoyed considerable prestige as a Muslim teacher, gathered together a band of supporters drawn from the Kanembu and the Shuwa Arabs and drove back the Fulani in 1808, and again, following a second invasion, in 1813. These services made him the most powerful man in Bornu and the *de facto* ruler of the country. In 1814 he established a capital for himself at Kukawa, west of Lake Chad. But he allowed the Sultans of the old Saifawa dynasty to remain as puppet-rulers; indeed it was not until 1846 that the last Saifawa Sultan was removed by al-Kanemi's son and successor, Umar. After 1814 the old empire of Bornu, given new life by al-Kanemi's reforming ability, was never seriously threatened by the Fulani, but al-Kanemi and his successors were never able to recover Bornu's western provinces, which the Fulani had captured and transformed into the emirates of Hadeija and Katagum.

From the early days of the *jihad*, Uthman dan Fodio had usually made his headquarters at Sokoto. Sokoto had never been more than a hunter's camp at the foot of the tamarind tree, which until about 1950 could still be seen in the enclosure of the mosque. It remained a mere camp until 1809 when Uthman's son Muhammad Bello, built the present town which continues to be the seat of the Sarkin Musulmi.*

Sokoto was so close to the western frontier of Shehu's newly won dominions, that it is not surprising that the year in which the town was built saw also the conquest of Dendi by Shehu's brother Waziri Abdullahi, who pursued the flying enemy across the Niger. 'When we came to this river', wrote Bello, 'the river was obedient to us so that we forded it. Again we crossed it a second time, on our going and on our return the water did not pass the soles of our feet.†[18]

From the Niger westwards, there was a considerable Fulani population many of whom were of the Torodbe clan, so Shehu had many sympathizers there. But his influence within the bend of the Niger was not great, though he exercised nominal suzerainty over Liptako of which Dori is the chief town.

Among Shehu's early followers there had been a certain Ahmadu Lobo, a Fulani malam or ulema of Massina, afterwards known as Seku or Shehu Ahmadu. When he returned from Gobir, burning with his master's zeal for reform, he and the disciples he had gathered round him were persecuted by the Ardo, the Fulani king of Massina, and the Arma of Jenne. This won for him the sympathy of a large part of the population, which so alarmed the Ardo that he sought the aid of his suzerain, the Bambara king of Segu, in quelling the swelling tide of unrest. Seku declared a *jihad* and, in spite of being greatly outnumbered by his enemies, he defeated them and freed Massina, for the first time since the seventeenth century, of the tutelage of the Bambara of Segu. Seku, the pattern of whose career followed so closely that of his master, sent two of his brothers to ask the blessing of Shehu Uthman, which was granted and afterwards gave rise to the

* Sokoto may have long been the name of the district. In a Bornu *mahram* of 1694 we hear of a certain Ayesha, the patroness of a Fulani tribe, who had the title Sokotoma, meaning ruler of Sokoto. (H. R. Palmer, *The Bornu, Sahara and Sudan*, London, 1936, p. 39.)

† Although this incident, recalling many similar ones in history (notably the passage of the Israelites through the Red Sea and that of Alexander the Great over the Pamphylian Sea), has come to be called the miraculous crossing of the Niger, it is not as improbable as it sounds. Barth was told that the Niger was sometimes fordable at several points between Tosaye and Gao, and Captain Hill of the Laird-Oldfield expedition found that at a point as far downstream as its junction with the Benue the Niger could be crossed on foot. (Barth, *Travels*, V 196; M. Laird and R. A. K. Oldfield, *Narrative of an Expedition into the Interior of Africa by the River Niger, 1832–1834*, 1837, I, 176.)

erroneous belief that Seku Ahmadu was one of Shehu's original flag-bearers. This won over to Seku's side those who had remained true to the Ardo whom they handed over as a prisoner. Seku was now the undisputed master of Massina but, eschewing the worldly title of Ardo, he, like his master, adopted the title of Amir al-Mu'minin, or Commander of the Faithful. Making his headquarters at a village he called Hamdallahi, he embarked on a career of conquest which ultimately made him master of a vast territory which for a time extended from Timbuktu to the Black Volta.

In 1812 Shehu Uthman divided the administration of the still expanding empire between his brother, Abdullahi, and his son, Muhammad Bello. To Bello, who retained Sokoto as his capital, went the provinces of Kano, Katsina, Zaria, Bauchi, and other territories further east, while Abdullahi, who in time made his capital at Gwandu, only fifty miles from Sokoto, was given control of the provinces to the south and west. The first provincial governors were the successful military leaders who had received a flag from the Shehu and been instructed to forward the *jihad* in particular territories. Some, as in Kano, were able to take over the old Hausa machinery of government; others, in an area of many pagan tribes such as Bauchi, had to create their own capital and administrative framework. Tribute, largely in slaves, had to be paid annually to Sokoto and Gwandu, and the governors had to furnish troops as required. So long as these services were punctually rendered the central government interfered little in the affairs of the emirates.

With the organization of his empire completed, Shehu felt that his life's work was done. He passed his remaining years in retirement finding, one cannot doubt, study and contemplation more satisfying to his unworldly spirit than the stirring events which he had designed and directed. His name will long be honoured in the land which he mastered in order to fulfil his high ideals.

As F. de F. Daniel wrote,

Shehu lived to see the conclusion of his life's work. He had found Muhammadanism under a ban: he left it supreme. The Fulani, from a tribe of nomad herdsmen, had become the ruling race throughout the Hausa states. A man of sincere faith and deep religious convictions, he had implicit confidence in his Divine call, and his personality inspired his followers with a confidence similar to his own. His simple habits and austere life made a profound contrast to the barbaric pomp affected by the pagan rulers. No soldier himself, he attributed his success solely to the hand of God. After the partition of his empire, he withdrew from the active conduct of affairs and devoted himself to a life of study, first at Sifawa, and later in the city of Sokoto. Here he died in 1817, and was buried within the city walls, where his tomb is still a place of pilgrimage.[19]

To be fully understood, the Fulani *jihad* needs to be seen in the broad context of Islamic history. There had been other revivalist movements in the past—those of the Almoravids and the Almohads in North Africa provide striking examples—and there were to be similar movements later in the nineteenth century: that of the Sanusiyya in Cyrenaica, for example, or the Mahdiyya in the eastern Sudan. In each of these movements, as in the Fulani *jihad*, one can detect common themes: 'the idea of a return to the Qur'an and the Sunna; the effort to restore the Islamic state in its original purity; the emphasis on moral austerity; and the use of the *jihad* as a legitimate instrument of reform.'

But the movement must also be seen in its local setting. Within the Hausa states the Fulani Muslims formed an 'intellectual elite'. Their revolution was 'an expression', as Thomas Hodgkin has pointed out, 'if not of Fulani "nationalism", at least of the sense of common purpose which a group with ties of education, culture and ideology, as well as language and kinship, is liable to generate.'[20] Finally there is some evidence in the literature produced at the time to suggest that the movement appealed to many of the common people in the Hausa states, who saw in it an opportunity to free themselves of corrupt and oppressive rulers.

Shehu was succeeded by his son Bello, whose reign of twenty years was largely occupied in crushing revolts against the new rulers of the country. He was an able administrator and unquestionably the greatest of the Sokoto sultans. His patronage of the arts attracted to his court scholars from far afield. Among those who came under his influence was al-Haji Umar Tall, the Tucolor *jihadi* who, in the middle of the century, won for himself a large kingdom on the upper Niger. As a young man he had spent some time in Sokoto on his way home from Mecca, and had married a kinswoman of Bello.

With the death of the original flag-bearers, the Fulani soon began to lose their religious zeal, and the rewards of victory, as so often in history, brought with them a weakening of all the qualities to which they owed their triumph over the Hausa states. As a Tripolitan Arab remarked to Clapperton, when they were poor the Fulani chiefs led their men into battle; since they had become rich they remained behind and sent them forward alone. Their great men became fief-holders, surrounded by slaves, eunuchs, and concubines, and farming the taxes of large districts where relations and favourites acted as their deputies. The *jihad* against their pagan neighbours still went on. In the 1820s the Fulani, using a shrewd mixture of diplomacy and force, established themselves in Nupe. In the 1830s they built up their power in Ilorin within the confines of Yoruba territory. Meanwhile, in the Benue valley, one of the flag-bearers, Adama, was laying the foundations of the great province that bears his name. The nineteenth-century Adamawa stretched far beyond the confines of modern Nigeria to include a substantial territory now lying within the Republic of Cameroun.

By the middle of the nineteenth century, many of the Fulani attacks on pagan people, especially in areas such as Bauchi or Adamawa, represented nothing more than raids for slaves. For slave-labour provided one of the foundations of the empire's economy. Great men settled their slaves on agricultural estates whose products were used to provide for their horde of hangers-on. The more followers a successful local ruler attracted round him the more insistent became the demand for raids. There is no doubt that some areas were almost depopulated by Fulani raiding. In the Kontagora district of Niger province in Northern Nigeria, for example, the present low density of population appears to be a direct result of the devastation caused by nineteenth-century slave raiders. In other parts, however, especially in the more mountainous areas, the local people seem to have become increasingly adept at warding off attacks.

In some parts of the empire, slave-raiding gave way to outright war. For the Fulani had never succeeded in subduing all the Hausa communities lying within the confines of their empire. In the west the Kebbawa, amongst whom the spirit of Kanta still lived, continued successfully to defy them in spite of their proximity to the main Fulani strongholds. Their principal town, Birnin Kebbi, had fallen to the Fulani early in the *jihad*, but although many Kebbawa had submitted, there was a considerable body of irreconcilables who, led by a certain Ismaila, preserved their independence at Argungu. Argungu was precariously situated between the twin Fulani capitals of Sokoto and Gwandu, but the Kebbawa succeeded in maintaining their independence until the coming of the British. Similarly, many of the Hausa of Katsina retreated northwards to escape Fulani domination. They established a centre for themselves at Maradi, which served as a base for devastating raids into Katsina territory.

Finally, the rulers of Sokoto and Gwandu also had to face occasional revolts from over-mighty subjects. Buhari of Hadeija, for example, was able to maintain his independence for several years in the 1850s, and in the course of his revolt 'spread terror and devastation to the very gates of Kano'.

Slave-raiding, revolt, and the strength of Hausa resistance, taken together with the swiftness of the Fulani collapse in the face of the British advance, have seemed to some historians to provide evidence of the complete decadence of Fulani rule in the latter half of the nineteenth century. On the other hand, it needs to be remembered that many parts of the empire remained peaceful, that the ties that linked the provinces to the capital remained unbroken, and that some of the later rulers showed remarkable powers of recuperation. The French traveller Monteil, who visited Sokoto in 1891, thought at first that the empire was on the verge of collapse, but admitted later that his prophecies were disproved by the energy with which the Sultan Abd al-Rahman warded off his enemies.[21] In the present state of knowledge—when a detailed study of the entire Fulani empire still remains to be made—a historian is wise to introduce a note of hesitation into his judgements. But it is at least possible to affirm that the Fulani empire of Sokoto and Gwandu represents one of the most remarkable states —remarkable for its intellectual origins, its size and administrative complexity—that Africa had ever seen.

25

The Last of the Caravans

'Trading is the true test of man, and it is in the operations of trade that his piety and religious worth become known.'—CALIPH UMAR.

THE need of the western world for the products of Africa and the mercantile instincts of its peoples, both north and south of the Sahara, combined to make foreign trade a dominant factor in the history of the north-western quarter of the continent. Trade bridged the Sahara, one of the world's most formidable barriers to human intercourse, and linked Barbary with the Sudan to the enrichment of both. The desert trade was a magnet with drew to the Maghrib the merchants of Europe, and filled the ports and roadsteads of the rugged Barbary coast, from Tripoli to Agadir, with Christian shipping. To the Sudanese it carried, together with the coveted wares of the Mediterranean, the culture of the Muslim north which, more than anything else, governed their social and political development. Trade, also, inspired the achievements by which, after centuries of frustration and disappointment, the interior was ultimately revealed to inquiring western minds. In the wake of the dauntless and triumphant explorers came their countrymen, in armed strength, to conquer and occupy, and gradually to alter the whole pattern of African life. No field of human activity was more profoundly affected by the coming of the European than the trade of the interior, from which until then he had been rigorously excluded. His roads, river-boats, and railways opened new outlets to the Guinea coast, drained away from the Sahara its carrying trade and ruined the caravan routes, the ancient arteries of commerce and culture. We shall do well, therefore, to take a last look at the trade of the interior as the great explorers found it and when its general character was still much as it had been for many centuries.

In the first half of the nineteenth century, the greater part of the caravan traffic between Barbary and the Western Sudan was still concentrated on the three great trade routes which must be numbered among the oldest highways in the world: the Taghaza–Timbuktu road in the west, the Ghadames–Air road to Hausa in the centre, and in the east the Fezzan–Kawar road to Bornu. On each of these roads there were long waterless stages which heavily laden caravans could only cross at great peril. Nevertheless, the test of time had proved them the safest as well as the shortest routes for merchants. Each represented about two months' journey for a camel caravan. From time to time lesser roads had been brought into use, but only to be abandoned through the failure of wells or pasturage, or owing to the vagaries of desert politics. On the three ancient highways there was greater certainty of finding water and grazing where they were expected, and in the face of this compelling circumstance neither war nor blackmail could force the toiling merchant caravans permanently to forsake them. They had endured through the ages.

To be really accurate, an account of trade and trade-routes needs to be based on statistical material. For the latter half of the nineteenth century an increasing amount of such material is beginning to come to light; the diplomatic archives of European powers, for example, contain the reports of consular officials stationed at the main ports of North Africa, one of whose tasks was to gather information on the trade of the interior. But for the period before 1850 such information as exists on the Saharan trade, particularly in the accounts of European travellers, is of a more impressionistic nature. The main lines can be detected, but it is not possible to assess the total volume of the trade along any one route.

Until the beginning of the seventeenth century the Taghaza–Timbuktu road, pre-eminent in the gold trade and still more important as a cultural highway appears to have been the greatest of the routes across the desert. In the late seventeenth and early eighteenth centuries the powerful Moroccan Sultan, Mulai Ismail, imported a large number of slaves from the Sudan as recruits for his standing army. Mulai Ismail's death in 1727 was followed by a generation of civil war, in which the slave army, the *Abid*, played so turbulent a part that later Sultans decided to dispense with their services. Consequently there was a decline in the numbers of slaves imported, a decline which affected the entire trade between Morocco and the Sudan. 'The Caravans to the South', James Matra, the British consul in Morocco, reported in 1788, 'have decreased very considerably for many years'. It seems possible that with the greater measure of political stability enjoyed by Morocco in the nineteenth century, the route to Timbuktu regained something of its old activity. At any rate, up to the 1880s the Saharan trade was a factor of considerable importance in the economy of Morocco.[1]*

The destruction, in the closing years of the eighteenth century, of Sijilmasa, which had been in decay since Leo's day, had deprived the Taghaza–Timbuktu road of its historic northern terminus. Its place had to some extent been taken by the neighbouring town of Abuam, but much of the trade had left Tafilelt. Some had gone to In Salah, the capital of Tuat, which was easily

---

* In his recent study of trade between Morocco and the Sudan in the nineteenth century, J. L. Miège estimates that the years 1858 to 1870 were the most prosperous period. During these years a number of Jewish merchants from the northern Sahara settled in Timbuktu. (J. L. Miège, *Le Maroc et l'Europe*, 1961, III, 94).

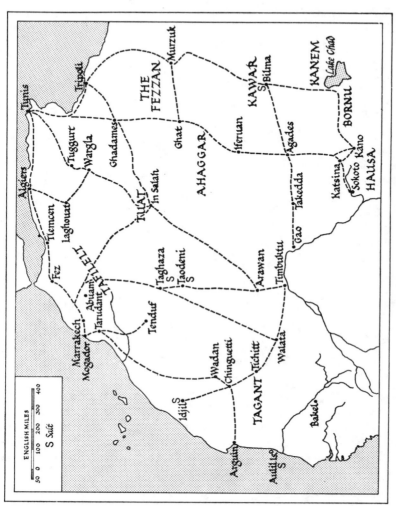

IX. Principal Saharan caravan routes

accessible from Morocco along the Wadi Saura, and some had gone west to Lektawa, in Wadi Dra'a, and to Wadi Nun, a new settlement near the coast and a few miles from Cape Nun, which had been founded by fugitives from the intolerable oppression of an avaricious sultan.[2]

Merchants trading from Wadi Nun and Abuam with the Sudan travelled through Akka, which had inherited Sijilmasa's business of fitting-out and equipping trans-Saharan caravans, and thence along the old road through Taghaza and Taodeni to Timbuktu. Instead of turning westwards at Taodeni to Walata (like Wadan, now in decay but still noted for the skill of its goldsmiths), the road followed the more direct route through Arawan. Here it was joined by two other roads: one running through Tuat and Mabruk to Timbuktu, and the other coming up from Sansanding on the upper Niger. Centuries of traffic had not lessened the dangers of the Taghaza–Timbuktu road. In 1805 a caravan of 2,000 men and 1,800 camels homeward bound from Timbuktu along this route perished of thirst, not a man or beast being saved.[3]

This road, which was controlled by the Berabish Arabs, owed its long-continued prosperity to the unequal distribution of gold and salt in the interior. Much has already been said about the gold trade and not a little about the traffic in salt, but only in so far as it touched the gold trade. To the African, salt was so infinitely the more important that it is no over-statement to say that gold was valued by the Sudanese almost entirely for its purchasing power in salt, their craving for which they were never able wholly to satisfy. It was the basis of their domestic, as it was of their foreign, trade, neither of which can be properly comprehended without an understanding of how starved they were of this essential to the well-being of man.

al-Bakri's statement that the Ferawi used to exchange gold for an equal weight of salt was probably not a gross exaggeration.[4] There is a similar statement about Mali on certain Jewish maps of the early sixteenth century which may or may not have been a repetition of al-Bakri, and only a century ago a European traveller in these parts, the Frenchman Raffenel, found himself so short of salt that he was fully prepared to entertain such a bargain.[5] Only those who have witnessed it can realize how intense is the craving for salt by those to whom an adequate supply is denied. In the Western Sudan it was a luxury which only the rich could regularly enjoy.

A limited number of natural salt deposits were to be found in the Western Sudan. In the Dallul Fogha in Dendi and the neighbouring *fadama* or marsh of Birnin Kebbi, for example, the soil was sufficiently impregnated with salt to make possible its recovery by evaporation. At various points along the sea coast from the Senegal to the Niger, marine salt could be obtained. But these were all meagre sources and adequate at most for a very limited export trade. For tribes who were unable to acquire salt by trade, it was possible to extract it in pathetically small quantities from the ashes of grasses, millet stalks and certain shrubs, and from cattle dung.*

It will be recalled that when the Songhai were driven out of Taghaza by the Moors in the sixteenth century they opened the now famous mines at Taodeni, which then became, and indeed to some extent still remain,† the principal source of supply for the countries of the middle Niger.[6] It was carried as far upstream as Bamako which Park found being supplied from Taodeni and with sea salt from the Rio Grande. Salt was also obtained from Sebka d'Idjil, in the desert to the north-west. But the desert was a precarious source on which to depend for a prime necessity of life. The mines were defenceless against raiders, supplies at the mercy of desert politics, and the miners likely to die if, as sometimes happened at Taodeni, provisions failed to reach them in time. By the beginning of the nineteenth century these hazards had led to the export of salt from Morocco to the Sudan, where the Moors bartered it at the rate of one pound of salt for one ounce of gold.

Timbuktu owed as much to gold and salt as did the ancient road of which it was the southern terminus. Neither growing nor manufacturing anything, it depended on imports for its food and on transit trade for its prosperity. It was essentially an *entrepôt*, deriving its importance from its situation at the point where the great highway of the Niger is most accessible from the Maghrib and its desert outpost, the oasis of Tuat. While the Taghaza road brought it salt and the trade goods of the Mediterranean, and the Niger rice, millet, gold, slaves, ivory, and kola nuts from Sansand-

---

* The French traveller Binger noted in the 1880s that towns lying between 8° and 10° 30′ N appeared to be best supplied with salt, as they were able to draw on the three main sources, desert salt, sea salt, and salt from local deposits. He found that in Kong, an important trading centre in the northern Ivory Coast, salt from Taodeni sold as cheaply as salt from the sea coast. (L. Binger, *Du Niger au Golfe de Guinée*, Paris, 1892, II, 375.)

† The people of Timbuktu still get their supplies from Taodeni.

ing and Jenne, a third road from the east linked it with Egypt. This road ran through Air and Ghat to Ghadames, the Cydamus of the Romans, the merchants of which still had a close hold on the trade of the interior. In Barth's time Timbuktu was importing kola nuts from Tangrela, far away in the hinterland of the Ivory Coast, and English cottons and cutlery from Mogador; it was also trading with the European factories on the Senegal and Gambia rivers through Sansanding and Bamako. The geographical extent and ramifications of its foreign trade were impressive.

The Ghadames–Air road is probably not less ancient than the Taghaza road. Where it passes over rocky ground the deeply worn tracks prove its antiquity and the great weight of traffic it carried. Its route seems never to have varied. Between Ghadames and Ghat it was, in the first half of last century, controlled by the fierce Azger Tuareg. Between Ghat and Air, where it passes over one of the worst bits of desert in the world, it lay in Kel Owi country; halfway, at In Azawa or Asiu, it was joined by the Tuat–Air road which traversed the Ahaggar massif and was controlled by the Ahaggar Tuareg. The main road entered Air at Iferuan. This was an important junction, for here the road was joined by the old pilgrim way from Timbuktu which entered Air at In Gall, passing thence through In Azawa, Ghat, Murzuk, Augila, and Siwa to Cairo. Owing to the country round Agades being unsuitable for heavily laden camels, the road has always skirted the capital, which lies a few miles to its west. The southern terminus of the road used to be Katsina, but when, following the Fulani *jihad*, Kano replaced Katsina as the chief market of Hausa, the road was extended to the former, but by way of Zinder and by-passing Katsina. Between Kano and Air it was controlled by the Kel Geres.

In the days of the Songhai empire Agades prospered as the chief *entrepôt* for the gold trade Gao carried on with Tripoli and Egypt. The Moorish conquest killed this trade and impoverished Agades, but left its political importance unaffected. What little prosperity remained to Agades in the nineteenth century was derived principally from the salt trade between Kawar and Hausa. The people of Agades owed their hold on this important and lucrative trade to their grazing grounds. These supported immense herds of camels, without which the salt traffic could not be maintained. Every autumn a vast caravan, known as the *Azalai* or *Taghalam*, set out from Air to fetch salt from Bilma, the capital of Kawar, for the Hausa markets. Probably nowhere else in the world could be found a commercial spectacle comparable with the *Azalai* which even as late as 1908, when it was in its decline, numbered no less than 20,000 camels.

Elaborate preparations preceded the departure of the *Azalai*. The assemblage of so many camels, mostly from the Kel Geres and Itesan tribes, alone took a long time. They congregated at Tabello, in central Air, where there was sufficient grazing to condition them for their arduous journey. Although the round trip to Kawar and back to Air took only three weeks, it demanded great endurance, and the route of the *Azalai* was marked by a vast accumulation of camel skeletons. So immense a caravan was naturally very vulnerable, a circumstance of which predatory Tuareg, not directly interested in it, took advantage, sometimes at great cost to the salt merchants.

The *Azalai* set out in October, commanded by the Sarkin Turawa of Agades, the vizier of the Amenokal or Sultan. It carried corn and cloth from Hausa to barter for salt, and immense quantities of fodder, there being no grazing in Kawar where the few local camels were fed on dates. Fachi, an outpost of Kawar, was reached in five days, and there the *Azalai* was joined by a caravan from Damagaram. It entered Bilma three days later. By a curious and unexplained phenomenon the 'singing' of a neighbouring peak used to give the people of Bilma two days' warning of the approach of the *Azalai*, as it did of any other exceptionally large caravan coming from the west.*

The return journey to Air with the salt followed the same route. After resting at Agades, a large part of the *Azalai*, with the Sarkin Turawa still at its head, travelled south to Sokoto and thence to Kano where the salt was sold for distribution all over Hausa and beyond. The camels returned to Air with cloth and corn.[7]

In the nineteenth century Kano was far more important than Timbuktu. Its population, predominantly Hausa but with a large foreign element which included a colony of rich Tripolitan Arabs, was estimated by Barth at 30,000; with the coming of the dry season and the opening of the trade routes, the number was doubled by the influx of traders. Kano was the centre of a rich

---

* This extraordinary phenomenon seems to belong to the same category as the singing sands, and in certain respects is comparable with two hills in Ross-shire which 'roar' to each other, according to Dr. F. Fraser Darling, 'when snow is down, an east wind blowing hard, the sky leaden, and the tops partly hidden'. (*A Herd of Red Deer*, London, 1937, p. 11.)

agricultural district which produced all the goods its teeming population required and a considerable surplus for export. But it owed its prosperity chiefly to the industry and extraordinary skill of its Hausa craftsmen, especially the weavers and dyers,* whose wares were in demand all over northern and western Africa.

The great advantage of Kano [wrote Barth] is that commerce and manufactures go hand in hand, and that almost every family has its share in them. There is really something grand in this kind of industry, which spreads to the north as far as Murzuk, Ghat, and even Tripoli; to the west, not only to Timbuktu, but in some degree even as far as the shores of the Atlantic, the very inhabitants of Arguin dressing in the cloth woven and dyed in Kano; to the east, all over Bornu, although there it comes into contact with the native industry of the country; and to the south it maintains a rivalry with the native industry of the Igbira and Igbo [Ibo], while towards the south-east it invades the whole of Adamawa, and is only limited by the nakedness of the pagan *sans-culottes*, who do not wear clothing.[8]

Most of the imports into Kano from the north came down the Air road, and the rest through Kawar and Bornu. Apart from salt and a coarse silk from Tripoli they consisted of a wide range of European trade goods: Manchester cottons, French silks, glass beads from Venice and Trieste, paper,† mirrors and needles from Styria, besides quantities of spices, sugar, and tea. Kano was also an important market for natron from Lake Chad, and kola nuts.

The kola nut, the *goro* of the African and the early Arab travellers, had been in use in the Western Sudan since very early times. The twin interlocking kernels were regarded as a symbol of friendship, and no present was complete without kolas. The nut consequently acquired a ceremonial importance, and it became customary to swear oaths on a kola. Its bitter flavour appeals strongly to the African, it is undoubtedly very sustaining and it is widely regarded as a cure for impotency. Although the heavy cost of transport always kept the price high and for long it was a luxury only the rich could afford, it became, and still remains, a necessity

---

* The skill of the dyers was held in such esteem that cloth used to be sent from Ghadames to Kano to be dyed for the Tripoli market. The brilliantly coloured leather-work of Kano always found a ready sale on the Mediterranean coast.

† Professor H. F. C. Smith has pointed out that 'in view of the large number of Arabic manuscripts that have already been discovered in Northern Nigeria alone, this item must have been of very great importance'. (A. A. Boahen, *Britain, the Sahara, and the Western Sudan*, 1964, 123.)

to a large part of the population. Moreover it was one of the few stimulants allowed to Muslims.

Kola trees were cultivated in the northern belt of the forest over an area that extended from Futa Jallon to northern Ashanti. From the producing areas they were exported northwards to Jenne and north-eastwards to Kano. Some were even carried across the Sahara for sale in towns such as Tunis where the Bey and his mamluks were reported in the 1840s to be consuming a large number.[9]

Travellers crossing the desert were forced to follow well-defined tracks. But south of Kukawa, Kano, and Timbuktu, the *entrepôts* of the Saharan trade, the network of trade routes became much more complicated. For within the savannah and forest belts of West Africa there lay a remarkable number of towns which derived a large part of their wealth from trade. Kong, for example, in the northern Ivory Coast had a population estimated by Binger as 15,000 in the 1880s.[10] It possessed its own cloth industry and traded in kola nuts, gold, and salt. Salaga, in northern Ghana, was regularly visited by Hausa traders. They came to purchase kola nuts and brought with them horses, and goods such as paper, swords, and scent, that had been brought across the Sahara. In Salaga it was also possible to obtain gold from northern Ashanti and European trade-goods, such as cloth and gunpowder, brought from the coast.[11]

Many small traders frequented these routes, men who hoped to acquire a modest capital from the profits of a few journeys spent trading in kola nuts and salt. (A trader at Gronmania, south of Kong, for example, could buy kola nuts locally at one cowrie a piece and sell them for 25 cowries each at Salaga two hundred miles to the east.[12]) It was not impossible, as the European explorers found, to travel alone, accompanied by a few servants. But the hazards of travel were considerable, and most small trains preferred to join regular caravans of merchants. Local wars often delayed travellers or forced them to change their routes. Travel was naturally easiest within the borders of the large well-governed states, most difficult in their turbulent border-lands.

In the development of inter-regional trade in the Western Sudan two peoples had played a dominant part, the Mande or Mandingo, and the Hausa. In the mid-nineteenth century, Hausa traders were to be found settled west of the Niger in the Mossi states, and in the trading centres of northern Ghana. The country to the west of the Hausa sphere of influence was controlled commercially by the Mande. During his visit to Kong, Binger described how Mande influence spread. A family of traders would go and settle in a pagan country. Their wealth, their literacy, and their religion as Muslims gave them prestige. The local chief would turn to them for advice, using them as judges and ambassadors. Having a horror of war, the Mande made use of the influence they acquired to encourage the flow of trade.[13]

The route from the Fezzan through the long oasis of Kawar to Bornu is the easiest of the trans-Saharan caravan routes. There is no conclusive evidence to show that it was used in prehistoric times, and when the Arab commander, Uqba ibn Nafi reached Kawar in 666, he was forced to turn back, after learning from the inhabitants that they knew nothing of the country further south. But it is clear from Arab geographers that by the ninth century the route was in use. As the power of Kanem-Bornu developed, the route must have become more secure and attracted more travellers. Indeed it is possible, as Boahen has suggested, that 'from about the beginning of the seventeenth century until the 1820s, the Fezzan–Bornu route was the most active of all the Saharan routes'. After 1830 the route was disrupted by a variety of political disturbances. The Karamanli dynasty of Tripoli, which had maintained strict control of the Fezzan and established amicable relations with Bornu, was overthrown; but the new Turkish governors, appointed by the Porte, found it difficult to make their power felt in the interior. Among the Arab tribes most affected by the breakdown of law and order was the Awlad Sulaiman. In the 1840s this tribe moved to the area north of Lake Chad and 'earned their living solely by plundering and raiding all and sundry'. The same area was further devastated by the frequent wars between Bornu and Wadai, while the oases of Kawan were raided by the Tebu of Tibesti and their hereditary and bitter enemies, the Tuareg of Air, disappointed raiders consoling themselves by robbing passing caravans. In these circumstances, traders found it more prudent to take the route that led through Air to Kano.[14]

Although the Fezzan–Kawar road carried a great deal of salt southwards from Bilma, it was essentially a slave route. Every European who travelled this blood-stained highway recorded his horror at the thousands of human skeletons with which it was strewn. They were mostly those of young women and girls, and were particularly numerous around the wells, showing how often the last desperate effort to reach water led only to death from exhaustion.

There had long been a big demand for negro slaves on the North African littoral, partly for local use, but more particularly for export to Egypt and Turkey. It will be no surprise to those who have sojourned in the Hausa country that Hausa slaves were more highly valued than any others, the men for their skill and intelligence, the women for their good looks, cheerfulness, and neatness. This preference extended even to Morocco where J. G. Jackson, early in the nineteenth century, and W. B. Harris, at the end of it, both recorded the high prices paid for Hausas in the local slave markets.[15]

In their own interests the slave merchants saw that their slaves were in good condition before they set out to cross the desert. The men, who were mostly youths, were coupled with leg-irons and chained by the neck, but the women and girls were usually allowed to go free. Only the strongest survived the desert march, and these were little better than living skeletons by the time they reached Fezzan. There they were rested and fattened for the Tripoli and Benghazi markets, where prime slaves could be sold at a profit of 500 per cent.

An important, but particularly hideous branch of the trade was the traffic in eunuchs, for whom, as guardians of the harem, there was a big local and foreign demand. It was customary in the Sudan to geld the most robust of the boys and youths captured in slave raids, and some tribes, notably the Mossi, punished crime with castration in order, no doubt, to foster a lucrative trade. Only about 10 per cent. of the victims survived the brutal mutilations which were performed in the crudest possible manner.* The Mossi were considered exceptionally skilled at the operation and they kept their method a closely guarded secret.† They and the Bornuese enjoyed international reputations in the trade in which the principal foreign buyers were Turkey, Egypt, and the Barbary states. Leo Africanus relates how he once bought eunuchs

---

* In 1919 this was confirmed to the author by a native of Kano, who recalled the gelding there of 100 Ningi pagans of whom ten survived, which, he said, was as good as could be expected. Barth, on the other hand, said that usually less than 10 per cent. survived.

† E. F. Gautier recalls the bewilderment of the French ambassador at Constantinople in 1900 at the arrival there of Mossi eunuchs from the French Sudan. (*L'Afrique Noire Occidentale*, Paris, 1935, 139.)

from some wild tribes on the coast of Tripoli.[16] But the trade was far older than that: in the ninth century, for example, the haematomaniac Ibrahim ibn Ahmad of Sicily one day slaughtered all his 300 negro eunuchs. Foreign buyers had to compete with a strong local demand, for eunuchs were as freely used in the Sudan as in any other Muslim country. According to Denham, the sultan of Bornu (where Turkish merchants would pay 250 to 300 dollars for a eunuch) had 200 in his harem.[17]

Before condemning the Sudanese for a barbarous and repulsive trade, we should remember that it was long practised in Christian Europe. During the Middle Ages large establishments, mostly under the direction of Jews, were maintained in France, notably at Verdun, for the supply of eunuchs to Muslim Spain. The *Soprani* of the Sistine Chapel, 'the musical glory and moral shame' of the papal choir, were not abolished until late in the nineteenth century, but the gelding of boys continued in Italy for some time after that.

In addition to the enormous demand for slaves for export to the Muslim north and the Christian south, there were gigantic local needs to be satisfied in the Sudan itself, where many a chief owned thousands of slaves. Consequently the raiding of pagan tribes in the hills and forests became a major occupation of the Muslims throughout the whole length of the Western Sudan. The raids were carefully planned and launched very secretly. A village would be surrounded at dead of night in overwhelming force, and, if the plan did not miscarry, not a soul would escape when the raiders fell on their unsuspecting victims at dawn.* Only the young men and women were taken. The older men, who had little value, and the aged and infirm of both sexes, who were unsaleable, were usually slaughtered. In Bornu Barth witnessed the appalling spectacle of 170 men in the prime of life being left to bleed to death after one such raid. Nearer the coast, where there were eager European buyers for any able-bodied negro, this would not have happened. All this ruthless savagery was perpetrated in the name of religion. As Lord Lugard truly said, 'It is the most serious charge against Islam in Africa that it has encouraged and given religious sanction to slavery.'[18]

Various factors contributed to the decay of the trans-Saharan caravan routes. In southern Morocco the 1880s were a period of

---

* On these raids it was customary for the mounted men to ride mares because stallions were apt to squeal or neigh and give the alarm to the village.

growing political unrest. From their bases in southern Algeria the French were beginning to make their influence felt in areas south of the Atlas that had always acknowledged the suzerainty of the Sultan of Morocco; at the same time, the nationals of other European countries, notably Spain and Britain, were attempting to establish trading posts along the Atlantic coast of the north-western Sahara in order to tap the trans-Saharan trade, and the presence of these foreigners naturally aroused the indignation of the local people. The powers of Europe then put pressure on the Sultan, urging him to restore law and order in the southern part of his domains; to meet this demand the Sultan embarked on a series of punitive expeditions, which served only to ruin the territories at which they were directed. In conditions of increasing insecurity and impoverishment it became more and more difficult for Moroccan traders to support their age-old commerce with the Sudan.[19]

Political disturbances were not their only misfortune. Since the later 1850s, Saharan traders had profited greatly from the sudden demand for ostrich feathers in Europe, the product of a change in ladies' fashions inspired by the example of the French Empress Eugenie. Between 1853 and 1864 the value of ostrich feathers exported from Mogador increased ten times. But in the 1880s competition from South African ostrich farmers, whose birds, carefully reared, produced finer feathers at a cheaper price, grew more intense, and in 1895 the Moroccan trade in ostrich feathers ended completely.[20]

Even more disastrous was the decline in the trade in slaves, for in the mid-nineteenth century slaves had provided about half the total value of all exports across the Sahara.* Ever since their own abolition of the slave trade in 1807, it had been the policy of the British to encourage other governments to follow their example. In 1842 the Bey of Tunis agreed to prohibit the import and export of slaves, and fifteen years later the Ottoman government applied the same regulations to all its domains, which included the province of Tripoli. The Moroccan government was

---

* The number of slaves exported annually across the Sahara has been estimated at about 10,000. 'Of these, until about 1860, 5,000 were exported to the Regency of Tripoli, about 2,500 to Morocco, and the rest smuggled into Algeria and Tunis. About 2,500 of the slaves exported to Tripoli were re-exported annually to Constantinople, Mytilene and Izmir in Turkey . . . to Cyprus, and even as far north as Prevesa and Aulona in Albania.' (A. A. Boahen, *Britain, the Sahara and the Western Sudan*, 1964, 128.)

less susceptible to pressure, but the French advance towards Timbuktu effectively prevented the export of slaves from the Sudan. Traffic in slaves continued longest along the most easterly of the Saharan routes, which ran from Wadai northwards to Kufra and Benghazi.* Not until after the Italian occupation of Cyrenaica in 1911 was the export of slaves from Benghazi finally abolished.[21]

As for other commodities of the Saharan trade imported into North Africa, gold was certainly an item of some importance in the middle of the nineteenth century. By the 1890s, however, the traffic in gold had ceased almost completely. With gold, slaves, and ostrich feathers, their great staples, removed, there was little left for the caravans to carry but a certain amount of ivory, of hides and skins, and perhaps some cotton cloth from Kano.[22] Already new and more efficient routes were being devised, for in the last years of the century the French and the British were extending their conquests deep into the Sudan. In 1883 the French reached the Niger and built a post at Bamako, in 1894 Timbuktu was in their hands, and within the next fifteen years they had begun to bring all the southern Sahara under their control. Meanwhile, the British advancing up the Niger struck at the heart of the Fulani empire, and occupied Kano in 1902 and Sokoto the following year. In 1906 the French completed a railway linking the Niger with the Senegal; five years later the British had finished the railway that connected Kano with the sea at Lagos.

But long before the railways had been completed, the signs of change could be observed. In 1874 the first Moroccan merchant was reported to have arrived at St. Louis, the capital of the French colony of Senegal, and twenty years later there were a hundred Moroccan traders in the town. In 1885 a delegate from Timbuktu arrived in St. Louis to explore the possibility of developing a trade between his town and the French posts on the Niger,[23] and by the 1880s most of the developing ports of West Africa were connected with Europe by steamship lines. The trans-Saharan

---

* This route did not come into use until early in the nineteenth century. According to J. L. Burckhardt it was pioneered by Arabs from Augila, who sought a more direct route to the Sudan (*Travels in Nubia*, 1819, 490). According to another source, however (a French agent who visited Benghazi in the 1840s) the initiative was due to the Sultan of Wadai, who sought a better outlet for his trade than the difficult route that passed west of Tibesti to join the main Kawar–Fezzan route. (M. Emerit, 'Les liasions terrestres entre le Soudan et l'Afrique du Nord au XVIIIe et au debut du XIXe siecle', *Transactions de l'Institut des Recherches Sahariennes*, Algiers, 1954, XI.)

route between Timbuktu and Morocco was certainly much shorter in simple mileage than the route from Timbuktu to St. Louis and from St. Louis by sea to the ports of Morocco, but the new route was infinitely safer, and eventually probably cheaper and swifter. Still more important was the fact that the new links with the sea put the countries of the Western Sudan in touch with markets they had never known before: from these markets in Europe and America came a demand for the agricultural products of the Sudan, and especially for groundnuts (peanuts). The groundnut is a plant of Latin American origin; its cultivation was first actively encouraged by the French in Senegal in the 1840s, and by the 1920s it had been introduced to all the countries of the Western Sudan. The unromantic groundnut has provided a greater and more reliable source of wealth than all the gold and all the slaves, the bundles of ostrich feathers, and the loads of ivory carried by camel-caravan across the Sahara.

The decline of the trans-Saharan caravan trade marked the beginning of a profound revolution in the life of the desert, a revolution that was basically the product of political changes, for the period between 1850 and 1930 saw the gradual extension of European rule over the entire Sahara. The French, advancing from Algeria and Morocco and from their colonies of Soudan and Chad, annexed the greater part of the desert; but Spain carved out a territory along the Atlantic coast of the Sahara, and Italy extended her colony of Libya to include Ghadames, Kufra and the Fezzan.

European rule meant the imposition of a peace such as the desert had never known before. Over large areas of the Sahara this pacification was the work of French officers, making skilful use of native allies. Thus the Chaamba, nomadic Arabs of the northern Sahara, notorious raiders in the past, provided many volunteers for the Saharan Camel Corps established by the French in 1902. 'Their work is what Chaamba nomads have always known best and loved most dearly, namely the pursuit and destruction of bands of robbers and smugglers from rival tribes and especially their traditional blood enemies, the Tuareg and Moors.'[24] The battle at which in 1902 the power of the Ahaggar Tuareg was completely shattered was fought by a French Camel Corps patrol composed mainly of Chaamba.

With the new peace came new methods of transportation. 'Of all the innovations introduced by the French into the Sahara',

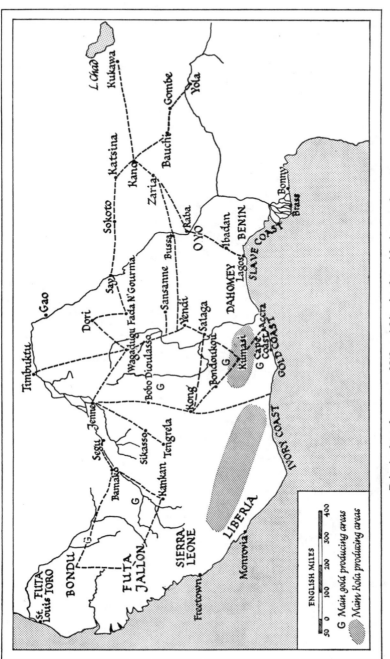

x. Principal trade routes of West Africa in the mid-nineteenth century

Capot-Rey has written, 'none, not even the peace nor the multi-plication of wells, has had such a profound effect on the conditions of life as the motor-car; to discover a fact of comparable import-ance one must go back to the domestication of the camel.'[25] For the slaves and serfs of the oases, the Haratin and the Bellah, the motor-car opened the door to the promised land, first to the cities of the North African coast, then—in the 1950s—to the camps, glittering with modernity, of the oil-prospectors and the mining engineers. Meanwhile, within many of the oases, wells fall in and irrigation channels become blocked for lack of labour to maintain them; and so the desert encroaches.

For the nomadic tribes, for the old aristocracy of the desert the disappearance of the trans-Saharan trade, the check on raid-ing, and the emigration of their serfs has meant 'a loss of prestige, a reduction of employment and a fall in income'.[26] Nomadism in the grand manner appears to be fading away, and both 'the warlike pastoral nomads and the sedentary poor are being driven towards the intermediate condition of semi-nomadism and indus-trial employment'.[27] The prospect is one that fills old Saharan hands with a sense of sadness and outrage.

Here are a people perfectly adapted to the natural environment, not only physically, through the sharpness of their senses, the sureness of their instincts, the speed of their reflexes, but also by their social organization and their sense of honour; and simply to obtain workmen for the oil fields, it is planned to transform these lordly people who command our respect by the dignity of their attitudes and the wisdom of their rare utterances into a rabble seeking jobs and doles.[28]

Whatever the social consequences, the isolation of the Sahara is becoming less and less apparent. Its significance as a barrier, too, is declining. New wealth—and few parts of Africa, it should be emphasized, have had such a sudden access to new sources of wealth as parts of the Sahara—is bound to create new commun-ities and lead to improved communications. Only a decade ago one could think of 'the ties which for countless centuries had bound Barbary to the Western Sudan' as being 'for ever broken'.[29] Today it is possible at least to envisage the desert being spanned by broad arterial highways, along which there may flow as great a volume of trade and more diverse a concourse of travellers than in the centuries of the caravans of the old Sahara.

References

CHAPTER 1: ARID NURSE OF LIONS

(pp. 1–13)

1. Herodotus, *The History*, II. 32.
2. J. Carcopino, *Daily Life in Ancient Rome*, London, 1941, 239.
3. Pliny the Elder, *Natural History*, VIII, 7.
4. ibid. VIII, 10.
5. Strabo, *Geography*, XVII. 3.
6. G. W. Murray, 'The Climate of Egypt', *Geographical Journal*, CXVII (1951), 422–34.
7. Horace, *Odes*, I. 22.
8. Sallust, *Jugurthine War*, XVII. 4.
9. Herodotus, op. cit. II. 32.
10. Pliny, op. cit., V. 1.
11. Herodotus, op. cit., III. 26.
12. L. C. Briggs, *Tribes of the Sahara*, London, 1960, 34.
13. R. Mauny, *Tableau géographique de l'ouest africain au moyen âge*, *Mémoires de l'Institut Français d'Afrique Noire*, no. 61, Dakar, 1961, 202–204.
14. Mauny, op cit. 204–8.
15. ibid. 208–11; R. Capot-Rey, *Le Sahara français*, Paris, 1953, 85–98.

CHAPTER 2: CARBUNCLES AND GOLD

(pp. 13–27)

1. Herodotus, op. cit. IV. 183.
2. ibid. II. 32.
3. H. Barth, *Travels and Discoveries in North and Central Africa*, London, 1858, I. 196–202.
4. H. Lhote, *Les Touaregs du Hoggar*, Paris, 1955, 64–75; R. Mauny, 'Gravures, peintures et inscriptions rupestres de l'quest africain', *Initiations africaines*, no. 11, I.F.A.N., Dakar, 1954.
5. H. Lhote, *The Search for the Tassili Frescoes*, London, 1958, 122–32.
6. Briggs, op. cit. 21.
7. F. R. Rodd, *People of the Veil*, London, 1926, 203.
8. Strabo, op. cit. III. v. 11.
9. Pliny, op. cit. XXXVII. 25, 30.
10. Athenaeus, *Deipnosophistae*, II. 22.

11. Frontinus, *Strategematicon*, I. xi. 18.

12. Herodotus, op. cit. III. 21.

13. Thucydides, VI. 34.

14. Pliny, op. cit. XXXIII. 15.

15. S. Gsell, *Histoire ancienne de l'Afrique du Nord*, Paris, 1921–9, IV, 140.

16. Herodotus, op. cit. IV. 195.

17. ibid. 196.

18. Strabo, op. cit. II. iii. 4.

19. ibid. XVII. i. 19.

20. The original text of Hanno is given in C. Muller, *Geographici Graeci Minores*, I, 1–14. It has been translated in full with a commentary in M. Cary and E. H. Warmington, *The Ancient Explorers*, Penguin Books, Harmondsworth, 1963, 63–68.

21. For a detailed discussion of the Periplus on conventional lines, see J. Carcopino, *Le Maroc antique*, Paris, 1943, 49–162.

22. G. Germain, 'Qu'est-ce le périple d'Hannon? Document, amplification littéraire ou faux intégral?' *Hespéris*, Paris, 1957, 247.

23. R. Mauny, 'La Navigation sur les côtes du Sahara pendant l'antiquité', *Revue des études anciennes*, LVII, Bordeaux, 1955; idem. *Les Navigations médiévales sur les côtes sahariennes antérieures à la découverte portugaise (1434)*, Lisbon, 1960, 1–25.

24. E. F. Gautier, *L'Afrique noire occidentale*, Paris, 1935, 123–7.

CHAPTER 3: ROMANS AND GARAMANTES

(pp. 28–44)

1. Sallust, op. cit. LXXX.

2. Tacitus, *Annals*, III. 74; IV. 23.

3. Tacitus, *Histories*, IV. 50.

4. Lucian, *De Dipsadibus*, II.

5. For a fuller discussion of the ethnology of the Garamantes, see Capot-Rey, op. cit. 171–2.

6. Pliny, op. cit. V. 5. For a detailed discussion of this expedition, see J. Desanges 'Le Triomphe de Cornelius Balbus 19 av. J.C.', *Revue africaine*, CI (1957), 5–45.

7. Tacitus, *Annals*, III. 73–4; IV. 23–4.

8. ibid. IV. 23.

9. ibid. IV. 26.

10. Pliny, *Natural History*, V. 5.

11. ibid.

12. Ptolemy, *Geography*, trans. E. L. Stevenson, New York, 1932, I. viii.

13. Rodd, op. cit. 318–29.

14. Caesar, *Bellum Africanum*, LXVIII.

15. Ammianus Marcellinus, *History*, XXXVIII. vi. 5.

16. G. F. Lyon, *A Narrative of Travels in Northern Africa*, London, 1821, 93.

For a discussion by modern scholars of the introduction of the camel into North Africa, see O. Brogan, 'The Camel in Roman Tripolitania', *Papers of the British School at Rome*, XXII (1954); S. Gsell, 'La Tripolitaine et le Sahara au IIIe siècle', *Mémoires de l'Institut National de France*, XLIII (1926); C. Courtois, *Les Vandales et l'Afrique*, Paris, 1954, 97–104.

17. R. G. Goodchild and J. B. Ward-Perkins, 'The Limes Tripolitanus', *Journal of Roman Studies*, XXXIX (1949), XL (1950).

18. Barth, op cit. I, 157.

19. The results of this expedition were published in *Monumenti Antichi*, XLI, Rome, 1951; see also Mortimer Wheeler, *Rome beyond the Imperial Frontiers*, Penguin Books, Harmondsworth, 1955, 121–33.

20. Pliny, op cit. v. 5.

21. Strabo, op. cit. XVII. iii. 19.

22. ibid. IV. v. 2.

23. R. H. Barrow, *Slavery in the Roman Empire*, London, 1928.

24. Seneca, *Letters*, LXXXVII. 9.

25. On Tin Hanan, E. F. Gautier and M. Reygasse, 'Le Monument de Tin-Hanan', *Annales de l'Académie des Sciences Coloniales*, VII, Paris, 1934; M. Reygasse, *Monuments funéraires préislamiques de l'Afrique du Nord*, Paris, 1950, 88; Mortimer Wheeler, op. cit. 133–7.

SAHARA AND SUDAN

CHAPTER 4: THE TUAREG AND OTHER PEOPLES OF THE SAHARA

(pp. 45–50)

1. Briggs, op. cit. 37.

2. ibid. 66.

3. ibid. 67.

4. Capot-Rey, op. cit. 168–70.

5. Briggs, op. cit. 168; Capot-Rey, op. cit. 172–5.

6. Briggs, op. cit. 126.

7. ibid. 151–5.

8. Lhote, *Les Touaregs du Hoggar*, 120–1.

9. Ibn Khaldun, quoted in G. H. Bousquet, *Les Berbères*, Paris, 1957, 53.

10. Ibn Haukal, quoted in Lhote, op. cit. 126–7.

11. On the history of the Western Sahara, see F. de la Chapelle, 'Esquisse d'une histoire du Sahara occidental', *Hespéris*, XI (1930).

12. Capot-Rey, op. cit. 191–2.

13. Lhote, op. cit. 344–6.

14. H. Macmichael, *History of Arabs in the Sudan*, London, 1922, I, 55–7.

15. Yaqubi, quoted in H. R. Palmer, *The Bornu Sahara and Sudan*, London, 1936, 209 n.3.

16. F. Wüstenfeld, *Jacut's Geographisches Wörterbuch*, Leipzig, 1866–1870.

17. Ibn Khaldun, *Histoire des Berbères*, trans. de Slane, Paris, 1925, II, 64.

18. Briggs, op. cit. 90.

19. M. Delafosse, *Haut-Sénégal-Niger*, 3 vols., Paris, 1912, II, 219.

20. For a summary of recent discussions about the position of the Jews in West Africa see Mauny, *Tableau géographique*, 459–60.

21. P. de Ceniral and T. Monod, *Description de la côte de l'Afrique de Ceuta au Sénégal, par Valentin Fernandes*, Paris, 1938, 85.

CHAPTER 5: PEOPLES OF THE SUDAN

(pp. 50–55)

1. J. H. Greenberg, *Studies in African Linguistic Classification*, New Haven, 1955.

2. R. G. Armstrong, 'The Use of Linguistic and Ethnographic Data in the Study of Idoma and Yoruba History' in *The Historian in Tropical Africa*, ed. J. Vansina, R. Mauny, and L. V. Thomas, London, 1964, 135.

3. B. Fagg, 'The Nok Culture', *West African Review*, December 1956.

4. T. Shaw, 'The Approach through Archaeology to early West African History' in *A Thousand Years of West African History*, ed. J. F. A. Ajayi and I. Espie, Ibadan, 1965, 36. See also J. P. Lebeuf and A. Masson-Detourbet, *La Civilisation du Tchad*, Paris, 1950.

5. On the megalithic and other archaeological sites in West Africa, see Mauny, op. cit. 56–187.

6. as-Sadi, *Tarikh as-Sudan*, trans. O. Houdas, Paris, 1900, 18.

7. ibid. 6.

8. J. D. Fage, 'Reflections on the early history of the Mossi-Dagomba group of States' in *The Historian in Tropical Africa*, 177.

9. One version of this legend is given in H. R. Palmer, *Sudanese Memoirs*, Lagos, 1928, III, 132–41.

10. Palmer, *The Bornu Sahara and Sudan*, 112.

11. Y. Urvoy, *Histoire de l'empire du Bornou*, Dakar, 1949, 21–26; see also Thomas Hodgkin, *Nigerian Perspectives*, London, 1960, 21.

12. M. G. Smith, 'The Beginnings of Hausa Society, A.D. 1000–1500' in *The Historian in Tropical Africa*, 342.

13. ibid. 88–90.

14. J. S. Trimingham, *A History of Islam in West Africa*, London, 1962, 35–6.

CHAPTER 6: THE ARABS

(pp. 56–66)

1. C. A. Julien, *Histoire de l'Afrique du Nord des origines à la conquête arabe*, Paris, 1961, 225.

2. Procopius, *Secret History*, XVIII. 9, quoted in Julien, op. cit. 272.

3. Ibn Khaldun, op. cit. quoted in Trimingham, op. cit. 18.

4. Ibn Battuta, *Travels in Asia and Africa*, trans. H. A. R. Gibb, London, 1929, 317.

5. Details of some of the other Arab geographers not mentioned here are given in Mauny, op. cit. 24–37. Translations of all Arab geographers who wrote about Africa are contained in Youssouf Kamal, *Monumenta Cartographica Africae et Aegypti*, 5 vols., Leiden, 1926–53, III, folios 1–4.

6. Ibn Haukal, *Opus geographicum anctore Ibn Haukal*, ed. J. H. Kramers, Leiden, 1938, I, 9–10.

7. J. O. Hunwick, 'Ahmad Baba and the Moroccan Invasion of the Sudan (1591)', *Journal of the Historical Society of Nigeria*, II, Ibadan, 1962, 311–28.

8. Barth, op. cit. IV, 406.

CHAPTER 7: THE ALMORAVIDS

(pp. 67–79)

1. Ibn Haukal, *The Oriental Geography*, trans. W. Ouseley, London, 1800, 21.

2. al-Bakri, *Description de l'Afrique septentrionale*, trans. de Slane, Algiers, 1913, 282.

3. Ibn abd al-Hakam, *Conquête de l'Afrique du Nord*, trans. A. Gateau, Algiers, 1942, 119.

4. On the site of Kumbi Saleh, see Mauny, op. cit. 71–4, 469–73, 480–2; Mahmud al-Kati, *Tarikh al-Fattash*, trans. O. Houdas and M. Delafosse, Paris, 1913, 76.

5. as-Sadi, op. cit. 18.

6. Mahmud al-Kati, op. cit. 75–6.

7. On the area covered by the empire of Ghana, see Mauny, op. cit. 508–10.

8. Ibn Khaldun, op. cit. II, 65.

9. al-Bakri, op. cit. 299–301, 317; Mauny, op. cit. 71–2, 481–3.

10. Ibn Haukal, *Description de l'Afrique*, trans. de Slane, *Journal Asiatique*, Paris, 1842, 243.

11. al-Bakri, op. cit. 311–12.

12. Ibn Khaldun, op. cit. II, 69.

13. al-Bakri, op. cit. 314.

14. ibid. 317.

15. Ibn Khaldun, op. cit. II, 71.

16. R. Dozy, *Spanish Islam*, trans. F. G. Stokes, London, 1913, 694.

17. E. Lévi-Provençal, 'Reflexions sur l'empire almoravide au début du XIIe siècle', *Cinquantenaire de la Faculté des Lettres d'Alger*, Algiers, 1932, 307–30.

CHAPTER 8: THE GOLD OF GHANA

(pp. 79–85)

1. Leo Africanus, *History and Description of Africa*, trans. J. Pory and ed. R. Brown, 3 vols., Hakluyt Society, London, 1896, II, 282.

2. al-Bakri, op. cit. 328–30.

3. al-Idrisi, *Description de l'Afrique et de l'Espagne*, trans. R. Dozy and M. J. de Goeje, Leiden, 1866, 8.

4. Ibn Khaldun, op. cit. II, 115.

5. al-Idrisi, op. cit. 7.

6. Yaqut, quoted in Delafosse, op. cit. II, 45–6.

7. al-Masudi, *Les Praires d'or*, trans. B. de Meynard and P. de Courteille, 9 vols., Paris, 1861, IV, 93.

8. A. da Cadamosto, *Voyages*, ed. and trans. G. R. Crone, Hakluyt Society, London, 1937, 22.

9. al-Bakri, op. cit. 325; Barth, op. cit. IV, 443.

10. al-Bakri, op. cit. 327.

11. Delafosse, op. cit. II, 162–70.

CHAPTER 9: MANSA MUSA OF MALI

(pp. 85–91)

1. al-Bakri, op. cit. 333.

2. D. T. Niane, 'So undiata ou l'épopée mandingue', *Présence Africaine* (1960).

3. al-Umaii, *Masalik al-Absar*, Paris, 1927, 79.

4. Ibn Khaldun, op. cit. II, 113.

5. On the foundation of Timbuktu, see as-Sadi, op. cit. 36.

6. Dulcert's *mappa-mundi* is reproduced in Youssouf Kamal, op. cit. IV, ii, 1223.

7. ibid. IV, iv, 1465.

8. ibid. IV, iii, 1305.

9. ibid. V, i, 1515.

10. ibid. V, i, 1504.

CHAPTER 10: IBN BATTUTA

(pp. 91–7)

1. as-Sadi, op. cit. 16–17.
2. On Sulaiman, see Trimingham, op. cit. 71–2.
3. On Takedda and its copper mines, see Mauny, op. cit. 139–41, 308–13.
4. Leo Africanus, op. cit. III, 802.
5. Ibn Battuta, op. cit. 321.
6. ibid. 323.
7. ibid. 332.
8. ibid. 329–31.
9. ibid. 335–6.
10. Abbé Bargès, 'Mémoire sur les relations commerciales de Tlemcen avec le Soudan', *Revue de l'orient*, Paris, 1853.
11. On the decline of Mali, see Trimingham, op. cit. 73–76, 147–8.

CHAPTER 11: THE CRESCENT AND THE CROSS

(pp. 98–108)

1. On the survival of Christianity in North Africa, see Julien, op. cit. 277–9, 322.
2. al-Bakri, op. cit. 70.
3. Mas Latrie, *Relations et commerce de l'Afrique septentrionale ou Maghreb avec les nations chrétiennes du moyen âge*, Paris, 1886, 268.
4. Ibn Khaldun, op. cit. II, 235 n.1.
5. Mas Latrie, op. cit. 20.
6. Ibn Haukal, *The Oriental Geography*, 16.
7. Mas Latrie, op. cit. 22.
8. R. W. Southern, *The Making of the Middle Ages*, London, 1959, 51; see also M. Bloch, 'Le problème de l'or au moyen âge', *Annales d'histoire économique et sociale*, V, Paris, 1933, 1–34; F. Brandel, 'Monnaies et civilisations: De l'or du Soudan a l'argent d'Amérique', *Annales: (Économies, sociétés, civilisations)*, I (1946), 9–22; M. Lombard, 'L'Or musulman du VIIe au XIe siècle', *Annales*, II (1947), 143–60.
9. Mauny, op. cit. 293–306, 375–7.
10. Youssouf Kamal, op. cit. IV, i, 1139.
11. Abbé Bargès, op. cit.

CHAPTER 12: THE QUEST FOR GOLD

(pp. 108–12)

1. On the Majorcan cartographers, see C. de la Roncière, *La Découverte de l'Afrique au moyen âge*, 3 vols., Cairo, 1924–7, I.

2. Malfante's letter is given in an English translation in Cadamosto, op. cit. 85–90.

3. de la Roncière, op. cit. I, 161.

CHAPTER 13: THE DISCOVERY OF GUINEA

(pp. 112–19)

1. Ibn Khaldun, op. cit. I, 187–8.

2. Mauny, *Navigations médiévales*, 1–25.

3. Mauny, op. cit. 26–33, 86–91.

4. J. H. Parry, *The Age of Reconnaissance*, London, 1963, 19.

5. R. H. Major (ed.), *The Canarian or Book of the Conquest and Conversion of the Canarians in the year 1402, by Messire Jean de Bethencourt, Kt.*, Hakluyt Society, London, 1872, 106.

6. H. V. Livermore in *The New Cambridge Modern History*, I (1957), 420.

7. For a discussion of Henry's motive, see J. H. Parry, op. cit. 35–6.

8. Mauny, op. cit. 17–19.

9. Gomes Eannes de Azurara (Zurara), *The Chronicle of the Discovery and Conquest of Guinea*, Hakluyt Society London, 1896, 1899, II.

10. Richard Jobson, *The Golden Trade*, London, 1623, reprinted Teignmouth, 1904, 34.

11. J. D. Fage, *Ghana: A Historical Interpretation*, Madison, 1959, 20.

12. ibid. 42.

13. Brandel, op. cit. I.

14. Quoted in C. R. Boxer, *Four Centuries of Portuguese Expansion, 1415–1825*, Johannesburg, 1961, 26–7.

15. A. F. C. Ryder, 'Portuguese and Dutch in West Africa before 1800', in Ajayi and Espie (ed.), op. cit. 226.

16. Quoted in R. Hallett, *The Penetration of Africa up to 1815*, London, 1965, 128.

CHAPTER 14: WANGARA

(pp. 119–31)

1. al-Fazari in Youssouf Kamal, op. cit. III, i, 510.

2. Ibn al-Faqih in Youssouf Kamal, op. cit. III, i, 558.

3. al-Bakri, op. cit. 331.

4. ibid. 333. al-Bakri states that Iresni lies 'to the west' of Ghiarou; Mauny, *Tableau géographique*, 302 n, thinks that this must be a mistake.

5. al-Idrisi, op. cit. 3, 7–9. For a summary of Muslim accounts about the gold of West Africa, see Mauny, op. cit. 300–6.

6. Malfante in Cadamosto, op. cit. 88.

7. For a more detailed account of the gold-bearing areas of West Africa, see Mauny, op. cit. 293–9.

8. The *Tohfut-ul-Alabi* is printed in Palmer, *Sudanese Memoirs*, II, 90.

9. Ibn Battuta, op. cit. 318.

10. al-Umaii, op. cit. 58

11. W. Bosman, *A New and Accurate Description of the Coast of Guinea*, Eng. trans., London, 1721, 70.

12. J. Dupuis, *Journal of a Residence in Ashantee*, London, 1824, xli n.

13. S. Purchas, *Purchas His Pilgrimes*, 20 vols., Glasgow, 1905–7.

14. de la Roncière, op. cit. I, Plate IX; see also Mauny, *Navigations médiévales*, 96–7.

15. al-Idrisi, op. cit. 7–9.

16. *The Book of Knowledge*, Hakluyt Society, London, 1912, 31.

17. Yaqut, quoted in Delafosse, op. cit. II, 46.

18. Delafosse, op. cit. I, 55.

19. Mauny, *Tableau géographique*, 302.

20. Cadamosto, op. cit. 21–23.

21. ibid. 24.

22. Jobson, op. cit. 131.

23. H. Labouret, 'Mutilations labiales des populations du Lobi', *L'Anthropologie*, XXXI (1921), 95–104.

24. E. G. R. Taylor, 'Pactolus: River of Gold', *Scottish Geographical Magazine*, XLIV (1928), 129–44.

25. On Lobi and its ruins, see Mauny, op. cit. 297. H. Labouret, 'Le mystère des ruines du Lobi', *Revue d'ethnologie et des traditions populaires* (1920), 177–96; H. Labouret, 'L'or du Lobi', *Bulletin du Comité de l'Afrique Française, Renseignements coloniaux* (1925), 69–73.

26. Leo Africanus, op. cit. III, 831–2.

27. Barth, op. cit. II, 82.

28. Mauny, op. cit. 306.

29. The Kano chronicle is printed in Palmer, op. cit. III, 111.

30. The relevant passages from J. de Barros, *Da Asia*, 24 vols., Lisbon, 1778, are translated by Crone in his edition of Cadamosto, *Voyages*, 146–7.

31. For a more detailed account of these expeditions, see Hallett, op. cit. 78–91.

32. M. Park, *Travels in the Interior Districts of Africa*, London, 1799, xxiii.

33. R. Caillié, *Travels through Central Africa to Timbuctoo*, Eng. trans., 2 vols., London, 1830, I, 283–4.

34. Mauny, op. cit. 364–5.

35. Lyon, op. cit. 148–9.

36. Dixon Denham and Hugh Clapperton, *Narrative of Travels and Discoveries in Northern and Central Africa*, 2 vols., London, 1826, II, 85.

This book has been edited and new material added by E. W. Bovill in *Missions to the Niger*, II, III, IV, Hakluyt Society, London, 1966.

37. R. J. Harrison Church, *West Africa*, 3rd ed. London, 1961, 406.

38. ibid. 144, 294–5.

39. J. J. Scarisbrick and P. L. Carter, 'An expedition to Wangara', *Ghana Notes and Queries*, No. 1 (1961).

CHAPTER 15: THE SONGHAI

(pp. 132–42)

1. as-Sadi, op. cit. 4–9. For a more detailed discussion of Songhai origins, see J. Rouch, *Contribution à l'histoire des Songhay*, *Mémoires de l'I.F.A.N.*, no. 29 (1953), 165–71.

2. For the criticism of Delafosse's statement, see Trimingham, op. cit. 85.

3. On Kukiya, see Mauny, op. cit. 120; on Gao, ibid. 48, 112–13; on as-Suk, ibid. 117–18, 487–8; on Takedda, ibid. 139–40.

4. al-Bakri, op. cit. 342; as-Sadi, op. cit. 5.

5. as-Sadi, op. cit. 103.

6. ibid. 22–23. On Jenne, see also Mauny, op. cit. 115–16, 494–5, 499–500, and C. Monteil, *Une Cité soudanaise: Djénné*, Paris, 1932.

7. Portuguese contacts with the interior of West Africa at this time are briefly described in de Barros, *Da Asia*, I, ii, 12, translated in Cadomosto, op. cit. 142–5.

8. On Sonni Ali's magical powers, see Rouch, op. cit. 183–4.

9. The historian, Mahmud al-Kati, accompanied Askia Muhammad on his pilgrimage. On the significance of his investiture, see Trimingham, op. cit. 98.

10. Rodd, op. cit. 26, 101; C. Jean, *Les Touareg du Sud-Est l'Aïr*, Paris, 1909, 87–89.

11. Barth, op. cit. I, 418; M. Abadie, *La Colonie du Niger*, Paris, 1927, 189.

12. Rouch, op. cit. 193–4, 199, 209.

13. A. G. P. Martin, *Les Oasis sahariennes*, Algiers, 1908, 142; Trimingham, op. cit. 133.

14. T. H. Baldwin, *The Obligations of Princes*, Beirut, 1932.

CHAPTER 16: LEO AFRICANUS

(pp. 142–54)

1. Leo Africanus, op. cit. I, 190.

2. The account given here of Leo Africanus's life and travels is based on the research done by R. Mauny for 'Note sur *Les grands voyages* de Léon l'Africain', *Hespéris*, XLI (1954), 379–94.

3. Leo Africanus, op. cit. II, 309.

4. ibid. III, 821.

5. Mauny, *Tableau géographique*, 497–9.

6. On the identity of the 'rich king' of Timbuktu, often confused with the Askia, see the note by H. Lhote, in Jean-Léon l'Africain, *Description de l'Afrique*, trans. A. Épaulard, Paris, 1956, II, 467.

7. Leo Africanus, op. cit. III, 824–5.

8. Caillié, op. cit. II, 49.

9. as-Sadi, op. cit. 22.

10. Leo Africanus, op. cit. III, 822.

11. ibid. 823.

12. ibid. 826–7.

13. This passage is omitted in Pory's translation, but is included in the French translation by Épaulard, II, 471.

14. Leo Africanus, op. cit. III, 828.

15. ibid. 831–2.

16. ibid. 832–5.

17. As Pory failed to give an accurate translation of this important passage, it has been translated from the French version by Épaulard, I, 5.

18. Cadamosto, op. cit. 94.

19. Leo Africanus, op. cit. III, 938.

CHAPTER 17: MULAI AHMAD AL-MANSUR

(pp. 154–9)

1. For a detailed account of the events leading up to the battle of al-Ksar al-Kabir, see E. W. Bovill, *The Battle of Alcazar*, London, 1952.

2. The principal Moroccan source for the reign of al-Mansur is the 18th-century historian, al-Ifrani, *Histoire de la dynastie saadienne au Maroc, 1511–1670*, trans. and ed. O. Houdas, Paris, 1886, 131–54. For other sources, see C. A. Julien, *Histoire de l'Afrique du Nord de la conquête arabe à 1830*, 2nd rev. ed., Paris, 1952, 210–23, 344–5.

3. For a more detailed account of al-Mansur's relations with England, see Bovill, op. cit. 43–48, 175–9.

CHAPTER 18: TAGHAZA

(pp. 160–4)

1. For a comprehensive account of the salt trade, see Mauny, op. cit. 321–36.

2. Ibn Battuta, op. cit. 317–18.

3. Leo Africanus, op. cit. III, 800.
4. as-Sadi, op. cit. 163–4.
5. ibid. 174; Mauny, op.cit. 331 n. 2.
6. as-Sadi, op. cit. 180.
7. ibid., 193.
8. al-Ifrani, op. cit. 154–5.
9. H. de Castries, *Les Sources inédites de l'histoire du Maroc*, 18 vols., Paris, 1905–36, *Première série—dynastie sa'dienne, Archives et bibliothèques de l'Angleterre*, I, 431.
10. as-Sadi, op. cit. 193.
11. Julien, op. cit. 214.
12. as-Sadi, op. cit. 216–17; al-Ifrani, op. cit. 155.
13. Mauny, op. cit. 331–2.

CHAPTER 19: THE DESERT ARMY
(pp. 164–72)

1. as-Sadi, op. cit. 217.
2. al-Ifrani, op. cit. 160–2.
3. Leo Africanus, op. cit. III, 991.
4. *The tragical life and death of Muley Abdala Melek, the late King of Barbarie*, Delft, 1633, quoted in de Castries, op. cit. III, 201.
5. Details of the expedition's equipment are given in the account of the anonymous Spaniard, published by H. de Castries, in 'La Conquête du Soudan par El-Mansour (1591)', *Hespéris*, III (1923), 433–88.
6. *Journal of the African Society*, XXXV (1936), 159.
7. de Castries, *Sources inédites*, I, 521.
8. ibid. I, 527.
9. ibid. II, 10.
10. ibid. II, 23.
11. J. Méniaud, *Haut-Sénégal-Niger: Géographie économique*, 2 vols., Paris, 1912, II, 207.
12. Leo Africanus, op. cit. III, 800.
13. Mahmud al-Kati, op. cit. 263.

CHAPTER 20: THE INVASION OF THE SUDAN
(pp. 173–83)

1. This account of the Moroccan invasion is based chiefly on Mahmud al-Kati, op. cit. 160–320, and as-Sadi, op. cit. 215–80. See also Hunwick, op. cit. 311–28.
2. Mahmud al-Kati, op. cit. 264.

3. as-Sadi, op. cit. 219.
4. Mahmud al-Kati, op. cit. 263.
5. *Antiquity*, vii (1933), 353.
6. This document was published by H. de Castries in *Hespéris*, iii (1923), 483–8.
7. de Castries, *Sources inédites*, ii, 66.
8. *Geographical Journal*, vi (1895), 219.

CHAPTER 21: THE FALL OF SONGHAI

(pp. 183–95)

1. as-Sadi, op. cit. 223.
2. A letter written by Mahmud to the *qadi* of Timbuktu at this time was discovered by E. Lévi-Provençal among the Arabic documents in the archives of the Escorial, Madrid, and published in *Arabica*, ii, Leyden, 1955, 89–96.
3. Hunwick, op. cit. 313, 322–3.
4. ibid. 324–5.
5. de Castries, op. cit. ii, 146.
6. For the later history of the Moroccan Pashas of Timbuktu the principal source is the anonymous work, *Tedzkiret en-Nisian* (translated by O. Houdas in 1899), a biographical dictionary of the Pashas of the Sudan from 1590 to 1750.
7. Mons. A****, *A Letter concerning the Countrys of Muley Arxid, King of Tafiletta*, Eng. trans., London, 1671, 17.
8. Julien, op. cit. 229. The principal Moroccan source for the reign of Mulay Ismail is the chronicle of al-Zayani, *Le Maroc de 1631 à 1812*, ed. and trans. O. Houdas, Paris, 1886.
9. Monteil, op. cit. 83.

CHAPTER 22: ADH-DHAHABI

(pp. 195–206)

1. as-Sadi, op. cit. 223.
2. al-Ifrani, op. cit. 167.
3. R. Hakluyt, *Principal Navigations of the English Nation*, 12 vols., Glasgow, 1903–5, vii, 99–100.
4. ibid. 100–1.
5. Quoted in P. Masson, *Histoire des établissements et du commerce français dans l'Afrique barbaresque*, Paris, 1903, 92.
6. Captain John Smith, *Travels*, 2 vols., Glasgow, 1907, ii, 163.
7. Mons. A****, op. cit. 15.
8. Ro. C., *A True Historicall discourse of Muley Hamet's rising to the*

three Kingdomes of Moruecos, Fes, and Sus, London, 1609, ch. xxv, quoted in de Castries, op. cit. II, 404.

9. For an account of Edward Wright and his work, see E. G. R. Taylor, *Mathematical Practitioners of Stuart and Tudor England*, Cambridge, 1954.

10. Purchas, op. cit. II, 168–70.

11. de Castries, op. cit. II, 177–9.

12. ibid. 200.

13. Purchas, op. cit. VI, 60–1.

14. Hakluyt, op. cit. VII, 88.

15. Ro. C., op. cit. quoted in Purchas, op. cit. VI, 108.

16. de Castries, op. cit. II, 226.

17. For an account of this expedition, see Jobson, op. cit. See also J. M. Gray, *A History of the Gambia*, Cambridge, 1939, 26–35.

18. Peter Mundy, *Travels*, 5 vols., Hakluyt Society, London, 1907–1936, V, 131.

19. Jobson, op. cit. 4.

20. de Castries, op. cit. III, 237.

21. ibid. 452.

22. ibid. 485.

CHAPTER 23: THE EUROPEAN PENETRATION OF THE INTERIOR

(pp. 207–22)

1. For D'Anville's ideas about the Niger, see his 'Mémoire concernant les rivières de l'intérieur de l'Afrique', *Mémoires de Littérature de l'Académie Royale des Inscriptions et Belles Lettres*, XXVI, Paris, 1759.

2. Sir Godfrey Fisher's *Barbary Legend*, Oxford, 1957, provides a scholarly corrective to many long accepted ideas about 'Barbary pirates'.

3. On Cecil's activities, see Hatfield House, Cecil MSS. 38, f. 59. For an account of the Salee pirates, see de Castries, op. cit. III, 'Les Moriscos à Sale'.

4. For a more detailed discussion of the reasons for European ignorance, see Hallett, op. cit. 125–35.

5. *Proceedings of the African Association* (1810), I, 7–8.

6. On the work of the African Association, see R. Hallett (ed.), *The Records of the African Association*, London, 1964, and *idem, Penetration of Africa*.

7. Park, op. cit. ch. XV.

8. ibid. ch. XVI.

9. For Rennell's ideas, see *Proceedings of the African Association* (1810), I, 534–7.

10. Frederick Hornemann, *Journal of Travels from Cairo to Mourzouk*, African Association, London, 1802. This book has been edited with much additional material by E. W. Bovill in *Missions to the Niger*, I, Hakluyt Society, London, 1964.

11. For a more detailed account of the genesis of Park's second expedition, see Hallett, *Penetration of Africa*, 321–31.

12. Park's *Travels in the Interior Districts of Africa*, was published with much additional material in 1816. For a discussion of the various reports on Park's death, see Hallett, op. cit. 340–6.

13. Reichard's theory was first put forward in an article in the *Monatliche Correspondence*, Gotha, v, May 1802, 402–15, MacQueen's in *A Geographical and Commercial View of Northern Central Africa*, Edinburgh, 1821.

14. On the Congo expedition, see J. K. Tuckey, *Narrative of an Expedition to Explore the River Zaire*, London, 1818; on the Senegambian expedition, W. Gray, *Travels in Western Africa*, London, 1825; on the Fezzan expedition, see Lyon, op. cit.

15. Denham and Clapperton, op. cit.

16. Hugh Clapperton, *Journal of a Second Expedition into the Interior of Africa*, London, 1829; Richard Lander, *Records of Captain Clapperton's Last Expedition to Africa*, 2 vols., London, 1830.

17. On the origin of the idea of a chain of mountains across West Africa, see the passages quoted in Hallett (ed.), *Records of the African Association*, 251-2, 255.

18. General Sir Rufane Donkin, *Dissertation on the Course and Probable Termination of the Niger*, 1829.

19. Richard and John Lander, *Journal of an Expedition to Explore the Course and Termination of the Niger*, 3 vols., London, 1833; abridged edition with additional material, R. Hallett, *The Niger Journal of Richard and John Lander*, London, 1965.

20. Many of Laing's letters written during the course of his expedition to Timbuktu have survived; they have been edited by Bovill in *Missions to the Niger*, I.

21. Caillié, op. cit. II, 49.

22. For a detailed account of the genesis of Richardson's and Barth's expedition, see A. A. Boahen, *Britain, the Sahara, and the Western Sudan, 1788–1861*, Oxford, 1964, 181–212. Boahen brings out clearly the diplomatic importance of Barth's mission.

23. Delafosse, op. cit. II, 317.

24. Barth's *Travels* were published in five volumes in 1857-8; they have recently been reprinted in a three-volume edition, and in an abridged form, *Barth's Travels in Nigeria*, ed. and introd. A. H. M. Kirk-Greene, London, 1962. Richardson's journal was published posthumously, *Narrative of a Mission to Central Africa in 1850–1*, 2 vols. London, 1853.

CHAPTER 24: BORNU, HAUSA, AND THE FULANI
EMPIRE OF SOKOTO
(pp. 223–36)

1. Ibn Khaldun, op. cit. II, 306, quoted in Hodgkin, op. cit. 74–75.
2. Ahmad ibn Fartua's chronicles have been translated by H. R. Palmer in two volumes, *History of the First Twelve Years of Mai Idris Alooma*, Lagos, 1926, and 'The Kanem Wars of Mai Idris Alooma' in *Sudanese Memoirs*, I. The original manuscripts were obtained by Barth in Bornu in 1853 and sent by him to the Foreign Office.
3. Palmer, *Sudanese Memoirs*, I, 22.
4. Palmer, *The Bornu Sahara and Sudan*, 243.
5. Palmer, *Sudanese Memoirs*, I, 18.
6. ibid. III.
7. Trimingham, op. cit. 127.
8. Traditions connected with Daura are given in S. J. Hogben and A. H. M. Kirk-Greene, *The Emirates of Northern Nigeria*, London, 1966, 145–50. (See note on p. 271 *infra*.)
9. M. Hiskett, 'The Historical background to the Naturalization of Arabic Loan Words in Hausa', *African Language Studies*, VI (1965), 20.
10. M. G. Smith, 'The Beginnings of Hausa Society', 346–7.
11. Palmer, op. cit. III, 111.
12. For comments on this State of Wangara, see Trimingham, op. cit. 128–9.
13. On the legends connected with Amina, see M. G. Smith, op. cit. 349; and Hogben and Kirk-Greene, op. cit. 215–18.
14. M. G. Smith, op. cit. 351.
15. Muhammad Bello, *Infaq al-Maisur*, quoted in Trimingham, op. cit. 152.
16. Palmer, *The Bornu Sahara and Sudan*, 246.
17. J. O. Hunwick, 'The nineteenth-century Jihads', in Ajayi and Espie (ed.), op. cit. 265.
18. E. J. Arnett, *The Rise of the Sokoto Fulani*, Kano, 1929, appendix 26.
19. F. de F. Daniel, 'Shehu dan Fodio', *Journal of the African Society*, XXV (1925–6).
20. Hodgkin, op. cit. 39.
21. Barth, quoted in Hogben and Kirk-Greene, op. cit. 488.
22. P.-L. Monteil, *De Saint-Louis à Tripoli par le lac Tchad*, Paris, 1895, 248–55, quoted in Hodgkin, op. cit. 313–17.

CHAPTER 25: THE LAST OF THE CARAVANS
(pp. 236–51)

1. Matra's report is printed in Hallett (ed.), *Records of the African Association*, 79–82. See also Boahen, op. cit. 104, and J. L. Miège, *Le Maroc et l'Europe*, Paris, 1961, II, 146–54.

2. On trade routes from Morocco, see W. B. Harris, *Tafilet*, London, 1895, 265, 305–6, and J. G. Jackson, *An Account of the Empire of Morocco*, 2nd ed., 1811, 282–8.

3. Jackson, op. cit. 285.

4. al-Bakri, op. cit. 327.

5. A. Raffenel, *Nouveau Voyage dans le pays des Nègres*, Paris, 1856, I, 284.

6. For a vivid account by a modern traveller who has accompanied a caravan from Taodeni to Timbuktu, see J. Skolle, *The Road to Timbuktu*, London, 1956.

7. For an account of the present salt trade of Kawar, see Capt. Grandin, *Bulletin de l'I.F.A.N.*, XIII (1951), 488–533.

8. Barth, op. cit. II, 126.

9. On the trade in kola nuts, see Mauny, op. cit. 248–9, 366, and Prax, 'Commerce de l'Algérie avec la Mecque et le Soudan', *Revue de l'orient*, IV (1849).

10. L. Binger, *Du Niger au golfe de Guinée*, Paris, 1892, I, 309.

11. ibid. II, 86.

12. ibid. II, 220.

13. ibid. I, 328.

14. On the Fezzan-Kawar route, see Mauny, op. cit. 435, and Boahen, op. cit. 106–8.

15. Jackson, op. cit. 247, and Harris, op. cit. 297.

16. Leo Africanus, op. cit. I, 161.

17. Denham and Clapperton, op. cit. I, 206.

18. F. D. Lugard, *The Dual Mandate in British Tropical Africa*, London, 1923, 365.

19. Miège, op. cit. III, 292–372.

20. ibid. III, 89, 361–2; IV, 382.

21. Boahen, op. cit. 132–59.

22. H. Schirmer, *Le Sahara*, Paris, 1893, 363–6.

23. Miège, op. cit. III, 369–72.

24. Briggs, op. cit. 203.

25. Capot-Rey, op. cit. 479.

26. R. Capot-Rey, 'The Present State of Nomadism in the Sahara', *Arid Zone Research:* Vol. XVIII, *The Problem of the Arid Zone*, UNESCO, 1962.

27. Briggs, op. cit. 268.

28. Capot-Rey, op. cit. 307.

29. E. W. Bovill, *The Golden Trade of the Moors*, first ed., London, 1958, 247.

Select Bibliography

NORTH AFRICA

There are two excellent introductory works on the geography and history of North Africa: J. Despois, *L'Afrique du Nord* (Vol. 1 of the *Géographie de l'Union Française*, Paris, 1964) and C. A. Julien, *Histoire de l'Afrique du Nord* (2 vols., Paris, 1956). The latest editions should be consulted. Both books contain comprehensive bibliographies.

C. B. McBurney, *The Stone Age of Northern Africa* (Penguin Books, Harmondsworth, 1960) is the best introduction in English to the pre-history of North Africa. S. Gsell, *Histoire Ancienne de l'Afrique du Nord* (8 vols., Paris, 1913–28) is one of the finest works of French historical scholarship produced in this century. It covers the history of the Maghrib up to the end of the first century B.C.; it should be supplemented by the results of recent research, details of which are given in the bibliography to the first volume of Julien's *Histoire de l'Afrique du Nord*.

C. Courtois, *Les Vandales et l'Afrique* (Paris, 1955) is one of the most important recent works on North African history. It is concerned not only with the Vandal invasion, but also with the position of the indigenous Berber people during the centuries of Roman rule.

On the Byzantine period in North African history C. Diehl, *L'Afrique byzantine*, though first published in 1896, is still the outstanding work.

Of the history of the Muslim states of the Maghrib, the second volume of Julien's *Histoire de l'Afrique du Nord* contains the most comprehensive account. E. F. Gautier, *Le Passé de l'Afrique du Nord* (Paris, 1937) is a stimulating and controversial interpretation of the early Muslim centuries.

H. Terrasse, *Histoire du Maroc* (2 vols., Casablanca, 1949–50) is the only good history of a single country. But although there is no adequate single work on Algeria or Tunisia, French scholars have produced many fine works dealing with aspects of these countries' history. The bibliography in the second volume of Julien's *Histoire de l'Afrique du Nord* provides an invaluable introduction to recent French research.

The *Encyclopedia of Islam* contains a mass of valuable historical material, with articles by leading scholars on the countries and peoples of the Muslim world, on the main towns, on the dynasties of the countries of North Africa, together with biographies of many of the important men in Muslim history. The *Encyclopedia* is in the process of being completely rewritten; wherever possible the new edition, sections of which are published every year, should be consulted.

THE SAHARA

The most comprehensive single work on the Sahara is R. Capot-Rey's *Le Sahara Français* (Paris, 1953); this book contains a detailed bibliography. The most useful general work in English is L. Cabot Briggs's *Tribes of the Sahara* (London, 1960).

On the Tuareg F. R. Rodd's *People of the Veil* (London, 1926) and H. Lhote's *Les Touaregs du Hoggar* (Paris, 1944) should be consulted.

F. de la Chapelle's article 'Esquisse d'une histoire du Sahara occidental' (*Hespéris*, XI, 1930) provides the best introduction to the history of the Sanhaja.

WEST AFRICA

J. F. A. Ajayi and I. Espie (ed.), *A Thousand Years of West African History* (Ibadan, 1965) provides the most comprehensive introduction to West African history.

For the history of West Africa up to 1600 R. Mauny, *Tableau géographique de l'ouest africain au moyen âge* (Dakar, 1961) is the essential work. It contains a comprehensive bibliography. In English the most important work on the Sudanic belt of West Africa is J. S. Trimingham, *A History of Islam in West Africa* (London, 1962).

Among West African regional histories the following contain material particularly relevant to the subjects discussed in this book:

M. Delafosse, *Haut-Sénégal-Niger* (3 vols., Paris, 1912).

J. D. Fage, *Ghana—A Historical Interpretation* (Madison, 1959).

T. Hodgkin, *Nigerian Perspectives* (London, 1960).

J. Rouch, *Contribution à l'histoire des Songhay* (Dakar, 1961).

Y. Urvoy, *Histoire des populations du Soudan central* (Paris, 1936).

Y. Urvoy, *Histoire de l'empire de Bornou* (Dakar, 1949).

EUROPEAN ACTIVITIES IN NORTHERN AND WESTERN AFRICA

The most important study of European activities in the Maghrib during the Middle Ages is still Mas Latrie, *Relations et commerce de l'Afrique septentrionale ou Maghreb avec les nations chrétiennes du moyen âge* (Paris, 1886).

C. de la Roncière, *La Découverte de l'Afrique au moyen âge*, (3 vols., Cairo, 1924–7) contains the most detailed account of the knowledge possessed by medieval Europe of the interior of Northern Africa.

Early European voyages down the coast of Western Africa are summarized in R. Mauny, *Navigations médiévales sur les côtes sahariennes antérieures a la découverte portugaise (1434)* (Lisbon, 1960).

J. W. Blake, *European Beginnings in West Africa, 1454–1578* (London, 1937) is the standard short account of the first century of European activity on the West Coast.

R. Hallett, *The Penetration of Africa up to 1815* (London, 1965), describes European activities in the interior of northern and western Africa principally in the eighteenth and early nineteenth centuries. A second volume will describe European penetration of the interior between 1815 and 1830.

A. A. Boahen, *Britain, the Sahara and the Western Sudan, 1788–1861* (Oxford, 1964) draws on a mass of unpublished material to describe British exploration in the mid-nineteenth century.

SUPPLEMENTARY BIBLIOGRAPHICAL NOTE

Among the works relating to the subject of this book published while the present edition was in the press the following should be specially noted:

N. Barbour, *Morocco* (London, 1965). The first history of Morocco by an English writer to appear for more than fifty years, this book provides an excellent introduction to the entire span of the country's history.

W. K. R. Hallam, 'The Bayajidda legend in Hausa folklore', *Journal of African History*, VII, 1 (1966). Much circumstantial evidence is brought forward to suggest that Bayajidda (see p. 225) represents the personification of a group of Berber political refugees, the supporters of Abu Yazid, a Kharijite rebel defeated by the Fatimids of Tunisia in the middle of the tenth century.

R. C. C. Laws, 'The Garamantes and Trans-Saharan enterprise in classical times', *Journal of African History*, VIII, 2 (1967).

M. Lewis (ed.), *Islam in Tropical Africa* (London, 1966). An important collection of studies, several of which deal with the history of Islam in West Africa.

C. W. Newbury, 'North African and Western Sudan trade in the nineteenth century: a re-valuation', *Journal of African History*, VII, 1 (1966). Evidence from French and British archival sources suggests that the caravan trade increased in the mid-nineteenth century, reaching its peak in 1875, when the total value is estimated at £1.5 m (imports and exports combined), then falling steadily away.

Marilyn R. Waldman, 'The Fulani *Jihad*: a reassessment', *Journal of African History*, VII, 3 (1965). An excellent study of the Fulani *jihad* in Northern Nigeria, with references to many other recent works on the subject.

Bibliographical Essay for the 1995 Edition
BY ROBERT O. COLLINS

This is a select bibliography to supplement *The Golden Trade of the Moors* as a guide to those who wish to return to Bovill's sources and the scholarship which has been written after his prosaic synthesis. Selection is always arbitrary and is rigorously intimidated by the space available and the eclectic knowledge of the editor. Thus, with few exceptions, I have limited the following selections to the principal monographs, which is a disservice to the numerous articles that have appeared in many prestigious journals but are of greater interest to the student and scholar than to the general reader. One would do well to consult the extensive bibliography in Nehemia Levtzion, *Ancient Ghana and Mali* (New York: Africana Publishing Co., 1980). To search for additional Arabic sources see: *Corpus of early Arabic sources for West African History*. transl. by J.F.P. Hopkins and edited and annotated by N. Levtzion and J.F.P. Hopkins (Cambridge: New York: Cambridge University Press, 1981); and *Chronicles from Gonja: a tradition of West African Muslim historiography*. Ivor Wilkes, Nehemia Levtzion, and Bruce Haight; Arabic texts edited and translated by Nehemia Levtzion (Cambridge: New York: Cambridge University Press, 1986).

For the intrepid reader who seeks to learn more of the trans-Saharan trade and the dynamic and cultural history of the Sahilian empires of the Western Sudan, two specific but not insurmountable problems await the traveler. The first erg (sand dune of the Sahara) to cross consists of those accounts of the empires of the Western Sudan and trans-Saharan trade in Arabic or French which are known to scholars but are not comfortable for readers of English readers who prefer to enjoy Bovill's prose.

The second obstacle to those who wish to trek with Bovill is perhaps more formidable. There is a dearth of water in that part of the world combined with a lack of understanding of the cultural history of the empires of *The Bilad as-Sudan*, the Land of the Blacks, a history which has spanned many centuries and the interminable plains of the African Sahil bound together by the river Niger. If one can put aside the potsherds and the paraphemalia of the archaeologists (See: Thurstan Shaw, "African archaeology: looking back and looking forward", *The African Archaeological Review*, vol. 7, 1989, pp. 3-31), to move down the centuries, if not the millennia, David Conrad and

Humphrey Fisher have, scouring the sources, dismissed the alleged demise of the Empire of Ghana supposedly caused by Almoravid Muslim hordes more interested in the riches of Iberia than the arid plains of the Sudan. "There was no Almoravid conquest of ancient Ghana. Instead the Almoravid period saw a strengthening of Islam in the Western Sahara and Sudan, highlighted by the peaceful conversion of Ghana (probably early in the twelfth century) and carried forward by the cooperative action, sometimes military, of black Muslims and the Almoravids, with the former tending to call the tune" (David Conrad and Humphrey Fisher, "The Conquest that Never Was: Ghana and the Almoravids", History in Africa, vols. 9 and 10, 1982, 1983. This quote is from vol. 9, 1982, p. 45).

Having resolved relations between the extensive domains of Ghana and the Almoravids, one must turn to the relevant sources in Arabic some of which have been translated into French and English. The Arabic sources fall roughly into two categories: The majority are concerned with the dynamic Arab conquests of the Maghrib and Spain and their subsequent Muslim rule of the Iberian Peninsula until their expulsion to North Africa by Christian Crusaders in 1492. The second sources in Arabic tend to be general histories of the Arab diaspora to the West such as Ibn 'Abd al-Hakim (d. 871-872), Kitāb futūh Misr wa' l-Magrib wa-akhbārihā, (The History of the Conquest of Egypt North Africa and Spain). ed. Ch. C. Torrey (New Haven: Yale Oriental Researches Series, iii, 1922); Al-Balādhurī (d. 892/3), Kitāb futūh al-buldān. ed. M.J. de Goeje (Lugduni Batavorum: 1863-1866); and Al-Ya'qūbī (wrote 891), Kitāb al-buldān. ed. M.J. de Goeje. Lugduni Batavorum: 1892 in Bibliotheca Geographorum Arabicorum, vol. vii and transl. by G. Wiet as Les pays (Cairo, 1937). There were others, but it is unknown whether Bovill was aware of these Arab accounts or made use of them.

Our knowledge of the empires of Ghana, Mali, and Songhay are through those travelers and merchants, including Arabs, who crossed the Sahara to observe and to do business with the kings of the Bilad as-Sudan. They were few, that is who wrote of their experiences, but those who did were extraordinarily perceptive and in their fashion, historians who gleaned from the oral and written traditions of the Sudanic peoples, most of our knowledge of the medieval kingdoms of the Western Sudan. There was the celebrated Arab traveler Ibn Battuta who traversed nearly the whole of the Muslim world including the Sahara and in 1352 the Kingdom of Mali: Ibn Batoutah, transl. from the Arabic by C. Defremery and B.R. Sanguinétti, Paris, 1865. Others followed including Leo Africanus (Al-Hassan ibn Muhammad al-Wizaz al-Fasi) who was captured by Christian corsairs and baptized in Rome as Giovanni Lioni. He completed in 1526 the most authoritative account of the Western Sudan between the writings of Ibn Battuta and the descriptions of the Sudan in the nine-teenth century by Heinrich Barth. Battuta's famous *The History and Description of Africa and the Notable Things Therein Contained.* transl. from the Italian by John Pory (1600), ed. by Robert Brown, London, 1816, and as *Description de l'Afrique.* new edn., transl. by A. Épaulard and annotated by A. Épaulard, Th. Monod, H. Lhote, and R. Mauny. 2 vols. (Paris, 1956). A major contribution on the Kingdom of Songhay was made by Abd al-Rahman al-Sadi, the Imam of Timbuktu in his *Ta'rīkh al-Sūdān.* (c. 1655), Arabic text and French transl. by O. Houdas. (Paris, 1911); and Ibn al-Mukhtār. *Ta'rīkh al-Fattāsh.* (c. 1665), Arabic text and French transl. by O. Houdas and M. Delafosse (Paris, 1913).

A bibliographical essay is not the court of legal or moral judg-ment, but a guide to those who wish to know more and have the arro-gance to leap to their own conclusions only to stumble on their own opinions. They are not alone. The Arab travelers who witnessed the empires of the Western Sudan and have contributed so much to our understanding of these kingdoms have been followed in the nine-teenth century by the Europeans who at first came, like Ibn Battuta or Leo Africanus, out of curiosity but were unwittingly the harbingers and more ruthless imperialists from Europe. These early European explorers were motivated more by "scientific" investigations (anthro-pology and sociology had yet to be invented) but displayed an inquis-itive love of Africa and its people which has provided the student and the scholar with a wealth of information and interpretation which has amplified and enriched the chronicles of the Arab travelers.

By general consensus the most perceptive of those Europeans who passed through the African Sahilian Sudan in the first half of the nineteenth century was Heinrich Barth. *Travels and Discoveries in North and Central Africa from the Journal of an Expedition Undertaken under the Auspices of H.B.M.'s Government in the Years 1849-1855* (Philadelphia: John Bradley, 1959). A German, Barth crossed the Sahara from Tripoli in 1850 as a member of a British expedition to return to Europe with a journal containing an immense amount of information on the Western Sudan collected from precise and pene-trating observations. Another German who made substantial contri-butions was Gustave Nachtigal who left Tunisia in 1869 crossed the Sahara and explored the Western Sudanic kingdoms in the Chad Basin and as far south as Bagirmi to return to Germany in 1874. Gustave Nachtigal, *Sahara and Sudan,* transl. and ed. by Allan G.B. Fisher and Humphrey J. Fisher, 3 vols.; vols. 1 and 2 (Berkeley: University of California Press, 1974, 1980); vol. 3 (London and Atlantic Highlands (N.J.): C. Hurst and Company, Humanities Press, 1987).

And then there were the British and the French. In 1822 the

British Government authorized an expedition consisting of Dr. Walter Oudney, Major Dixon Denham, and Lieutenant Hugh Clapperton, R.N. to cross the Sahara to the Niger. Denham explored the Sudanic Kingdom of Bornu west of Lake Chad. Oudney and Clapperton continued to the southwest. Oudney died, but Clapperton reached the Sultanates of Kano and Sokoto before returning with Denham to England in 1825. The French were represented in these early European probings into the Sahara and Sudan by René Caillié who was the first European to visit Timbuktu in 1828 and return alive, crossing the Sahara with a caravan of 1,400 camels vividly described in his *Travels through Africa to Timbuktu and Across the Great Desert to Morocco. Performed in the Years 1824-28* (London: H. Colburn and R. Bentley, 1830).

In the latter half of the nineteenth century those who came to explore also came to conquer and were hardly considered by the Africans of the Sudan as the beneficent burdens of the White man. There were, however, many colonial administrators and officials, both British and French, who not only had empathy for those that they ruled but sought out the cultural history and customs of their subjects. The cynics have remarked that this was merely a means to facilitate the collection of taxes while retaining law and order supported by the thin red line and the Maxim gun. In their official duties these colonial administrators learned much of the Sudanic kingdoms and wrote prolifically about them during the twentieth century, particularly in the interwar years. There was M. Delafosse's. *Haut-Sénégal-Niger (Soudan français)*. 3 vols. (Paris, 1912), which was followed by numerous works on Ghana, Mali, and Songhay. Charles Monteil wrote extensively on the Western Sudan during the interwar decades whose most perceptive work was perhaps *Une cité soudanaise: Djenné. métrople du delta central du Niger* (Paris, 1932). Representing the British during his service and long residence in Northern Nigeria as a colonial administrator was H.R. Palmer, author of *The Bornu Sahara and Sudan* (London, 1936). All of these works provide enormous amounts of information from these men, and others, acquired as colonial rulers which is why they should not be ignored but placed in the context presented by the scholars, rather than the administrators, who wrote of the Sahara and Sudan after the Second World War.

At the end of empire in Africa in the 1960's there was a flood of intellectual energy and inquiry into the African past precipitated by the rapid expansion of African studies programs in European and American universities and the phenomenal growth of colleges and universities within Africa itself. Y. Urvoy, *Histoire de l'empire du Bornu* Dakar, 1949, complimented and revised Palmer's work of the 1930's, but it was only the beginning of an exhaustive list of books, articles, and conference papers which requires even greater selectivity of the works of the principal contributors, some of whose most interesting ideas and interpretations were presented at what has now become commonplace in the academic world—the international conference where scholars combine controversy with mutual admiration. The papers produced at these conferences, in which the Sahara and the Sudan have been a constant theme, have often gone unpublished, but the principal participants, not surprisingly, have built upon the foundations laid down by the previous contributors to the history of the Sahara and Sudan—the early Arab chroniclers, the later seminal works of Ibn Battuta, Leo Africanus, Al-Sadi, Heinrich Barth and the works of the colonialists, Delafosse, Monteil, and Palmer.

After Urvoy, Raymond Mauny became one of the pioneers of the postwar school of Sudanic historiography. He is best known for his *Tableau géographique de l'Ouest africain au Moyen âge* (Dakar, 1961). Cheikh Anta Diop, *l'Afrique noire précolonial* (Paris, 1960), has perhaps been overshadowed by his more controversial views in journals and conference papers where he has argued the place of Africa in the larger world beyond the continent. J.S. Trimingham, who began his career as a Christian missionary, is another who sought a greater understanding of Islam in Africa in numerous books among which his most useful contribution to the Sahara and Sudan is *A History of Islam in West Africa* (London, 1962), which should be read in conjunction with Peter Clarke's more recent work, *West Africa and Islam: A Study of Religious Development from the Eighth to the Nineteenth Centuries* (London, 1988). Within this group of post-World War II scholars, Nehemia Levtzion, previously cited, remains one of the most widely read and respected historians of the history of the Sahara and Sudan. But there were others whose contributions cannot be ignored: L. Cabot Briggs' work on the tribes of the Sahara (1960); R.C.C. Law on the trans-Saharan trade (1967); S.M. Cissoke on the Mandingo (1969); J.D. Fage's thoughtful essays on the early Western Sudan (1959, 1964); the writings of M. Hiskett on the Habe Kingdoms (1960) and the role of currency so vital to the trans-Saharan trade (1966); the numerous contributions in journals and papers by J.O. Hunwick on the Western Sudan; those of H. Lhote on the Tuaregs who controlled the caravans that crossed the Sahara; the work of R. Pageard on Segu, the Bambara, and Mali.

The reader may be frustrated that I have avoided providing the specific citations to the articles, conference papers, and ephemera which would be of interest to the more diligent student depending on the particular subject in time and place but which space does not permit. The specific references can be found in the usual bibliographical references or now more commonly by the computerized holdings more commonly found in any research library. To those who do not have access to these resources, as Bovill certainly did not, the bibliography complied by Nehemia Levtzion in *Ancient Ghana and Mali*. New York, Africana Publishing Co., 1980, remains the best guide for the general reader.

Robert O. Collins
Santa Barbara, California
August 1994

Index